Reflections from Yellowstone and Beyond

Forty-three Years as a Seasonal Ranger

By

Orville E. Bach, Jr.

Illustrations by Margaret C. Bach

Copyright © 2016 by Orville E. Bach, Jr.
Illustrations Copyright © 2016 by Margaret C. Bach
All rights reserved

Library of Congress Control Number:

ISBN: 978-0-9767473-1-4

Published by
Blue Willow Press
197 Lamplight Drive
Bozeman, MT 59718

Ordering Information:
bluewillowpress@yahoo.com
406-388-0272 or 406-579-7908

Printed in the USA by
Morris Publishing®
3212 East Highway 30
Kearney, NE 68847
800-650-7888   www.morrispublishing.com

To my sister,

Alice Bach Robinson

Front Cover: Twilight at Grand Prismatic Spring

By Margaret C. Bach

TABLE OF CONTENTS

Map of Yellowstone	vi
Preface	viii
Acknowledgements	ix
Introduction	x

Part I HIKING THE HIGH COUNTRY

Eagle Peak and Unsolved Mysteries	3
Fishy Stories and Lake Wyodaho	10
Close Call Along the South Boundary	18
When the Going Gets Tough the Tough Change Plans	22
Along the Crest of the Tetons	30
Grizzlies in the Mist	41
When the Yellowstone High Country was Green	51
Across the Two Ocean Plateau	61
To the Headwaters	73
Are There Angels in the Backcountry?	82
Nine Days Through Glacier's Mountain Splendor	86
The Winds—a Spectacular Wilderness in Need of Care	97
Hoodoo High Country	111

Part II WILDERNESS WATER ADVENTURES

A River-Lake Combo Wilderness Trip	118
The Smith—Finally!	124
A Sinking Feeling on Yellowstone Lake	133
Journey to the Everglades	139
Troubles on the Snake	147
The Northern Lights	154
Backcountry Companions and the "BC Syndrome"	157
Abrams Creek-- A Secret Wilderness	162
Yellowstone of the East	169
Wild Times on Wild Waters	182
Call of the Loon	193
A Napali Coast Wild Adventure	204
Journey Down "Lost Paddle" Creek	217

Part III THROUGH THE SEASONS

    Autumn
        Way Down in the Fall in Bear Valley   228
        Of Wolves and People—Encounter at Cougar Creek   235
        Mary Mountain and the Shutdown   241

    Winter
        GP at 25 Below   251
        A Frigid Late-Night Winter Duty   256
        A Winter Ordeal High in the Smokies   263
        Slough Creek Solitude   269
        Late Winter Wildlife Adventures at Old Faithful   275
        A Late Season Ski and Diminishing Winters   282
        Moonlight Skiing   287

    Spring
        Spring Comes to Old Faithful   290

Part IV GEOLOGIC WONDERS

    Please Don't Be Critical of Old Faithful   296
    On Protecting Thermal Resources   300
    Adventures at Norris Geyser Basin   306
    Strange Incidents at West Thumb and Old Faithful   311

Part V TO LEAVE THEM UNIMPAIRED

    The Treasure of an Undeveloped Shoreline   317
    The Gallatin Crest—the Need for Wilderness   320
    Has Yellowstone Exceeded its Carrying Capacity?   324
    This Horse Should Stay in the Barn   328
    Memories of the Yellowstone Cutthroat Trout   332
    Ten Ways to Advance in the Park Service   336
    Where the Grizzly Walks   343
    Humor in Uniform   347
    The Value of Public Lands   356

Epilogue   361
Appendix   362

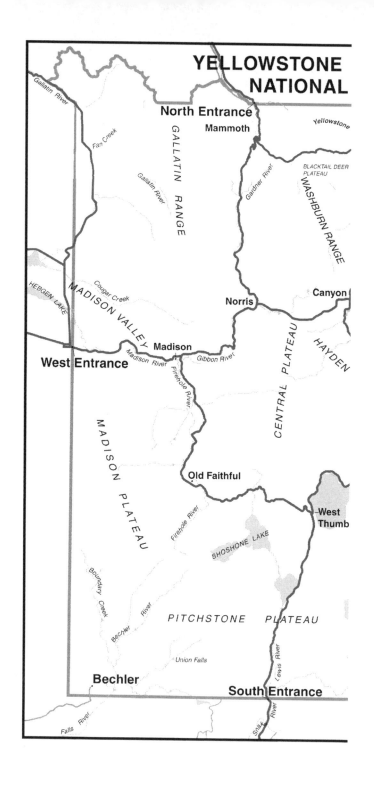

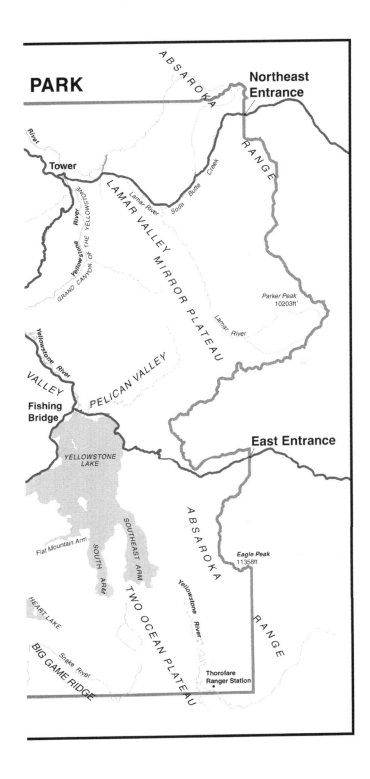

Preface

I have been blessed over the span of forty-six years to work seasonally in three national parks: Yellowstone, Great Smoky Mountains and Glacier. All but three of those summers have been spent in Yellowstone, and the year 2016 marked my 43rd year working as an Interpretive Park Ranger for the National Park Service, as well as the 100th anniversary of the creation of the National Park Service. Working with dedicated colleagues, serving a diverse array of visitors in a unique setting, and exploring the parks' backcountry certainly produces some interesting adventures—thus the stories contained in this volume. I write them from my own personal views and experiences, not as an official representative of the National Park Service.

I trust that these stories will strengthen your conviction to help protect and preserve not only Yellowstone, our nation's "Mother Park," but indeed *all* of our national park units and wild country everywhere.

Acknowledgements

After 31 years of traveling back and forth across the country between East Tennessee and Yellowstone, my wife Margaret pleaded, "Just plant me in one place." In 2006 we planted ourselves year round near Bozeman, Montana, and Margaret is now enjoying the flowers and gardens she could not grow when we lived each summer at Old Faithful. I am grateful to her for putting up with my forays into the park to backpack, ski, canoe, and continue to work as an interpretive ranger.

I deeply appreciate my dear friends and family, who have accompanied me on backcountry trips into Yellowstone in all seasons, and for allowing me to write about our adventures and misadventures in this volume.

I continue to be amazed by the quality, passion and expertise of the employees I am privileged to work with, including the National Park Service, Yellowstone Association, and the park concessions and guides.

Thanks to Tami Blackford of the National Park Service in Yellowstone for providing the map in this book. The following people were kind enough to read over the manuscript and offer helpful comments: Margaret Bach, Alison Bayr, Jim Lenertz, Steve Hixson, and Clyde Austin. John Hooker and Tom Gerrity pored over the manuscript in detail, and contributed many valuable suggestions.

My journal keeping over the years has not been the best. I would therefore like to thank Al Duff, Hank Barnett, Clyde Austin, Rod Busby, Steve Hixson, Tom Gerrity, Jim Lenertz, and John and Deb Dirksen for helping me to sort out the details from our many excursions into the backcountry. Even with all of this wonderful assistance, I take full responsibility for any errors.

My sister, Alice Bach Robinson, is the person most responsible for my passion for Yellowstone. When she was a student at Auburn University she decided, with the consent of our wonderful parents, now deceased, to have a summer adventure in 1959 by boarding a train, and traveling from Alabama to Yellowstone all by herself. When she returned she made a scrapbook of her summer escapades. I came across that scrapbook when I was a junior at Auburn in 1968, and after three summers of working for the Alabama Highway Department in Montgomery, I decided I too wanted a taste of adventure. Margaret and I headed to Yellowstone, and our lives were changed forever. It is therefore my pleasure to dedicate this book to my sister Alice, the "pioneer" of our family!

Introduction

The Greater Yellowstone Ecosystem (GYE) represents one of the largest wild and intact ecosystems in the temperate life zone on our planet. Most of the stories in this volume emanate from the park and ecosystem, but this book is primarily a collection of stories that celebrate wilderness. That's why I added "and Beyond" to the title of this book, as I have included a few stories about wild places beyond the GYE. Back in the 1970s, Yellowstone's Grant Visitor Center had a room comprised of "listening chairs." There, visitors would listen to a wonderful message extolling the many virtues of wilderness, as they gazed out across the far reaches of Yellowstone Lake—the world's second largest natural lake at such a high elevation. Unfortunately, as visitation grew, it became impractical to continue using listening chairs at the Grant Visitor Center, and they were removed. However, I truly loved the messages those chairs delivered, and I continue to incorporate them into my evening programs to this day.

The one line in that message that I agreed with the most was, "we need wilderness as much as we need food and water." The backcountry of most of our national parks such as Yellowstone is managed as wilderness, but in 1964 the Wilderness Act was passed by Congress, which set aside almost 110 million acres coast to coast. The act passed by a vote of 434-1, and President Lyndon Johnson signed it into law. What a wonderful gift to our children and grandchildren that law has been. However, since 1964 our nation's population has increased by 67 % from 192 million to 322 million. It is obvious that not only do we need to be good stewards of our existing wilderness areas, but we need to protect what little wild country we still have in our nation. Designating additional wilderness areas, as well as establishing more national monuments/parks, will be critically important for the well-being of our children and grandchildren. The great ecologist and conservationist Aldo Leopold once extolled the importance of wild country with these quotes: "I am glad I will not be young in a future without wilderness," and "Wilderness is a resource which can shrink but not grow."

I am no longer a young person, but I truly believe in wild country more than ever for our children and grandchildren. I hope that these stories about adventures in the wild will inspire you to not only be good stewards of wilderness, but to work hard to protect more. Our children's children will thank us.

Part I

Hiking the High Country

John scans for route to the confluence of Broad Creek and the Yellowstone

Eagle Peak and Unsolved Mysteries

On a cold blustery June morning in 2003 I was sitting in a small Livingston café sipping coffee with my good friend Jim Horan. We were sharing Yellowstone stories from trips that we have both enjoyed over the years. Jim is the epitome of a rugged wilderness traveler. He has served as a Yellowstone backcountry ranger, and is an accomplished skier and backpacker. He has completed trips that I can only dream about, such as backpacking the entire length of the Pacific Crest Trail, and the Continental Divide Trail in single seasons, along with many treks abroad. I had just shared with Jim my story about encountering a black wolf at Heart Lake Geyser Basin in March of 1973 while on my 18-day winter ski trip, and how officials with the National Park Service at the time had refused to believe that I had actually seen a wolf.

At the time I was serving in the Air Force at Malmstrom Air Force Base in Great Falls, Montana, and frankly was not aware that wolves were assumed to be completely missing from the Yellowstone region. I had briefly encountered the wolf during a blizzard, and did not have an opportunity for a photograph. However, if I had only suspected how rare this sighting was, I could have at least photographed tracks the wolf made in the mud around the thermal pools. Jim said that he completely understood how I felt when the officials dismissed my wolf sighting. "I once saw something in Yellowstone and no one believed me either," he said. "Really? What did you see?" I asked. "I'm not going to tell you," Jim replied. "Why not?" I asked. "Because you won't believe me either," he said.

"Jim," I replied, "what do you mean I won't believe you? You're the real deal. Given all of your backcountry experience, why in the world would I not believe you?" Despite my persistence, Jim would not budge. "I'm just not going to tell you because you will be like my other friends and simply not believe me." "Jim," I said, "this is getting ridiculous. Of course I'll believe you. Now, tell me what you saw!" Jim took a sip of coffee, placed the mug down on the table, settled back into his chair, then looked me squarely in the eye with a serious expression, and replied, "I saw Bigfoot." I was right in the middle of taking a sip of coffee from my mug and choked a bit. "Bigfoot!" I exclaimed, fighting back a grin on my face.

"See, I *told* you that you would not believe me," Jim calmly stated. I paused, shook my head and finally managed, "Jim, let me put it this way: I believe that *you* believe that you saw Bigfoot. But never mind that, I want to hear the details. Where did you see it? And did you take any photos or see any tracks?" "No photos or tracks," Jim replied. "It all happened so quickly. A friend and I were descending Electric Peak, and were on a ridge above Cache Lake. We looked down and clearly saw a large hairy beast in a meadow walking on two legs, just like a human. It was only for a few seconds, then it disappeared into the trees."

"Did you report the sighting to the Park Service?" I asked. "Are you kidding?" Jim replied. "My friends don't believe me. Why would the Park Service?" "Well, I see what you mean. They sure didn't believe my wolf sighting in 1973. Jim, how do you know that what you saw was not a big grizzly rearing up on his hind legs?" I asked, hoping to rescue him from his frustration. "Butch," Jim started out with a rather sarcastic expression, "how many times have you seen a grizzly in Yellowstone taking long strides on two legs while swinging his front legs as though they were arms?" "Okay, Jim," I replied. "You have convinced me that you saw what you say you saw. Let's just say that I will keep an extra ear to the ground and eye on the horizon on all my future trips into the Yellowstone backcountry!"

The subject of Bigfoot did not come up again for the next couple of years, even when Jim and I were on backcountry outings such as a late fall backpack trip up and over The Thunderer, and down Cache Creek in the northeast section of the park, and taking overnight winter ski trips up Slough Creek, and Daly Creek in the northwest corner of the park. But then came the summer of 2005.

Three times my friends and I had attempted to reach the summit of Eagle Peak, Yellowstone's highest mountain at 11,358 feet, and three times we had failed. On our last attempt in August, 2003, we had tried to ascend the Trappers Creek drainage to reach a saddle close to its summit, but we had encountered horrendous deadfall, a result of the huge fires of 1988. We had instead climbed Colter Peak, and found the views from near its summit so spectacular, that we swore to never mention the words, "Eagle Peak" again.

As someone once said, "never say never." My friends and I mapped out a good backcountry trip for late July, 2005. Our plan was for the four of us to paddle two canoes down the Southeast Arm of Yellowstone Lake, stash the canoes, then backpack south on the Thorofare Trail until we reached Mountain Creek, then hike up toward Eagle Pass, and set up a base camp about three miles inside the park boundary. From this spot, in September of 1987, my friend Hank Barnett and I had hiked up a tributary of Mountain Creek, and climbed up to a saddle just below Eagle Peak. We would've made the summit except for electrical storms that rolled in, and a tight time schedule. This time around my group would include John and Deb Dirksen, and Hank Barnett. Actually, the goal of reaching the summit of Eagle Peak was secondary. We simply loved being out in "The Thorofare," thought by many to be the wildest country in Yellowstone.

5 Reflections from Yellowstone and Beyond

Our trip proceeded smoothly as we finally reached our campsite along the northwest side of Mountain Creek. The weather on this late July day was absolutely superb, and even the mosquitoes were not giving us much trouble. Yellowstone Lake had been a paddler's dream with calm conditions. Wildflowers along the trail were at a peak, with glorious displays of pink, yellow and blue. The Delta wolf pack had announced its presence with howls reverberating off the walls of the Two Ocean Plateau. We had just finished having dinner, and were settling around the campfire as darkness enveloped us. Suddenly, we heard the most gut-wrenching sound that any of us had ever experienced in the Yellowstone backcountry emanating from the dense brush across Mountain Creek. The sound was almost impossible to describe, other than to say it sounded half-animal and half-human. It was loud and sort of a combined scream/roar.

John Dirksen up to this point had spent over forty summers of his life backpacking in Yellowstone, and he had never heard anything remotely similar to this. I had spent well over 400 nights out in Yellowstone, and had never heard anything like it either. Furthermore, I had never seen John get so visibly upset in the backcountry, even when facing grizzlies, a stampeding herd of bison, or treacherous waves on Yellowstone Lake. John grabbed his ax and his bear spray. "I think we need to take turns standing watch tonight," he announced. "Whatever made that sound we just heard might try to do us some considerable harm." Just then the sound re-emerged, this time about 100 yards further down the stream, but still on the other side of the creek.

That evening we stayed up for a long time, keeping a large campfire burning well into the night. When we finally did retire, we pulled our tents close together, and placed our bear sprays in handy locations. I don't think any of us had a very restful sleep on this night. The following morning broke clear and quite cool. A low fog drifted over the meadow adjacent to our camp. We quickly built a fire and began preparing breakfast. Then, from across the creek, we heard the loud, spine-chilling sound *again*! How could I possibly describe it? Something like, "Argghhhh…Ugghhh…Aieee," like a crazed Tarzan call. We couldn't get packed up for our trip up Eagle Peak fast enough! We pulled our backpacks with food high above the ground, and hung them on the food pole, typically provided at backcountry campsites in Yellowstone. We half expected them to be taken by the Mountain Creek Creature, as we called it, but later that afternoon when we returned to camp, everything appeared to be untouched and in good order.

The day had been spectacularly beautiful, and we had succeeded in climbing to within about 100 yards of the summit of Eagle Peak before being blocked by a vertical wall. We found no strange creatures up high, just a few bighorn sheep prowling the slopes. As we packed up and then made our way down the trail leading to the Upper Yellowstone River, we frequently discussed the eerie sounds we had heard at Mountain Creek. Naturally, I had shared Jim Horan's story about Bigfoot. What creature produced those sounds we heard? Was it one of Yellowstone's large animals—a moose, elk, bear, wolf, or cougar—suffering from some type of terrible injury? We just didn't know. The mysterious sounds we heard up Mountain Creek haunted us, but the subject of Bigfoot did not come up again for a while—not until one late August evening the following summer.

The interpretive ranger staff at Old Faithful was having the annual season-ending cookout at Nez Perce patrol cabin, located about halfway between Old Faithful and Madison, and about one mile from the main road. We had finished up dinner, and everyone was sitting around the large campfire. It was time for Yellowstone stories. When it came my turn, I told them all about our trip the previous summer, and the chilling sounds that we had experienced. When I finished my story, everyone gathered around the fire was chuckling. That is, *almost* everyone.

Longtime National Park Service employee and geologist Scott Bryan (author of "The Geysers of Yellowstone") was not laughing. "Well, this is interesting," he said. "What do you mean, Scott?" I asked. "I don't think I've ever told this story to anyone before tonight," he began. "During the late summer of 1972 I worked for NPS Maintenance. I recall that a crew had been assigned to do some work on the blister rust (an exotic fungus that damages high elevation whitebark pine trees) in the vicinity of Mountain Creek. The crew had travelled in with supplies by boat to the dock at Trail Creek patrol cabin, and then packed the remaining 12 miles or so to their work site. Then something very strange happened," Scott continued. You could hear a pin drop. Every person around the campfire had their eyes and ears directed at Scott. "A couple of days later we get a call from the Foreman of the blister rust crew. He said that the crew had become so spooked from strange sounds they kept hearing from camp each night, that they refused to work, and demanded to be taken out of the backcountry."

I noticed a bunch of laughs and chuckles from around the campfire, but Ranger Tim Townsend was not laughing. "How many of you have heard of Bob Jackson?" Tim asked. Of course, we all had heard of "Action Jackson." Bob Jackson was another one of those legendary Yellowstone backcountry rangers who had spent decades patrolling Yellowstone's wilderness terrain in all seasons. He had spent many years stationed at the Thorofare Ranger Station, located at the most remote spot in the lower forty-eight states as determined by a National Geographic map survey. "Well," Tim continued, "I've heard Bob tell stories about him being up on top of The Trident, above 10,000', and seeing some hairy creature on two legs stalking sheep."

The following April I reported for my spring duty at Old Faithful Visitor Center. I always enjoyed this time of year, given the fine skiing that typically still existed in the area, along with the opportunity to view grizzlies appearing in the Upper Geyser Basin. I soon ran into Tim, who at the time worked as a law enforcement ranger year round at Old Faithful. "Well Tim," I half-joked, "have you had any bigfoot sightings this winter?" After the initial warm "welcome back," Tim's expression grew serious. "Actually, we did have some strange things happen this winter." "What do you mean?" I inquired. "Well," Tim continued, "a couple of concession employees were skiing up on the plateau coming back from Summit Lake, when they were overcome with the strange sensation that someone or some *thing* was following them. When they turned around they saw a large dark object that they said appeared to look just like a Sasquatch. When it noticed it was being watched, it quickly disappeared into the trees."

"Did they go back and take photos of the tracks?" I asked. "No, it was snowing and blowing so hard that their own ski tracks were filling in," Tim replied. "However, another employee was skiing up above Black Sand Basin this winter, and came across some very large and mysterious tracks, but she didn't have a camera with her. By the way, have you seen Bob Jackson's bigfoot accounts on the web?" "I don't know what you are talking about," I replied. "Well, since Bob has retired he has contributed some fascinating accounts of his bigfoot observations, one of which matches the story Scott told at the cookout last summer about the blister rust crew down in Thorofare." "Tim," I said, "I just don't know what to make of all this. If there really is a Bigfoot out there, you would think we would come up with the evidence." "Well, lots of folks think they have plenty of evidence," Tim countered. "I guess you could say this is just part of Yellowstone's wild mystique!"

I recently listened to an interview with Bob Jackson on "Larry Battson's Wild World" radio show that I found online, and was recorded on August 9, 2013. Ironically, in his narrative, Jackson reported seeing a Bigfoot very close to where my friend Jim Horan made his observation, and then what is truly scary is Jackson not only accurately described the same sounds that John, Deb, Hank and I heard, but Jackson heard them in almost the identical location up Mountain Creek! Jackson also described coming across tracks in the snow on some of his lengthy ski patrols—tracks over six feet apart (about the length of a cross country ski) that simply did not match any known animal in Yellowstone, but *would* conceivably match those of a large creature on two legs taking long strides.

Does a Bigfoot type creature actually live deep in the wilds of the Greater Yellowstone Ecosystem? I'll admit, I'm a skeptic, but I simply cannot explain away the inexplicable sounds we heard up Mountain Creek. Neither can I dismiss what my friend and highly experienced backcountry traveler Jim Horan saw. Bob Jackson, in my opinion, was the essence of a Yellowstone backcountry ranger. I once asked legendary Yellowstone Ranger Jerry Mernin what he thought about Jackson's accounts of seeing Bigfoot. Mernin simply chuckled and said that long periods in the backcountry can have a "weird" effect on you. Well, as one who has spent lots of time in the Yellowstone outback, I have to agree; however, part of the "weirdness" is how much more your senses become attuned to your natural surroundings.

Yes, I'm a skeptic but I also have an open mind. My ten-year old grandson likes to go around telling his friends that "my Pawpaw (that's me) believes in Bigfoot!" All I know is the Greater Yellowstone Ecosystem is the largest, intact ecosystem of its kind in the temperate life zone on planet earth. I doubt that we have uncovered all of Yellowstone's mysteries out there, and we probably never will. There are many places where a human foot has never been placed. One thing I know is certain: there are some eerie and mysterious sounds that no one can seem to explain out there in the wilderness of Greater Yellowstone!

Dunanda Falls on Boundary Creek

Fishy Stories and Lake Wyodaho

In April of 2012 I attended a presentation by Jonathon Klein, Resource Specialist with the Beaverhead-Deerlodge National Forest, to the Madison-Gallatin Chapter of the Montana Wilderness Association in Bozeman, Montana. Jonathon's topic dealt with the number of high country lakes in wilderness areas that are barren of fish, but subject to pressure from anglers to stock them. I found his presentation both fascinating and thought-provoking, and it reminded me of my own evolution of thinking about backcountry lake fishing. During the early 1970s, when I lived in Great Falls, Montana, I almost singly focused on those wilderness lakes that offered good fishing possibilities. There was one particular lake situated in very rugged terrain high in the Lincoln-Scapegoat Wilderness Area just below the Continental Divide that I was determined to get to. On some maps the lake had no name, though others listed it as "Bighorn Lake." According to fishing guidebooks, this lake was almost impossible to reach, as there were no maintained trails leading into it, but it contained lunker rainbow trout. I couldn't wait to get there.

In late September of 1973 we were experiencing a glorious period of Indian summer, and I decided to head for the high country with my little "Benji-like" dog Sam. Our destination was the difficult to reach "Bighorn Lake." I packed my tent, sleeping bag, food for the two of us, and my fishing gear, and headed up the Alice Creek road, not far from Lincoln, Montana. My plan was to hike up an old unmaintained trail until I reached the top of a ridge along the Continental Divide. Once on top, I would hike along the ridge for several miles, then attempt to find a route to drop down into the cirque that held this lake.

The aspens along Alice Creek were at their golden peak on this glorious fall day, and the hike up was quite enjoyable; however, as is so often the case, I did not make the progress I had anticipated. It was a long hard struggle through rough terrain before I finally emerged above timberline atop the ridge, which was quite narrow and consisted mostly of loose rock. I had planned to make it to the lake before dark, but upon studying my topo map, I knew that was now going to be a tall order. Sam and I gave it our best try, but we simply ran out of daylight. The day had been surprisingly warm, especially for this late in the fall, and this high above 8000'. I had a two man tent, which required stakes, but with all of the loose rocks, I was barely able to plant the tent stakes into the talus. I had food and water for both of us, the tent was staked out, and the weather was mild, so I remained optimistic. I figured we would simply visit the lake the next morning, and then retrace our steps back. My outlook drastically changed later that night.

Around 10:00 p.m. a steady wind developed that gradually turned into a gale. This part of the Rockies is notorious for high winds, which is true all along the eastern front of the Northern Rockies in the Bob Marshall Wilderness Complex. The wind velocity continued to increase and eventually must have been approaching fifty mph. I knew we were in trouble. As the tent began to shake violently, I observed something that I've never seen before or since. All of the friction from the flailing of the nylon tent was causing sparks to shoot off the end of Sam's nose! He didn't seem to be in any pain, but just watching the sparks fly off the poor pup's nose, and listening to the deafening roar of the wind outside, frightened me. Given the fact that I had staked the tent out in loose rock, I knew that we didn't have a chance, and sure enough, by around midnight, the tent collapsed on us.

At first, I just tried to curl up in my sleeping bag and sleep anyway, but with the constant loud flapping of nylon all around me, it was impossible. Therefore, I decided to get *out* of the tent to escape the mental torture. I attempted to wad the tent up to prevent the thing from flapping, but a huge gust of wind came up and almost knocked Sam and me off of the ten foot wide ridge, which contained steep drop-offs on both sides. I grabbed my backpack and sleeping bag to keep them from blowing away, but in doing so, I had loosened my grip on the folded tent. And away it went! That blue nylon tent simply took off for the heavens. As I squinted my eyes in the semi-darkness on top of this ridge, I could see the tent headed upward and toward the northeast. It probably eventually settled somewhere in a field around Browning, Montana!

Sam and I burrowed down into the loose rock, curled up in my sleeping bag to keep warm, and simply waited for first light. I don't know about the dog, but I got zero sleep on this rather harrowing night. It was a *long* windblown night, and when first light arrived, we tucked our tails and headed back along the ridge toward Alice Creek. We made it out, but our attempt to reach Bighorn Lake had failed miserably!

A couple of years later, I tried to reach Bighorn Lake again with a friend and Air Force colleague, Kent Meyer. Rather than drop into the lake from atop the Continental Divide, we attempted to follow a drainage *up* to it. This attempt was also a failure. We wandered into horrendously dense vegetation, which was jam-packed with huckleberry bushes loaded with their ripe fruit. This made for fine munching, but judging from the many steaming piles of fresh grizzly scat, the bears were gorging on the delectable berries as well. And it's *their* home! We decided to abandon this route as well. I played lots of harmonica tunes in that dense jungle on *that* day! I had suffered my most serious grizzly bear encounter only one year earlier in Yellowstone (see "Are you a Stander or a Runner?" in *Tracking the Spirit of Yellowstone.*), and did not relish another such incident.

My third attempt at Bighorn Lake would be the charm. In September of 1977, I teamed up with my old backpacking buddy, Al Duff, for a week-long backpack trip. We made our way up to that same narrow ridge where I had lost my tent, and this time found a route down into the lake. Once there we were shocked to stumble upon a rather well-traveled trail that was not shown to exist on maps. When I arrived at the shore of the lake, I will never forget what I saw. After so many trips into the backcountry of Yellowstone and Glacier National Parks, I was accustomed to a pristine natural setting, *especially* when traveling to a place as remote as this lake. However, that was *not* the case here! There were old burned out fire rings all around the lake, which was disappointing enough. But what *really* galled me was finding the outfitter camps in place. There were actually tent platforms that had been constructed with logs cut from the immediate vicinity. I realized that all of the distasteful impact at this otherwise gorgeous wilderness lake was the result of pressure from outfitters bringing in fishing parties. These folks had basically made their *own* trail here, and it was not to simply appreciate the wonderful solitude and beauty of this wild place. Rather, it was first and foremost to *catch fish*. I did indeed see some hefty looking trout surfacing, but I had no luck in catching any. When it comes to angling skills I'm pretty average, and these trout appeared to be well-educated! These fish had apparently seen many a lure and fly float past their noses, which was the last thing I had anticipated. I think it was right then and there that I questioned the connection between wilderness lakes and fishing, particularly if the lake had been artificially stocked with fish.

During Jonathon Klein's presentation on fishing and high country lakes, he said that it is always very easy to tell whether a lake contains fish or not. If the lake is barren, chances are you will see absolutely no sign of human visitation—no unsightly fire rings, litter, or beaten-down paths along the lake shore. On the other hand, if the lake contains a good fish population, he said it is a challenge to minimize the impact from the many backcountry hikers and horse parties who go there to fish.

Klein said that it is not always that easy to resist pressure from anglers to stock high country lakes that have historically been barren of fish. In fact, he told a story about a friendly argument he once had with one of his colleagues in the U.S. Forest Service. When Jonathon made his case that wilderness lakes that were historically barren of fish should remain that way, his colleague gave him a strange look then asked, "What do you do with your time when you go to such a lake, read a book?" When Klein told this story his audience erupted with laughter. After all, this was the Montana Wilderness Association not the "Backcountry Anglers Society." The audience was first and foremost appreciative of *wilderness* values. The very idea that someone would travel to a gorgeous high country wilderness lake, and find it boring, since there was no fishing available, was undeniably a humorous thought. Which brings me to some of my adventures of reaching wilderness lakes within the Greater Yellowstone Ecosystem—like Lake Wyodaho.

Over the years, the Cascade Corner down in the Bechler country of southwest Yellowstone, with its lush vegetation and many waterfalls, has always been a special backcountry destination for me. On numerous occasions while traversing the Bechler Meadows, I have gazed up at the edge of the Pitchstone Plateau, and wondered what Lake Wyodaho looked like. Glancing at a topo map, it certainly looked like an appealing place, though there is not a maintained trail that leads to it. After all, the lake sits right on the lip of the steep-edged plateau near the mouth of the spectacular Bechler Canyon. I figured that just the view of the Tetons alone from atop the plateau would be worth the climb up to the lake.

I recall once in the late 1970s asking long-time Yellowstone ranger Terry Danforth about this lake. Danforth related to me that at one time the lake had been stocked with trout, and there was a very popular side trail that anglers had beaten up to the lake from the Bechler Meadows. "That was a long time ago though. There are no longer any fish in the lake, and no one bothers to go up there anymore," he concluded.

Danforth's observation regarding the connection between fish and backcountry use raised the same exact point that Jonathon Klein addressed decades later: Should lakes in the backcountry be stocked with fish? For example, nearly half of Yellowstone's waters were barren of fish when the park was established in 1872. These barren waters included not only many small lakes, but big bodies of water such as Lewis Lake, and Shoshone Lake. Even the famous Firehole River above Firehole Falls was devoid of any fish.

Early park managers changed that by introducing non-native fish, such as brown trout, brook trout, rainbow trout and lake trout, into many lakes and streams. In recent decades the park's fisheries management has focused on protecting and preserving Yellowstone's native fish, the cutthroat trout, but the damage has been done. Take the lake trout for example. This fish has been called a "fresh water shark," because a single mature lake trout can eat *over fifty* native cutthroat trout per year. The first lake trout was caught in Yellowstone Lake in 1994. It was probably introduced by 1980. I can almost picture someone back then catching a bunch of lake trout from Lewis Lake, placing them into a bucket of water, and then driving the short eight miles over to Yellowstone Lake to release them (see "Memories of the Yellowstone Cutthroat Trout.")

Over the years I have continuously maintained a list of prospective hiking destinations in Yellowstone, and Lake Wyodaho was always near the top of the list, but I just never got around to hiking up to it. That finally changed in the summer of 2011, when Clyde Austin and I managed to find a route to it. Clyde, who is originally from Greeneville, Tennessee, and four years my elder, is quite the guy. He worked hard for most of his life, then finally tried a backpacking trip to relieve the stress and was hooked. Clyde is a venerable old East

Tennessee mountain boy who loves to travel off-trail in his beloved Great Smoky Mountains. I also love to travel off-trail but *not* in the Smokies (see "Lost" in *Tracking the Spirit of Yellowstone*).

Each summer Clyde usually comes out to the Northern Rockies for about a month of backpacking, and on several occasions, we have teamed up for some great trips. In mid-August of 2011, Clyde had just completed a rather lengthy excursion in Glacier with some friends, and had a few remaining days before he had to fly back east. He gave me a call and wondered if I had any suggestions for a four-day trip. "Clyde," I responded, "I have just the perfect trip. Have you ever heard of Lake Wyodaho?" "Nope, but I assume it must be close to the Wyoming-Idaho border," he astutely responded. After I told Clyde of my long-held ambition to visit this lake, he was as eager as me to make the trip.

Rather than approach our destination from Bechler Ranger Station, which is where most backpackers begin trips into the Bechler country, we opted to begin our trip from what is probably Yellowstone's least-visited trailhead, along the west boundary that leads to Buffalo Lake. In fact, the only reason that I could find this way into Yellowstone is because former Park Geologist Rick Hutchinson (see "Memories of Rick Hutchinson" in *Tracking*) once was heavily involved in monitoring the Boundary Creek Thermal Area near the park's west boundary, and showed me a route that he had found through the maze of primitive roads in the Targhee National Forest, which borders Yellowstone to the west. As interest increased regarding the possibility of geothermal drilling near the park's west boundary, Rick wanted to collect data, such as water temperature, discharge, chemistry, and any eruptive activity on the myriad of thermal features there. He wanted to have a baseline of information just in case he had to provide evidence that drilling would harm Yellowstone's thermal basins. Fortunately, as of this writing drilling has not occurred along the west boundary, but there is still interest, and therefore risk.

Thanks to visionaries like President Theodore Roosevelt, who worked tirelessly in the early 1900s to establish many of our great national forests in the West, Yellowstone has buffer zones all around it. I have found that when you hike and backpack along the park's north, east and south boundaries, the natural beauty contained within the park vs. the national forest cannot be differentiated. But, this is definitely *not the case*, in the Targhee along the park's west boundary. For unknown reasons, during the 1970s officials in leadership positions with the Targhee National Forest apparently decided to thumb their noses at Yellowstone's leaders in the National Park Service, and ordered immense clear cuts all the way to the park boundary. The logging operations were so massive that the twenty some-odd miles of border of Yellowstone along the west boundary with the Targhee National Forest can clearly be seen from space!

Needless to say, lots of logging roads had to be constructed all through the predominately lodgepole pine forests, and Rick had managed to find a route through them that eventually led to within one-half mile of the park's west boundary trail. Once you found this trail, it was only a couple of miles to Buffalo Lake, and from there the Boundary Creek trail could be followed south to access the thermal basin, as well as the beautiful Bechler country with its huge meadows, and many streams and waterfalls. Rick's map was very accurate, and the first time I used it, I was able to make it almost to the park boundary, just as Rick described. However, as I have made subsequent trips, I have noticed that the Forest Service has made changes on some of the old logging roads, and the closest that you can now get to the park's west boundary is about 3.5 miles

So with some of those old maps in hand, Clyde and I headed down through the Targhee National Forest to navigate our way to as close to the West Boundary trail as possible. Amazingly, Yellowstone's official "Backcountry Trip Planner" actually shows this trailhead on their map, as it is listed as 9K8. Unfortunately, it appeared to us, at least on the surface, that the Targhee folks still aren't too concerned about their neighbor to the east, because we did not find a single sign or trail marker to help visitors find their way to this trailhead. Furthermore, once you *finally* figure out the chopped off logging road where you begin the hike toward the park, you basically have a moonscape to walk through for about three miles all the way to the park boundary. Rather than the diversity of trees and age structure that you walk through in a wild forest, you are walking through an ugly field of stumps and slash piles. It just so happened that the days Clyde and I walked into Yellowstone, and then back out of it along this route, we were experiencing a mid-August heat wave, and thanks to the Targhee not providing any buffer zone whatsoever—not even a few hundred yards—we had no shade to duck under. With all of the black obsidian volcanic rock, we felt like we were hiking somewhere in Hawaii Volcanoes National Park!

The park boundary was rather conspicuous. We suddenly left the moonscape behind, and walked into a fine, diverse lodgepole pine forest. Now, we had a sun-dappled forest complete with shade to walk through. "You know," Clyde remarked, "this reminds me of the transition you make when driving from Pigeon Forge, Tennessee into the Great Smoky Mountains National Park." I chuckled at the remark, as I indeed recalled the transition from the wall to wall tacky billboards along the roads in the tourist trap town of Pigeon Forge, to the wall of lush green vegetation inside the Smokies' park boundary. "Thank God for our national parks," I remarked.

Once inside the park, we quickly found the west boundary trail, which led us to the cutoff trail over to Buffalo Lake, home to one of the park's oldest patrol cabins. The old cabin appeared the worse for wear due to the weight of the heavy snows. This region of Yellowstone, high up on the Pitchstone Plateau, can receive 80 to 100 inches of measurable precipitation due to the storms that blow in from the southwest. That equals many feet of snow in these parts, and it appeared that the old cabin roof was sagging a bit. Yellowstone has about forty backcountry patrol cabins, and given its location, Buffalo Lake receives relatively light use from rangers on patrol. Clyde and I stopped on the shores of the lake to have lunch, and we were immediately attacked by hordes of mosquitoes. Usually by mid-August such pestiferous insects are mostly gone, but not this particular year.

The trail from Buffalo Lake going south along Boundary Creek is a great backpacking trip, and is one of the least traveled trails in the park. Along the way, we encountered the very significant Boundary Creek thermal area, with its many hissing and bubbling springs, mud features, and steam vents. One of the true highlights of this trail is the "Roman Baths," where Boundary Creek spills into some huge, circular shaped bowl-like formations. On a warm day these pools make for a wonderful swim. I decided to give it a try, but my swim was rather short-lived. The waters were so icy that my body went numb after only a few minutes.

We reached our backcountry campsite right along the banks of the creek, and set up our tents just as darkness was settling into the forest. By this point near the edge of the plateau, we were walking through a rich forest replete with spruce and large aspens. Boundary Creek was now a virtual whitewater cascade. After dinner, we were forced to duck into our tents due to the clouds of mosquitoes.

The next morning we took the short cutoff trail to the overview of Dunanda Falls, a 150 foot sheer drop of Boundary Creek. There are dozens of superb waterfalls in the Bechler Country, and Dunanda is one of the best. Clyde decided to rest at the overlook, and I opted to leave my backpack with him, and hike down to the foot of the falls to sample the view from below. The day was already shaping up to be another unusually warm one, especially for mid-August, so I decided to take a dip at the foot of the falls to cool off.

By the time we reached our campsite down in the meadows, we found the mosquitoes out in full force, so we quickly set up our tents, hung our food, and ventured out from camp to scout out our next day's route up to Lake Wyodaho. After dinner Clyde gave up slapping mosquitoes, and ducked into his tent. I was determined to enjoy the evening campfire, but basically had to practically stand next to the fire engulfing myself in the smoke to escape the little bloodsuckers. Soon I gave up the fight and retired early as well. Thank goodness for mosquito netting!

The next morning the temperature was much cooler, as one would expect in mid- to late August in Yellowstone. What a relief! On this day we would venture several miles from established trails in our pursuit of a route up to Lake

Wyodaho. Along the way, we crossed a stream that dropped through a narrow rugged gorge, and I noticed a waterfall at the head of the canyon. From here we began our slow climb up the plateau. Clyde was ahead of me, and I heard him yell, "Bear!" When I reached Clyde, I was relieved to see a medium-sized black bear, rather than a grizzly, ripping open a log in search of insects. I was surprised to see that this area had experienced a forest fire not that long ago, and there was now a nice ground cover of shrubs and berry bushes that provided excellent bear habitat.

Upon reaching the top of the plateau, we found the view of the Bechler Meadows below, and of the majestic Grand Tetons to the south, as rewarding as we had hoped. I was surprised to see the vast meadows still so verdant this late in the summer, obviously reflecting a rather wet summer, which also helped explain the mosquito problem we were having. As we walked around the lake, we felt like the first explorers or pioneers to ever visit here. There was not so much as a footprint to be seen anywhere, not a single shred of evidence that anyone had ever been here. Clyde and I spent a couple of hours just soaking in the beauty and solitude of this very special place, and frankly I was thankful that this body of water no longer supported any fish populations that had once apparently attracted hordes of anglers according to Ranger Danforth.

Our last campsite turned out to be our best, as we again camped along Boundary Creek, but this time with the cooler weather, we were able to relax around our campfire without the annoying buzz of mosquitoes in our ears. The hike back to our car was quite enjoyable until we reached the "Targhee Moonscape."

In subsequent years I have taken other trips to remote lakes barren of fish in the Greater Yellowstone Ecosystem, especially high in the Lee Metcalf Wilderness. I fully appreciate the passion of anglers who enjoy hooking wild trout in the backcountry, but I find myself in total agreement with Jonathan Klein. If a wilderness lake is historically barren of fish, then for goodness sakes, let's keep it that way!

Close Call Along the South Boundary

I have always considered traveling off trail in the Yellowstone Country a great adventure. In fact, when I am leading walks for visitors, I often explain the rating guide my friends and I use for hiking in the park: the heavily-traveled nature trails near the roads are the "front-country." An example of this would be the trails around the Upper Geyser Basin at Old Faithful to view the world's greatest collection of geysers. The short trails within a mile or two to popular destinations such as Mystic Falls and Fairy Falls are the "front-back country." Such trails are wide and heavily traveled. Once you progress to the narrow, less-traveled trails to destinations several miles from the road, you are in the "back country." A good example of this would be the 7.5 mile trail to Summit Lake. Although this trail begins near the Old Faithful area, the most congested part of Yellowstone, very few people hike up this trail. However, the wildest part of Yellowstone is the "back-back country," the approximately 97% of the park that does not contain roads *or* trails.

Some of my very favorite backpacking trips have occurred not within the boundaries of Yellowstone National Park, but rather just outside the park boundary in the wilderness areas that surround the park. Much of this terrain along the north, east and south boundaries is quite spectacular, and not that difficult to negotiate, especially above 9000'. There are several reasons that I love backpacking in the wilderness areas along the park's boundary. First, you are typically close to timberline, where the views and wildflowers are simply breathtaking; second, being off-trail, you rarely see another soul, which provides a deep sense of wildness and solitude; and finally, since we are just outside the park and off-trail, there is more flexibility when it comes to selecting campsite locations.

I had always had my sights set on a trip along the southern boundary. I had traveled along the Big Game Ridge country near the south boundary, but wanted to explore the Huckleberry Ridge country farther west. In August of 2008, I teamed up with my hiking friends John and Deb Dirksen, and Clyde Austin to give it a try. My friends often kid me that I have nine lives. Well, I definitely used up one of them on this particular trip. Our plan was to begin at the Sheffield Creek trailhead near Flagg Ranch at an elevation of 6800,' and climb up to the top of Huckleberry Mountain at an elevation of 9500'. My youngest daughter Alison worked one summer in Grand Teton National Park, and had told me about an old, historic lookout located atop Huckleberry Mountain. She said that you can always tell if there is anyone staying there by simply looking at the seldom-used parking lot at the trailhead. "If no one is parked there, then you can be pretty certain that the lookout is yours for the night," she told us.

From the lookout, we planned to try to stay above 9000,' and follow Huckleberry Ridge, which finally drops down to the Snake River at an elevation of 7000' near the confluence with Coulter and Harebell Creeks. From there we would follow the Snake River trail out to the South Entrance. Our trip distance would total about 30 miles, and involve over 4000' of climbing. The high country along Huckleberry Ridge was new country to all of us, so we were excited. Also, I had not traveled along the Snake River here for many years, so it was time to get reacquainted with that country as well.

The day that we began our trip was a typical warm August day. Much of this area burned in 1988, so shade was rare, making the 2700' climb up to the top of Huckleberry Mountain rather brutal. Not only would we stop to drink from cold streams and springs, but we would also douse our heads with the ice cold water. When we finally reached the top, we could understand why Alison had strongly recommended this hike. The views to the west of the Grand Tetons and Jackson Lake were absolutely spectacular.

We climbed into the old log lookout, and were both impressed and dismayed. We were impressed by the craftsmanship evident in the building of this old historic structure many decades ago; however, we were dismayed by its lack of attention and upkeep. It appeared that the critters had taken over the place, and was really not fit to stay in. We opted to pitch our tents down at the base of the lookout, and sleep where we knew we would not have to worry about mice crawling across our faces all night. In fact, when I returned from this trip, I penned a letter to the Bridger-Teton National Forest urging them to preserve this really unique historic lookout, now abandoned.

Our evening was spent basking in the glow of the view over the Tetons. It was practically impossible to look away from those jagged peaks, as the sun set behind them. Of course, the next morning, the Teton Range was bathed in the early morning light of the rising sun. What a spectacle! After breakfast we packed up, and descended back down the trail until we reached an elevation of about 9000'. We then headed north along the top of Huckleberry Ridge. It was our intention to follow this ridge to its end, all the while staying high in subalpine meadows.

We spent our second night on the edge of a flower-filled meadow overlooking the Snake River Valley below, and in the distance, the prominent Mount Sheridan with Heart Lake below. Our little campsite had it all: a cold spring, some trees for shade, a beautiful meadow, and stunning views from our high vantage point. On our third day we continued to wander through mostly open country along the top of Huckleberry Ridge. Everything was so lush and green, yet the bugs were not a problem. We observed deer and elk, and were constantly on the lookout for bears or their fresh sign, but really did not notice any.

Early in the afternoon we finally reached the point where Huckleberry Ridge began to slope down toward the Snake River. From an elevation of 9300' we began our slow and steady descent through a forest that was open enough to allow for relatively easy travel considering we had no trail. About halfway down the ridge, we noticed a lake in the distance below us. We checked our map and noted that this lake was unnamed. By now it was the warmest part of another hot August day, so we decided to make the lake our lunch destination. I was determined to take a swim in it to cool off.

The lake was situated at an elevation of 8300,' and was quite pretty with mostly open country around it, but with an ample supply of shade trees for our lunch stop. As we ate our lunches I noticed fish rising in the lake, which truly intrigued me. How did these fish get here? There was no trail anywhere near this lake, and there were no tributaries connecting it to any major streams. Given the remote location, we felt certain that this lake was rarely ever visited.

After lunch, I put on my trunks and eased out into the water. I was surprised at how cold it was. I expect this with streams, but on this hot day I just thought the lake would be a bit more comfortable. I suspect there were several ice cold springs feeding this lake. After treading water a bit, I noticed a neat little isthmus that extended out into the lake. It appeared to be about 60 yards away, so I decided to swim over to it. Clyde, John and Deb remained on the shore to relax in the shade. I have always considered myself a good swimmer, and whenever I have tired from swimming, I would simply ease onto my back, take deep breaths, and float until ready to continue swimming again.

But on this day there was something different happening to me. I don't know if it was due to the water being extra cold, or if I was having some type of physical problem. Physically, I thought I had performed quite well to this point; after all, we had to climb up a 2700' ridge in the blazing sun the first day, and I had handled that just fine. But as I tried to swim toward the point, I was quickly running out of gas. I was tired and gasping for each breath. I tried to slow up and try different strokes, such as the backstroke and scissors, but nothing seemed to help. I was so terribly out of breath, that I stopped swimming and reverted to my tried and true solution—lying back and floating so I could rest. However, in order to float, you have to take deep breaths, and fill your lungs with air. I could not do this. I was gasping for each breath, and it was only getting worse.

I have never had asthma, but I imagined an attack would feel something like this. I simply could not get a breath, so therefore I could not float, which meant I had to keep kicking my legs and waving my arms in the water, making matters worse. Finally I realized I could no longer swim, and could not float, so I weakly yelled, "John, I'm in trouble!" John has always impressed me with his physical strength, so it was only natural for me to yell his name. I'm sure that my "yell" sounded half-hearted though, because I was just about down to my last breath. I yelled it once more, and then I could no longer keep myself up. I started to sink straight down, and it was only through the Grace of God that my feet touched bottom just as the water level reached my chin!

I was actually able to stand on the lake bottom with just the tip of my nose protruding out of the water. I just stood there in that spot for minutes on end, taking deep, deep breaths until finally, *finally,* I had caught my breath, and was able to begin a weak-kneed walk along the lake bottom toward shore. All the while I was struggling, John, Clyde and Deb simply stared at me. They told me later that they thought I was "joking." I told them in no uncertain terms that I don't joke about such matters, and if they *ever* again heard me murmur the words, "John, I'm in trouble," I sure as hell mean it!

When I finally pulled myself out of the cold water, I just lay back on the grass and thought to myself, "What if that water had been a foot deeper? What would've happened?" I had no idea, but it is scary to think back about just how exhausted and helpless I was when I completely ran out of breath. I've only had this happen one other time, and that was about two years before this particular trip, when I was skiing solo into Slough Creek Valley. Of course, on that occasion I simply stopped skiing though I remember thinking at the time, "Why are you so breathless?" I have had physicals that don't show up any problem with my heart. Clyde is certain the cold water had a lot to do with it. Since this incident, I have swam on several other backcountry trips without feeling any tiredness or loss of breath. However, I learned a lesson from this close call. I never *ever* attempt to swim out across open water to an island, point, etc. like I was trying to do at this lake. Rather, I simply swim along the shore or in circles.

After I had sufficiently recovered from my very close call in this unnamed lake, I was ready to leave it! We continued our descent until we had reached the Snake River Valley, and made camp near the Snake Hot Springs. After dinner, we forded the river and explored the mouth of Forest Creek Canyon, a very beautiful and verdant gorge, but very difficult to access.

The following day we finished our trip along the South Boundary Trail to the South Entrance road. Our loop trip, most of it at high elevations, and just outside the park boundary, had provided us with a spectacular backcountry experience, though I'm thankful that I managed to survive the close call in that ice-cold, unnamed lake.

When the Going Gets Tough, the Tough Change Plans

Backpacking the Yellowstone high country can be a challenging endeavor. Thus, the old saw, "When the going gets tough, the tough get going" often comes into play. However, with my group of hiking companions, on more than one occasion, we have had to modify that adage. In the summer of 2010, I had a great trip planned with John and Deb Dirksen, Hank Barnett, Steve Hixson, and Clyde Austin. We had received a special permit to make a loop trip on the Two Ocean Plateau. Our plan was to hike down the Thorofare trail along the east shore of Yellowstone Lake, then ford the Yellowstone River near the confluence of Cabin Creek. We would then head east until we reached the Passage Creek trail that would take us up high on the plateau. However, when we arrived at the banks of the Yellowstone River, we knew we were in trouble.

We always try to take our annual "big" backpack trip around the first of August, because typically the weather and trail conditions are favorable. Spring runoff is over, and streams are normally fordable. However, due to an unusually long, cold and wet spring, we found the Yellowstone River quite high. John and Deb have spent over forty summers backpacking in Yellowstone, and they were not concerned. They had made many early season fords over the years. The rest of our group was not as confident as we studied the deep swift water where the trail crossed the river. Suddenly a backpacker appeared on the other side of the river. This guy appeared to be quite an athlete. We estimated his height to be 6 feet 5 inches. He hoisted his backpack, and headed out into the river. We were surprised to see the water come all the way up to his waist as he slowly made his way across the river.

I walked over and asked him about the ford. "Well, it's pretty deep and swift out there, but you just have to take it slowly, one step at a time," he replied. I looked at his long legs, and confirmed that the water line on his shorts was almost to his belly button. "Hey Deb," I called, "Come over here." I stood Deb next to the young man. I wanted to see just how high that water would come up on Deb. The water line on the man's shorts was just about equal to Deb's arm pits! It didn't faze her. "I'll just put my backpack in a plastic bag, and if I need to, I'll inflate my sleeping pad, and John can help pull me across," she said. "We've done that before." John and Deb were comfortable with the plan, but Hank, Steve, Clyde and I just shook our heads. It wasn't so much that we didn't think Deb could make it, we were concerned whether *any* of us could make it safely across the deep swift waters of the Yellowstone River!

We huddled our group and held a little pow wow to discuss what we should do. We had a time constraint to deal with. John and Deb worked as volunteers in the park, so they were flexible. However, Hank, Steve and Clyde all had a plane to catch after our trip was over. While we always allocate "cushion days" in our trips for unexpected circumstances, those typically only covered a couple of days. Due to the length of this trip, we had already made arrangements with the park concession for a boat pickup in the Southeast Arm at the point where motorboats are permitted to travel. We had spent the previous night near Cabin Creek patrol cabin, and had visited with backcountry park ranger Tim Kanaus, who John, Deb and I knew from his days working at Old Faithful. We finally decided, with much regret, to bag our planned loop trip on the Two Ocean Plateau, and head back to talk to Tim to see what he recommended for changing our backcountry use permit. We reached Tim just in time, as he was loading up his pack horses and heading out. Tim agreed with our decision not to attempt the ford, and suggested that we consider going up Mountain Creek, then over Eagle Pass, the park's highest, into the Washakie Wilderness in the Shoshone National Forest, finally exiting at the Eagle Creek trailhead about eight miles east of the park's east entrance. This alternative especially appealed to me, because while I had been up Mountain Creek before, I had never hiked across Eagle Pass and out via the expansive Eagle Creek Meadows. Also, we thought we might attempt to scale Eagle Peak, the park's highest, though Tim told us he thought there was still too much snow up there to make it to the top. Tim called the backcountry office on his radio to change our permit, and also to cancel our boat pickup. This was a huge relief, because if we had not been able to get through, and the boat had made the scheduled trip, we would have been responsible for the full payment.

Ironically we ended up camping at the same site where our group had encountered the spooky and mysterious sounds a couple of years earlier (see "Eagle Peak and Unsolved Mysteries.") However, this time we heard no such sounds. It was here that Deb's boots gave out. John had found the boots at a garage sale, and they appeared brand new, but apparently several years of non-use had caused the glue to deteriorate. As a result the boot soles were coming apart. However, John, ever the handyman, used a role of thin rope, and some glue to repair the boots. By the next day the boots were like new again!

As we approached Eagle Pass, we could clearly see that Tim had been correct about the snow up high on the shoulders of Eagle Peak. There was no way we could safely attempt to make the climb to its summit. We camped in Eagle Creek Meadows, and with the spectacular mountain backdrop, I felt as though I was in Glacier. We had a difficult time catching a ride back to our vehicle, but eventually succeeded. Our trip turned out to be successful, though it was completely different from what we had planned.

Likewise, we had to change gears on our 2009 trip as well. This time our group consisted of John, Deb, Clyde, Beth Kreuzer from the Old Faithful Backcountry Office, and me. We were in the middle of an off-trail trip that my friends like to call a "Butchwhack." I had gotten the bright idea to attempt to duplicate a trip that Jim Lenertz and I had made in 1977 to the confluence of

When the Going Gets Tough, the Tough Change Plans 24

Broad Creek and the Yellowstone River in the bottom of the Grand Canyon of the Yellowstone. Unfortunately, while my mind still can cover very difficult terrain, my body increasingly has trouble. In 1977 Jim and I were in our prime. I was only 31, and he was 38 and tough as nails. One summer's day I was visiting Jim in his trailer, and he led me to his park topo map. "Butch," he began, as he pointed with his finger, "I want to camp right here and see what the fishing is like." His finger was pointing to the junction of Broad Creek and the Yellowstone River out on the Mirror Plateau, one of the largest backcountry regions in the park. There was not a trail anywhere *near* the confluence. Jim and I had once backpacked down to Seven Mile Hole on the Yellowstone River at the bottom of the Grand Canyon of the Yellowstone, and had enjoyed some great fishing. However, we traveled a maintained trail on that trip. "Jim," I exclaimed, "How in the heck do you propose reaching this spot? There are no trails!" "No problem," he calmly replied, "We'll just hike along the southeast side of the canyon until we reach the ridge that leads down to the river."

I knew that all of this terrain was covered with dense forest, but I also knew that Jim was a master with a map and compass, and enjoyed navigating his way through the woods to reach a destination. Of course, we only had two days off, which were Friday and Saturday. Jim and I always had a big disagreement regarding one aspect about our trips. I always preferred getting a jump start by heading out as soon as we got off work on Thursday afternoon, and spending two nights out and coming out late on Saturday, or even Sunday, since our shift typically did not begin until the afternoon. But not stubborn Jim. He preferred heading out at daybreak on Friday, and coming back out late Saturday. We obtained a permit for undesignated camping, and made it to the confluence on Friday with plenty of time left over for fishing, which was excellent. Then we went back out the same way, and made it home on Saturday, just as Jim had planned. Most of that hike consisted of bushwhacking through mature and dense spruce and fir forest replete with deadfall, not to mention that we had to negotiate a 1200' drop to the bottom of the canyon with no trail. The distance each way was about 12 miles. To this day I have absolutely no idea how we covered that distance and terrain in only two days, and still had plenty of time to fish both days!

The reason I wanted to go back in 2009 had nothing to do with fishing. Rather, I wanted to attempt to hike upstream on Broad Creek to its confluence with Shallow Creek in a deep canyon with unique thermal features. I recalled thermal activity on Broad Creek when I had made the trip with Jim, but our minds were focused on one thing—fishing! My biggest problem in talking my friends into taking this trip was the fact that my mind still thought it was 1977 and I was 31 years old instead of 61! After obtaining our backcountry use permit for undesignated camping, we headed out from Artist Point attempting to duplicate the route that Jim and I had covered over three decades earlier.

Fortunately, at least we had planned for more than the two days that it had taken Jim and me. Our plans were to make it down to the confluence of Broad Creek and the Yellowstone River, then travel upstream on Broad Creek and eventually make our way out through Pelican Valley, and exit at the trailhead near Mary Bay on Yellowstone Lake.

After two full days of navigating our way through dense forest, we finally came to the point where we would begin our steep 1200' descent to the bottom of the canyon. I recalled that Jim and I had found a decent animal trail to follow on our 1977 trip, but there was no sign of it this time around, and in fact, it was hard to imagine one ever existed given the steepness of the terrain. Some of this forested area had burned in the last several years, so when we would attempt to grab on to any type of vegetation to keep from tumbling, we would become coated with black charcoal. At times we were sliding on our butts more than walking on our feet. As we *finally* neared the bottom, I heard John behind me exclaim, "Whose idea was it to come down here?" I turned around to take my medicine, but immediately broke into laughter. John's face was completely black. Apparently John had taken a full on face plant fall on the descent. Coincidentally, I had just finished reading an account of polar explorer Ernest Shackleton's voyage of the Endurance that became trapped in ice. In an effort to reach help and save his crew, he sailed to South Georgia Island in a small boat, then miraculously hiked over the island's mountains in an amazing 36 hours to reach the whaling station of Stromness. When the fellow in the station opened the door he was taken aback by Shackleton's appearance. He and his crew had been using an old whale oil stove to keep warm, and their faces were completely black. Clyde had read the same book. We both smiled and Clyde said, "John, you look just like Ernest Shackleton when he arrived at the whaling station!" John did not laugh or smile. He was not a happy camper at the moment.

However, once we finally reached the bottom and found a grassy level bench next to the river where we could camp, everyone's spirits improved. At least until we walked over to take a look at Broad Creek, where it flowed into the Yellowstone. The creek was roaring, and the canyon walls were almost vertical. Clearly, there was no way we would be able to hike upstream to the thermal area. We now knew that our planned itinerary would have to change. As we looked around there were steep canyon walls rising above us on all sides. There was no easy way out in any direction. We were in a hole, "Butch's Hole," as Clyde named it forever more. I thought back to how Jim and I had reached this "hole" in one day, enjoyed fishing and camping, and made it back to Old Faithful the following day back in 1977. How did we manage that? I had no idea. I made a suggestion that we should climb back out of the hole the next day the same way we had come down. However, John, with his face still black from his face plant immediately vetoed it. Clyde seconded the veto. "No way am I going back up that cliff," he said. He pointed at the steep slopes rising above Broad Creek to the northeast. "Let's try to get back up on the plateau that way," he said as he was studying his topo map. "It looks like there are some nice meadows along Burnt Creek where we can camp tomorrow night, then we'll work our way through Hot Springs Basin, and eventually to the trail and Wapiti Lake." We had campsites reserved at Wapiti Lake, and also one near Fern Lake north of Pelican Valley. But first we had to get there.

The rest of the afternoon we managed to relax and soak in the incredible beauty of our surroundings at this tri-canyon junction. We tried to not think too much about what we had facing us the next couple of days. Later that afternoon we walked over to take a closer look at Broad Creek, since we would have to ford it the next morning. The crossing appeared treacherous. If we slipped and fell, the swift waters of Broad Creek would quickly flush us right out into the raging torrent of the Yellowstone River, which would probably spell death. Beth and I found a spot up into the canyon that appeared to be wide enough to ford, but John quickly vetoed it. "We've got to find a place to tie off a rope," he said. "And the only place we can do that is here," as he pointed to a narrow spot with a tree on both sides. Beth and I looked at the deep, swift waters and just shook our heads. We did not agree, but John had much more experience with high water stream crossings than any of us. Despite the good weather that we were enjoying along with the splendor of our wild setting, I think most of us had a restless night attempting to sleep.

The next morning after breakfast our group packed up camp and headed over to Broad Creek. John tied a rope off on a stout tree, then Clyde volunteered to wade into the swift waters and take it to the other side. After the rope was tied off to trees on both sides, John told everyone to watch his technique for fording. He held on tightly to the rope, which was about chest high, but leaned downstream so he could plant his feet in the streambed, and prevent the current from sweeping him off of his feet. John made it look easy, but I knew it was not. Each time one of us crossed John shouted, "Lean back, lean back!" The technique worked as none of us lost our footing. John made the last crossing after he untied the rope, and then pulled himself over to the other side. I have always relied on a stout hiking pole for my "third leg" whenever I have encountered a difficult, high water ford, but in this situation John's technique was what we needed. We absolutely had to have the rope to hold onto given the fact that we faced grave consequences if we had slipped and been swept out into the Yellowstone River.

We now faced a 1500' climb back up to the plateau on the north side of the canyon through which Broad Creek flowed. As we slowly made progress, I would stop to catch my breath, and gaze down into "the hole," fully realizing that as beautiful as it was, I would never attempt a return trip. As I neared the top, I had to agree that this ridge had been a bit easier to negotiate, plus it had not burned, so we had more vegetation to grab onto, and any slips along the way would not produce another "Shackleton moment." We walked along the canyon rim above Broad Creek, and were amazed to see a major waterfall come into view. We were not aware of any waterfalls of this size along Broad Creek. Given its unique hourglass shape, Beth suggested the name, "Chalice Falls." We all heartily endorsed the name. By late afternoon we found our way to the open meadows along Burnt Creek, which provided a nice setting for our undesignated camp. At the close of the evening, while we felt disappointment that our goal of hiking up the Broad Creek Canyon had not been met, we were relieved to be out of "the hole" and back on top of the plateau.

As we made our way to Wapiti Lake and Astringent Creek for the next two nights, and eventually out through Pelican Valley to the trailhead, we had two more interesting events. One was observing a grizzly at a distance grazing on thistle out in the open meadows of upper Pelican Valley; the other was a rather humorous incident that I have not lived down to this day. It is only recently that solo tents have come onto the market. For most of my backpacking life I have typically teamed up with a friend in a two-person tent. One person would carry the tent, the other would carry the poles and stakes to divide up the weight. The old mountain ranger Jim Lenertz was my mentor in many ways. One of the best tips Jim ever came up with was a "pee bottle." "Why does anyone want to get up in the middle of a frigid night, and crawl out of his tent when you don't have to?" Jim exclaimed. I decided to give it a try and found myself in total agreement with Jim. The little portable urinals are available at most backpacking supply stores. There is a men's model called the "Little John," and a woman's model called "Go Girl."

Our last evening was spent at a designated campsite near Fern Lake, and I was glad that it would be my last time sharing a tent with Clyde. When sleeping two guys to a tent, it has always been my custom to trade ends so you don't wake up in the middle of the night with your partner's face two inches from yours. However, Clyde's feet sweat a lot in his boots, and as a result we had a serious problem with foot odor in our tent! Of course, Clyde was not too keen about my use of the Little John. He was afraid of an accident with such a device, and opted to crawl out of his tent when nature called. Along with my little portable urinal, I also keep my water bottle handy. Typically, I use a flexible bladder, also called a Platypus, that I like to place in the top of my backpack with a tube, so I can frequently sip on it as I'm hiking. As daybreak neared, and I had endured my last evening of Clyde's snoring and smelly feet, I started to get up. To my shock, I immediately felt wetness all around me. I knew that it had not rained during the night, so my first fear was my Little John had somehow opened up! Thankfully, that was not the case, as I quickly realized that the tube on my Platypus had come off, thus releasing about a liter of water in the tent. Apparently, I had rolled over on top of it during the night.

(I am now careful to place the Platypus *outside* of my tent, and only run the tube in to sip on.) I realized that most of the water had pooled under Clyde's sleeping bag. Since Clyde was still asleep, my plan was to ease out of the tent, retrieve a towel from my pack, and attempt to blot up the water before he woke up. However, my plan did not work. As I emerged from the tent I heard Clyde scream, *"Butch! Butch!"* "Clyde, relax it's not what you think!" I yelled back, trying to calm him down.

Since this was the last day of our trip, I knew that some dampness on our sleeping bags would be no cause for concern, but convincing him that it was water, and not something else was not easy. Clyde has a strong East Tennessee mountain accent and mine is Deep South. I guess the two of us going back and forth over my *Platypus* must have sounded pretty amusing, because I could hear the guffaws booming out from John and Deb's tent, and especially Beth's. To this day Clyde still gives me a hard time over taking him to "Butch's Hole," and the perceived tent disaster. I think this was the last trip I ever took where I shared a tent. We all now use solo tents that weigh only about two pounds, and you just can't beat them. No smelly feet from your neighbor. No snoring. And any tent disasters will be of your own making. As to Chalice Falls, Deb remains pretty convinced that it is an undocumented waterfall. However, Lee Whittlesey, Mike Stevens, and Paul Rubinstein, co-authors of "The Waterfalls of Yellowstone" are convinced we were looking at Golden Fleece Falls, first documented by former Park Geologist Rick Hutchinson. We haven't been back to check it out, and frankly I doubt that we ever will, considering the hardship of getting there. Such are the trials and tribulations when the going gets tough and you change plans!

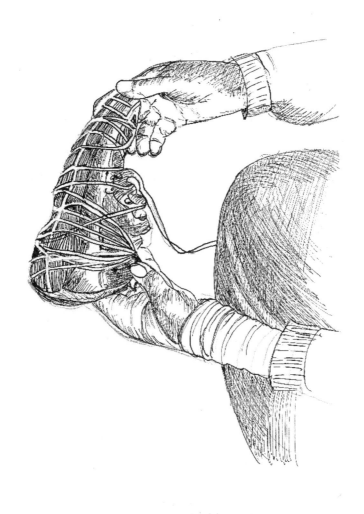

John's amazing repair job on Deb's boot near Eagle Pass

Along the Crest of the Tetons

It is amazing that after spending almost forty years working next door to Grand Teton National Park, I had never hiked the Teton Crest trail there. In fact, my time in Grand Teton's backcountry had been quite limited. Jim Lenertz and I enjoyed a couple of great trips, one a river to lake combo canoe trip (see "A River-Lake Combo Wilderness Canoe Trip"), and we had also completed a loop backpack trip in the remote northern section of the Tetons, going up Webb Canyon over Moose Basin Divide, and back down Owl Creek. When Margaret and I worked for the Yellowstone Park Company in 1968, we actually rode horses back to Lake Solitude from the Jenny Lake Corral (no longer in operation.) But I just did not think the Tetons were "wild enough," especially compared with Yellowstone. I think this attitude can be traced back to a trip I took with a fellow ranger, Jim Jones, during my first summer working for the NPS at Norris Geyser Basin in Yellowstone in 1974.

Jim and I knew that Lake Solitude had become "Lake Multitude," and we wanted to experience a wild and remote corner of Grand Teton's backcountry. We studied topo maps, consulted our supervisor John Stockert, and found just what we were looking for. John had many years of experience working in Grand Teton before arriving in Yellowstone, and highly recommended Hanging Canyon. So Jim and I planned to begin our trip by hiking up to Laurel Lake, which sits on a bench about 800' above String Lake. From there we would travel cross country, eventually climbing up to the entrance of Hanging Canyon. John had gushed about the jewel-like lakes in this spectacular trail-less canyon: Arrowhead Pool, Ramshead Lake, and Lake of the Crags.

Our bushwhack up to Hanging Canyon was rugged, but we were young and full of energy. When we arrived at Arrowhead Pool, we found the spectacular setting equal to John's descriptions. We hiked to the end of the canyon at Lake of the Crags, which is surrounded by huge peaks—Rock of Ages, The Jaw, and Mount St. John, the latter two above 11,400'. We set up camp at Lake of the Crags, and to this point our trip had exceeded our expectations. However, nothing could have prepared us for the next morning. Just after first light we woke up to loud chatter. It sounded as though a brigade of soldiers was marching through our camp! Here we were in this trail-less remote canyon camped at 9600' and it sounded for all the world like we were waking up at the Town Square in downtown Jackson! We looked outside our tent and saw a long line of folks marching past us—all carrying climbing gear. "So this is what it's like to backpack in the Tetons," I thought to myself. Despite the spectacular scenery I looked down on the Tetons as almost a "city mountain park" overrun with too many folks in the backcountry. Also, at this point in time, the Tetons had no grizzly bears, other than an occasional bear drifting south from Yellowstone into the northern range. Soon the Tetons moved to a "camping zone" system, where a specific number of backpackers could stay within a designated zone, as opposed to the one party per campsite system featured in Yellowstone. The final straw occurred when the park began requiring each backpacker to take a bear canister along, despite the presence of "bear boxes" provided at most camping zones. I had never had a problem finding a tree limb from which to hang my food if food poles were not provided, so why the need for bear canisters unless you were going to be camping above timberline? I had made up my mind that the Tetons with its big crowds was simply not wild and big enough to satisfy my wilderness cravings. However, in the summer of 2012 I finally retreated from that stubborn position.

I can credit my backpacking buddy Clyde Austin. "Butch," he drawled in his best East Tennessee mountain dialect, "I just don't understand you. I've backpacked all across the West, and I can tell you that the three most spectacular mountain backpack trips are Glacier, Grand Teton, and the Wind Rivers. I know you've been to Glacier, but I just can't believe you never backpacked in the Winds, or especially the Teton Crest, since it is right next door to your beloved Yellowstone!" "Clyde," I mused, "you have a point—it *is* close by!" Incidentally, I finally made it to the Winds in the summer of 2015 (see "The Winds—a Spectacular Wilderness in Need of Care".) I really cannot bestow all the credit for finally backpacking the Teton Crest solely to Clyde. My younger daughter Alison had worked a summer in the Tetons, and had visited Alaska Basin several times. She had also scolded me, "Dad, you have *got* to make it up to Alaska Basin and the Teton Crest if for no other reason than to see the wildflower display!" Down deep I knew that the mountain scenery and wildflowers would indeed be stunning. Soon our trip planning was underway, and we managed to obtain a backcountry use permit that contained just the trip we wanted.

Our group would include most of my reliable backpacking friends: Clyde, John and Deb Dirksen, Hank Barnett and Steve Hixson. Our trip itinerary would take us from the top of Rendezvous Peak to Marion Lake, and along the Teton Crest Trail to Death Canyon Shelf, through Alaska Basin, over Hurricane Pass, on to the South then North Fork of Cascade Canyon to Lake Solitude, over Paintbrush Divide, to Grizzly Lake, and finally through Paintbrush Canyon exiting at String Lake. John and Deb had balked at the idea of riding the Jackson Hole Aerial Tram to begin our trip. They wanted to begin near Teton Pass, and access the Teton Crest Trail from there. I tend to be a wilderness purist, so it did seem that we were "cheating" by taking the shortcut to the top of the mountains via the tram. However, our time frame did not allow for the Teton Pass alternative, since our trip included several day hikes to distant peaks and lakes. Also, I had to admit that being transported some 4000' from the valley floor up to an elevation of 10,450' was not a bad way to begin to begin a trip for a bunch of old folks.

Besides, this was the Teton Range, not Yellowstone. While over the years grizzly bears and wolves had made their way into the Tetons, I was still skeptical of its wild character, so why not fork out twenty bucks, go modern, and use the tram? No need to be a purist here!

As soon as we got off the tram I felt as though we were in downtown Jackson. There were hordes of people walking about taking in the sights of the valley far below. Paragliders were launching. "This is the last time I'll ever do something like this!" I heard Deb mumble to John. However, as soon as we moved away from the congested viewing deck where the tram offloads and began hiking down the trail, we lost the crowds and our spirits lifted. It was a blue bird day and the surrounding views of the Tetons were indeed breathtaking.

We had allocated eight days and seven nights for our backpack trip, and on this day we had a hike of seven miles to reach the multi-party campsite at Marion Lake at an elevation of 9200'. We followed an undulating trail through meadows filled with wildflowers—especially blue lupine and red paintbrush, before reaching our junction with the Teton Crest trail. A mule deer hopped through the meadow as we neared Marion Lake, situated in an idyllic setting with patches of timber, flower-laden meadows and steep cliffs nearby. However, once our trail reached the lake, it appeared that each tent site was occupied. We had a permit to camp here, but were wondering if there would be a place for us to pitch our tents. We finally came to the last spot at the far southwest end of the lake. My first reaction to the Tetons' "camping zone" system was not favorable. There just appeared to be too many folks at this one small lake.

Backpacking regulations for the high country of the Tetons does not allow fires, which is understandable given the fragile alpine vegetation. Therefore, we had camp stoves and freeze-dried meals. It had been very difficult to stuff eight days of food into the bear canister, but I managed to do it. After dinner just before sunset, we decided to take a walk around the lake, and ran into a rather stout backpacker who was packing 45 revolvers on both hips. I immediately knew that something was amiss because the Marion Lake camp zone was full. The fellow told us he had somehow lost his partner along the trail and he was trying to find a campsite. I asked to look at his permit and it turns out that they were supposed to camp at the Middle Fork Granite Canyon zone. He had walked right past it about two miles back. When I pointed this out the fellow seemed understandably concerned since daylight was dwindling. Chances are his partner was back in the campsite they were assigned. This fellow had a really big, heavy looking backpack. I was tempted to ask him why in the world he felt the need to pack along not one but *two* heavy revolvers in Grand Teton National Park. Visitors with guns do show up in the national parks now since legislation was passed by Congress to allow it, but in my opinion it is unwise to carry heavy guns into the backcountry. The interesting thing is, the law allows you to carry a gun in a national park, but it is illegal to *use* it! I'm sure this fellow felt the guns offered protection against bears, but from all of the expert testimony I've heard, shooting a bear with a gun is about the last thing you would want to do. It is practically impossible to hit a vital spot that quickly kills a bear. You would most likely injure the animal, and the enraged bear is going to take his anger out on you. Even if you do hit a vital spot, bears have been known to easily live long enough to fatally maul the shooter. Bear spray on the other hand is relatively lightweight, and it will blind and disable the animal, allowing sufficient time for the hiker to move away. I was an expert marksman in the Air Force, but I would much rather pack along a light canister of bear spray that shoots out a cloud of pepper spray, than carry a heavy gun that frankly would require a lucky shot.

The next day we faced an eight mile hike to Alaska Basin, where we had planned to camp for two nights. Along the way we hiked along the Death Canyon Shelf, and I have to say the scenery was simply out of this world. The wildflower display was the most spectacular that I have ever seen anywhere. The meadows were absolutely *carpeted* with wildflowers of all colors, and if you were able to pull your eyes away from that, we had stunning views of Death Canyon below and the prominent Grand Teton in the distance. We simply had to stop, take off our packs, sit down and take in nature's majesty all around us. The flowers were apparently at a peak given our travel date of late July, and the moisture in the mountains this late in the summer was helping the display. I had frankly been surprised at just how large the snowfields were this late in the summer.

I think it was at this point that I realized I had perhaps misjudged the Grand Tetons as a backpacking destination. Not only did we have views of magnificent wild mountain country in all directions, but surprisingly, there were no other hikers or backpackers around—just us. We surmised that lots of folks like to ride the tram up, hike over to Marion Lake for the night, and then hike back for the tram ride back down. If so, this was fine with us as we relaxed in solitude on Death Canyon Shelf. We were unanimous in our agreement that we wished we had come to this camping zone, rather than crowded Marion Lake for our first night. Our first day's hike would've been lengthened by three miles or so, but what a grand place to camp!

As we gazed at the mighty Grand rising above the horizon about ten air miles to the north, it was interesting to realize that in the coming days we would be hiking completely around it. We would pass below its west side but by the time we ended our trip at String Lake, we would be looking up at the east side of the Grand. We were looking forward to our stay in Alaska Basin for not only the grand scenery with its lakes, flowers and peaks, but also because we would have two nights. A layover day is always enjoyable. You get up in the morning, and instead of having to pack up all of your gear, you trade the 45 pound backpack for a simple daypack with a lunch, and head out for the day!

Our trail climbed to Mount Meek Pass above 9700,' and we were treated to a great view of Mount Meek (named for the famed mountain man, Joe Meek) immediately to our west, and what appeared to be a sudden drop-off from our high plateau directly ahead. When we reached the edge of the drop-off, we gained our first good view of Alaska Basin with its myriad of lakes below. To reach the basin the trail made a dramatic descent on a series of tight switchbacks known as the "sheep steps."

Once at the Basin we picked out a wonderful campsite with views of the surrounding peaks and nearby lakes. With no campfires allowed in this fragile high country, our evening entertainment centered around the incredible alpenglow on the peaks immediately above us. Buck Mountain, at an elevation of 11,938,' dominated the skyline, as it lit up like a huge lampshade with the setting sun. I had read that the Grand lights up like a candle in the distance when viewed from Sunset Lake in Alaska Basin, but from our campsite it was Buck Mountain that put on the show.

The next morning we awoke to another bluebird day, and we looked forward to a relaxing time of hiking, and not having to pack up and move camp. John and Deb decided they wanted to explore the many lakes scattered throughout Alaska Basin, and the rest of us decided to climb Static Peak. If we made it all the way to the summit at an elevation of 11,303,' it would be the highest ground that Hank, Steve or I had ever hiked (though Hank and I would top that in the Wind River Mountains in the summer of 2015.) Clyde had hiked above 19,000' in the Andes before. Our camp was situated at an elevation of about 9500,' so we faced a climb of about 2500,' which we would tolerate much easier without our heavy backpacks. We followed the Alaska Basin Trail, which led us up out of the basin, and over Buck Mountain Pass at 10,400.' Along the way the trail wound through meadows laden with flowers, especially pink elephant head, aster, and red Indian paintbrush.

Once over the pass, we encountered large snowfields, which we navigated with the help of our hiking poles. The trail hugged the massive shoulders of Buck Mountain and Static Peak, and provided sweeping and stunning views of the country to the southwest, especially Prospectors Mountain, and the Death Canyon Shelf upon which we had earlier hiked. Of particular interest was Rimrock Lake, appropriately named as it is tightly tucked into a high cirque beneath Prospectors Mountain. I recalled the story John Stockert once shared with me about attempting to reach this lake. John took many amazing day hikes during his tenure in Grand Teton; however, he never found a route to access Rimrock Lake. As I looked at it across the valley, I could certainly understand why. The size of the lake was rather significant, but it appeared that to reach it you would almost have to be lowered there by a helicopter!

There was really no maintained trail heading up to the summit of Static Peak, but the scramble was not that difficult. However, the wind was howling with such a velocity, as to throw you off balance. We held our hats in our hands, and stayed low to the ground, as we gradually made our way to the top. There were fires burning in Idaho that had the potential to obscure our mountain views, but during the week of our trip, we were extremely fortunate that the prevailing winds were causing most of the smoke to drift to the south of the Tetons. The views from the top of Static Peak were therefore magnificent. The four of us were giddy as we gazed at the pinnacle of Buck Mountain, less than a mile away. The top of the mighty Grand seemed much closer than its distance of five air miles from us.

Our trip back down to Alaska Basin was relaxing as we occasionally stopped to revel in the wild beauty around us, from tumbling streams, to meadows full of colorful flowers to rugged peaks. Amazingly, we did not see another soul the entire day. We spent another tranquil evening enjoying dinner, followed by the spectacular low light show on Buck Mountain. Our layover day had been a joyous one, and we looked forward to one more during our trek.

The next day we again shouldered our backpacks, and began an 1100' climb up to Hurricane Pass at an elevation of 10,700.' From the top we had a wonderful view of the Grand (13,770') and the Middle Teton (12,804') to its south. The trail switch backed down past Schoolroom Glacier, so named for its textbook glacial characteristics, such as moraines, crevasses and a proglacial lake at its base. I was impressed by its size in 2012, but I found later that the glacier had decreased by almost half of its size in the last 50 years, and will most likely disappear within the next 25 to 30 years.

Below Hurricane Pass we entered the south end of the South Cascade Canyon camping zone, and selected a great campsite at 9600' elevation near the junction of a maintained spur trail that leads up to Avalanche Divide. Given the fabulous day hike choices from here, we had planned to spend our second and last layover day at this spot. On this evening, we were treated to a magnificent alpenglow on both the Grand and the Middle Teton above our camp. Once again, we had the area to ourselves. I think it was on this evening that I began to completely change my attitude about the wildness and serenity of the backcountry of Grand Teton National Park. Here we were in one of the most magnificent settings I have ever experienced in the wild in my life, and yet we had the solitude and peace that are so important to a quality wilderness experience. The camping zone concept employed by the NPS in Grand Teton seemed to me, at least on our trip, to be an outstanding way to manage a wild area that many people want to visit. The camping zone had obvious spots for tents, and were spread out over appropriate distances. The quantity of backpackers within the zone was limited, thanks to the requirement of obtaining a backcountry permit. The individual tent sites were basically selected on a first-come, first-served basis. Either we were arriving at each camping zone early, or there were not that many other backpackers on the trail during our trip, because we had our pick of campsites in each zone for the entire trip. The camping zone concept and backcountry permit system here was a marked contrast to the horrendous system of management we encountered three years later in the Wind Rivers (see "The Mighty Winds—a Wilderness in Need of Care.")

The next morning we departed camp sans all the gear for another blissful day of exploring the high country. We followed the spur trail up to Avalanche Divide through some of the most stunning mountain scenery I had ever seen. The trail climbed through verdant meadows and whitebark trees, with snowcapped peaks, and vertical walls rising above us on all sides. A lavender flower known as Parry Primrose was prevalent throughout the meadows. I had now bought in completely. No wonder Clyde and Alison had given me a hard time for not making it to this wild mountain paradise sooner! Upon reaching Avalanche Divide at an elevation of 10,680,' we obtained a wide-ranging view of the peaks around us, dominated by the South Teton at 12,514,' and the Middle Teton at 12,804.' We now had a decision to make. We could either descend 700,' and explore the shoreline of Snowdrift Lake, or we could attempt to angle along a steep slope for about a mile to reach Icefloe Lake, which was tucked into a cirque and hidden from view. After poring over our topo map we were convinced that Icefloe Lake at an elevation of 10,652' was the highest lake in the Teton Range. This fact, plus the lake being hidden from view with no trail to it, was simply irresistible, though none of us relished beating up our feet with the mile-long side hill approach.

The lake did not come into view until the last possible moment, as we topped over a large snowfield, which sloped away to the shore of the lake. We were rewarded not only with the view of this hidden high gem of the Tetons, but directly overhead rising some 2000' was the summit of the Middle Teton, and the Grand was also in view just over one mile away. In fact, with binoculars, we could easily spot climbers on both peaks, especially the Middle. Frankly, we had no desire to trade places with any of them. We prized right where we were, on much firmer terrain than those climbers above us.

We returned to our camp, and decided to pack up our gear, and hike a few more miles down the trail. We knew that the trail coming up Cascade Canyon from Jenny Lake to Lake Solitude (aka "Lake Multitude") was by far the busiest in the park. Since no camping is allowed at Lake Solitude, Clyde suggested that we camp at the north end of the camping zone just south of the trail junction with our trail, the South Fork Cascade Canyon trail, and the Cascade Canyon trail. In this manner we could get an early start, and beat the hordes coming in from Jenny Lake the following morning on this popular day hike, perhaps enjoy some actual solitude at Lake Solitude for an early lunch, then head over Paintbrush Divide before the crowds arrived.

As we began our descent down the canyon, we were treated to scenes of waterfalls spilling over the walls of the canyon from the melting snowfields above. We passed a trail crew that was building a retaining wall from the available rocks at a sharp switchback in the trail with a steep drop-off. The quality and expertise of their work was amazing. I thanked them for keeping this trail in such great condition. "Thank you sir, we appreciate the compliment," the young man on the trail crew replied to me.

The quality of this wilderness backpack trip had far exceeded my expectations, but another unexpected surprise was the vibrant health of the whitebark pine forest. While most of the mature whitebarks in Yellowstone are gone (see "When the Yellowstone High Country was Green,") we were continually being treated to large, healthy trees. We stopped at one huge tree and I took a photo of John giving it a bear hug. We had not seen trees like this in Yellowstone since the late 70s. After the trip was over I called Roy Renkin, Yellowstone's vegetative specialist, and asked him about the marked difference in the health of the whitebarks between the two parks. Roy attributed the health of the Teton whitebarks to more moisture from a larger snowpack in the Tetons, and also perhaps a different point in the age cycle of the forest compared to Yellowstone. The moisture helps strengthen the trees' resistance to pine bark beetles, which seem to be more prevalent due to the general warming throughout the West. What we were seeing and enjoying could be only a short-term reprieve for this majestic tree, but it was like going back in time to the 70s in Yellowstone's high country.

As the trail lost elevation in the forest, we were in the midst one of my very favorite plants—huckleberry bushes! As anyone knows who has ever picked these delectable treats, much patience and time are required. Deb always prepares many delicacies over the campfire using dried foods, but on this trip in fragile alpine country most of us were eating freeze-dried meals. However, on this evening she prepared a scrumptious huckleberry cobbler on her camp stove, utilizing the many berries we had picked. It was to die for.

The next day would be by far our most difficult. Not only did we have about 11 miles to go, but from our camp at 8000' we had to climb over 2700' to the top of Paintbrush Divide on our way to Grizzly Lake, where we had a permit to camp for the night. On this day I would fully understand why so many folks stick more to day hiking in the Tetons rather than backpacking. For one thing, even though this was our sixth day of the trip, our backpacks were not appreciably any lighter. That's because our dry food did not weigh much to begin with. The weight in our backpacks was more from necessary gear, such as tent, sleeping bag, clothing, etc. When you plan an eight day trip at such high elevations you have to go prepared, and the weight quickly adds up.

My daughter Alison had actually *run* the Teton Crest trail in one day! Jim Lenertz covered most of the Tetons via day hikes when he worked here in 1967. Ditto for John Stockert. My former supervisor at Old Faithful, Katy Duffy, co-authored a guidebook, *Teton Trails*, and most of her hikes consisted of day hikes sans backpack. There are definitely advantages to backpacking in the mountains. I just love immersing myself for 24 hours each day in the wilderness, but Lord on this day my body was rebelling.

We climbed 1000' and made Lake Solitude for lunch. Just as Clyde had predicted, we practically had the lake to ourselves, as there was only one young couple present beside us. We knew that within the next two or three hours this would not be the case. It had been 44 years since Margaret and I had ridden horses here with friends when we worked at Canyon Village, but I remembered the setting as though it had only been the previous year. We relaxed on the granite boulders and enjoyed our lunch, as we gazed at the west side of the mighty Grand towering over Cascade Canyon. I was surprised at the number of trout rising in the lake at this time of day.

After lunch we faced a 1700' climb up to Paintbrush Divide. As we rounded one switchback after another, I realized that this trail's reputation was well-deserved. The views down on Lake Solitude, Cascade Canyon, and the Grand were simply dazzling. Normally, when I am gradually ascending a trail that provides such splendid mountain views, I don't seem to get so physically whipped. But I guess we had just covered too many miles on this rather warm day, because I was absolutely wiped out. Not Hank or Steve; they whizzed on up the trail as though they were floating on a cloud. I thought back to a trip I had taken only a few years before that featured a similar trail—the "Beaten Path" in the Beartooths, which climbs 4000' from Rosebud Lake up to Fossil Lake. I was amazed that I never felt tired backpacking that trail, because the climb was gradual, and the ever-changing views of the canyon walls and waterfalls spectacular. But on this day heading up to Paintbrush Divide, the mind was not able to conquer the body. I found myself stopping and gasping for breath every hundred yards or so. At least my eyes were feasting on fabulous scenes.

John and Deb did not appear to be as whipped as me, but they were also taking their time as well. When we finally reached the top, Steve and Hank had obviously been waiting for quite some time. They were bundled up in coats while the three of us were still decked out in shorts and tee shirts. After a short break, we headed over the divide, and immediately gasped at what we had to negotiate. There were still some very large snowbanks remaining, plus the narrow trail dropped straight down tucked against sheer vertical walls. With a stiff breeze blowing and such tight quarters, keeping our balance with our backpacks was a challenge. We were in rugged country with no ropes or handrails. One slip here could easily produce serious injury. Once we safely emerged from the cliff, we encountered a long, steep snowbank. This we had not anticipated. Again, one slip crossing this would lead to a slide into sharp boulders.

We had a permit for camping off trail at Grizzly Lake, which we could see far below us during our descent on the Paintbrush Divide trail. However, after making it down the cliff trail and through the snowbank, we were now faced with a steep 800' drop to the lake. With snowbanks and springs nearby, we decided to pitch our tents on a flat bench for our camp, and hike down to the lake the next morning sans backpacks. From an aesthetic point of view, the bench provided a better setting than the lake would have. Our campsite overlooked Grizzly Lake, and rising directly above us was Mount Woodring at 11,590.' Later that evening, the alpenglow on its slopes was impressive, as we eased into our tents for a comfortable night's sleep. It had been a long and arduous day.

The next morning after breakfast we descended to the lake, and experienced a brief shower for the first time since we had left Marion Lake. Along the shores of this pristine lake we marveled at the sight of several streams tumbling into the lake, verdant gardens full of flowers, and trout rising. Despite the attributes of this beautiful high mountain lake, we saw absolutely no evidence of human visitation.

Our seventh day took us to yet another fabulous campsite located at an elevation of 9700' near Holly Lake. This time instead of alpenglow, we were treated to an incredible orange sunset over the distant waters of Leigh Lake and Jackson Lake far below us. Apparently the prevailing winds had changed, blowing some of the smoke from the fires burning in Idaho our way, thus providing the orange haze at dusk.

Our final day would consist of a gradual descent of over 2800' to trail's end at String Lake. The highlight of our hike on this day was picking a quart of huckleberries to take home to Margaret. We love to use them in pancakes! Once we reached String Lake, we were back in the crowds and heat. It was tough to take after spending eight straight days mostly above 9200' in the cool, fragrant high country of the Teton Range. My attitude had been completely adjusted. The grandeur of this high mountain trek and the quality of the wilderness experience ranked this backpacking trip one of my best ever. My hat is off to the NPS backcountry managers in Grand Teton National Park.

Cascade Canyon as viewed from the Paintbrush Canyon Trail

Grizzlies in the Mist (or You Want Me to Pick You Up *Where*?)

From January of 1970 through June of 1974, Margaret and I lived in Great Falls, Montana, while I was stationed at Malmstrom AFB. I could not help but notice the *huge* blank spot on the map south of Glacier National Park that was called the Bob Marshall Wilderness, or affectionately "The Bob" by locals. Just who was this Bob Marshall fellow? I actually became very familiar with this man's legacy before I ever explored the wild country named for him.

During the early 1970s William Kemsley had introduced an excellent magazine named *Backpacker Magazine*. The backpacking craze was just taking off, and I enjoyed the magazine's articles about gear, great places to hike, and especially a series called "Elders of the Tribe." I kept waiting for one to appear on Bob Marshall, and one day decided to propose writing it myself. "Hell yes, we would love such a story!" was Kemsley's enthusiastic reply, so I set about gathering as much information as I could about this incredible champion of the wilderness, who died in 1939 at the young age of 38. I even traded correspondence with Bob Marshall's brother George, who lived in California during the early 1970s. My article appeared in the summer, 1974 issue of *Backpacker*. However, I still had not taken a lengthy trip into the Bob, only short day hikes along the perimeter of its vast acreage. Most of my extensive trips had been in Glacier, and especially Yellowstone, since I had been working on a Sierra Club trail guide for the park's some 1000 miles of trails. I was aching to go deep into the Bob.

My tour of duty with the Air Force was approaching an end, and I was due to begin work as a National Park Service Ranger in Yellowstone in early June of 1974. My good friend and Air Force colleague, Al Duff, with whom I would take many backpacking trips into Yellowstone, and I planned a 70 mile long trip across the Bob in mid-May prior to my leaving the Air Force and Great Falls. We knew that we would encounter significant snow this early in the season in the mountains, so we packed along lightweight plastic snowshoes. However, we had no idea just how *much* snow we would have to deal with!

The plan was for Margaret to drive Al and me to Holland Lake on the west side of the Bob, where our trip would begin. We would climb into the mountains, and eventually make our way out to Lincoln, Montana on the south end (now the Lincoln-Scapegoat Wilderness) where Al's wife Susan would pick us up. But as they say… "the best laid plans of mice and men!" We started our hike in gorgeous spring conditions at Holland Lake at an elevation of 4031,' but as we climbed over 2000' to Upper Holland Lake, we transitioned back into winter! Along the way we donned our snowshoes. There was nothing to be seen but deep snow everywhere. In fact the trail sign, "Entering the Bob Marshall Wilderness" was almost completely covered in snow, indicating a depth of five feet. High above us on the slopes of Mount Waldbillig, we heard a loud roar. When we glanced up we watched an avalanche cascading down the slopes, which really spooked us. This reminded us that taking a trip in May exposed us to a variety of challenges. Not only could we expect to encounter some very difficult stream crossings due to the snow melt this time of year, but in the high country we faced the dangers associated more with a winter trip, such as avalanches and hypothermia.

Spring may have been busting out down around 4000' at Holland Lake, but that night at Upper Holland Lake we pitched our tent in the snow. There was no bare ground in sight. I was reminded of the scene in the movie "Jeremiah Johnson," where the old mountain man "Bearclaw" played by Will Geer gazes down at the valley from his beloved snow-covered high country and says, "Winter stays long this high. It's green and muddy down below, some folks like it—farmers mostly." We weren't farming anytime soon, but we certainly hoped to get back to boots on solid ground, but for the time being we were snowbound. While it didn't snow that evening, we were enveloped in clouds, which kept the temperature from plunging much below the freezing mark.

The next morning we awoke to find ourselves in a foggy, dreary mist. After a quick breakfast, we strapped on our snowshoes, and began the 600' climb up to a pass at 6600,' before descending down to the Pendent Lakes. On our topo map these lakes, surrounded by big peaks, appeared to provide a scenic setting worthy of a calendar photo shoot; however, when we arrived in the basin, we could not see a single lake. Nor could we see any alpine meadows replete with wildflowers. In fact, all we saw was white—everything was snow-covered, including the lakes. We thought that by wearing snowshoes we would be fine with all of the snow, but as we began our gradual descent along Pendant Creek and later Big Salmon Creek, we soon encountered big problems.

Given the warming temperatures, the streams were running very high. Each time we came to a stream crossing, we had to unfasten our snowshoes, attach them to our backpacks, then climb down a four foot snow bank to reach the raging stream, figure out a way to get across the stream, then climb up the snow bank on the other side, refasten the snowshoes, and start the routine all over again. The leather straps with buckles were not easy to put on and then take off. Our travel therefore became very exasperating, and our tempers flared each time we rounded a bend to face yet another stream crossing. On several of the crossings, the stream was simply too deep and swift to ford, so we had to find a tree fallen across, and then shimmy our way over to the other side.

I'm embarrassed to say that I probably used more colorful language on this particular day than on any other trip I have taken. At least, that is what Al tells me, I don't recall. All I remember is, I was simply trying to avoid slipping off one of those logs into the streams below, which would have definitely been life-threatening! To make matters even worse, the fog refused to lift, severely restricting our visibility.

Even though we were now losing elevation, we were still in the snow. We eventually made camp in the snow once again. We managed to find a decent supply of firewood for our campfire, plus it really wasn't that cold. After all, this was mid-May, and the days were getting longer. Our main problem continued to be negotiating the stream crossings.

The next morning we awoke to another gloomy day. The combination of cold snow and mild weather was producing a low fog, which along with a light mist falling from above, completely engulfed us, and really obscured our visibility. I had once taken a long trip in Yellowstone over the snow, but there you have orange trail markers to look for. Here, we could only look for clearings, and obvious avenues through the trees, which hinted there might be a trail there. This significantly slowed our progress. So, amid the fog, the stream crossings, and the wet mist falling from the skies, what other challenges could we possibly face? Well, how about grizzly bears?

After yet another stream crossing, we were reattaching our snowshoes when I heard Al say, "Butch, look over to your right." I glanced over to where Al was looking, and observed a *very* fresh set of grizzly tracks coming out of the woods, and heading right down our direction of travel. What was worse, there was also an accompanying set of cub tracks. "Just great," Al moaned. "Now we have grizzlies in the mist to contend with." We both knew just how dangerous an encounter with a sow and cub in this fog could be. I had run into a sow and cub with my friend Rod Busby near Fawn Pass in Yellowstone the previous September, and Al had heard me describe what a close call it had been. Given the fact that our visibility was extremely limited, we relied on making noise to prevent another such encounter. It appeared that the sow and cub were heading for the low country just like us. The fog was so thick that on several occasions, we thought we saw dark objects moving immediately ahead of us, causing our hearts to skip a beat. Perhaps it was only our imagination playing tricks on us, or maybe the bears were indeed ahead of us, barely out of our very limited range of vision. After a while though, we were able to relax, as the bears' tracks headed off to the left away from our trail.

I really didn't mind the snowshoeing, but having to constantly take them off and put them back on due to the stream crossings was taking a toll on our wits. Therefore, it was quite a relief when we reached Albino Creek, where we found a few spots of bare ground large enough on which to actually pitch our tent, and build a campfire. It felt great to finally get out of our snowshoes and walk around a bit. We retired for the evening with high hopes of not having to put our snowshoes back on the rest of the way down to Big Salmon Lake.

The next morning we awoke to a steady rain. Rather than venture outside, and attempt to build a campfire in the wet and cold, we simply brought our granola bars and dried fruit breakfast inside the tent. Alas, no hot coffee on this morning. To make matters worse, once we departed camp, we found ourselves right back in the snow, and having to deal with constant stream crossings again. The frustration of having to put the snowshoes on and off finally got to us, so we decided to simply try walking on top of the snow in our boots. It worked for about one hour until it warmed up, then we started to sink to our knees. So rather than continue post-holing, we returned to our familiar miserable routine with the snowshoes.

Finally, by about 3:00 p.m., we emerged from the snow at an elevation of 4400,' where Brownie Creek flows into Big Salmon Creek. We now had about four more miles of stress-free walking on bare ground to our planned campsite along Big Salmon Lake, one of the largest wilderness lakes in the lower 48 states. The lake is rather narrow and measures five miles long. By the time we reached camp, the rain had slowed considerably. Al started a campfire and given the calm conditions, the smoke wafted out over the lake, and just hung there.

After dinner I leaned back against a tree to escape the light rainfall, and gazed out across the vast expanse of Big Salmon Lake. "Al," I said, "I'm certain that we are the first visitors of the season to this lake." "No question about it," he remarked, "but who else would be dumb enough to snowshoe into here in the spring, and deal with all of these stream crossings?" Al had a point. We had seriously miscalculated the extent to how much snow we would encounter. We had figured it would be limited to the higher mountain pass areas, but the vicinity around Big Salmon Lake had been the first snow-free area we had found since leaving the trailhead behind at Holland Lake.

We gathered around the campfire for a very important discussion. We knew that we were in big trouble. "Al," I began, "I have always enjoyed traveling over the snow either by ski or snowshoe, but I just can't take any more of this on and off routine every 100 yards." "I feel the same way," Al said. "We've got to come up with a different plan." Our original plan had been to turn to the south at Big Salmon Lake, and head up the South Fork of the Flathead River, and on to Danaher Creek, eventually coming out near Lincoln, Montana, where Al's wife Susan was to meet us. However, we knew this route would take us back up above 6600,' and back into the nightmare of deep snow and numerous streams to cross. There was simply no way that we could make it out to Lincoln anywhere close to the date we had projected, when Susan would be there at the trailhead to pick us up. Susan would probably have Search and Rescue teams out looking for us.

We knew that we only had one option, and that was to turn to the north and follow the South Fork Flathead River *downstream* some 45 miles, until we reached an isolated U.S. Forest Service ranger station at Spotted Bear, on the far south end of Hungry Horse Reservoir. This route would keep us at lower elevations, and from all indications out of snow. Also, since this appeared to be a major trail, hopefully there would be footbridges in place for stream crossings. But there was a big problem with this plan as well. According to our topo map, it appeared that the only way for an auto to reach the Spotted Bear station was via a remote 55 mile long dirt road from Hungry Horse, Montana. This early in the spring season, we wondered if the road would even be open and passable, and if it was, would there even be a ranger stationed there yet? And, then of course, our huge problem—how in the world would we get word to Susan to not drive to Lincoln to meet us, and instead head for the south end of Hungry Horse Reservoir? Our only hope was to pick up our pace, get to Spotted Bear just as soon as possible, and hope there was a ranger present who would have a phone so that we could catch Susan before she left.

The driving distance from Great Falls to Lincoln was only 90 miles, and would have required less than two hours. However, to get to Spotted Bear from Great Falls, would require a drive of some 260 miles, and would most likely take well over six hours. We hated to even ask Susan to do this, but on the other hand, the worst possible scenario would be if we ended up at Spotted Bear, and she ended up at the trailhead out of Lincoln! Obviously, this was the age before cell phones, not that it would even make any difference today given the remote locations involved. So we headed out into what really would be the big unknown. Neither of us had ever been on this trail, or for that matter, had ever visited the long and narrow Hungry Horse Reservoir. I had certainly heard of it. How could you forget a name like that?

For all we knew, the station would be deserted, and the dirt road to Spotted Bear a muddy quagmire with a locked gate across. But as Al had said, at least we had a chance. As I heard legendary Yellowstone ranger Jerry Mernin say on more than one occasion, "It would be an adventure!" As we left Big Salmon Lake behind, it was encouraging to continue to have firm soil under our boots rather than having to deal with the snowshoes. This allowed us to make excellent progress, as our trail followed right along the gorgeous South Fork of the Flathead River. Furthermore, the weather had finally cleared, and would stay that way for the remainder of the trip. Occasionally, the river flowed through a gorge, and our trail stayed up high on the rim. We passed Forest Service patrol cabins along the way, but they were locked up tight with no evidence of recent activity. That night we camped at a sharp bend in the river with large meadows known as Little Salmon Park, and enjoyed clear conditions for the first time on the trip. The pink alpenglow on the surrounding peaks was both welcome and spectacular. Our trip enjoyment, however, was somewhat muted. We had worried minds.

The next day broke clear and beautiful, and it would be our biggest day in terms of miles covered. By the end of the day, we would hike nearly 20 miles, and would have made more if we had not had to endure so many treacherous stream crossings. Our hope for footbridges had not come to fruition. Dozens of very large streams cascaded down the mountains from both sides of the trail, emptying into the roaring South Fork of the Flathead River. Streams with strange names: Damnation Creek, Hungry Creek, Snow Creek (appropriate for *this* trip!), Jungle Creek, Hodag Creek, Slick Creek, Lost Jack Creek, Addition Creek, to mention just a few. We lunched at Black Bear Creek and violated the "Rod Busby stream crossing rule." My old hiking buddy Rod and I used to have this argument. I would usually want to relax and enjoy my lunch *before* the ford. Rod would never do this. He would only have lunch *after* the crossing. More than once we had lunch on opposite sides of the stream.

I guess the prime problem was back in those days we did not have lightweight footwear such as Crocs or "river shoes." Flip flops were worthless, so unless you wanted to haul along a waterlogged pair of sneakers, which we did not, we had to hang our heavy hiking boots around our necks and make the stream crossing through rocky, ice-cold waters barefooted. It was absolutely a miserable experience that we both dreaded. Al and I choked down our lunch as we gazed out at Black Bear Creek, our most treacherous stream crossing yet. "I guess my old buddy Rod was right," I mused to Al. "Looking at what we have to contend with has ruined my lunch!" We found some sturdy branches to use to steady our balance, took off our boots and socks, tied them around our necks, and hoisted our backpacks as high on our shoulders as we possibly could. We then eased into the deep, icy waters. The water was flowing so swiftly that we could feel rocks banging against our legs and feet, but we made it across.

We hiked on into the darkness of night and did not stop until after 9:30 p.m., when the trail paralleled steep canyon walls at least 30' above the river. We figured we needed full visibility to continue lest we make a misstep and plunge into the gorge. We had stopped just short of the primitive U.S. Forest Service air landing strip at Meadow Creek. That left us with about 12 miles to cover the next day to reach Spotted Bear. We figured if we got a good early start we might stand a chance of making it there in time to place a phone call to Susan *before* she left her house and headed for Lincoln. We had instructed her to pick us up fairly late in the afternoon. Of course, even if we made it to Spotted Bear in time, we knew that three other things had to work for us: 1) the dirt road from Hungry Horse to Spotted Bear had to be passable; 2) A ranger would actually be present at the remote Forest Service station at Spotted Bear; and 3) the place would have some type of phone or radio communication capability. I did not even want to consider what the odds were that all pieces of the puzzle would fit together for us! From a physical standpoint we were ready to hit the sacks on this evening. But we again retired with worried minds.

The next morning at first light we gathered up our gear, gulped down some oatmeal, and hit the trail. On this our sixth day of the trip, we still had not seen another human being. However, that was about to change. Just before noon we rounded a bend in the river, where I noticed an unusual assortment of color off to the right of the trail about 75 yards away. Upon closer examination we realized that we were looking at someone lying on his stomach aiming a revolver in the opposite direction from us. Whoever this was had not seen us. We took out our binoculars to take a closer look, and this guy looked just like an old prospector defending his claim. He was wearing a red and black flannel shirt, a beat up old cowboy hat, and he had a thick, black beard. "Al, we need to make sure we don't surprise this character, since he has a gun," I whispered. "Hello there," we said in not too loud of a voice so as not to surprise the fellow. It didn't work. The guy jumped about two feet off the ground, whirled around, and uttered "What thuh...." Then he looked at us, thankfully with his gun lowered, and said "Where in hell did you guys come from?" He obviously was not expecting any visitors from this end of the trail, which came from the high country still covered in snow.

"Well, we have our story, but why don't you tell us yours," Al answered. It turns out that this fellow was named Sam, and he worked for an outfitter who brought customers in for wilderness pack trips, and when conditions allowed, drop float trips. For the latter, the outfitter packs in rubber rafts over 25 miles to a backcountry camp along with dudes on horseback. The dudes then float the South Fork Flathead, which is designated as a Wild and Scenic River. There is no road access to the upper reaches of the South Fork, which is a tribute to the sheer size of the Bob Marshall Wilderness. Sam was in early ahead of his co-workers to reconnoiter things—check on the river's flow, begin setting up and preparing camp, gathering firewood, etc. The season's first pack trip was still a couple of weeks off. "I just like to come back here early, to get out here in the backcountry," Sam said. "I figure I was born about 150 years too late!" As for the gun, Sam was taking target practice at pocket gophers out in the meadow. "You guys are the first folks to come into this country this season, you know," Sam added. "Yeah," I answered, "I think we figured as much."

We told Sam of our predicament, but he did not seem to know any more about whether we would run into anyone down the way any more than we did. When he had ridden in on horseback, he did not pass directly by the Spotted Bear station. Furthermore, from our brief conversation, we were not even certain that he was aware of current road conditions. "Good luck," he wished us as we continued down the trail. "Have a great season in the wilderness," I responded. Despite our best efforts we did not reach Spotted Bear Station until 3:00 p.m. due to the rugged terrain we encountered. When we walked up to the front door we could not believe our eyes! The station was open and a ranger was on duty. We quickly went inside as we knew we were right on the edge of when Susan would be departing her home for Lincoln. We had noticed that there were no telephone poles, but we still hoped there would be some way we could attempt to get word to Susan. Sure enough, the ranger station had a "radio- phone."

The ranger handed the unit to Al with instructions on how to use it. As Al dialed I just held my breath and said a little prayer that Susan had not yet left. When Al said, "Hi Susan," I gleefully exhaled. I sat down in a chair because I figured this was going to be a rather lengthy conversation. However, Al got right to the point and I heard Susan exclaim, "You want me to pick you up *where?"* When Al hung up the phone he turned to me and said, "Butch, she said she was headed for the door when the phone rang. If we had been five minutes later she would now be on her way to Lincoln!" Al had instructed Susan to get a map out so they could together go over the rather complicated directions on how to find her way in to Spotted Bear. We knew that poor Susan would have to negotiate the hardest part of the trip along very primitive dirt roads well after dark. We asked the ranger what time he thought she might make it in. "You'll be lucky if she gets here before midnight. You folks should just plan to camp here tonight, rather than attempt to drive all the way back to Great Falls," he said.

The rest of the afternoon Al and I just relaxed. We set up our tents, enjoyed a nice meal, and rested around the campfire to wait on Susan. We were extremely relieved in one sense. Thank goodness we had caught Susan before she had headed up to Lincoln. However, we still had concerns. I could only imagine how difficult it would be to drive by yourself to this isolated place in the night. We were confident she would safely make it from Great Falls to Hungry Horse, but it was that 55 mile stretch of winding, twisting, narrow dirt road that concerned us. Also, the map seemed to show a maze of logging roads along the way, so we were concerned that Susan could make a wrong turn in the dark. The ranger also expressed this concern, and wished us the best of luck as he closed up the station for the night.

Midnight came and went and no Susan. We threw more logs on the fire. 1:00 a.m. passed and still no sign of any car lights approaching this remotest of outposts. It was time for another silent prayer. 2:00 a.m. passed and we were growing extremely concerned. But shortly after the 2:00 o'clock hour, we observed some headlights in the distance. Susan had made it! She said it was extremely slow going in the pitch black wilderness, and maze of dirt roads. She had also encountered a severe rockslide that extended all the way across the road. She had managed to barely skirt along the edge of the road to make it by, even though there appeared to be a steep drop off below the road. The amazing thing to me was, Susan was completely at ease with this assignment of rescuing her husband and his friend out in the middle of nowhere. No cross words. No complaints. No gripes. As far as I was concerned she was qualified for Sainthood. For her reward Susan got to sleep in her truck for the rest of the evening.

The next morning before we could get packed up and ready to pull out, the ranger walked over to us. "I'm afraid I have bad news," he began. "A rock slide has blocked the road in and it may be late in the day before crews get up here to remove the debris." "Oh, that slide was already there last night," Susan casually replied, "and I managed to make it past in the dark, so I'm sure we'll be able to make it through this morning." I could only grin and shake my head. Of course, it turned out Susan was correct. It was a tight squeeze but we made it. "This was more of a challenge at 1:30 in the morning in the pitch dark," Susan mused. By late morning we pulled up to the Hungry Horse café where I attacked the biggest stack of huckleberry pancakes I had ever attempted. I had finally reached deep into the heart and soul of "The Bob," and found it to be every bit as wild and remote as I had imagined. In future years I would return for more backpacking expeditions into what is now called "The Bob Marshall Wilderness Complex," which includes the Great Bear Wilderness, the Bob Marshall Wilderness, and the Scapegoat Wilderness, an area of more than 1.5 million acres. Our first trip into The Bob had been a remarkable adventure. Only a few weeks later Margaret and I took up residence at Norris Geyser Basin in my very first year as a seasonal ranger in Yellowstone. Al and Susan have continued to be great friends over the years and we continue to enjoy grand adventures with them.

Examining a huge whitebark pine in 1977 near Jones Pass in Yellowstone

When the Yellowstone High Country was Green

During my first summer as a seasonal ranger in Yellowstone in 1974, most of my duties involved giving guided interpretive walks to Echinus Geyser (which erupted about every 80 minutes then), and roving the Back Basin and Porcelain Basin. Everywhere I walked at Norris, I could not help but gaze up at the massive outline of Mount Holmes on the western skyline. I had never climbed to its 10,336' summit, which had a fire lookout stationed there for the summer fire season. By late July when the snow had sufficiently melted away, my friend Al Duff came down from Great Falls to join me for a backpacking trip to the high country, beginning with a climb of Mount Holmes.

As soon as I got off duty at 4:00 p.m. on Thursday, we headed in from the Grizzly Lake trailhead. It was about six miles to Winter Creek meadows, and from there, we traveled up a very primitive, rarely-used trail toward Trilobite Lake. Long-time seasonal ranger Ted Weight had raved about the scenic setting of this lake. He would often take his son there on his days off to fish for brook trout. Al and I had requested and received a non-designated backcountry permit, which meant that we were going to be staying away from established campsites. Most of the trips that Al and I took during the 1970s were of this variety, which involved traveling off-trail. Basically, in order to obtain such a permit, you had to demonstrate to the district ranger in charge of the region that you had the knowledge, skills and gear to travel off-trail, and that you were willing to accept the strict requirement to "travel light on the land," which included not building any campfires. The route that our permit covered allowed us to venture off trail from Mount Holmes, going north past Echo Peak, Three Rivers Peak and Gallatin Lake, until we reached a maintained trail at Bighorn Pass. From there, we would follow the Bighorn Pass trail east and exit at the trailhead at Indian Creek campground, located about ten miles north of Norris.

Such permits today are a bit tougher to obtain, mainly because of the many bear management areas (BMAs) that were created beginning in 1983. BMAs were established by Yellowstone Park officials, when biologists became alarmed over the decline in the grizzly bear population during the 1970s. The park was going through a difficult transition, where the attempt was made to remove all garbage and unnatural foods from bears. Research had shown that human travel in ideal grizzly habitat could actually cause the bears to abandon good sources of food. The BMAs allowed park officials to carefully manage human use in such areas. There were 17 different BMAs established in the park that in different degrees restricted recreational use in areas with seasonal concentrations of grizzlies. As of summer 2016 the area that Al and I traveled through in July of 1974 is called the Gallatin Bear Management Area, and off-trail travel is not allowed between May 1 and November 30. This restriction was placed into effect due to the high concentration of grizzly bears that biologists had observed throughout the Gallatin Range. Of course, when Al and I took our trip we were not aware of this, and to us it was simply another wild area of Yellowstone's backcountry. We did see grizzly sign but we did not see any bears on our trip.

The trail that we attempted to follow into Trilobite Lake became so grown over and tangled with deadfall, that we decided to veer up the slopes of the east shoulder of Mount Holmes to escape the jungle. We knew that the lower lake was situated at an elevation just under 8400' so we attempted to get to this level and follow it, since the trees were much more sparse here than below. It had been our goal to camp at the lake for the night, but by 8:00 p.m. darkness was setting in, and it appeared that the vegetation was about to become more dense. Therefore, we selected a spot on the edge of a small meadow to camp in. It was not level, but other than that was not a bad campsite with a nice view to the east. The trip up had been a tough one, and for dessert we added some powdered instant pudding to ice cold spring water in a Nalgene bottle, and shook it into a nice thick treat that helped to warm us up prior to crawling in our bags for the night.

The next morning we made it to Trilobite Lake by 9:00 a.m. I decided to fish for brook trout, but on this day the fish were not too interested in any of the lures I had to serve up. Incidentally, Trilobite Lake and Trilobite Point (10,011') just to the southwest, are named for the extinct marine anthropods that lived in ancient seas millions of years ago. We did not see any fossilized imprints of trilobites on this trip, but I did the following summer when I took a day hike to the summit of nearby Antler Peak (10,063'). Looking back, that day trip to Antler Peak was a tribute to the prowess of youth. I biked eight miles to the trailhead (climbing 800'), then hiked seven miles, climbing almost 3000' to the summit. Most of the hike up was off-trail. Then I made the return trip to my quarters in Mammoth. Such are easy feats when you are in your 20s! I recall the feeling of contradiction that day, as I examined fossilized sea shells and trilobites from my perch near the summit of Antler Peak high in the Gallatin Range. I remember thinking to myself, "Here I am on top of a mountain, looking at fossils that were on the ocean floor at one time in the past!"

From Trilobite Lake, Al and I climbed about 400' in less than one mile to an unnamed lake, though the obvious unofficial name should be "Upper Trilobite Lake." Of the two, the upper lake is the more impressive, since its shoreline is not as densely forested, and the rugged shoulder of Mount Holmes juts up almost vertically from its shores. "Al," I said, "this country up here has the look and feel of the Glacier high country!" Al, who had spent a lot of time in Glacier, agreed. We were now high enough to enjoy the beauty of Yellowstone's whitebark pines that flourished at these elevations. Whitebarks have five needles to the clump, and therefore provide the visual image of a "bushy" conifer, rather than the more pointed triangular shapes of the spruce and fir. When these elegant trees are mature, they provide pine cones that contain nuts that grizzlies feast on in the fall, due to the nuts' high caloric and fat content.

From the upper lake we now faced a climb of almost 3000' in less than a mile through boulders and talus. The established trail to the summit was on the other side (southwest) of the mountain, and is not nearly as steep. We had taken the adventurous route for sure. With backpacks on it was one of those "take three steps, rest, take three steps, rest" types of climbs. As we neared the summit, and the fire lookout station came into view, we noticed the fire technician was on duty, and was looking through the window on the other side of the lookout, so he did not see us approaching. When we knocked on the door he just about jumped out of his skin! He invited us in for a cup of hot chocolate, and told us that he had never seen anyone else "crazy" enough to climb up the north side of the mountain.

After chatting and resting a bit, we donned our packs and headed off down the summit into the valley to the west and northwest. We visited a small pocket lake nestled on the east side of the White Peaks where we had lunch, then proceeded north past Echo Peak to the saddle just north of Three Rivers Peak that provides access to Gallatin Lake. The passage was easy and we descended to the lake, which serves as the headwaters for the Gallatin River, one of the three primary sources of the mighty Missouri River, the other two being the Madison River (which also begins in Yellowstone), and the Jefferson River.

We set up our tent in a meadow about 75 yards away from the lake, and had the intention of relaxing and taking in the spectacular view of 9,958' Three Rivers Peak. However, storm clouds continued to build up, and shortly after 4:00 p.m., a tremendous thunderstorm rolled over us. We had made it to the lake ahead of schedule, which allowed us to duck into our tent to escape the fierce storm. Lightning hit the cirque walls above us, blasting stone out, which then clattered down the slopes. The electrical aspect of the storm eventually subsided into a heavy rain, which continued on throughout most of the evening. So much for the relaxing around camp, and enjoying the alpenglow on Three Rivers Peak! We had managed to hang up our packs and bring in a few cold snacks with us into the tent, so that became our supper.

The next morning was clear, fresh and just beautiful. We broke camp and began the short two-mile jaunt over to Bighorn Pass. Traveling along at an elevation just under 9000,' we were treated to stunning wildflower displays in the meadows, and a lush green forest of spruce, fir, and whitebark pine. Once we reached the maintained trail, we picked up our pace and made good time down the eight mile stretch to the trailhead at Indian Creek Campground. As we descended from the high country through first forest, and then large meadows, Al and I were already making plans for a longer trip the following summer. Our short three day backpack excursion into Yellowstone's higher elevations had truly whet our appetite for more. There was something magical about walking through verdant high country forests interspersed with flower-laden meadows. The following summer Al and I would embark on a fabulous eight day journey into what we felt was the best high country Yellowstone had to offer.

I was transferred from Norris Geyser Basin to Mammoth for the summer of 1975. It actually turned out to be one of the best summers of my career, at least in terms of the variety of interpretive duties that I had. Margaret and I enjoyed our quarters near a moose bog filled with aspens, and great views of nearby Mount Everts, and also of the rugged peaks north of the park. Just looking at the snow-clad peaks all summer kept my excitement high for our planned trip at the end of my season. Since my college was on the quarter system at the time, and classes did not begin until well into September, I had a nice gap between the date my Park Service employment ended, and when I had to be back in the classroom. When early September arrived, Margaret would spend time up in Great Falls with Al's wife Susan, and Al and I would head for the high country.

Each day at the Mammoth Visitor Center, the staff kept a logbook of the day's activities, and I vividly recall my entry as my last duty day of the season came to an end: "The Eagle Peak Expedition now begins!" Al and I had pored over topo maps, and had decided to follow this itinerary: We would drop off a vehicle at the Heart Lake trailhead on the south entrance road and then Margaret and Susan would drive us to Eleanor Lake near Sylvan Pass on the east entrance road. Our plan was to climb up to the top of the mighty Absaroka Range that runs north and south along Yellowstone's east boundary, and attempt to hike along the top of this ridge all the way to the summit of Eagle Peak, the park's highest at 11,358'. From there we would descend Beaverdam Creek to Yellowstone Lake and skirt the Southeast and South Arms on our way to Heart Lake, eventually coming out at the trailhead about 15 miles north of the park's south entrance. We figured we had about 60 miles to cover, much of it off-trail, and we had allotted eight days for the trip. Once again we had to obtain a backcountry permit that allowed off-trail travel and undesignated campsites.

Planning a big trip like this in September is risky due to the weather. As an example, Rod Busby and I had taken a big September trip through the Thorofare in 1972, in which a fall weather front rolled in that dumped unending rain and snow for the entire trip. However, Al and I had a charmed weather event in September of 1975. High pressure prevailed for the entire eight-day trip, with only a couple of brief showers encountered.

Beginning our trip from the high elevation of 8466' at Eleanor Lake helped when we started our off-trail climb toward Top Notch Peak, which tops out at 10,238.' Once we reached the top of the ridge above 9400,' we were once again in the enchanting world of high country with alpine meadows, and a luxuriant verdant forest comprised almost exclusively of the magnificent whitebark pine. Even though we were into September, we found the high country still lush with snowbanks still in place, and mountain streams flowing. The main reason that I titled this chapter "When the Yellowstone High Country was Green," is just that. It really did used to be green. This high elevation forest was the picture of health. My time in Yellowstone began in 1968, and it seems that with few exceptions, the next two decades featured heavy winter snows followed by wet summers. Such was the case in 1975. Obtaining drinking water on top of the Absaroka Ridge was not a problem, thanks to the abundance of snow banks.

I am often asked about changes that I have observed over four decades of working and backpacking in Yellowstone. Lots of great things have occurred—the return of the wolf, fewer elk which has produced a healthier northern range, a better road system that bypasses fragile thermal basins, recovering grizzly bear and mountain lion populations, to mention just a few. However, there are two things that I would have to say are much worse: one is the loss of Yellowstone's native cutthroat trout population (see "Memories of the Yellowstone Cutthroat") and the other is the die-off of the whitebark pines in the higher elevations. The illegal introduction of the non-native lake trout was the culprit regarding the loss of cutthroat, and I'm afraid that humans have played a significant role in the loss of the high elevation forest given the significant change in climate that I have observed in such a short period of time (see "A Late Season Ski and Diminishing Winters.")

For the duration of our trip the visibility in all directions was incredibly clear. From the top of the Absaroka Ridge along the park's east boundary, it is truly uplifting to see such a continuation of wild country to the east, which is the Washakie Wilderness within Shoshone National Forest. Not all national parks are so fortunate to have wild buffer zones on most of their boundaries as does Yellowstone. The almost unlimited visibility helped us to appreciate just how big and wild the Greater Yellowstone Ecosystem is. The reason for the clarity was the fact that few if any forest fires were burning anywhere near Yellowstone. Such is certainly not the case during the last couple of decades. Given the abundance of fires throughout the Rocky Mountain West each summer, unless wind conditions are favorable, it is rather unusual to find such clear conditions in late August and early September. In fact, when visitors ask me to advise them as to the best time of year to visit Yellowstone, I tell them around mid-June. At that time fires have usually not started up so the skies are clear. Other good reasons for a June visit include better chances of seeing animals in the valleys, since snow is still in the high country, less crowds, lush green meadows, and spectacular waterfalls. The downside would be reduced availability of hiking trails that are open, and a better chance for inclement weather.

Al and I felt as though we were literally walking in the clouds as we followed the top of the Absaroka Ridge from Top Notch Peak past Mount Doane and to a saddle below Mount Langford for our first camp. We made the big mistake of not filling our water bottles before retiring into our tent. The next morning the temperature was below freezing, so not a drop of water was trickling out of the snow, so we had to melt snow for our breakfast, and to fill our bottles.

On this day we had intended to stay on top of the ridge and hike over the top of Plenty Coups Peak at 10,940,' and Atkins Peak at over 11,000,' before dropping down to a small lake just below Mount Schurz. However, when we rounded Mount Langford, the sight of that rugged high ridge on the skyline was downright intimidating. The ridge had continuous steep undulations, and with our binoculars the section around Mount Atkins appeared rather technical. Therefore, we opted to drop down off of the ridge into the headwaters of Beaverdam Creek, and work our way along that stream south until we reached the nose of a forested ridge that we would climb back up to the lake. In the process we had to descend over 2000,' but the payoff was a walk through an enchanting combination of rolling meadows, and fine forest, with streams tumbling along the way. The forest here was healthy, with no recent burns and the amount of deadfall to contend with was minimal.

After hiking about four miles we were having a tough time spotting the ridge protruding to the west that we needed to climb up, but thanks to a small meadow we were able to gain a view. We then climbed up the nose of that ridge about 1200' to a lake that Al and I had referred to as "Schurz Lake," since it sits at the base of the mountain by that name. However, I have seen other sources refer to this lake as "Glade Lake." In September of 1975 I thought it was the most beautiful high country lake that I had ever seen. At an elevation of over 9600,' this body of water was nestled in sort of a hanging garden, with stupendous peaks rising above it to the west, and each evening these peaks would catch the rich hues of gold and pink from the setting sun. The alpenglow was fabulous, but the reflection in the lake was even better.

Once we reached "Schurz Lake" we had hoped to map out our route for climbing Eagle Peak. On our topo map, it looked deceptively easy for a couple of young fellows still in their twenties. It appeared that we could simply climb up the ridge to the east of the lake, and then follow it to the 11,139' summit of Mount Schurz. From there, we hoped to see a clear route over Mount Humphreys, and on to the summit of Eagle Peak. However, reaching the summit of Mount Schurz was no small feat. We first tried the east ridge, but were blocked by huge boulders. We backed down and returned up the north face, but again came upon a jumbled technical boulder field extending almost vertically to the top. Once again, we retreated to the saddle, had lunch, then circled around to the southwest face for our final attempt. This time we made it to within 50 vertical feet of the summit. The last pitch looked feasible, but rather technical, but by now we were simply too exhausted to attempt it. So we headed back down to camp, gathered up our stove and freeze-dried meals, and proceeded over to the sheer drop-off at the outlet of the lake to have dinner.

Since we were well into the fall in the high country, there was no outflow from the lake. We could only imagine how impressive the waterfall here would be during the peak of the snow melt. It appeared that this seasonal waterfall would measure about 600,' but getting here by foot at the time of peak snow melt would be quite a challenge. As we sipped hot chocolate gazing down to the bottom of the cirque, we watched a big bull elk moving along this headwater tributary of Beaverdam Creek. The next morning we worked our way down the ridge, and found our way to Beaverdam Creek, and followed it all the way out through forest, and eventually dense willows, until we reached the Thorofare Trail. Bushwhacking through willow brush is never a relaxing matter given the concern about jumping a moose or grizzly at close range.

After four full days of traveling cross-country, it was great to finally be back on a maintained trail, at least for a little while. However, right off, we faced a tough ford of the Yellowstone River, just south of Cabin Creek patrol cabin, where Rod and I had gratefully received permission to stay during our rainy and snowy fall trip only three years earlier. We weren't surprised that the river was still running high this late in the season given the heavy precipitation over the previous winter, spring, and summer. We found a good cottonwood branch to use for our third leg, took off our boots, stripped down to our undies, and waded through waist deep water to reach the other side. We then walked a couple of miles through large meadows before reaching Trail Creek, where it was time to once again leave the trail, and follow the little stream about one mile to its outlet at Trail Lake. Upon reaching the shore of the lake, we were immediately spellbound by the beauty of the spectacular backdrop of Turret Mountain, and the Absaroka Range, as well as the lush forests and meadows surrounding the lake. We selected a spot to pitch our tent next to Trail Creek, which tumbled down from the mountains into the lake on its southwest shore. Al tossed a lure out five times and reeled in five cutthroat trout. I then tried five casts and also caught five cutthroat. Trail Lake was absolutely full of this native fish, which the ospreys, eagles, otters and grizzlies depended on as a key food source. That evening after dinner, we enjoyed yet another display of alpenglow on the high peaks as the sun slowly set in the west.

The next morning we bushwhacked through the meadow a mile back to the maintained trail, which we would enjoy for the rest of our trip. We covered 12 miles for the day, and camped near the mouth of Grouse Creek on the South Arm of Yellowstone Lake. That evening we enjoyed yet another gorgeous alpenglow on the Absarokas. From our campsite, we cast a loving glance up to the top of the ridge just below Schurz Peak, where we had spent two glorious days and nights. We wondered aloud if and when we would ever get back to that very remote, extremely difficult to reach, little piece of heaven. That evening we were serenaded by the flocks of ducks and geese that were stirring to the shorter, cooler days of fall.

The next day we made a rather easy pass over the continental divide, and continued past Outlet Lake, eventually reaching the west side of Heart Lake, just as a thirty minute rain shower rolled in. It was the only precipitation we received during our eight day trip. We spent two splendid days and nights at Heart Lake, which I have always felt featured some of the most diverse and dramatic scenery in Yellowstone. Near our campsite we had the fascinating Heart Lake Geyser Basin and Witch Creek to explore. The lake itself with its winding shoreline is gorgeous; and then you have massive Mount Sheridan at 10,308' rising majestically above the lake's west shore.

The next morning broke clear but due to the rain shower, nearby thermal basin, and cold temperatures, a heavy fog hung over the lake. Al and I had planned to hike up to the summit, a 2868' climb in three miles, where a fire lookout station was located. Mount Sheridan was one of the few named mountain summits I had yet to visit, and our desire to climb it was our primary reason in spending two nights at Heart Lake. However, with the heavy fog over the lake, we could not even see the top half of the mountain, so we decided to postpone our climb until after lunch.

Instead, we walked over to the patrol cabin located on the north end of the lake, where I had spent several nights in March of 1973 during a blizzard, to see if a ranger was on duty. We found the cabin locked up tight, so we assumed he/she was out on patrol or on lieu days. However, the aluminum canoe behind the cabin was unlocked, and had paddles and life jackets underneath, so having just completed my second season with the Park Service, I gave myself permission to take a spin. Al and I took out our fishing rods, and decided to wait out the fog with a bit of fishing. We did have success with catching cutthroat, but nothing like what we experienced at Trail Lake. While we were out on the lake, the sun finally burned through the fog and a clear, bluebird day was at hand.

After eating lunch we began our hike to the summit. Margaret had made me a neat sleeping bag stuff sack that doubled as a light daypack, so I used it to carry along water, snacks, and a rain jacket. It was a tough climb, but not having to lug our relatively heavy backpacks along certainly made the hike more enjoyable. When we reached the summit, we walked over to the lookout cabin, and found a veteran by the name of Jim on duty. He had served a couple of decades there, and made us feel very welcome. After all, he did not receive many visits, since it was a 22 mile roundtrip hike from the trailhead.

Amazingly, almost 20 years later in 1994, I hiked up to the fire lookout station on Mount Washburn with Margaret and our friends Hank and Nancy Barnett. There was Jim, the lookout from Mount Sheridan! I asked him why he had traded locations, and he said that Mount Sheridan was too lonely; he enjoyed visiting and providing information to the *many* visitors who daily hike up to one of Yellowstone's most popular destinations. I had not seen Jim since that 1975 September day, but *incredibly* he remembered our visit! Incidentally, as of 2016, the fire lookouts at Mount Holmes and Mount Sheridan are no longer staffed. Only Mount Washburn lookout is staffed, partially because of the large amount of visitation it receives.

What a view from the summit of Mount Sheridan! The entire body of Heart Lake lay before us. We could see steam rising from thermal basins, large golden meadows, and in the far distance, that magnificent Absaroka Mountain Range along the park's eastern boundary that Al and I had only days earlier traversed. However, looking back, I think the most impressive sight that day from the top of Mount Sheridan was pretty similar to the scenes Al and I had taken in from Mount Holmes, Top Notch Peak, Mount Langford, and just below Mount Schurz: it was a view of thousands and thousands of acres of rolling, *green* forests.

Our trips to the Yellowstone high country those two summers of 1974 and 1975—in the Gallatin Range in the park's northwest corner, in the Absaroka Range along the park's eastern border, and concluding with the Red Mountains in the south end of Yellowstone, had exposed us to an amazing abundance and variety of elevations carpeted in green. Most impressive to us though, were those whitebark pines up in the high country. I captured many images on film of the September, 1975 trip, and I recently had them digitized so I could enjoy looking at them, and comparing the images to more recent photos I have taken of Yellowstone's high country. The contrast between those images separated by only a few decades is simply stunning.

Obviously fire has always played a significant role in the ecology of Yellowstone's forests at all elevations. However, something else is going on these days in Yellowstone. So much of the high country forest is either dead, dying or burned. It bears little resemblance to the land I observed first hand in the late 60s and 70s. Clearly, Yellowstone has a much warmer climate today than it did only forty years ago, which permits greater infestations of insects such as the mountain pine beetle. There are still places today in the Greater Yellowstone Ecosystem where you can find healthy forests in the high country, such as along the Teton Crest in Grand Teton National Park. Some plant biologists attribute this perhaps to those high peaks receiving more snow and moisture, which in turn allows the tree to resist the mountain pine beetle. However, most of the high country inside the boundary of Yellowstone National Park has dramatically changed from the time when Al and I embarked on our great adventures. We have watched a transition in color to mostly gray from when the high country was *green!*

Al Duff on Mount Schurz above the S.E. Arm of Yellowstone Lake

Across the Two Ocean Plateau

By the summer of 2013 there was still one huge blank spot on the topo map of Yellowstone National Park that was calling to me for exploration—the Two Ocean Plateau. Rod Busby and I had sampled a taste of the plateau when we traversed it in early September of 1969 during a four-day, 70-mile "forced march." We started at the Heart Lake trail, skirted the tip of the South Arm of Yellowstone Lake, climbed up and over the plateau via the Passage Creek trail, and hiked the last 30 miles along the Snake River to the South Entrance. Why did we backpack 70 miles in only four days? Well, we had just completed our summer work contracts, and it was all the time we had before we both had to get back to school. Plus, we were highly motivated to see this country, and we were *young!* It was the first true big overnight wilderness trip for either of us and it made a huge impression. In many ways it was the trip that changed my life, as I truly came to appreciate and love the lure of wild country. And when you cross the Two Ocean Plateau of Yellowstone, you are *most definitely* in wild country!

The Two Ocean Plateau consists of approximately 60 square miles of high country (mostly above 9000') and really only has the one trail that crosses it. I wanted to explore the far reaches of the plateau beyond the trail. In other words, I wanted to take a big off-trail adventure, and go all the way to the highest point of the plateau at an elevation of 10,045' near a small unnamed lake. A large portion of the plateau is managed as a bear management area (BMA), and off-trail travel is not allowed except by special permit.

Our trip would be taken in early August, 2013, and would include four participants: John and Deb Dirksen, Hank Barnett, and me. Hank and I decided that we wanted our trip to be a combo "surf and turf" trip, consisting of a canoe paddle down to Monument Bay at the very southern tip of the South Arm of Yellowstone Lake. From there, we would don our backpacks, and head up the Passage Creek trail. Once we reached the highest elevation, we would leave the trail, and make a big loop heading south until we reached the Southeast Arm, and the Trail Creek trail that would lead us back to Monument Bay and our canoe. John and Deb on the other hand felt they had not hiked enough during the summer. They had spent several weeks at Mary Mountain patrol cabin as VIPs (volunteers in parks) building a new log cabin outhouse. Therefore, they decided to backpack in via the Heart Lake trail, and meet us at Monument Bay. We all agreed that two days should be sufficient time to get there. Paddling and backpacking generally proceed at the same pace; however, Hank and I were planning to bring in some food and drinks that are generally not carried on your backs!

We stopped by Grant Visitor Center to pick up our boat permit, and backcountry permit. We had previously received permission from District Rangers to hike and camp off-trail on the plateau. By the time we reached the

Grant boat dock, it was 4:00 p.m. and a weather warning had been issued. It appeared that thunderstorms were due to roll over the lake within 30 to 45 minutes. Hank and I launched our 15' Coleman canoe in calm conditions, but as predicted, after about 30 minutes the wind began to blow, and a good chop developed. By now we had covered perhaps two miles, and pulled over into a nice, protected cove to wait out the storm. The motto on Yellowstone Lake is and always will be, "Take what the lake gives you!" If you are on any kind of schedule, when the lake is calm, you'd better have your canoe in the water.

The timing of the storm was perfect though, as we were both famished. We donned our rain gear, picked out a nice log under a tree, and started up our little propane stove. Next we cracked open a cold beer (tough to do *this* when backpacking), toasted yet another great trip, and waited for the beef stew to heat up. This is yet another advantage in canoeing—our beef stew was the real stuff, not the dehydrated variety—and it was delicious! We knew that we were only a couple of miles east of the Grant Village developed area, but just looking around, it felt as though we were in the middle of the Alaskan wilderness. Such is the wonderful advantage of a pristine shoreline (see "The Treasure of an Undeveloped Shoreline.")

The storm appeared to skirt us for the most part, and we only received a smattering of light rain. As expected, the wind soon dissipated, and it was time to get back out on the water. We were entering that special time of day when canoeing conditions are often ideal. Before long the huge lake resembled a massive sheet of smooth glass. As we approached Breeze Point with the sun hanging low in the western sky, I could not help but recall my adventure of encountering a swimming mountain lion here during a canoe trip in 1996. On this day all was quiet as we approached the point. Rather than take the wide loop around the point, we opted to pull our canoe across a narrow isthmus to reach the other side of the lengthy spit of sand. We looked back at the steam rising from West Thumb Geyser Basin, and then rounded the point.

Given our late start, we knew that we needed to take advantage of these calm conditions. We had a campsite reserved at campsite 7L4, named "the ravine," and we managed to reach it just after sunset. We figured we were about at the half-way mark of our 25 mile journey to Monument Bay. We enjoyed a small campfire for a short time, marveling at the starry skies, and the fact that we had yet to see another human being since leaving Grant behind. Across the way we could make out the dark outline of Frank Island, the largest island on Yellowstone Lake. It appeared much closer than the two miles separating us.

The next morning was clear and beautiful with calm waters. We knew we faced the challenge of crossing the mouth of Flat Mountain Arm. Ideally, we would dip into this arm, and follow the shore as much as possible. Unless conditions were rough though, we intended to dart across a narrow portion of the arm, which measures only about one-half mile across. One of the chief advantages to starting a canoe trip from Grant boat dock is, you tend to be in the lee of the prevailing southwest winds most of the way down to Monument Bay. When you canoe from Sedge Bay down the east shore of the lake, you have just the opposite situation, as those southwest winds sweep across the entire breadth of the lake, which can create some really rough conditions.

As we approached the mouth of Flat Mountain Arm, the southwesterly winds had really not come up yet, so we made a quick crossing, and soon we made our way to Plover Point, one of my favorite spots on the lake. Here the land juts out to the east, and provides a great view down into the South Arm. With binoculars we could barely make out one of our destinations before entering Monument Bay, and that would be Peale Island—a spot very close to my heart. Plover Point is typically a popular campsite for larger boats with motors, since the 5 MPH zone begins at this point going south into the arm. However, on this day, no one else was around as we pulled our canoe alongside the dock for a break.

Suddenly, the southwest winds arrived. Thanks goodness we had made it to Plover Point, because from this point on we would be in the protected lee along the west shore of the South Arm. We figured we had about eight miles between Plover Point and Peale Island, but we felt good about the progress we had made. We knew the last two miles to Peale Island would be more of a challenge, since the bottom of the South Arm broadens out and you lose protection from the winds.

With choppy waters about all you can do is get down on your knees, spread your gear out on the bottom of the canoe to lower the center of gravity, and then get in sync with your paddling partner. It took Hank and I a good hour battling the wind and choppy conditions to reach Peale Island, and as soon as we paddled around to the lee side we found placid waters. What a relief to pull our canoe up into the lagoon of this almost exotic place, and then soak in the setting. Peale Island is a very difficult place to reach, but what a wild and remote paradise. The Absaroka Range provides a stunning backdrop to the east, especially late in the day when the mountains are lit up by the golden and pink colors from the setting sun. It was on Peale Island that I heard my first elk bugle in September of 1969, and caught about ten straight cutthroat trout on ten casts before getting bored. I had heard that the cutthroat were making somewhat of a comeback from the devastating impact caused by the illegal introduction of non-native lake trout (see "Memories of the Yellowstone Cutthroat Trout"), and had purchased a fishing permit to find out for myself.

Hank and I had made good time coming down the arm, and we were not due to meet John and Deb until late afternoon, so while Hank stretched out on the shore for a nap, I launched my canoe to try my hand at catching some cutthroat. I used the same type flies and lures (with a single barbless hook) that I had used on previous trips prior to the lake trout disaster. However, I did not get a single strike in over an hour of fishing. By late afternoon it was time to pack up our gear back into the canoe, and continue our paddle over to the very southernmost tip of the South Arm at Monument Bay, where John and Deb had a designated backcountry campsite for the evening. As we entered the bay there stood John, directing us into the deepest part of the channel that would lead us close to our campsite. After hugs and greetings, we beached our canoe, and began toting our gear over to the campsite. As usual, John had selected an outstanding location. There were trees for shade, flower-laden meadows surrounding us, and a small stream trickling down from the mountains. We had not told John and Deb that we were bringing in steaks, beer and soft drinks for the evening. We even had a grill to use in the fire pit.

After Hank and I cracked open a soft drink for Deb and beers for the guys, we discussed our trip plans going forward. We learned that their two days along the trail from Heart Lake had been beautiful, but uneventful as far as unusual wildlife sightings were concerned. After our hearty dinner Hank and I paddled our canoe over close to a dense grove of old spruce trees, and pulled it ashore, hiding it, and locking it to a tree. We then put up our tents and took seats on logs around the campfire to share our life experiences over the past year. We had not seen each other since our last trip a year earlier—an eight day journey along the Teton Crest trail in Grand Teton National Park.

The next morning began with an eerie fog blanketing Monument Bay, indicating that the air temperature had dropped below that of the shallow waters in the bay. I have always been amazed at the range of temperatures in the high, dry elevations of Yellowstone. After breakfast we loaded up our backpacks, and headed east to pick up the Passage Creek trail, which would climb about 1400' in eight miles to the top of the Two Ocean Plateau. We knew this would be one of our tougher days, though we would be on a maintained trail for the entire day. After being confined to a 15' canoe for the last two days, it felt great to be backpacking again and using a different set of muscles.

Along the way we passed an elk skull with large antlers. Since this area was certainly not a suitable wintering area, we wondered when and how this elk had met its fate. We guessed that the big bull elk had succumbed to wolves in late fall after the rutting season. During this time the bulls are all wired up for mating and do not spend much time or energy eating. The cows on the other hand continue to graze, so it comes as no surprise that by late fall it will be the large bulls that are more susceptible to being taken by wolves as opposed to the cows. Looks can be deceiving to the human eye, but the wolves know the score.

On our way over to the Passage Creek trail, we passed the ancient cement monument that was erected in the early 1900s to mark the southernmost point of Yellowstone Lake. When Yellowstone was created as a national park in 1872, the south boundary was set up to be ten miles south of the most southern point of Yellowstone Lake. The marker was erected to determine that point.

We steadily climbed through sections of the old Chipmunk Burn, which burned 11,000 acres in 1941, as well as the Snake Complex fire that burned in September of 1988. The scenic landscape consisting of 25 to 75 year-old conifers served as a reminder of the important cycle that natural fire represents in Yellowstone.

We made camp that evening alongside the gurgling Passage Creek surrounded by lush meadows and huge spruce trees. Our camp just had the look and feel of mosquito country; however, for the second consecutive summer, the mosquitoes on our early August trip were practically non-existent. For dinner Deb served up a delicious meal from her varied selection of dehydrated foods. No steaks and beers on this evening, but our meal was delectable just the same. Deb would never dream of spending big bucks on purchasing freeze-dried dinners; rather, she does her own drying of meats and vegetables over the fall and winter, and by late May she has an ample supply for a summer in the backcountry.

After breakfast we continued our steady climb, and by mid-morning, we reached the top of the continental divide, leaving Passage Creek behind in a narrow gorge far below. We didn't realize it at the time, but Passage Creek was the last source of good drinking water we would see for the rest of this day. When we reached the high point of the trail atop the continental divide, we stopped for a snack break. John, Deb and Hank found a log on which to sit; however, I walked over to a boulder that I remembered from my last visit to this spot in September of 1969 with Rod Busby. Tears welled up in my eyes. I vividly remembered standing right here with Rod, and looking out across the vast wilderness as far as the eye could see in every direction. From this high vantage point, I could see the far reaches of Yellowstone Lake, and wild, unspoiled mountain country in all directions. I realized on this day, just as I had over 44 years ago, that we were standing in the middle of one of the wildest, most remote spots left in the temperate life zone on the planet. That moment long ago was a life changing event for me, and it moved me on this day, as I stayed at this spot by myself remembering that first truly wild journey, so long ago, deep into Yellowstone's wilderness.

We cris-crossed the continental divide walking from the Atlantic side to the Pacific side, and then back to the Atlantic side. I have always thought it fascinating how the nation's continental divide snakes and winds through Yellowstone National Park. We soon came to a very large meadow with a small lake that marked the spot where we had planned to leave the trail and turn toward the east in search of a U.S.G.S. benchmark (named "Lynx" on topo maps) that marked the highest point on the Two Ocean Plateau at 10,045.' After enjoying lunch in the meadow, we took out our maps and compasses, and set a course that we all agreed would take us in the direction of the Lynx benchmark. We filtered water from the small lake because as we headed up on top of the plateau we weren't sure what sources of water we would find at such high elevations.

We walked over a mile through a long meadow, and spooked dozens of elk grazing in this ideal habitat. "Backcountry elk sure behave differently from front-country elk," I whispered to Hank, as they bolted away upon sensing our presence. As we approached a scattering of trees I heard Hank exclaim, "Hey, I thought we were going to travel *off trail* on this trip!" Ahead of us was one of the finest animal trails we had ever come across in the park, made by elk migrating back and forth from the high country. Trail crews could not have produced a better trail to follow. Along the way we passed huge whitebark pine trees—long dead, but their massive trunks still standing. "If only these old trees could tell us stories about what has passed beneath their canopies," I thought.

We decided that our goal for the evening would be a small unnamed lake at an elevation of 9100'. On the map it looked very enticing. We could envision sky blue waters surrounded by rolling green meadows, and fine stands of spruce and fir. Well, we had everything about right except for the "sky blue waters!" We were now high on the plateau where there was no running water, only stagnant pools and "lakes." Our lake of destination was ringed with a scummy, muddy shoreline, as it was obviously a frequent watering hole for the many elk that passed through. In fact, right after we set up our tents, we watched a young bull come in for a drink. We froze and did not make a sound, and the elk did not detect our presence for several minutes before he finally bolted off. In order to find some half way decent water that would not clog up our filters, we had to walk about ten yards out on a log into the lake to escape the scum, foam and mud at the shore. Thank goodness for water filters!

Up until this evening our weather had been perfect, but we could tell from the building cumulous clouds throughout the afternoon, that we were going to have a rough night. Sure enough, right after dinner all hell broke loose, as a thunderstorm rolled right up on top of us, and stalled for most of the evening. Throughout the night we were treated to quite the play on our visual and audible senses from brilliant flashes of light and raucous claps of thunder.

We were almost surprised that the next morning broke clear and quite cool. Our first order of business was to take our tents down, and hang them over tree limbs to dry in the sun's early morning rays. This was the day we planned to reach the top of the plateau, so we were thrilled to have mostly clear skies. Often by early August forest fires can cause very hazy skies, thus obscuring distant views, which would be a shame here. However, despite the fact that fires were burning to the west of us in Idaho, prevailing winds were pushing the smoke far to the south of us. We knew that we had to climb almost 1,000' in slightly less than four miles to reach the Lynx benchmark. Our goal was to get there by lunch and take a lengthy break.

The high point of the plateau was fairly easy to discern, so no intensive map reading was necessary. Once we reached it, we all set out to find the official United States Geological Survey benchmark, which measures about three inches in diameter. After several minutes Hank located it. It read "Lynx" with a date of 1955 on the round brass marker. Right next to the benchmark was a nice little grove of trees that would provide shade for our lunch stop, and just beyond the trees was a decent-sized unnamed lake. "Hey," I proclaimed. "This has *got* to be the highest lake in Yellowstone National Park!" We pulled out our topo map, and studied it for a few minutes and we all agreed. We also decided that if this lake was not officially named Lynx Lake, then it certainly *should* be given the namesake of the benchmark only about 40 yards away.

As we relaxed in the shade of the stunted alpine firs, we marveled at the views in all directions. We were not standing on the summit of a mountain, but we felt as though we were on top of the world, or at least the top of Yellowstone! To the south we enjoyed a fabulous view of the Grand Tetons; to the east the Absaroka Range dominated the horizon; to the north we could view Yellowstone Lake below with the Gallatin Range visible some sixty miles away. We felt extremely blessed to have such great weather and visibility, as we recognized that we could just as easily have been dodging lightning bolts and electrical storms up this high.

After lunch we filtered water and filled all of our containers, as we figured the hike along the top of the plateau would be a dry one. From Lynx Lake we changed directions. After hiking due east all morning, we now turned and headed north. Our goal was to hike about four miles, and eventually descend over 1200' to Badger Creek and meadows, where we were certain we would find good water for our camp. This portion of the hike was perhaps the highlight of the entire trip. The going was easy and the views in all directions unending. I could even hear Julie Andrews singing, "The Hills are Alive…with the Sound of Music!"

Later that afternoon we reached the edge of very steep cliffs all around us. We appeared to be on the edge of an old lava flow. At first we were concerned as to how we would make our way down, but as is usually the case, we found a good animal trail. I'm not sure a trail crew could have constructed a much better switchback route down off of that cliff! After descending about 800' we came to a wonderful lush meadow replete with wildflowers and springs popping out of the ground, providing us with ice cold, delicious drinking water. I took off my backpack, reached down to get a long drink from the spring, and then I just stretched out in the cool grass with the warm sun beating down. I reached over to sniff the fragrance of purple monkshood wildflowers on their long stems. Even the mosquitoes were not bothering us. "Does it get any better than this?" I thought to myself as I relaxed in this wild and remote little meadow paradise.

So far this day of off-trail travel had gone as good as it possibly could, but that was about to change. At this lower elevation we now encountered sections of dense forest with lots of tangled blowdown, and this slowed our progress considerably. We were gradually heading down a north-facing slope so with the retention of moisture here, the dense vegetation was not surprising. Later that afternoon, we *finally* reached the edge of the last steep slope that provided us with a view of Badger Creek a mile away coursing through a big verdant meadow below. However, the 500' descent would be a horrendous struggle. In poring over topo maps we knew that much of the Two Ocean Plateau had burned in 1988, and we had carefully planned our route to miss the burn areas as much as possible. But there was no way to miss it here where fires had burned all the way across from west to east.

Typically, about 35% of dead trees fall within ten years of the burn. That figure doubles in another five years. It had been 25 years since the big fires of 1988 swept over much of Yellowstone. We now had to make our way through about one mile of those fallen logs, which ranged from knee to waist high. Given our remote location we repeatedly urged each other to take our time and be extra careful. A crippling injury here would simply be disastrous! Take our time we did, and it was rather late in the afternoon when we *finally* all emerged out of the giant "pick-up-sticks" maze into a gorgeous green meadow with Badger Creek flowing through it.

We selected our tent sites and then headed off in different directions to take a bath before the sun set. Taking a bath in the backcountry is a fairly simple procedure. First you dig out of your pack a wash cloth, some biodegradable soap, and a small cooking pot to scoop water out of the creek with. Then, you find a secluded spot behind some bushes. If you get to camp early enough on a sunny day, a black plastic sun shower comes in handy, as you get to wash your hair and body with warm water instead of the typically icy stuff. We did not have enough time for this, though we did have a few more minutes of direct sunlight to help warm and dry our bodies. One absolute no-no in backcountry etiquette is to actually bathe in the stream or lake itself, as that causes pollution. The technique of transferring the water out of the stream with your pot, and then disposing of your dirty bath water on land helps keep the streams and lakes pure.

As I was drying off I looked upstream and marveled at the fact that even down in this meadow, the very prominent Turret Mountain was still in view to the east. Even though during the day we had enjoyed gazing at many different prominent peaks such as Eagle (the park's highest at 11.358'), The Trident, Table Mountain, and Colter Peak, Turret Mountain seemed always to dominate the view, as it would this evening, catching the pink and golden rays of the setting sun. Now that we were clean, our tents were set up, and Turret Mountain was bathed in alpenglow, our attention turned to our ravenous appetites! Deb

Dirksen has always been a fabulous backcountry cook, and she once again lived up to her legendary reputation by somehow transposing a bunch of dehydrated meat and vegetables into a scrumptious and filling culinary delight!

The area we were camped in just looked like ideal grizzly country. Even though we had not seen any fresh evidence, we took every precaution. John located a dead tree over 100 yards away from our camp with some tall horizontal limbs to serve as our food pole. We also pitched our tents well away from our cooking area. Yellowstone's designated backcountry campsites complete with food poles serve backpackers well and guarantee solitude; however, it is always somewhat of a concern as to what type of campers recently used the site. What if a messy camper trashed the campsite a few nights before you arrived? This is certainly one problem we did not have to worry about on Badger Creek. In fact, subconsciously, we wondered just how many other humans had even set foot here. That is part of the thrill that being so far removed from a maintained trail will produce.

The next morning, our sixth day, again broke wonderfully clear. We knew this day would be the toughest of our trip, because we had to contend with about four miles (as the crow flies) of dense vegetation ending with our longest trek yet through a burn replete with deadfall. Our progress was slow as we climbed 400' back up above 9000,' but with good weather and fine wild scenery of the big mountains to our east, we weren't complaining. By late afternoon we finally reached the spot along the top of the plateau that we had been anticipating and somewhat dreading. We had to descend from 9200' down to 7800'—a drop of 1400' in only one mile. Such a drop anywhere off-trail would be tough, but we had to work our way down a steep northeast-facing slope that had completely burned over in 1988. We had to once again confront the danger of climbing over waist-high logs. Our progress was painfully slow, especially since our destination for the evening—Trail Lake, was visible throughout the descent.

The closer we got to Trail Lake, it seemed the higher the blowdown became, though I'm sure our legs were just getting wearier. Finally, we followed Trail Creek directly to the spot where it flowed into the lake. We considered camping here but the lakeshore was too wet and marshy. We eventually found a spot not quite as wet and suitable for our camp. Amazingly, we found no mosquitoes in this area that had all the appearances of a mosquito hell.

Trail Lake is a good-sized lake as it is at least one-half mile across. I first visited here in 1975 with Al Duff, and we caught about one cutthroat per cast. The next time I visited was in 1989 when I watched John Dirksen catch five cutthroat in five casts. I'm really not a fishing enthusiast, especially when it comes to catching cutthroat trout. They have always been so easy to catch that I found it to be boring. However, I do recognize the importance of the native cutthroat to the Yellowstone ecosystem, so I was very curious to see what the fishing was like in August of 2013. Unfortunately, I caught no fish and saw practically no activity or rising on the calm water that evening. It is hard for me to imagine how lake trout could have migrated up tiny Trail Creek into Trail Lake, but perhaps that is what has happened, though there was no confirmation of that from fishery biologists in the park.

As we set up camp we marveled at the alpenglow that was beginning to glow on Colter Peak and Turret Mountain looming high above us less than five miles to the west. One of the luxuries that we insist on bringing on our backpack trips are lightweight folding chairs, so we enjoyed yet another one of Deb's delicious meals as we relaxed and gazed out at our fabulous backdrop.

The 1988 fires swept across the forests around Trail Lake. When John Dirksen and I visited here in 1989, the burned snags had not fallen yet, so we had no deadfall to contend with, plus we encountered the most incredible display of white lupine I had ever observed. It is common to have an explosion of wildflowers a year after a wildfire burns through an area. But now, 25 years later, we had the "pickup sticks" jungle to contend with for one mile before we reached the maintained Trail Creek trail. At one point I looked back and all I could see was Deb's hand sticking out of dense willow amid blowdown. I then heard, "Help, please" from somewhere behind the protruding hand. Deb with her short legs has always been a trooper when it comes to crawling over waist high logs.

Soon we emerged from the willow and blowdown, and found ourselves on a maintained trail once again complete with trail markers. We had mixed feelings. We realized that the most adventurous portion of our journey—the off-trail segment—was concluded. Of course, we still had seven more miles to camp. Then John and Deb had about 18 miles to still hike out, and Hank and I had 25 miles to travel by canoe. On this our seventh day, we had not seen another human being, but that was about to change.

We stopped at Trail Creek patrol cabin along the shore of the Southeast Arm to have lunch. There was shade, an ice-cold spring nearby, and even a picnic table in front of the cabin. The cabin appeared to be unoccupied, but during our lunch we saw two kayaks approaching. A man and a woman beached their craft, walked up to us, and introduced themselves as NPS volunteers. There simply are not enough backcountry rangers to adequately patrol the park's vast wilderness, and these volunteers help fill the void. While they do not have law enforcement authority, they do carry park radios in the event they come across a visitor in trouble or witness a violation of park regulations. In the case of an emergency a call on the radio would get a uniformed boat patrol ranger on the scene, though it could take a little while. The couple had quite a bit of experience in Yellowstone's backcountry, so we enjoyed trading stories for a while before we bid them good bye. They were staying at the cabin for the evening. After we left the cabin, I joked to John, "John, maybe you need to trade with them. You and Deb patrol the Southeast Arm in kayaks, and let them build the outhouse at Mary Mountain." John managed to chuckle but I think he was thinking the same thing.

Once we reached our camp at Monument Bay, we retrieved our canoe and had an early dinner since we all had to cover more miles before dark; otherwise, it would be tough to make it out in two days, which would allow both Hank and Deb to make it back to their teaching duties on time. After dinner we all hugged each other since we knew it probably be next July before the four of us would get back together. Hank and I pushed off in our canoe and waved once more to John and Deb, then headed for Peale Island. We took a brief break before enduring the two miles of choppy waters to reach the west shore of the South Arm.

In setting up our permits we had reserved a campsite north of the mouth of Flat Mountain Arm. It was our hope that we would reach the mouth close to sunset after winds had died down and the lake was calm. Our trip along the west shore was uneventful until we reached Plover Point. We knew we would no longer be in the lee of the prevailing winds if they were still blowing. As we rounded the point we were immediately met with stiff winds despite the lateness of the day. The prevailing southwest winds were directly in our face, and waves were splashing into Hank's lap in the bow. We stayed close to shore, and continued on in hopes that the wind would quit, but it did not. Finally, after proceeding a mile past Plover Point, and with darkness settling in, we pulled over and discussed our options. The wind was not letting up at all. If anything, it was increasing. The only usable campsite was back at Plover Point, which was not occupied when we passed it. We hated the idea of facing the mouth of the Flat Mountain Arm the next morning on our last day, but we knew that we had no choice. We turned back and arrived at the Plover Point campsite just as it was getting dark.

I had never camped at this spot and had always wanted to, but not on these terms. We had the spot all to ourselves and after pitching our tents, we built a roaring fire in the metal fire pit. Despite the fact that skies were clear, the winds only grew stronger, and were now blowing directly out of the south. We had to really anchor our tents on the gravel spit where we were camped. All night long the winds blew, and as I tried to sleep, all I could think about was how rough the waters would be the next morning. Despite the loud winds and crashing waves all night, I finally dozed off.

My slumber was wrecked when I heard Hank shout, "Butch, wake up, we've got to make a run for it." As I blinked my eyes awake, I noted two things: first, I could still hear the waves crashing, and the wind blowing, and second, it was still almost dark as the sun had not yet come up. However, Hank had already been up, and had walked around the point to scout out the lake's condition heading over to the mouth of Flat Mountain. What he found shocked him. The wind was still roaring up the South Arm directly from the south, but that meant that on the north side of Plover Point we would be in the lee of the wind, and at present, the waters were calm.

I have taken many trips on Yellowstone Lake, and the one thing I have learned is to expect the unexpected. *Normally,* at dawn air currents are quite still. When the wind does come up, usually around 10:00 a.m., they blow from the southwest. But not on this morning. Hank had already taken down his tent. I rolled out of my bag, hurriedly stuffed the bag and tent into my dry bag, then stuffed a granola bar into my mouth, and headed for the canoe. I could see Hank was anxious to hit the water. He knew that our window of opportunity could end at any moment.

We had to actually launch our canoe into the water on the south side of the point where the wind was raging, and waves were crashing; however, as soon as we rounded Plover Point and reached the north side, we were completely protected from the wind and found calm waters. When we reached the mouth of Flat Mountain Arm, we decided to venture a ways into the arm rather than cut directly across the mouth. We felt that the conditions were just too strange, and although the lake was presently calm, it could change at any time.

In fact, the calm conditions persisted throughout the morning, and by lunchtime we reached the Grant boat dock. After eight days in the wilderness, it felt odd to see folks busily milling about the dock, and walking along the lakeshore. But I have found over the years that in Yellowstone all you have to do is walk (or paddle) a few hundred yards in just about any direction, and you find yourself in a magnificent and unspoiled wilderness. Hank and I realized that we had just come from terrain that perhaps no other human had ever set foot on. In fact, we could not help but ask ourselves, just how many folks had ever visited "Lynx Lake," Yellowstone's highest? A dream of mine for many years had finally been realized. We had crossed the Two Ocean Plateau.

To the Headwaters

The Yellowstone River is the last free-flowing, undammed major river in the lower forty-eight states. I would wager that most folks believe the river begins where it flows out of Yellowstone Lake at Fishing Bridge in Yellowstone National Park. However, the river actually begins about 60 miles further south at the base of Younts Peak in the Teton Wilderness within the Bridger-Teton National Forest. Over the years I had backpacked many times along Yellowstone's south boundary, but had never ventured into the Teton Wilderness. My friends John and Deb Dirksen had done so several times with rave reviews and were ready to return, so finally during early August of 2014 a trip there was planned. Several of my faithful backpacking companions from Tennessee, Hank Barnett, Steve Hixson and Clyde Austin, were unable to join us, so it would just be the three of us.

I met John and Deb during the afternoon at Old Faithful, and we drove our two vehicles to near the end of the Pacific Creek road, which begins in Grand Teton National Park, and ends in the Bridger-Teton National Forest. We found a wonderful campsite along Pacific Creek in a grove of large cottonwoods. By then it was 10:00 p.m. and John and Deb promptly went to bed in their van, but I decided to venture out of my trusty Ford Ranger 4WD pickup, sit on the tailgate, crack open a cold one, and enjoy the absolutely incredible starry skies above from our quiet and remote location. I don't know if I have ever seen the stars any clearer than they were on this very cool evening. The Milky Way seemed so close I felt as though I could reach out and touch it. It felt so wonderful to be here on the threshold of the vast Teton Wilderness, which is buttressed to the north by the backcountry of Yellowstone National Park, and to the east by the North and South Absaroka Wilderness Areas in the Shoshone National Forest. After studying the skies for over half an hour, I eased into my down bag in the bed of my truck, and quickly dozed off.

The next morning broke clear and cool as it would for most of our trip, save the last day. The air contained the fresh fragrance of cottonwoods, and my ears joyfully picked up the incessant cries from a nearby osprey nest. After positioning John and Deb's van, we piled all of the gear into my truck, and headed for Turpin Meadows, from where we would begin our trip. We were surprised to see the number of horse trailers at the trailhead, but we knew this wild country was big enough to easily absorb lots of folks. It was obvious though that this was primarily horse country, and backpackers numbered in the minority. By the time we hit the trail the day was rapidly warming up, and the horseflies were becoming a nuisance. Then we encountered a difficult ford of the North Fork of Soda Creek. We had just passed a backpacker who warned us of the ford, as he had lost his footing and gone under, completely soaking all of his gear. We saw the deep hole he must have stepped in and were careful to avoid it. Still, the water was deep, swift and cold, even for this late in the summer. The past winter's snowpack in these parts had ranged up to 140% above normal and the stream flows showed it.

We found a nice campsite along the creek with a great view of Smokehouse Mountain to the east. We named our campsite "Beaver Lodge" for the sizeable lodge nearby constructed by nature's grand engineers. As we sat down for dinner we were surprised to see two backpackers approaching on the trail. After trading a few comments we invited them to visit for a spell around our campfire. Both were through hikers on the very rugged Continental Divide Trail (CDT.) Deb likes to joke that the name should be ACDT for "Almost Continental Divide Trail," since much of the trail traverses terrain far from the actual Continental Divide. Through hikers on long trails such as the Pacific Crest, Appalachian Trail and CDT typically have "trail names." One fellow was a 46 year old with the trail name of "Wolverine," since he hailed from the state of Michigan. The other fellow was 34 and his trail name was "Viking," since he hailed from Norway. The two had only recently joined up as they neared Yellowstone. Neither had ever been to the park and had planned to spend several days attempting to visit the highlights. Given our many years in the park, we gave them an earful as to what they should not miss. Wolverine took copious notes. After a short visit, the two continued down the trail. These guys were averaging over 20 miles per day. John and Deb and I could only shake our heads in disbelief, as we had our hands full trying to cover about 10 miles per day for the next eight days!

The following day John and Deb were eager to show me Big Spring, where the entire Soda Fork River originates right out of the ground. However, we were not sure what to expect along the way. During the summer of 2012 much of this area burned during the widespread North Fork Fire here. In fact, we recalled seeing the smoke from that fire during our wonderful backpack trip on the Teton Crest Trail. The previous day an outfitter on horseback had passed us on the trail, and John inquired as to the condition of the forest up to Big Spring and Crater Lake. "It's all burned up," the cowboy gruffly answered. However, about an hour later a solitary backpacker approached us and John asked the same question. "Oh, it is just wonderful," the young fellow answered. "Thanks to the fire opening up the forest canopy, now you can actually see the huge canyon walls and distant peaks, and the wildflowers are absolutely spectacular!" "Did the area around Big Spring burn?" John asked. "No, it is still mostly green," the young hiker responded. At the time I had told John how interesting it was to get two very different answers. It seemed to be the "half-full" vs. "half-empty" argument. However, by the time we reached the burn area, we definitely had to side with the young backpacker rather than the cowboy. As so often occurs after a cleansing burn, nutrients are released into the soil, sunlight is opened up to the forest floor, and a veritable explosion of blooms takes place. In fact, the wildflower display here was on an equal par with many of the displays I observed in the summers following the huge fires of 1988 in Yellowstone. The flowers were thick, varied and profuse, with all colors represented. I was especially impressed by the fields of holly hocks.

When we reached Big Spring I could understand John and Deb's zeal for this natural attraction, as the entire river just bubbled up right out of the ground at the base of a steep hill. Flowers were abundant, and most of the large trees had been spared by the 2012 fire. A very old rustic sign hung on one of the largest trees and read, "Big Spring is thought to be the outlet of Crater Lake, 2 miles to the east." By now thick clouds had gathered, and a steady drizzle had set in, reducing the enthusiasm we had felt upon our arrival. Plus, now we had to ford the river, as there was no practical route above the spring. This ford has to rank as the coldest I have ever experienced, but then it was the first time that I had ever forded a river only a few yards from where it gushed out of the ground! Our plans had been to camp at Crater Lake two miles away with a 1000' climb. However, we could not help but notice a fine campsite in a meadow below. There were large spruce trees that could serve to protect us from the rain that had started. The three of us had a brief summit, and decided to call it an early day and make camp here.

The decision turned out to be a good one as the drizzle continued through supper and the big trees offered great protection. There was also an abundance of firewood for our roaring campfire, as well as a fabulous view of the surrounding mountains. The evening was topped off by Deb's dinner of pizza followed by apple crisp for dessert. As the evening waned the rain stopped and the stars came out. On this our second night out, we felt ourselves becoming immersed in this wild country. No one was near us in this deep and remote spot.

The next day broke bright and sunny so after a hearty breakfast of egg McMuffins, we decided to stroll down to see Big Spring in the splendor of the bright sun. After some photos we returned to our camp, packed up and began the 1000' climb up to Crater Lake at an elevation of 9300', then on to Ferry Lake at 10,000,' where we decided to stop at a spring to have lunch. The amount of snow still up here this late in July was amazing. Our lunch spot featured great views of the Tetons, the surrounding mountain ranges to the south and east, as well as Ferry Lake situated mostly above timberline. We observed five bull elk walking across a huge snow field before topping out on top of a divide. We could only watch with envy at the speed and ease in which those elk covered that distance and elevation gain.

After lunch we continued to climb up to the top of the pass where we would reach a trail junction. We began to notice copious piles of grizzly droppings, where bears had apparently spent a lot of time grazing in the lush alpine meadows. We now turned to the north and headed into Woodard Canyon. With all of the abundant snow still melting in the high country, we passed one waterfall after another, as we descended the canyon and eventually entered a lush, mature forest. At that point the trail became extremely difficult to follow, primarily due to the complete lack of trail maintenance. Each time we encountered a large tree across the trail chest high, we had to struggle through the very dense vegetation to get around it. I could not help but empathize with the trail crews who worked here. First, the government shutdown in early October of 2013 had probably put a big dent in their trail clearing progress during the previous fall, but I mostly felt sympathy for the crews having to use hand-pulled crosscut saws instead of chain saws. This was after all the Teton Wilderness, where any mechanization is illegal. Yellowstone's backcountry is *managed* as wilderness but since it is not officially designated as wilderness under the 1964 Wilderness Act, trail crews are allowed to use chain saws to clear trails.

Woodard Canyon proved to be a very tough and long hike, and the off and on showers did not help. By late afternoon we finally arrived at the confluence of Woodard Creek and the Yellowstone River, near its headwaters. We had indeed paid a price for stopping early at Big Spring rather than climbing to Crater Lake, but we still were pleased with our decision. We found a small clearing in the forest for our campsite, which contained a fine view of majestic Younts Peak, which rises to an elevation of 12,165'. What a mountain! The peak has the appearance of a huge cone that steeply rises well above timberline, and feeds the north fork and south fork of the Yellowstone River. We had made it to the mighty Yellowstone's headwaters! I felt remorse that this mighty peak was not inside the borders of Yellowstone National Park, as it would rank as the park's highest and grandest peak. Eagle Peak, the highest peak in the park, does not even begin to compare with Younts, as Eagle is nothing more than a high point along a high ridge line. Younts, on the other hand, stands alone as a mighty and imposing peak, dominating the landscape, though nearby Thorofare Mountain at 12,068' is no slouch either. That evening we were treated to an alpenglow that lit up Younts like a lampshade. Dinner consisted of zucchini soup followed by chili cornbread. We didn't stay up long around the fire on this night. We were tired and ready to crawl into our warm cocoons.

The down bags came in handy as the temperature the next morning, July 31, read 26 degrees! We had decided the night before to postpone our ford of the Yellowstone until the next morning for two good reasons: first, it appeared that the area across the river did not afford as nice a clearing for a camp, and second, we figured that early in the morning the ford would be easier with a lower stream flow after a cold night.

On this day we would hike about ten miles along the east side of the Yellowstone River. We were getting deeper and deeper into the wilderness and frankly, we felt as though we were the only people on the planet. Apparently very few folks travel down Woodard Canyon, and then along the Yellowstone River. Throughout the day we enjoyed views of the rugged canyon walls above the river, punctuated with occasional waterfalls tumbling down. Grizzly signs in the form of tracks and droppings were becoming more abundant. As I hiked along the river I tried to picture what it would be like to paddle a pack raft here, legal since we were south of the national park boundary. However, after every nice stretch the river would suddenly enter a narrow canyon with raging rapids, or run into logjams stretched across the entire stream. I could not help but feel that this relatively new outdoor activity may be more troublesome and hazardous than some of its ardent supporters might be willing to admit.

By late afternoon we reached our planned destination for camp near the confluence of Castle Creek with the Yellowstone. We erected our tents in a fine meadow, and then hiked over to the river's rocky shores to build our campfire and cook our meal. Since this was the fourth day of our trip we all needed to take baths and wash clothes. We headed in different directions for our brief, but satisfying baths, then we did some laundry before supper. In both cases we always use an old gallon milk jug to scoop the water out of the river (rather than bathe or wash directly in the river) then use biodegradable soap. By now the three of us had our camp chores down to a fine routine. My job at each camp was to gather firewood and prepare a fire. I had to be careful to select the correct size wood so Deb would have a good bed of coals on which to cook. Deb, of course, had one main job and that she did fabulously as our camp cook. John had a variety of duties including finding a good limb from which to hang our food bag, and then tossing a rope over that limb, not always the easiest task. He also had a more complicated job erecting his tent and setting out the pads and bags for both he and Deb. By comparison, my solo tent went up in a flash. On this evening Deb cooked up chicken enchilada corn cakes for dinner. The valley was beginning to widen, so from our camp we enjoyed great views of the massive ridgeline known as Yellowstone Point, as well as Hawk's Rest, our destination for the following day. We stayed up around our campfire long enough to enjoy the stars before we retired to our tents.

August first, our fifth day, broke clear with a chilly temperature of 29 degrees. The scenery on this day would simply be stupendous as we continued to follow the Yellowstone River through an ever widening valley replete with large meadows, surrounded by huge canyon walls and distant mountain peaks. If there was a theme to this day Deb had suggested it. She called it "A Walk through Beaver Heights." Never had any of us seen such an abundance of beaver activity, as we passed one dam and lodge after another. No wonder this country was referred to as "The Thorofare" by the mountain men who passed through here in pursuit of beaver pelts during the fur trade era in the 1820s-30s. Our destination for this evening would be a meadow next to the Yellowstone

River near the historic Hawk's Rest patrol cabin. I had heard many stories about this famous old U.S. Forest Service cabin. My friend and colleague Bronco Grigg, who now works for maintenance in Yellowstone, was once a backcountry ranger stationed at Hawk's Rest. Bronco told me about the weird dreams that all seem to have while stationed there. I had also read the book, "Hawk's Rest," by Gary Ferguson, who also spent part of a season at the cabin and likewise told of the "strange dreams." John and Deb had been through this country two years earlier, and had told me about a very friendly older couple with the first names of Val and Cindy who had been stationed at the cabin. We hoped to find them in residence.

Before we reached Hawk's Rest, which is actually the north end of a high ridge that overlooks Bridger Lake and the seven-mile long Yellowstone Meadow, we encountered an old horse camp that Deb referred to as the "tombstones." She called it that because of the dozens of trees which had been sawed off about four feet high. At first I couldn't figure out why in the world the trees had been cut that way, but then it occurred to me that this was a busy outfitter's camp during the fall hunting season. Apparently the outfitters had purposely cut the trees in this manner to provide support for the big wall tents that would be erected. Given the incredible wild scenery we had enjoyed it was easy to forget that we were not inside Yellowstone National Park, which would never allow trees to be cut in this manner for the benefit of commercial outfitters.

We reached Hawk's Rest about 4:30 p.m. and when the cabin came into view I was impressed to see an American flag flying in front of the structure. We could see two people working next to the cabin, and John said, "Ha, it looks like ole Val and Cindy are still stationed here!" We walked up to see them and the couple did indeed remember John and Deb from two summers ago. Val was working on a plumbing problem at the cabin, and John, ever the handyman, had some good suggestions on how to fix the problem. Val took us for a tour through the rustic, two-room cabin, and then invited us to have a seat on the front porch, from which a wonderful view of the Yellowstone River and the Two Ocean Plateau could be enjoyed. I told him that this was the first patrol cabin I had ever seen that had an American flag flying, and Val proudly told me that he had constructed the flag pole by hand.

Val then brought us all a glass of wine (apple juice for Deb), and I proposed a toast to "wild country and Hawk's Rest." After a nice visit we decided we needed to head down to the meadow to set up our tents. Val and Cindy, quite the gracious and friendly hosts, invited us to return to the cabin to cook our dinner, visit, and Val said a special surprise would await us.

After we established our camp and hung a rope high on a tree limb for food storage, Deb and I decided to take a quick hike over to the south end of Bridger Lake. I had seen this very remote lake only once, when Rod Busby and I walked down to the north shore while on our cold and soggy September backpack trip in 1972. The Bridger Lake vicinity marks the most remote spot in the lower 48 states as determined several years ago by National Geographic, based on the fact that it is well over 20 miles in any direction to the nearest road. Frankly, when I heard this I thought it rather sad that we can't get any farther from a road in the lower 48!

We headed back up to the cabin, and once inside immediately saw the "surprise." Cindy had baked a fresh apple pie! Deb cooked up another great dinner on their gas stove, and then it was time for the pie. Val served up some fresh decaf coffee, and the evening was complete....at least so we thought. I had noticed a rather well-worn guitar in the tack room sitting in a case that contained a wealth of stickers from various locations around the West. Val pulled it out and announced that it was singing time. His voice produced some wonderful and melodious tunes and his yodeling was top rate. We soon realized that Val was no amateur, and had in fact toured with some famous musicians, including spending some time with Willie Nelson. We all joined in on many old western favorites, such as Home on the Range, Cool Water, and Ghost Riders in the Sky. Val then surprised us all by giving us a copy of one of his CDs from his singing and performing days. As the wonderful evening drew to a close, Cindy urged us to come back up to cook breakfast the next morning.

When daybreak rolled around and the thermometer read 28 degrees, we were glad for the invitation. A warm cabin would be a welcome place for Deb to prepare breakfast. After we completed our meal we thanked the Geisse' for their wonderful hospitality. Val and Cindy were the consummate hosts and it was obvious that they served a very important function staffing the remote Hawk's Rest patrol cabin. As we crossed the bridge across the Yellowstone River, we realized that we had completed the top end of our loop trip, and would now be heading south. As we walked the trail along the river we were amazed by the many fresh tracks from wolves and grizzlies, probably made during the early morning hours, and in fact within very close proximity to our tent sites.

On this day we would come to a natural feature that I had always wanted to visit—the "parting of the waters." At this spot right on the continental divide a stream, Two Ocean Creek, tumbles down from the slopes of the aptly named Two Ocean Plateau. The stream divides and one fork is named Atlantic Creek as it flows down into the Yellowstone River, which eventually flows into the Missouri, then the Mississippi, and empties into the Gulf of Mexico, Atlantic Ocean near New Orleans. The other fork, named Pacific Creek, eventually flows into the Snake River, to the Columbia River, and into the Pacific Ocean near Astoria, Oregon. After spending time visiting this unique landmark, we hiked another three miles until we reached a nice meadow with a nearby stream for our camp. A brief rainstorm passed over, and then I built a roaring fire to gather around to warm up and prepare dinner by. As I was scrounging around looking for firewood, I came across a rather elaborate shelter constructed of many tree branches that had been stacked in a manner to provide protection from the elements. It was certainly not something some casual backpacker would build. The structure reminded me of episodes of the TV series "Survivorman" with Les Stroud. I pondered what the story was behind this shelter. Either Les Stroud filmed an episode here and this was his demonstration, or indeed someone had perhaps been trapped in a raging snowstorm, and the shelter perhaps allowed them to survive the experience. Later, after dinner, a young fellow from Germany approached us in camp asking if we knew where the "parting of the waters" was. He had somehow missed the turnoff to the short spur trail that led up to Two Ocean Creek.

The next morning again broke clear, and we enjoyed hiking along Pacific Creek until we reached a confusing trail junction. The trail along Pacific Creek simply disappeared, unless you count a beaver trail through the willow. We were, after all, following a major trail used by large horse parties with pack animals. The tiny beaver trail into the willows was clearly not that trail. Therefore, we veered to the left on the large and obvious major trail. Next thing we knew we were gazing down at Enos Lake. Talk about confused! We stopped for lunch to study our maps, which for this particular section, were not very precise. How we had lost the major Pacific Creek trail was a mystery, but at this point we decided that it would actually be simpler to turn to the south and loop back to Turpin Meadows, rather than turn back and try to locate the Pacific Creek trail. None of us had ever been to Enos Lake, and it was indeed an interesting landscape. It appeared that in the not too distant past Enos Lake was surrounded by dense forest, but then in the early 1980s a severe microburst storm, similar to a tornado, leveled most of the forest here. The resulting tangle of dead and down trees had been a nightmare to trail crews in the Teton Wilderness.

Then, the huge fires in 1988 burned up the downed trees in the Enos Lake vicinity and today, since most of the forest originally consisted of spruce and fir trees, the entire area is basically open meadows full of wildflowers. Lodgepole pines reproduce from fire, but spruce and fir do not. The seeds have to blow in from distant trees that were not burned. Two or three hundred years from now Enos Lake may again be surrounded by dense forest. We decided to make our last camp of the trip along a small stream at the head of a meadow. As soon as we finished dinner the fine weather we had enjoyed for the past seven days took a dramatic turn. Almost without warning an intense electrical storm rolled across the high plateau to our west known as Gravel Ridge, and we barely had time to cover our packs and dive into our tents before the bottom dropped out. There would be no lengthy fireside chats on this evening. Lightning flashed and thunder roared throughout the night. During the night I assumed that the storms would pass over, but I was surprised to wake up to a steady, cool rain the next morning. The rain would continue throughout the day. Granted, if we had to have a rainy day to contend with, the last day would be our choice. I have often noted though that days like this frequently produce ethereal sights and views, and with the clouds hanging in the valleys and clinging to the mountaintops.

Later in the day we entered a large meadow perhaps within two miles or less of trail's end, and I noticed what appeared to be a large stump protruding out of the grass that just did not seem to belong. I asked Deb for her binoculars, and as soon as I put them to my eyes I saw that it was a beautiful sow grizzly standing upright peering directly at us! We then saw two other smaller bears— her yearlings, standing upright. They had apparently picked up our scent before we had spotted them. The big sow turned her two yearlings around, and all three ran off into the forest at the edge of the meadow. Naturally, we proceeded with extreme caution to ensure we did not surprise the bears around a bend in the trail, but the viewing of these majestic animals right at the end of our trip served as the climax of what had been an incredible journey. The beauty and diversity of the Teton Wilderness had indeed exceeded my expectations. What a fabulous portion of the Greater Yellowstone Ecosystem it represents!

Are there Angels in the Backcountry?

I have had some close calls in the backcountry. I almost drowned in the Clarks Fork my first summer in the park in 1968, and I had a frightening encounter with a grizzly sow and cub on Fawn Pass in 1972. Both of these incidents were detailed in my first volume. In this volume I describe two more, one on Yellowstone Lake, and the other at a lake along the south boundary. My friends tell me I have nine lives. Granted, exploring wilderness has its risks, but given some of the strange events I have observed, I sometimes wonder if there are angels out there. There are two incidents in particular that seem to just about fit that criteria.

During my tour of duty with the Air Force in Great Falls, Montana in the early 1970s, winters were much more severe than they are today. Winters were cold, long and snowy. Waiting for spring to finally arrive was very frustrating. Just when you thought it was safe to venture out to one of your favorite fishing holes to land some tasty trout, along would come yet another spring snowstorm. This waiting game has a name—it is called "cabin fever." My fishing friend, Larry Welton, and I were chomping at the bit to head to a remote lake that we had picked out on our map that supposedly had good populations of trout. The only way to access this lake was via a long primitive dirt road that dead-ended at its western edge. It was our plan and our hope to be the very first anglers to reach the lake as soon as it broke free of ice sometime in May.

Finally the weather warmed sufficiently, and we decided to give it a try. The lake was located in the rugged mountains of Lolo National Forest at an elevation of just under 5000,' so we weren't sure if the primitive road would even be passable yet. The distance from Great Falls was over 125 miles, so we were taking a gamble attempting to reach it this early in the season. The primary roads getting there were just fine, but when we reached the primitive road, it appeared that the snow had *just* melted off. There was no evidence that any vehicles had yet traveled it. With high hopes we began to slowly make our way along this road in Larry's Volkswagen van, which with the engine directly over the drive train, had excellent traction as long as we did not encounter deep snow. As the narrow road gained elevation through the forest, we began to notice more snow in the trees, and soon we encountered stretches of snow still remaining across the road. However, to our delight the snow was not deep enough to deter our progress, and the fact that no other tracks were visible provided proof that we would indeed be the first anglers to reach the lake following a long winter. As we continued to make progress the only remaining mystery would be perhaps the most important, and that would be whether or not the lake itself had broken up and was ice-free.

We finally came over a small ridge where we could see the end of the road at the edge of the lake, which was totally free of ice! We parked the van and could hardly wait to get out our little two man rubber raft, load up our fishing gear, head out, and start pulling in our catch. Since this was the only road into the lake, and we were the first folks to venture in, the lake was eerily quiet and peaceful. We were laughing and joking and making bets as to how long it would take us to catch our limit as we finished pumping up the raft. Just as we were about to launch it, we heard a booming voice behind us, "Excuse me gentlemen, but I need to talk to you."

We turned around and there to our shock stood a man in a uniform. I immediately assumed that he was a Montana state fish and game warden, and began to reach for my fishing license. "I don't need to see your fishing licenses," the man said. "I need to see your life jackets." In our excitement packing for this trip, Larry and I had completely overlooked getting our PFDs. "Sir, I guess we forgot and left them at home," I said. The man looked out across the somewhat choppy waters of the lake. "Well gentlemen," he said, "I'm afraid that you will not be able to launch that raft if you do not have your life jackets."

At this point Larry and I thanked the man, and he waited as we deflated our raft. The man then walked back into the woods and disappeared. We looked at the rather rocky and shallow shoreline, and realized that it would be fruitless to attempt to cast our lines from the banks of the lake. We promptly packed up our gear and decided to head toward home. We knew of a small lake near Lincoln which we had fished before, and knew that it had steep banks from which we could cast our lures. We were also certain that we would *not* be the first ones in to fish *that* lake for the season. As we drove back out the primitive road and neared its junction with a secondary road, it suddenly dawned on me that there were no other tire tracks on the road but ours. "Wait a minute Larry," I exclaimed, "where did that guy come from? No one else has driven in here! And this is the only way to reach this lake. There were no cabins back there. Did you see where he came from or where he went?" "No," Larry responded, "he just appeared behind us, then disappeared into the woods." When we arrived back at the beginning of the primitive road, Larry slowed down and we just looked at each other and shook our heads. To this day we have no idea who this man was or where he came from.

Over the years I have been very thankful that this mysterious person showed up when he did. Larry and I were caught up with cabin fever. We were young, excited, and somewhat inexperienced. It was a very cool, windy day, the lake's icy waters were choppy, and we had no business trying to fit both of us into that little two-man raft, *especially* without life jackets! I eventually learned that a "two-man" raft really means a one-man raft, and a "four-man" raft is really for two people. But as strange as this backcountry incident was, it paled in comparison to a misadventure that involved my younger daughter Alison. While working in Grand Teton she had already had some close calls, both times descending from the summit of the Middle Teton. Once she got "cliffed out" because she took the wrong route down, but the scariest occurred when she began sliding down a steep snowfield that ended at a boulder field. The snow was frozen and was more like packed ice. As she picked up speed she tried to use her ice axe to arrest her slide, but the axe would not dig into the ice-covered snowfield. Luckily, she had taken lessons at the Exum climbing school, and remembered the instructor's advice as to what to do in such a situation. She turned over on her stomach, and utilized her hands and feet as "claws," leveraging all of her weight, as if applying four ice axes simultaneously. The technique worked—barely, as she arrested her slide only a few feet above the boulders. However, her "angel" moment would occur several years later, when she and two friends attempted to make a day run along a section of the Teton Crest trail.

Alison and her friends had completed the rather famous Bridger Ridge Run, a twenty mile race along the top of the Bridger Mountain Range near Bozeman, Montana, numerous times, and had decided that a similar day run in the Tetons would be a great experience. First they parked one car at Teton Village at the base of the aerial tram at Rendezvous Mountain, then drove to the Paintbrush Canyon trailhead at String Lake, where they would begin their run. Since they were starting at daybreak, it was not possible to begin the run from the top of the tram, as it did not open until hours later. The total distance for their day's run would be 35 miles, but the three experienced runners expected to easily reach the tram at the top of Rendezvous Peak by late afternoon for the ride down. In fact, the three young ladies had planned to meet my older daughter Caroline for dinner in Jackson that evening. Margaret and I did not even know of Alison's plans. Margaret and I were in West Yellowstone with my sister Alice attending an outdoor concert when my cell phone rang. It was Caroline. She told me of their plans to meet at 5:00 p.m. but it was now 7:00 p.m., and she had not heard anything from Alison. "Dad," Caroline said with obvious alarm in her voice, "Something has gone wrong. I think you need to call the rangers in Grand Teton, and ask them to put together a search and rescue team."

As Caroline filled me in on the details of their run, all kinds of thoughts swirled in my head. I knew that the girls would have carried good gear for a day run, but they obviously were not prepared to spend the night out in the mountains. Something had obviously gone wrong, but where in the world could they be? It was now dark, and I really did not have a clue what to do other than worry my head off.

Truth be told, the three girls were fine except one of Alison's friends had come down with an acute upset stomach that had significantly slowed their progress. When it became obvious that they would never reach the aerial tram in time to catch the last ride of the day, they had to come down a different way. Their only alternative for exiting the high country was to hike down the Death

Canyon trail. By the time they made it off of the ridge to the canyon floor it had become dark. Of course, they knew that when they made it out, they would still have problems. The trailhead is located along the remote and narrow Moose-Wilson road, which at night is rarely traveled.

With it now dark and still four miles to go to reach the trailhead, the three girls could not believe their eyes. An elderly lady suddenly came into view approaching them on the trail. The lady told the girls she was a volunteer for the National Park Service, and was heading up the canyon to camp for the night. When the lady heard the girls' predicament, she pulled out her car keys. "Here," she said. "Use my car as necessary this evening, and just return it tomorrow." The girls looked at each other in disbelief, then graciously accepted the lady's incredible offer.

As soon as they reached Teton Village, Alison called Caroline who then called me to let us know that they were safe. The girls then drove to Teton Village and spent the night. The next morning they dropped the lady's car off at the trailhead with a thank you note and a full tank of gas. When Alison told me this story I could not help but compare it to my strange incident with the mysterious game warden at the remote lake. What was this older lady doing four miles in on the Death Canyon trail in the dark? And how many folks would so willingly hand over their car keys to three young women who were complete strangers? I have never seen a lady in her sixties hiking in the woods in the dark, but I suppose you could simply say it was an unusual coincidence. However, to this day, I cannot explain the "game warden" appearing at the lake!

Nine Days Through Glacier's Wild Mountain Splendor

I received my introduction to Glacier National Park in northern Montana when Margaret and I spent two months in the backcountry there working at Granite Park Chalet in the summer of 1970. I was enthralled by its wild mountain beauty, and could not wait to take an extended backpacking trip. The opportunity arrived in July of 1971, when I was stationed at Malmstrom Air Force Base in Great Falls, Montana. My old Yellowstone hiking buddy Rod Busby had just graduated from Washington State University, and was awaiting his assignment in the U.S. Army. We studied topo maps and finally came up with what we thought would be the perfect loop trip. We would start from the Camas Creek trailhead on the North Fork Road south of Polebridge, head into Trout Lake, Arrow Lake, then travel off-trail to Camas Lake, climb Heaven's Peak, descend to McDonald Creek, then hopefully find the Loop Trail leading up to Granite Park. From there we would follow the highline trail north to Goat Haunt on the U.S.-Canada border, and conclude our trip by hiking over Brown Pass to Bowman Lake, exiting back on the North Fork Road about 25 miles north from our starting point.

Backcountry regulations have dramatically changed over the years in most national parks in order to protect and preserve the resource, and also to ensure a quality wilderness experience for visitors. In the summer of 1971 a backcountry permit was required in Glacier, but campsites were simply selected on a first-come, first-served basis. I know from experience that today it is very difficult to obtain a permit and reserve campsites between Logan Pass and Goat Haunt. I parked my trusty 1964 Chevy II at the Camas Creek trailhead, and Rod and I headed down the trail with the goal of camping at Arrow Lake for the night.

The hike into Trout Lake was somewhat spooky, considering the fact that only four years earlier the tragic "night of the grizzlies" occurred, when two young women were killed on the same night by two different bears—one at Trout Lake, and the other at Granite Park. Also, just like 1967, the park was in the middle of an extended warm and very dry weather pattern. That horrific August night had a lasting impact on the mindset of backpackers entering grizzly country. The only way I could resolve it in my own mind, was to remind myself that both of those bears had been habituated to human foods, and that the current population of grizzlies in Glacier as well as Yellowstone were wild, natural-feeding bears. I also realized that you have to accept some risk when you enter grizzly country, just as we do when we drive down a busy highway or board an airplane.

We hiked by Trout Lake and observed the infamous log jam at the west end of the lake, prominently mentioned in Jack Olsen's riveting book, *The Night of the Grizzlies*, that documented the details of that dreadful night of August 12, 1967. We camped our first evening at Arrow Lake. I rarely pack along fishing gear on long backpacking trips now, but on this trip I had a small spinning rod and easily caught and released several trout. We probably would have fried a couple up for dinner, but we were extra sensitive about producing food odors in our camp, so our meals consisted entirely of the rather bland freeze-dried variety.

The next morning broke clear, cool and beautiful. Even though it was mid-July, the mosquitoes were not bothersome at all, and the wildflowers were nearing a peak. Above Arrow Lake the maintained trail ended, but we had planned to bushwhack the next three miles along Camas Creek to reach Camas Lake where we hoped to camp. A maintained trail now extends from Arrow Lake to Camas Lake, but in 1971 the trail ended at Arrow Lake. Hiking and backpacking in Glacier is dramatically different from most of Yellowstone. The vegetation is typically quite dense—almost jungle-like, especially on the west side of the divide. Much of Yellowstone, on the other hand, sits on a volcanic plateau, which tends to feature a more porous soil, and more open lodgepole forests. Glacier's rich, moist soils are perfect for spruce and fir trees, as well as an abundance and variety of deciduous undergrowth. As a result a much higher percentage of a grizzly bear's diet in Glacier consists of plant matter, compared to grizzlies in Yellowstone, which tend to consume more meats and insects. Having worked, hiked, and backpacked in both parks, I have always considered a surprise encounter with a grizzly more likely in Glacier because of its dense vegetation and steep narrow terrain.

Such was the concern as Rod and I continued our climb of some 1000' from Arrow Lake to Camas Lake. It didn't take long for us to encounter a grizzly, but thankfully it was not at close range. We were climbing along a steep and rocky ravine with Camas Creek raging below, and for a brief period we weren't sure the terrain was going to allow us to reach the bench above us. We feared getting "cliffed out," but when we finally managed to pull ourselves up to more level ground, the vegetation opened up, and off to our right on a snowfield above us, we caught the movement of two bears. It was a grizzly sow with her yearling cub, and they were gleefully at play, though the poor cub was getting tossed about unmercifully in the snow by Momma. Too bad the cub didn't have a sibling to play with because the wrestling match was decidedly one-sided. What an endearing sight! A sow and her cub at play in this spectacular mountain wilderness, and there appeared to be no other humans near—just Rod and I on the side of this mountain to revel in this wild exhibition.

When we reached Camas Lake we were astounded by the beauty of its setting. The steep verdant slopes of Heaven's Peak rose above us to the southeast, the precipitous Rogers Peak to the southwest, and off to the west we had a great view of jewel-like Evangeline Lake, situated in a cirque. Colorful wildflowers were everywhere, especially the showy beargrass – a tall plant in the lily family that features white clusters of blooms resembling snowballs.

The next morning we awoke to a light fog over Camas Lake, which the sun soon burned away. The weather appeared to be locked in a stable high pressure pattern, which meant hot, dry and dusty conditions down low, but absolutely perfect hiking conditions up in the high country. The lure of exploring Evangeline Lake was strong, but we were locked into a rather tight schedule. Though we had built in a couple of "cushion days," we decided to use them later in the trip, rather than make a detour 180 degrees against our planned direction of travel. Also, we faced the uncertainty of how we would handle the challenging off-trail segment we were now confronted with. From Camas Lake we had planned to climb up and over the north shoulder of Heaven's Peak, at which I had spent many hours gazing while working at Granite Park the previous summer.

As we ascended the very steep ridge gaining 2000' along the way, we spotted a fire lookout tower that I did not know even existed. When we finally reached it, we found the door to be unlocked, and the facility empty but rather clean. Once we gazed over the edge of the ridge from atop the lookout down at the steep and densely vegetated east slopes that we would be required to negotiate to reach McDonald Creek and the valley floor, we promptly decided to spend the night inside the lookout structure. Our "top of the world" view was amazing—lakes below to the west, and an almost endless array of peaks, ridges and valleys in all directions.

It did not appear as though this lookout had been used for years, though once the sun had set we discovered that the old Coleman gas lantern had fuel and still functioned. Perhaps the lookout was still put to use during severe fire seasons, which frankly we seemed to be approaching. I later read that this lookout was abandoned in 1952, and the trail leading to it had fallen into disuse, and nature had mostly obliterated it over the years. We certainly saw no evidence of a trail during our bushwhack up the slope to reach it. As the night fell we walked outside the building to avoid the lantern's glare on the glass windows. I could not help but wonder if the guests at Granite Park Chalet, six air miles away as the crow flies across the valley, would notice the glow on this evening emanating from Heaven's Peak Lookout.

The next day would undoubtedly be the toughest of the trip for both of us, but especially me. We had planned to camp at Granite Park, rather than pay the rather steep price to sleep inside the chalet, but we did hope to make it there in time to feast on one of the fine dinners (ham, turkey or roast beef) that I had so enjoyed the previous summer with Margaret as the cook. However, now that we had used up a cushion day by staying at the lookout, the pressure was on to make it all the way down to the valley bottom, and then back up the other side to reach Granite Park on this day, *and* in time for dinner. It would be a daunting task, consisting of an off-trail descent of 3,400' to McDonald Creek, then hopefully locating the maintained Loop Trail, and climbing back up 3,400' to the chalet.

As Rod and I began our descent from Heaven's Peak Lookout, we found the going extremely difficult given the steepness, and the thick vegetation. Obviously the trail that led to this lookout during its use was not on this side of Heaven's Peak! We probably spent more time falling and rolling through the vegetation than we did walking, but *finally* we reached McDonald Creek on the valley floor. By then we were both somewhat dehydrated. There was then a little tablet called a "Fizzie" that would transform a drink of cold water into a delicious carbonated fruity delight. We must have each gulped down three pints of Fizzie drinks. Today's backpackers use Gatorade, Kool-Aid, crystal light, etc., but I do wish that Fizzies were still around.

After we forded McDonald Creek, which was no easy matter this early in July, I soon discovered to my dismay that the descent from Heaven's Peak was going to be the easiest part of our day! At least I could fall and roll my way down through the jungle. Climbing *up* through the jungle was a different matter. I was hot, exhausted and totally in the grips of the dense vegetation. I would experience a similar horrible feeling on only one other occasion, and that would be deep in the trail-less backcountry of Great Smoky Mountains National Park 17 years later (see "Lost" in the first volume). I can easily say that the two most ecstatic moments of my backpacking life occurred on these two trips. Finding my way out of the Smokies ranked as #1 since I was traveling solo, but # 2 was on this trip. Rod and I were climbing uphill through the jungle hoping against hope that we would run into the Loop Trail that leads to Granite Park. Our topo map was of little use in the dense vegetation, and GPS technology was not yet around. The Loop Trail climbs almost 3000' in five miles from the trail head at Packer's Roost to Granite Park, so the thought of missing the trail, and attempting to bushwhack all the way up to the chalet was wearing on us. Then, like a pot of gold suddenly appearing at the end of a rainbow, there it was: this strange, four-foot wide neatly manicured path amidst the brush and fallen logs! Rod and I literally threw our hats into the air and began jumping up and down whooping for joy.

When our giddiness died down, we still faced a lengthy, steep climb, and for some reason Rod still seemed full of energy, yet I felt completely enervated. After enduring several days of bland dried meals, we had counted on enjoying a fine dinner at Granite Park Chalet on this evening. However, I was not sure I could make it up there in time to place our order. "Rod," I moaned, "You seem to have a lot more in your tank than I do. Why don't you go ahead of me and order our dinners. If I'm late just save me a plate of food." "Okay, but traveling solo we need to be extra careful not to surprise a bear," Rod wisely cautioned. Looking back, splitting up in grizzly country, especially in dense vegetation with huckleberry bushes was a dumb thing to do. Obviously, I was allowing my appetite for a fine meal to trump common sense. I guess the fresh memory of Margaret's fine home cooking at Granite Park the previous summer was clouding my judgement!

I actually managed to make it up to the chalet in time for dinner, though I didn't catch up with Rod until I walked into the dining room. I enjoyed munching on some huckleberries for my dinner appetizer on the way up, and I think that helped bring up my energy level—that and constantly being alert to not surprise a bear, which thankfully, neither of us did. The meal did not quite match what Margaret prepared, but after four days on the trail, it was quite scrumptious. After dinner we headed down to the campsite. Of course, it was in this backcountry campground that the other horrible and tragic fatal mauling had occurred. It seemed peculiar that our backpack route would take us by the scene of both fatal grizzly maulings only four years earlier. It certainly was not by design. However, during the previous summer that I worked at Granite Park, I was actually involved in the park's commitment to preventing *any* human foods from coming into contact with bears. While there were no guarantees, Rod and I had convinced ourselves that there were no more bears in the area habituated to human foods. That thought, plus the fact that we were absolutely wiped out from our strenuous hike all the way from Heaven's Peak Lookout to Granite Park in a single day, allowed us to sleep well.

The next morning Rod and I strolled back up to the chalet for breakfast and met a ranger on patrol. It was at this point that we learned that our route along the "high line" was closed due to huge snow drifts still in place at the notorious Ahern Drift. The news came as quite a shock. Neither of us had anticipated the trail not being passable. I knew from my past experience while working at Granite Park that the drift tended to stay over the trail well into the summer, but we had assumed we would be able to cross it. Apparently it was much deeper and wider after a big snow winter, thus making the crossing too treacherous. We now had to come up with a different plan as to how we were going to reach Goat Haunt, and continue our planned itinerary. Our only solution was to hike up and over Swiftcurrent Pass, and down to Many Glacier. From there, we would simply have to hitchhike our way up to Waterton National Park in Canada, then hike south along Waterton Lake until we reached Goat Haunt.

We hiked as fast as we could as we had no idea how successful our hitchhiking attempt would fare at Many Glacier. Luckily, we found two hotel employees who were headed to Waterton on their days off, and were willing to take us along. The only difficulty we faced was at the border, where Canadian agents grilled the two employees as to our credentials. For a few minutes I thought they were going to let the two employees go but make us get out of the car. However, when we told the agents our story, plus I added that I was in the

USAF at Malmstrom, he let us pass through. As soon as we arrived we donned our backpacks, and quickly headed down the trail along the west side of Waterton Lake. We were thrilled to actually find a beautiful campsite halfway down the lake just before sunset. We started a campfire, enjoyed a dinner of freeze-dried beef stew, then relaxed knowing that we would reach Goat Haunt the next morning, and thus put us back on schedule. However, the evening would not stay relaxing!

After darkness had descended on us, a boat arrived at our campsite. A gruff looking cowboy got out, walked up to us and said, "You fellows are probably not going to want to stay here tonight. We have a big group with ten horses coming in, and this is where we are going to stay tonight." Apparently the campsite that Rod and I had found was primarily used by horse parties, and the group coming in had no other campsite to go to this late in the day. The cowboy did not run us off; however, we knew that we did not want to share a campsite with such a huge horse party. So Rod and I donned our backpacks, and headed off in the dark toward Goat Haunt—not the best time of day to hike in grizzly country!

When we arrived at Goat Haunt, we were surprised to find hikers' shelters, which contained bunks. All we had to do was roll out our ensolite pads and sleeping bags, and crawl in. Surprisingly, there were no other backpackers staying here, so even with our late arrival, we had the place to ourselves. The next morning we could see why. Goat Haunt is almost like a little settlement in the wilderness. Here you have a ranger station, boat ramp, where the daily boat ride from Waterton docks, and the bunks. Really, why would a backpacker searching for wild country camp here, when just up the trail there were gorgeous lakes surrounded by rugged mountains? After breakfast we loaded up our packs, and headed up the trail, and soon passed through an open meadow that provided a stunning view of Mount Cleveland, which at an elevation of 10,466' is Glacier's highest peak. That elevation seemed low compared to Yellowstone's highest Peak—Eagle Peak at 11,358,' but that is misleading, because the entire Yellowstone volcanic plateau is so much higher than the glacial carved valleys of Glacier. After all, it is the *tallness* of the peak that really counts. From our vantage point just below an elevation of 4400,' Mount Cleveland rose an impressive 6,266' above us!

We were now actually a bit ahead of schedule, so we could relax. We were planning to hike six miles to Lake Francis, but when we reached Lake Janet at the three mile mark, we found that the campsite was open with no one around, and the mountain backdrop was spectacular. What was the rush? It was not even lunchtime, but we decided to relax, take it easy, and absorb our magnificent surroundings on a bluebird day.

Along about noon, a party of five backpackers, three young fellows and two young ladies, walked into our camp. The group appeared to be very energetic, and I guess we appeared somewhat tranquil stretched out in our sun-dappled camp. "Did you fellows stay at Goat Haunt last night?" one of the guys asked. "Yep," Rod answered, "we're taking it easy today." "Well, we're on our way up to Hole-in-the Wall for a couple of days; why don't you come on up and join us?" He went on to say that they were concession employees, and had a few days off. "Thanks," I answered, "but we had to take a detour from the highline trail, so we are going to enjoy these lakes." A couple of the guys looked at us in disbelief. "Man," one said while pointing to the high mountains above us, "Hole-in-the-Wall is way up there in that cirque near the top of the mountain. It's like the most remote campsite in Glacier, and you're on top of the world. Why the hell would you want to stay down here?" I just shrugged my shoulders. "It's gorgeous down here too," I said. At that, the group charged up the trail, full of vigor and excitement.

The next morning we found it hard to leave our little piece of paradise. We knew that we had two more evenings to camp before our trip ended at Bowman Lake, so we figured our last night should be spent about half-way down the trail along the shore of Bowman Lake, but we weren't sure where our next camp on this evening should be. However, after we hiked the three miles to Lake Francis we quickly made up our minds. The huge peaks behind the lake contained massive snowfields, with Dixon Glacier tucked in the cirque of The Sentinel. As a result mighty waterfalls were spilling over the hanging canyon, and cascading down the slopes leading to Lake Francis. "Rod," I mumbled as I gazed up at the incredible mountain scene before us, "I thought the scenery at Lake Janet was spectacular, but this is even more amazing!" We studied our topo map, and quickly decided that we would not find a better place to camp between here and Bowman Lake, so we decided on yet another short day that would again allow us to relax in a majestic mountain setting.

During the afternoon we strolled around the lake to marvel at the peaks and waterfalls above us, along with the grand wildflower show. Once again, we had this lake to ourselves for the evening. This was our seventh day of the trip, and up until this point, we had experienced only bright, warm sunny weather. However, that evening the weather changed dramatically. I will readily admit that I am a "fair weather" backpacker. I really don't enjoy hiking and camping in the rain. On the other hand, I absolutely *love* an evening thunderstorm, especially when it occurs after dinner has been consumed, time around the campfire has been enjoyed, and you are nicely ensconced in your tent for the evening. Well, on this evening we would experience one of the most powerful and lengthy thunderstorms that I have ever observed while in the backcountry. The only other one that would compare to it occurred about seven years later while I was camped in a cirque below Mount Chittenden in Yellowstone with Jim Lenertz (see "The Thunderstorm," first volume).

This storm was one for the ages. For *hours* an intense electrical storm simply parked over this little corner of Glacier National Park. The lightning strikes were relentless. The deafening roar of thunder reverberated off the slopes above Lake Francis. For quite some time Rod and I did not even attempt to sleep. Instead, we gathered at the tent window, and gazed in awe at the lightning strikes. Suddenly, it occurred to me where the majority of those strikes were hitting. "Rod, isn't that the area where that group was headed? Up there at Hole-in-the-Wall?" "O my gosh," Rod replied. "I can't even imagine what it must be like up *there* tonight!" It was one thing to enjoy the spectacle of a mountain thunderstorm from down in the valley where Rod and I were apparently safely located. But we could not comprehend what it would be like to be camped practically on top of a mountain, where the focal point of the lightning strikes appeared to be centered. We discussed their plight for some time, and we really came up with no reasonable solutions for such a dire predicament. We could only hope and pray that the group was safe, and would get through the evening unharmed. At some point, despite the sound and fury of the storm, we dozed off.

The next morning broke clear and sunny. It was the perfect way to follow such a weather event. Everything seemed so fresh and vibrant. The forest took on a sweet fragrance from the evening's heavy rainfall. The birds were chirping. All seemed right in the world. But as we turned our gaze up to Hole-in-the-Wall 1200' above us, we hoped that our wilderness comrades had survived the night, and were enjoying this delightful morning in the mountains as we were. On this day we figured we had about eight miles to cover, which included a 1000' climb up and over Brown Pass, and then down to Bowman Lake. Not a bad day at all, and given our surroundings, we were in no hurry to leave.

Our first task was to get our tent and other gear dried out while we enjoyed a relaxing breakfast on this bright and cheery sunny morning. After we had eaten, and just as we were finishing packing up our gear, we glanced up to see the aforementioned group of five approaching us, as the trail ran right by our camp. We were taken aback by their collective appearance. The group had lost their stride from before. They were moving along rather slowly. Each member of the group appeared gaunt and rather pale. Apparently and understandably, they must have not slept at all during the night's storm. Their eyes appeared glazed over. I did not say a word as they slowly made their way through our camp, but Rod, remembering the bit of ridicule a couple of them had directed our way at not joining them, could not resist. "Say," Rod bellowed out quite loudly, "How was Hole-in-the-Wall last night?" The group just kept moving along slowly, but finally one of the ladies murmured softly: "It was horrible, just horrible." As I watched the group gradually disappear down the trail, I turned to Rod and chuckled, "Man, you are blunt, but thank goodness they survived. That bunch sure looked like they were rode hard and rolled up wet! And thank the Lord we did not go up there with them!"

We reluctantly departed our second night of paradise in this verdant valley with lakes surrounded by towering peaks, and began our trek up toward Brown Pass. As we neared the top, the meadows were carpeted with a vivid display of bear grass. Once over the pass, we were treated to a fine view of a huge waterfall tumbling down near the trail, but as we continued our descent toward Bowman Lake, the true prize soon revealed itself: the mighty and majestic Hole-in-the-Wall Falls gushing out from a hole in the mountain. I felt as though I had been transported into Yosemite Valley. I never dreamed that we would see waterfalls of this caliber and height in Glacier! There were actually two falls, both forks of Bowman Creek, and each well over 1,300' high, flowing out from the Hole-in-the-Wall basin above. I'm sure the view from that campsite up there must be fabulous, but as we continued our descent to Bowman Lake, we could not imagine a more spectacular scene anywhere in Glacier that matched what we were enjoying. It felt as though Yosemite and Glacier had come together in this one special valley!

Our last camp on Bowman Lake was quite peaceful. Across the placid lake waters, we could barely obtain a view of the high peaks that we had so enjoyed over the past eight days. We were now in a different setting—down low in a deep forest. We had mixed feelings on our last evening. We felt a sense of pride and joy that we had pulled the trip off, even with the challenge of getting around the blocked Highline Trail, but sad to see it end. However, we still had one more rather unusual surprise yet to come—at least for me, and it was a pleasant one indeed. Our last day, the ninth, consisted of an enjoyable but routine seven mile hike through the dense forest along the shore of the lake. Our challenge for this day would be how in the world we would find a ride back to my car. The North Fork Road was a rather primitive low travel road to begin with, but to complicate matters, there was a five mile spur road into Bowman Lake. So first, we had to hitch a ride down the little spur road just to reach the North Fork Road near the tiny settlement of Polebridge. Then we would need to get a ride some 20 miles back down to where my car was located at the Camas Creek trailhead. Due to this concern, we had departed camp quite early, and when we reached the road at the end of Bowman Lake, we managed to locate a fellow willing to take us out the five miles to the North Fork Road. But he was headed north up to Kintla Lake, so he let us out at the junction. Now we needed a ride going south. However, it seemed that the rare vehicle that came along was going north—to camp either at Bowman Lake or Kintla Lake. It seemed that *no one* was traveling south.

We were now back down in the low country and away from the lush forest. It was terribly hot, dry, and dusty. The few vehicles that had passed us going north had stirred up an awful cloud of dust that descended on us. Finally, after about two hours, a pickup truck with a bunch of guys stopped. "We are headed down to our ranch, but we only have room for one of you," the young cowboy said with a smile on his face. Since it was my car at the trailhead, I told Rod I would take the ride. In order to save room I left my backpack with Rod, grabbed my canteen, and hopped in the truck. I turned to tell Rod, "I'll be back just as soon as I can." As we pulled away, I looked back, and Rod looked kind of pitiful sitting there on the side of that hot, dry, dirt road, as the dust cloud engulfed him.

It turned out that the small ranch was only about a third of the way to my car, and they pulled up to the front of their white clapboard home. All the young guys jumped out of the truck, and one turned to me and said, "Mom has lunch on, so we can't take you down the road until we eat. Come on in." I walked inside the small home, and found a large dining table set with big bowls and plates. A stately woman with white hair emerged from the kitchen and said, "Welcome to our home! Today, we are having fresh potato soup and cornbread, with lemonade. I hope you enjoy it!" It was a good thing that those cowboys were as hungry and thirsty as I was, because I was not embarrassed when I consumed two large bowls of the best potato soup I've ever had! However, with each spoonful, I could not help but envision Rod sitting on the side of that hot, dusty road.

When I finally reached Rod later that day he looked worse for wear. He appeared to be hot, sweaty, covered in dust, and not in the best mood. "What took you so dang long?" he blurted out. To this day I still can't remember the excuse that I came up with. It took me about a year before I mustered the courage to tell him the full story of how I was enjoying a great lunch, while he was eating dust on that road. However, time heals all wounds, and Rod now emits a loud guffaw when we reminisce about our adventure in Glacier. All of our memories tend to focus on those mighty glacially carved cirques, peaks and valleys. It is indeed a land of mountain splendor!

Rod scrambling off-trail toward Camas Lake in Glacier

The Winds—a Spectacular Wilderness in Need of Care

Located at the southern tip of what is generally considered to be the Greater Yellowstone Ecosystem is one of the most spectacular mountain wilderness areas in North America—the Wind River Range in the Bridger Wilderness. Several of my friends had admonished me for years that I had never backpacked through this stretch of rugged peaks that rise along the Continental Divide. Finally, through the urging of my friend Clyde Austin, my friends and I planned an 8-day trip in late July of 2015. Since Clyde had been through these mountains several times, he offered to provide a suggested route and join me, John and Deb Dirksen and Hank Barnett—all old backpacking buddies, for the trip. In fact, the previous summer while trekking through the Teton Wilderness with John and Deb, we had encountered several through hikers on the Continental Divide Trail (CDT) who had raved about the Winds. One hiker from Norway who had hiked in mountain ranges all over the world, including Patagonia, told us that the Winds were right at the top of his treks in terms of sheer stunning beauty. I was ready to see them for myself!

Clyde pointed out that while many breathtaking mountain ranges, such as the Grand Tetons, are easily viewed from a road, the only true way to see the Winds was to hike into them. That's because the range is sort of in the middle of nowhere, many miles away from the main highways such as U.S. 191 that runs through Pinedale, Wyoming. We heartily endorsed Clyde's suggested one-way route of beginning at the Elkhart trailhead, and ending at Lower Green River Lake. Our trip would cover about 70 miles of hiking. Along the way we planned to camp one night at Hobbs Lake, three nights at Island Lake (where we would enjoy two day hikes sans backpacks), one night at Elbow Lake, and the last two nights along the Green River. We decided on this route since we would begin our hike at a rather high elevation of 9400,' and end our trip at an elevation of 8000'. Since the logistics were rather brutal, we wisely decided to utilize a shuttle service out of Pinedale.

We knew that nearly all of our hike would be above 10,000,' so the weather conditions can either make or break a trip such as this. Fortunately, for the most part, we had a favorable forecast, except for the second day when a quick cold front was due to blow through. When we reached the large parking lot at the Elkhart trailhead, I was rather dismayed to see how many vehicles were present. We saw only one horse trailer, which indicated to me that this country was primarily utilized by backpackers. I thought back to one year earlier, when John, Deb and I showed up at the Turpin Meadows trailhead to begin our 8-day trek through the Teton Wilderness. That parking lot had also been full, but there were many more horse trailers present. We found that the vast Teton Wilderness had easily absorbed the apparent large number of visitors, as we never found the trails crowded at all. We hoped that this would be the case in the Winds.

After a few miles of hiking through spruce and whitebark forest, we soon reached an elevation of 10,400' at a rocky outcropping known as Photographer's Point. Here the incredibly jagged peaks of the Winds came into full view in the distance. The one peak that would dominate our view for the next several days was Fremont Peak at an elevation of 13,745,' named for the famous explorer John Charles Fremont, often referred to as "Pathfinder." Fremont had referred to this peak as "Snow Peak" in 1842 on his South Pass Expedition, and had diverted his itinerary to attempt climbing it because he thought it was the highest peak in the Winds, and possibly the entire Rocky Mountain chain. Actually, the highest peak in the Winds is Gannet Peak, which at an elevation of 13, 804' is also the highest peak in Wyoming, 34' higher than the Grand Teton, and there are many peaks above 14,000' throughout the Rocky Mountain chain from Colorado up into Canada. Although we would travel within only four air miles of Gannet Peak, we would not be able to see it due to the huge, jagged peaks that rise above Titcomb Basin. I often think of the southeast corner of Yellowstone to be the most remote place around regarding distance to the nearest road; however, on our trip through the Winds, we would at times be in a similar situation, over 20 miles from the nearest road of any type. In fact, in order to climb Gannet Peak, a roundtrip backcountry trek of over 40 miles is required, making it the longest approach for any state highpoint (climbers are flown onto a glacier at the base of Denali).

After 8.5 miles of hiking, we reached our destination for the evening, Hobbs Lake. The view from our campsite included an overview of the lake with the craggy peaks along the Continental Divide serving as an impressive backdrop. Hank and I were breaking in new, ultra-light internal frame backpacks, and so far we were pleased with their performance. After years of using a heavier external frame backpack, I had finally decided to go for lighter gear. Clyde had warned me to expect problems with mosquitoes, but on this day and evening, there were few around. The winter throughout northwest Wyoming and southwest Montana had produced a very dismal snowpack. It almost seemed like it was late August instead of late July, as we gazed out at the light snowpack still visible on the distant peaks. I figured that the unusually low snowpack might play into our favor regarding fewer mosquitoes, and also trail conditions. After dinner we relaxed around our campfire, and watched the late evening alpenglow on the peaks surrounding us. It truly felt great to be back out in the wilderness, especially surrounded by these incredible mountains.

We woke up the next morning to a changing weather pattern, as the cold front was obviously on its way, with increasing cloud cover and low temperatures. After a hearty breakfast of Deb's own version of egg Mcmuffins, we headed north toward Island Lake along perhaps the rockiest trail I have ever traversed. At times, it was almost as if we were bushwhacking cross country. We reminded ourselves to be extra careful not to turn an ankle or worse; the only way to enjoy the spectacular mountain surroundings was to occasionally stop walking, and just gaze around. Our slow progress did have the benefit of placing us at Seneca Lake just in time for our lunch break. Now we could stop worrying about fitting our next step on the rocky trail, and just sit back and marvel at the amazing scenery before us. With the intense blue waters of Seneca Lake below us, the jagged line of mountains dominated the view to the east. In fact, we felt as though we were looking at the huge spiny back of a giant dinosaur along the skyline!

It was tough to leave our lovely lunch spot, but we hoped to make camp before the full force of the cold front blew through. By 3:30 p.m. we came to a bench overlooking Island Lake, and the huge peaks in the distance, but despite our rather early arrival, there were already tents in place in several locations around the lake. By now the skies were darkening, and a cold wind was sweeping over the landscape. We quickly found some established campsites where fire rings were located, and began pitching our tents as the wind picked up, and the temperature plunged. Just as I pulled my rainfly over my tent, a sideways snowstorm hit. Hank, Clyde, and I all had solo tents, and John and Deb had their two-person dome tent. We all dove inside our tents to weather the storm, which now featured ominous dark clouds, fierce winds, and snow pellets. It was hard to believe that the date was July 27, as we had gone from a cheery partly-sunny summer's day to just the type of storm that can quickly kill an unprepared hiker. This storm was a perfect example of why hypothermia is often called the "killer of the unprepared." Our grassy, green camp area was soon transformed into a snow-covered wintry like setting. "Looks like the cold front has arrived," Hank announced from the safety of his tent several yards away from mine.

Fortunately, the storm blew through quickly, just as the weather forecast had predicted. We were pleased to see some blue skies emerging, but the temperature remained low. John announced that his thermometer showed the temperature at 30 degrees—an amazing drop of over 25 degrees in a matter of a few minutes. We emerged from our tents, but now we faced the challenge of trying to keep warm as dinner time was approaching. I put on just about every piece of clothing I had brought, including my light down coat and rain jacket. I walked around our campsite, and was frankly dismayed by what I found. First off, despite the preponderance of spruce and whitebark present, there was simply no firewood to be found. As I walked around I came across five fire pits, two large gallon cans, a plastic whiskey bottle, old underwear, wads of toilet paper scattered about, fish heads and fish carcasses, and bits and pieces of aluminum foil. The place looked terribly overused, hammered down, and frankly poorly managed—at least compared to similar backcountry areas in

Yellowstone and Grand Teton National Parks. I could not help but envision what Island Lake must have looked like when Fremont set up his base camp here prior to scaling the peak now named in his honor. Given the wind and low temperature, I knew that a campfire and protection from the elements would be a necessity for us to be able to prepare our dinners. One of the fire pits was located in the lee of a large boulder, so Deb set up her kitchen there while I continued my search for a decent amount of twigs and sticks to at least have a small fire. Our plan worked and we enjoyed a fine meal of chicken chow Mein prepared by Deb.

After dinner a young man and woman in U.S. Forest Service uniforms entered our camp. I could not really tell what type of workers they were from their appearance. The young man had an old round straw hat with no band or insignia showing. His shirt had the USFS patch but there was no name tag. If he was a ranger rather than a laborer, he certainly did not bear any resemblance to the rangers in the National Park Service. Nevertheless, the young man stated that he would like to see some of our tents moved farther away from the main trail. He said that camps were supposed to be at least 200 feet away from the trail. John and Deb had selected a tent site that had obviously been used many times before under a tree, and there was an existing fire pit nearby. Nevertheless, the young man said they were only about 150 feet from the trail. Clyde was told that his tent was "on the edge." Hank and I had selected existing tent sites (which also had fire pits nearby) that were closer to 200 feet from the trail. Both John and Deb, and Clyde complied with the young man's request and moved their tents to other, though less desirable, utilized tent sites. Later that evening we gathered around our small fire, but as the temperature plunged, one by one members of our party headed for their tents. By 9:30 p.m. I was the only one left but then it started to snow again. As I poured water on the coals I belted out a few strains of "Let it Snow." As I headed for my tent, I could hear John singing "Let it Snow, Let it Snow, Let it Snow" as well.

The next morning started out very cold, at least for late July. John said his thermometer read 20 degrees, and his water bottle was frozen solid. Fortunately the sun came out and warmed things up. After breakfast we packed our lunches in our daypacks, and headed toward the far reaches of Titcomb Basin and Titcomb lakes, a distance of about 4.5 miles. It was an absolutely glorious day. The sun's warmth along with the deep blue skies in this spectacular alpine setting made for a wonderful day. The high meadows were covered in flowers, with the ever-present purple elephant head dominating. At the far end of the basin, we stopped for lunch on the granite boulders, and marveled at the spiny ridge of the mountains high above us. Along the way we passed numerous other folks on the trail, as well as backpacker camps, as the basin is obviously a very popular destination for hikers.

That evening Deb prepared the best meal of the entire trip—homemade pizza. While she was getting it ready, Hank, Clyde and I hiked almost one mile back up the steep trail in an attempt to find a few dead limbs for our campfire. The weather was producing very cold evenings, and since fires were permitted, we intended to enjoy their warmth, plus Deb had included them in her cooking plans. We did wonder, however, why campfires were even allowed in this particular area, since firewood was not just scarce, it was simply nonexistent. I thought about sites in Yellowstone where, once available dead and down wood became scarce, backcountry rangers changed their designation to NWF (no wood fires.) Deb served up some brownies, cooked up in her backcountry version of a lightweight Dutch oven. As the glow from the embers of our campfire dimmed, a bright moon rose over Island Lake, lighting up the peaks surrounding us. We observed three mule deer grazing in the meadow nearby, our first wildlife sighting of the trip. The Winds contained grizzlies so we carried bear spray; the messy conditions we found when we arrived in our camp area was cause for concern. The clear night meant that the temperature would again plunge during the evening. My stocking cap came in handy, as did a tip from Hank that I should stick my lightweight down jacket in the foot of my sleeping bag to provide just enough extra insulation to stave off cold feet.

The huge mountains to our east blocked the early morning rays of the sun, so it was tough to get up early. Usually we would emerge from our warm cocoons around 7:15 a.m. just as the sun was peeking over the mountains. After breakfast, we packed our daypacks for the day's ambitious hike to the top of Indian Pass, a climb of 1600'. According to trail signs we would cover 14 miles for the day. We left camp by 9:30 and passed several gorgeous lakes as we steadily climbed toward Indian Pass. Our trail basically disappeared as snowfields and boulder fields covered the trail. We could only imagine the snow in this basin in a summer following a more normal winter snowpack. Thanks to our topo maps and Hank's GPS, we managed to negotiate our way across the snowfields until we finally neared Indian Pass, located in a notch between Harrower Peak and Jackson Peak, with the mighty Fremont Peak looming over us. We marveled at the sight of Harrower Glacier, and could not wait to reach the pass where we expected to see the huge Knife Point and Bull Lake Glaciers. As we crossed the last snowfield leading to the pass, we were surprised to find a full bottle of Canadian Mist whiskey laying in the snow. I picked it up, took off the cap and took a sniff. The stuff was real alright, but the top had been previously removed, so we decided to leave the "treat" in its place. Perhaps someone was attempting to summit Fremont Peak, and this bottle of whiskey was to be their celebratory reward on their way back.

John, having just completed a grueling hike with Deb in the Teton Wilderness, had decided to relax in camp for the day. Clyde hiked with us up to the beautiful Indian Basin lakes, then decided to head back to camp. So for

Hank, Deb and me, the elevation of 12,060' at the pass marked the highest elevation any of us had ever set foot on by trail. The day was sunny and glorious, so we lounged at the pass and enjoyed our lunch amidst these crown jewels along the Continental Divide. Our only disappointment was that we were unable to see the big glaciers our maps had promised just over the pass. Apparently, as in many other areas in the northern Rockies, global warming had resulted in a meltoff over the years, causing these glaciers to retreat. It appeared that we would have to hike quite a distance down on the other side of Indian Pass to possibly see what was left of them, but given the long day we already faced, we decided that our great view of Harrower Glacier would have to suffice. Our hike back down to our base camp at Island Lake was long but sweet, given the unending beauty of peaks, flower-filled meadows, and sky blue lakes. We did not run into the number of hikers we had the day before, which was not surprising given the difficulty of finding and following the trail up above timberline.

We made it back to camp by 6 p.m. rather tired and hungry. I immediately built a fire with our remaining sticks we had collected the previous day, and Deb commenced cooking one of my favorite meals—tuna cakes and garlic mashed potatoes. Just as she served up this delicious meal to the five of us sitting around our little campfire, our dinner was suddenly interrupted by the young man wearing the USFS uniform. He strode up to us, obviously upset that we were using the fire ring that was apparently within the 200 foot border of the trail below, although our tents were off in the distance. Of course, we were using this existing fire ring for two reasons—one, it was in the lee of a large boulder which had protected us against the cold winds the previous evening, and two, we always attempted to cook well away from where our tents were located when in grizzly country. The young man lit into us. "You are still camping too close to the trail," he barked. When John tried to explain why we were using this fire ring to prepare our dinner, he quickly interrupted him by saying, "I find this quite annoying! I expected more from you guys, but you are just like all the others! I'm giving you a ticket! I'm going to come in here and close this whole place down!"

While he was talking Deb extinguished the fire, and John scattered what few sticks we had left, all the while attempting to offer an explanation as to why we were using this fire ring, but to no avail. The young man cut him off each time. "Who is going to take the ticket?" the young fellow snarled. At this point we all realized that this young man was obviously having a really bad day, and it was no use to try to communicate with him. "I'll take it," Clyde offered. Clyde then gave him the requested information and the young fellow promptly handed him the ticket and marched off. "Butch," Clyde began, "I don't know about you, but I plan to protest this ticket!" Hank had been over at his tent performing some errands during most of the encounter, but arrived saying he had heard most of the comments. "Right now, let's try to finish our dinner, which has already gotten cold," Hank suggested. "We can then discuss our options, but we need to make certain we don't let this incident ruin our trip," he added. I managed to choke down the delicious meal, now cold, despite my anger. We all finished eating in silence.

After dinner we gathered up the few sticks that John had scattered, and wandered over to another existing fire ring that was over 200' from the trail, but closer to our tents. We built our campfire, gathered around and the discussion started. We all vowed to not allow the behavior by this USFS employee to ruin our trip, but we had things to get off our chests. "Do you realize that among this group we have over 200 years of backcountry experience?" Clyde pointed out. "We have already disposed of much of the trash we found in this campsite, and we never leave a trace," he said. "We did not deserve to be treated in this way," he added. I threw in my two cents worth, "You know, most of my wilderness experience has taken place in national parks, including Yellowstone, Grand Teton, Glacier, Great Smoky Mountains, and the Everglades, but I have also traveled in USFS wilderness areas including the Lee Metcalf, the Teton Wilderness, the Absaroka-Beartooth, and the Boundary Waters Canoe Area Wilderness. I sure don't recall any of the established campsites and fire rings being 200' from a trail and 100' from a lake!" "Well, what I object to the most," Clyde chimed in, "is not that we received a ticket, but rather the behavior in which it was handled. I'm going to write a letter."

Hank had been silent to this point, but now he spoke up. "No Clyde, *I'm* going to write the letter. I have extensive training as a National Park Service law enforcement backcountry ranger, having served in Crater Lake, Great Smoky Mountains, and Yellowstone. That guy followed poor protocol, and I'm going to write the District Ranger in charge of this wilderness, not to just reprove of his behavior, but hopefully to encourage them to get the young man some decent training as to how to carry out his job." Hank proceeded to explain to us how the situation *should* have been handled by a competent ranger. "First, you don't walk in and interrupt a group's dinner. Second, you *listen* to the visitors you are about to ticket. You don't continually interrupt and cut off what they are trying to say, especially as it pertains to the violation. John was trying to explain why we used the fire pit in the lee of the big boulder to keep warm and to also cook a safe distance from our sleeping area, but the fellow refused to listen. Third, you don't *elevate* the situation. He walked in among five calm, nice visitors, who by earlier moving their tents were trying to be compliant, and displayed a hot temper. You know, lots of folks these days really don't like the federal government. That young man, whether he realizes it or not, is *the very face* of the federal government. If he continues that behavior, one of these days he is going to walk into a very volatile and dangerous situation and get hurt.

Finally, you don't walk in and tell five strangers that they are unethical. As I looked around at the five of us, I don't think I could find a more ethical group of wilderness visitors!"

Hank then took a close look at the ticket and found that it had been improperly filled out. There was no box checked as to how Clyde would proceed regarding payment of the ticket, and Hank later found that the code for the federal regulation stated on the ticket did not exist. Later that evening as we gathered around our fire, we agreed to discuss the incident one last time before continuing our trip. We wondered why these two young USFS employees had not bothered to remove the several fire rings if they were within 200' of the trail. We wondered about all of the litter. We had already burned trash, old underwear, toilet paper, and fish carcasses. Why didn't they gather the two gallon cans and plastic bottle for packing out? While Hank had focused on the behavior of the young USFS employee, I pondered out loud that it may be time for the Bridger Wilderness to take a look at how other busy wilderness areas are managed. Places like Yellowstone, Grand Teton, and The Boundary Waters Canoe Area Wilderness. These areas all were carefully managed and permits were required for use. It was obvious to all of us that the Bridger Wilderness was being loved to death based on the large number of backpackers present, and the heavy impact the users had as we had observed at Island Lake. Finally, Hank issued an ultimatum: "Okay, no more talk about this. My wife has a question she always poses when the conversation begins to drift in a bad direction: "I wonder if it's snowing in the Smokies?" (Hank lives only about thirty miles from Great Smoky Mountains National Park, and the highest peaks can easily be viewed from his back yard in Dandridge, Tennessee.)

Our good luck with the weather continued as our fifth day began clear and cool again. It was time to finally break camp from the beaten-down, over-used environs of Island Lake. This would be our toughest day as we would cover ten miles with full backpacks, and gain and lose a significant amount of elevation. Also, for the first time of our trip, the temperatures soared, and as we hiked above timberline there was absolutely no shade to be had. By lunch time when we reached Upper Jean Lake, most of us promptly filled our hats and caps with its icy water, and poured it over our heads in an effort to cool down. I had to chuckle as only a few days earlier we had been trying to avoid hypothermia during a snow storm. Now we were attempting to avoid heat stroke! Even though the hike on this day was tough, the unending views of so much spectacular mountain scenery seemed to ease the physical effort. Mind over body, as the saying goes. We reached our planned destination for the evening, Elbow Lake, by our targeted time of 4:00 p.m. Given the rolling terrain in this treeless country, there would be no problem in finding a suitable place to camp which met the 200 foot rule from water or trail. Of course, there would be no campfire on this evening, as there was not so much as a twig for fuel—nothing but rocks and grassy spots.

We had heard all of the dire warnings about how bad mosquitoes were in the Winds, but so far the presence of these pesky bloodsuckers had been minimal. That was about to change. I guess the higher elevation and more recent presence of snow made the difference. We all donned long pants, long-sleeve shirts, mosquito head nets, and applied some repellent. Their abundant presence interfered with dinner, but as the evening alpenglow began to appear on the flanks of Elbow Peak, the coolness of the evening caused their activity to die down. Once the golden colors disappeared off the top of the peaks, we headed for our tents for a night of rest in the high country. We were all very tired given the long day of hiking, elevation changes and heat.

The next day our good weather continued as we headed west toward Summit Lake. It was apparent that a high pressure ridge was in place over the Wind River Range, bathing the mountains and meadows in bright sun each day. We passed a fellow on the trail going in the opposite direction, and carrying a huge backpack. It appeared that he was prepared for anything, as he had crampons and an ice axe attached to his pack. He said that he was out for two weeks, and reduced his weight somewhat by eating fish along the way. "You know, Summit Lake doesn't look like much," he said, "but I caught a big fat golden trout that was almost more than I could consume!" Although none of us had brought along any fishing gear or purchased a fishing license, I could easily believe the man's story. Several times as we passed lakes I could see fish rising, and in fact, when I tossed seed heads into the water, the fish struck at them—a sure sign that it would probably not be too difficult to catch a fish in these waters.

We made Summit Lake for lunch and relaxed in a shady spot that had obviously been used many times as a campsite. There was a fire ring present. In the distance we could see Green River Pass. We knew that once we crossed it we would begin our descent from our many days above 10,000'. I always do much better on a level or downhill trail, so I was pleased that our climbing had come to an end. After topping the pass our trail dropped into a narrow canyon with spectacular vertical walls on both sides, and Trail Creek accompanying us along the way. Our targeted destination for the evening was somewhere in the vicinity of a trail junction referred to on the map as Trail Creek Park. However, as we hiked along we realized that in this rugged terrain it would be impossible to find any campsites that met the criteria of being both 200 feet from the trail and 100' from the stream. We did pass a few obvious campsites with established fire rings, but alas, they did not meet the required distances.

Once we reached Trail Creek Park we were relieved to finally see a few level areas of terrain above the trail; however, while the established campsites here met the 100' distance rule from any stream, they did not appear to be at least 200' from the trail. Once you walked over 200' from the trail the terrain began to rise up into the steep slopes. I walked off the distance from the campsite with fire ring to the trail and measured 180'. We decided to risk another ticket by camping here, since there was nothing else available. The campsite turned out to be our favorite for the entire trip for several reasons. First, there was abundant dead and down firewood now that we were back down in the forest. Second, we had some great views of the sheer canyon walls rising above us, which turned golden in the late evening sun. Third, amazingly, there were no mosquitoes present—a huge plus! Finally, we had some ice-cold springs not far away for our supply of water. Deb prepared a fine dinner cooked on the fire in her little Dutch oven. All was well in the world on this superb evening in the wilderness. For the first time in many nights, we enjoyed the sound of a stream, as Trail Creek tumbled nearby.

The next day was met with great anticipation, because our trail would soon come alongside the famous Green River, and eventually we would be able to look back at the majestic Squaretop Mountain. Over the years I had seen many posters and photos of this recognized peak that rises above the Upper and Lower Green River Lakes and valley. I had always wanted to see it first hand, but the thing is, this area is simply in the middle of nowhere. During my many years of working summers in Yellowstone, we would often make it down to the Tetons and areas south of Jackson, Wyoming, but it was tough to justify making the long trip to the headwaters of the Green River. But my interest in the Green River was robust for other reasons. I had once taken a fabulous canoe trip down the Green River, as well as read Colin Fletcher's book, *River: One Man's Journey Down the Colorado, Source to Sea,* describing his long journey from the Green's headwaters. At age 67 Colin actually backpacked up to Green River Pass, and then began his long descent down the Green until he reached a point where he could launch his raft. He then soloed the rest of the way. Having floated down the Colorado River twice through the Grand Canyon in *really big* rafts, and not solo, I have always considered his journey simply amazing.

When we reached the Green River near Three Forks Park, I was astounded by its beautiful green color, a result of glacial silt. Its color reminded me of three other streams I had visited deep in the wilderness—Broad Creek in Yellowstone, and the Little Colorado River and Havasu Creek in the Grand Canyon. Our plan on this day was to hike about 10 miles and camp somewhere near the Green River above Upper Green River Lake, as this would leave us with only 7 miles on our last day. Clyde had "warned" us that the last two days would consist of a 17 mile "slog" through forest to eventually reach our exit point; however, we scolded Clyde for his comments. Our hike was anything *but* a slog. The scenery was absolutely magnificent every step of the way. Our trail wound through old-growth forest with some *huge* spruce trees. While I fully understand and appreciate the role of forest fires in the wilderness, I was thankful that fires had not burned here. The big trees were just so majestic, and the shade they offered was appreciated, especially since so much of the old-growth forest in Yellowstone had burned in recent decades. The terrain continued to be rugged, and we could only chuckle when we would pass established campsites with fire rings that backpackers obviously used. The sites, of course, were not far from the trail. Anyone attempting to comply with the 200' from trail rule along here would have to hang a hammock from a tree!

Soon we emerged into open meadows along the Green River, and there behind us was the monumental Squaretop Mountain rising above the entire valley. What a truly spectacular sight! The photos and posters were great, but there was simply nothing like seeing its full range of beauty, as it seemed to stand as a sentinel over the Green River valley. As the day lengthened and we neared the ten mile mark, we had been searching for a legal campsite. There were plenty if only the 100' distance from the stream rule applied. However, when combining both that with the 200' distance from the trail, it was absolutely *impossible* to find a legal campsite. Once we even attempted to ford the Green River, since it was the only way to get over 200' from the trail. However, the river was too deep, and the bank consisted of deep muck. On another occasion we stopped and all headed out in different directions, trying to find a somewhat level spot back in the forest that met the criteria. As we wandered about we accidentally became separated. John and Deb and I thought that Hank was ahead of us and Clyde behind us; actually, Hank had circled back through the forest in his search and was now behind us. As the day lengthened and everyone was tiring (our group was not a bunch of spring chickens—at the time Clyde, John and I were 73, 70 and 68 respectively), we came to a small island of trees that contained an established campsite with fire ring. The site was about 150' from the trail and perhaps about 75' from the banks of the river. It would have to do, ticket or no ticket. John, Deb and I decided to plop down in this site and wait. About thirty minutes later Hank and Clyde showed up and we all agreed to stop at this spot. There was nothing behind us that worked and looking further down the trail, the terrain only became rougher. To hopefully avoid receiving another ticket, we decided to not put up our tents until it was almost dark, and then we would take them down first thing the next morning.

The view from our campsite along the Green River was perhaps the most breathtaking of any in all my years of backpacking, but it was not our most pleasant evening. For one thing the mosquitoes returned and matched the level of activity that we had suffered at Elbow Lake. On came the head netting, which was a pain when attempting to eat dinner. Second, even though the green color of the Green River was lovely, the glacial flour present made for some extra work on our water filter. And finally, knowing that we could not get 200' away from the trail and 100' away from the water, we felt like "outlaws" in a hideout at the campsite. As planned the tents went up late, and by then the mosquitoes had won out anyway. Into the tents we all dove.

Our last morning we continued hiking north toward our exit trailhead located at Lower Green River Lake. We first came to Upper Green River Lake, and noticed that a couple of canoes were present. I was surprised at just how rugged the terrain was on either side of the trail. It was a good thing that we had not pushed on the previous evening in our attempt to find a "legal" campsite. There were none. It was difficult to walk for more than a couple of minutes without turning around to view Squaretop Mountain. We did it many times and snapped lots of photos. When we reached the larger Lower Green River Lake, I had halfway expected to see powerboats and jet skis zipping about, especially since we were coming out at the trailhead and road campground on a Sunday. However, I was pleasantly surprised to note that the lake was apparently off limits to any motors, except right at the north end, which was the boundary of the wilderness. We did see a few kayaks and canoes on the lake. The river connecting the two lakes had a swift flow to it, yet a few folks had paddled upstream from the Lower to the Upper Lake. Once we hiked about halfway along the Lower Lake, we began to pick up lots of day hikers, enjoying a hike from the campground. My son-in-law Christoph once told me that you can always tell when you are getting close to a trailhead when you start smelling the many fragrances of perfumes and colognes! Given the rugged terrain and limited level camping, I was rather shocked when we encountered two men on horseback trailing two pack horses. I moved off the trail then inquired, "Where are you fellows heading for the night?" "Trail Creek Park," came the reply. "Do you fellows get out here very often?" I asked. "Yes, we live near here," the man answered. "Well, how in the world do you manage to find campsites that are 200' from the trail and also 100' from lakes or streams?" I asked. "Oh, all the USFS cares about is that you not get too close to water. They could give a (expletive) about how far from the trail you are," the man said. I then told him of our experience to which he seemed quite surprised.

Our trip had safely come to an end. We had been incredibly fortunate with the weather that we had enjoyed for eight days, save one brief blast of a cold front with snow. I found later that the weather just north of us in the Tetons and Yellowstone had been very inclement. Then, the day *after* our trip a rainy front moved over the Winds. I was amazed at the long, primitive road that we had to drive from Green River Lake campground out to highway 191. We had about 25 miles of primitive, rutted dirt road, followed by another 20 miles of secondary road. Hence, the reason why you have to hike into these mountains to truly experience them. Motors won't cut it. Besides, as Ed Abbey famously said, "Yes sir, yes madam, I entreat you, get out of those motorized wheelchairs, get off your foam rubber backsides, stand up straight like men! Like women! Like human beings! And walk—walk—WALK upon our sweet and blessed land!" This we had done and we felt enriched physically, mentally and spiritually.

It was a Sunday, or we would have paid the District Ranger at the Pinedale, Wyoming U.S. Forest Service office a visit. However, we intended to be in touch by letter. Hank would make his points regarding the behavior of the young USFS employee who had issued us a ticket. I intended to voice my opinions as to how the Bridger Wilderness was currently being managed. It is simply too majestic, too spectacular to not go the extra mile to ensure that its wilderness quality will remain for our children and grandchildren. There are excellent management models nearby to emulate—Grand Teton National Park and Yellowstone National Park, not to mention the excellent stewardship and management provided by the U.S. Forest Service for the Boundary Waters Wilderness Canoe Area in Superior National Forest in northeastern Minnesota.

Addendum

Hank, Clyde and I did write letters. Hank sent his to the District Ranger in Pinedale, Clyde sent his to the Supervisor of the Bridger-Teton National Forest in Jackson, and I sent mine to my U.S. Senator Jon Tester, Montana (D). Hank received a reply from the District Ranger who defended the young man's actions, and said that we should have received a ticket the first time he found our tents within 200 feet of the trail. Clyde never received a reply. I received a reply from Senator Tester that my letter had been forwarded to the supervisor of Bridger-Teton National Forest with a note to keep him up to date regarding the response I receive. As the book goes to print I still have not received a reply.

Squaretop Mountain above the Green River

Hoodoo High Country

With 2.2 million acres Yellowstone is a huge park. Then toss in the fact that most of the park is surrounded by wilderness. The Greater Yellowstone Ecosystem comprises about 18 million acres. Finally, consider that 98% of the park is undeveloped and managed as a wilderness. For someone like me who loves the backcountry, working as an Interpretive Park Ranger and getting only two days off each week can be maddening. Each summer Jim Lenertz and I would study his topo map and dream about all of the wild corners of the park we longed to visit. He placed a red line along all of the routes he had trekked—many off-trail, and an "X" where he had camped. I eventually did the same thing on my own map which is now old, yellow and tattered. In the summer of 1979 there was one place we both particularly wanted to visit—Hoodoo Basin, way up in the Absaroka high country along the east boundary that borders the North Absaroka Wilderness in the Shoshone National Forest. But with only two days off, how could we get there and back? We managed to come up with a plan.

On a mid-July day Jim's trusty 1972 yellow K-5 4WD Chevy Blazer was loaded up and ready to go as soon as we completed work at 4:00 p.m. We drove out the East Entrance, and through the Wapiti Valley to Cody, a distance of 110 miles from Old Faithful. We then took the Sunlight Basin Road another 30 miles until we finally dropped down from Dead Indian Pass and reached a spur road along Sunlight Creek. From here we would drive into the backside of the rugged Absaroka Mountains as far as the old primitive road would take us. Jim had his good friend George and his son from Arizona visiting with him at the time so they joined us for this adventure. We really had no idea if we could make it all the way up to Hoodoo Basin and back during our brief time off, but we were going to give it our best shot.

The first time that I traveled the Sunlight Basin Road was in the summer of 1968, and it was little more than a jeep trail with deep ruts in it. Monied interests knew the potential for increased travel if the road could be upgraded, providing a viable route for tourists to take between Cody and Cooke City, basically connecting the East Entrance with the Northeast Entrance. The name was upgraded to the Chief Joseph Scenic Highway, which was a good choice since it was in this region where Chief Joseph and his band of 2000 horses and 800 people, including elderly men and women and children, completely gave General Oliver Howard and the U.S. Calvary an embarrassing slip. The road construction project to widen and pave the road was eventually completed, thus providing a loop for tourists to take going in and out of the park via these two entrances. But during the late 1970s this road was the definition of "off the beaten path."

Jim and I had attempted to obtain information about accessing the park from this remote location, but little was available. Most backpackers who ventured into the Hoodoo high country came in by way of the Lamar River and Upper Miller Creek, but this route covered a roundtrip distance of 48 miles, and would require much more time than we had available. We did call a U.S. Forest Service office in Cody, and the ranger there simply told us to expect a very rough road along Sunlight Creek. "That road is a low priority for us this time of year," he told us. "It will be later this summer before we do any maintenance on it as we get closer to hunting season in the fall. Practically no one goes back there anyway until fall." He told us to expect washouts and trees across the road. Therefore, we carried an axe with us. Even if we were able to drive deep into the forest on the old road, we did not want to be vulnerable to a windstorm blowing down trees and blocking our trip back out. We had to be prepared. And sure enough, we were not far along that dirt and gravel road before we began to encounter significant problems. The spring snow melt had indeed washed some sections of the road out, and portions of Sunlight Creek were literally coursing right down the middle of the road! Jim's K-5 handled these sections well though our progress slowed considerably. Then, as promised, we began to encounter downed trees across the road. We all took turns chopping the trees and pulling them to the side to allow passage.

After driving about 12 miles down the primitive road, we finally reached a point on our topo map called "Lee City." There was no evidence of any "city" here in this old mining region, but from this point on the road was simply impassable, so we pulled over and parked the truck. We had hoped to drive the old road all the way to the end where the trail began, but even with high clearance and four-wheel drive we could drive no further. Darkness had settled into the forest around us and all was eerily quiet. I fully believed what the U.S. Forest Service ranger had said about the almost nonexistent summer travel on this lonely remote primitive road. In fact, I had just finished reading Edward Abbey's novel, "The Monkey Wrench Gang," and I felt like we were in that book—stealthily sneaking along a dark backroad under the shroud of secrecy. We pulled out our tents and pitched them. There was plenty of flat space around and the roar of Sunlight Creek would provide a refreshing audible backdrop as we drifted off to sleep. We had a big day ahead of us and goodness knows, no one was going to bother us this evening. Not back here!

The next morning Jim locked up his truck, and we said a little prayer over it that it would be spared from vandals. The previous summer Jim had driven up to the Beartooth in June to enjoy a day of backcountry skiing. When he returned late that day he found his truck sitting on the ground. Thieves had removed all four wheels from his K-5. Such an act of thievery is bad enough, but to do so in a remote area early in the summer when few people are around borders on a hanging offense in the minds of many westerners. Fortunately for Jim, there just happened to be another person who had just driven up and seen his predicament, and offered to drive him into Cooke City to get some expensive assistance.

After a quick breakfast we hoisted our packs and enjoyed a pleasant, rather level hike along Sunlight Creek. At the turn of the century there had been some sporadic mining activity here but nothing of any value was ever found. We passed two places on our topo map listed "Hardee's Cabins" and "Painter Cabin." The former was now nothing but a pile of debris, but the foundation of Painter's cabin was still visible with trees growing right in the middle of it. Both Homer Hardee and J.R. Painter were early prospectors in this region. At the Painter cabin the old road ended, and we soon came upon a sign that read, "Yellowstone Boundary—5 miles." Soon we entered the North Absaroka Wilderness, and we knew that our trail was due to turn north and climb over 2,600' to the park boundary and the Hoodoo high country. However, we first had to contend with a difficult ford of Sunlight Creek. There was still plenty of snow up high, and the snowmelt was in full force. The length of the crossing was not the problem, it was the depth of the water, and the velocity at which it was moving. One slip here and the power of the stream would sweep us downstream, and possibly into a logjam, trapping us underwater. Therefore, each of us utilized a sturdy branch to use as our "third leg" for the crossing. Jim with his thin but wiry frame had always handled troublesome stream fords well, so he ambled across ahead of us and tied off a rope on a tree. With the rope and a hiking staff, the rest of us managed to make it across safely. However, as tough as this ford was, we did not factor in the time of day. It was still early morning. On our return trip out we would face this ford again, but late in the day. We never even thought about what a tremendous difference the time of day would have on fording this stream.

Our climb had begun in forests of lodgepole mixed with cottonwood, and on our way up we transitioned through spruce and fir to whitebark pine. So even though we frequently had to pause to catch our breath, the jaw-dropping scenery kept our minds off of our fatigue. The combination of deep blue skies, snow-capped peaks, and verdant flower-filled meadows took away what little breath we had remaining at our break stops on the way up. We eventually climbed above timberline and reached the park boundary at an elevation of 10,470.' From here we enjoyed clear views of the Beartooth Mountains to the north and the craggy Absarokas to the east and south. Some folks say that July is "mosquito month;" others label it "wildflower month." From the time we topped the ridge at the park boundary, we found ourselves wading through a veritable sea of wildflowers. All the colors were spread out before us— yellows, reds, blues, purples, pinks, whites. In all of my 46 years of hiking the high country, I have seen the flower display this spectacular on only one other trip, and that was an early August backpack trip along the Teton Crest of Grand

Teton National Park in the summer of 2012 (see "Along the Crest of the Tetons.")

Somehow I had anticipated that the Hoodoo Basin high country would have a different appearance. I knew about the wind-eroded goblin formations for which the basin gets its name nearby, so I just was not expecting such a carpet of colorful plants up here. We found our designated campsite which did not appear to receive much use at all. There was no food pole available and only a few stunted alpine firs at this high elevation (I suspect that a food pole is in place today). We pitched our tents and gathered in a semi-circle to eat our dinner. After the day's long climb we were beat. Not only had we climbed 2,600,' but we had covered a distance of about 14 miles. The soup, crackers and freeze-dried lasagna hit the spot.

While enjoying our dinner we gazed out across some of the wildest country in the lower 48 states. Jim, who is always looking through his binoculars for wildlife, saw it first, "bear! 2 o'clock!" he said with some alarm in his voice. About 300 yards below us a large grizzly bear was grazing and digging away in the alpine meadows. The wind was in our favor as the bear appeared to be totally unaware of our presence. We watched the bear for about 20 minutes before it gradually disappeared over a hill below us. Seeing the bear motivated us to look harder for a "bear tree" in which to hang our food, and we eventually found an old dead weathered whitebark pine tree, which almost always contain good horizontal limbs—perfect for hanging food bags.

During the decade of the 1970s there was no such thing as bear spray. About all you could do was take every precaution to keep your food odors away from your tent and sleeping area, hang your food, gather in decent numbers, and say the "backpacker's prayer" before retiring for the evening. There were four of us so once we had our food secured, I felt that we would be fine. Now, if I had been camping under the same circumstances by myself, I doubt I could've slept much at all, since we had just seen a grizzly close to our camp. Over the years I have taken many solo day hikes, but my backpacking trips almost always involve a party of several friends.

The next day, rather than dayhike from our camp, we decided to simply relax in camp and enjoy the immense beauty that the 360 degree view provided. Given the very long drive back to Old Faithful, we had decided to hike all the way back out to the truck on this day. Given the condition of the primitive road, we wanted to give ourselves plenty of time to negotiate our way back to Cody where we would pick up paved roads. On the previous day our trail had climbed up and around numerous huge snowfields in ravines. We had every intention of utilizing that snow and gravity on our way back down.

I had taken some June backcountry ski trips with Jim in the Beartooths before, but I had never tried my hand at glissading. This would be the day and what a joy it was! The whoops and hollers reverberated through the mountains as the four of us "boot-skied" our way down the slopes. What had been an excruciatingly slow and painful climb the day before, was now a recreational thrill. There was no one around for miles in this spectacular mountain wilderness, as we playfully descended the slopes from Hoodoo Basin. What could be more exhilarating on a gorgeous day? But as we neared the bottom of our descent, our joy turned to concern.

The previous morning we had managed to ford Sunlight Creek with difficulty. But this time we were approaching the stream late in the afternoon after a full day of warmth, which had produced lots of melting snow. As a result we found the stream raging out of its banks and completely unfordable. We discussed our options. One was to simply stop on the north side of the stream, camp for the evening, and attempt the ford the next morning. After a cool night perhaps the water level would be significantly lower and manageable for fording. However, we would not be able to make it to work in time if we did this. Therefore, we selected the second option, which was to search up and down the stream to hopefully find a tree that had fallen across. There would be no tossing of a log across this stream on *this* afternoon. We would have to get lucky.

Our plan was for Jim and I to explore the stream upstream in search of a tree bridge; George and Jerry would search downstream. Each pair would explore for 30 minutes and report back at the trail. There were no tree bridges within our view so we had no idea if any even existed. However, luck was on our side. Jim and I heard Jerry shouting and whistling after only about 10 minutes, so we headed back to the trail crossing and worked our way downstream to where a newly fallen spruce tree stretched across the stream. The crossing was still fraught with danger. The tree was a good six feet above the raging torrent, so we absolutely could not slip off the tree during our crossing. Thankfully there were a sufficient number of branches protruding above the trunk of the tree to hold on to while we deftly maneuvered our way across.

The stream was our final challenge. There were no new fallen trees to deal with across the jeep road as we made our way back out to the Sunlight Basin for our long drive back to Old Faithful. We had found a way to pull it off. With our short window of opportunity, we had managed to visit the Hoodoo Basin high in the Absaroka Range along the remote eastern boundary. It was everything I could have hoped for and only enhanced my appreciation for this wild Yellowstone ecosystem.

John and Deb near the southern tip of the Southeast Arm of Yellowstone Lake

Part II

Wilderness Water Adventures

A River-Lake Combo Wilderness Trip

Despite what some folks might say there are some excellent opportunities to explore the wilderness in Yellowstone and Grand Teton by canoe. Shoshone Lake at 8050 acres is the largest backcountry lake in the lower 48 states; Yellowstone Lake at 134 square miles is the second largest lake in the world above 7000,' and features over 140 miles of undeveloped shoreline. That is a lot of wild country to explore, and I have enjoyed some truly great trips on both lakes. But one of the more unique and special expeditions by canoe that I ever took in the Yellowstone Country began just below the South Entrance of the park. During the mid-1980s over the July Fourth weekend, Jim Lenertz and I embarked on a memorable 35 mile canoe trip that included paddling down one river and across four lakes, with two portages to boot. After studying several topo maps for a few days, a hobby I'm rather addicted to, I had approached Jim with my trip suggestion. "Now Jim," I began, "hear me out. I know you think I come up with some strange trips, but I think this one might work." We had just taken a canoe trip down the Big Hole River in southwestern Montana in which we hit a log and turned over. Jim had lost his cooler and fly rod, so I wasn't sure I could talk him into getting right back in a canoe. I pulled out my topo map of Grand Teton National Park and rolled it out. "Look here Jim," I said. "I've never heard of anyone completing this trip, but I think we could do it. What if we launch our canoe at Flagg Ranch, paddle down the Snake River, camp at Wilcox Point, paddle along the west shore of Jackson lake, camp on Little Grassy Island, paddle to Bearpaw Bay and portage to Bearpaw Lake, paddle across it, then portage to Leigh Lake, paddle to the west end of the lake and camp at the mouth of Leigh Canyon, then paddle over to the outlet, portage over to String Lake and paddle to the south end of the lake to conclude our trip? What do you think?" Jim looked at me with that half-crazy grin of his and said, "Bach, only you could come up with a trip like that. What the heck, let's go for it!"

During the next week we made arrangements to secure a boat permit, and make backcountry campsite reservations. As soon as Jim and I got off work on our Thursday, we first headed to String Lake to park Jim's truck, then returned in my vehicle to Flagg Ranch and launched our canoe on the Snake River. We had allocated four days and three nights for the expedition. Since some portages would be involved, we packed much lighter than we typically do for a canoe trip. We had no cooler on this trip. This eight mile stretch of the Snake does not contain any rapids, but it does feature some sharp turns, and of course, you always have the threat of strainers from trees that may fall across narrow channels in the river. The fact that there is no whitewater here plus you have two miles of lake paddling at the end (often into the wind) helps to explain why few people float this section of the Snake, especially in a raft.

From Flagg Ranch the Snake River immediately heads west leaving the highway well behind. The views of the Northern Teton Range were impressive as we wound our way around islands, sand bars, and cottonwood trees. At times the river would send us straight into a cliff, requiring the use of aggressive draw strokes to prevent a collision. As we passed under overhanging cliffs we were not surprised to see flocks of cliff swallows emerging from their nests and flying overhead. "Maybe they will eat up all the mosquitoes for us," Jim quipped. Soon we had rounded Steamboat Mountain and the joy of negotiating river currents was displaced by the hard work of paddling directly into the wind on Jackson Lake. We had about three miles of lake paddling before we reached our campsite at Wilcox Point. We camped the first night at the mouth of Webb Canyon, and marveled at the size of grizzly tracks along the lakeshore. It was not the first time Jim and I had camped here. In years past we had made the 15 minute paddle from Lizard Creek Campground across the way in order to provide access to a wonderful loop backpack trip up Webb Canyon over Moose Basin Divide at nearly 10,000,' and back down Berry Canyon to Wilcox Point.

Wilcox Point and Fonda Point directly across the lake were named for two rangers, Gail Wilcox and John Fonda, who tragically died while on a backcountry ski patrol on March 9, 1960 to measure snow depths, record wildlife sightings, and shovel snow off and away from patrol cabins. Such winter patrols used to be more common in Yellowstone and Grand Teton before the advent of snowtel sites, which now electronically measure snow depth, and overflights to count wildlife. Rangers Stan Spurgeon, Wilcox and Fonda had been transported by snow plane (the predecessor to snowmobiles) to the north end of Jackson Lake, where the Snake River flows into it. They had planned to make a loop trip of about 35 miles, which included staying overnight at Lower Berry patrol cabin at the mouth of Berry Canyon.

When the three rangers reached the Snake River channel, Ranger Spurgeon expressed a concern that he did not like the appearance of the snow, but he selected a spot where the ice appeared to be solid and well-packed from strong winds. Spurgeon rapidly skied across the frozen channel. Ranger Wilcox followed in the same tracks and also made it across just fine. However, Fonda broke through. Rangers Spurgeon and Wilcox immediately crawled out to where Fonda had broken through and extended a ski pole to Fonda. However, the ice gave way, and both Wilcox and Spurgeon fell into the icy water. The temperature on this day was well below zero. Spurgeon managed to pull Wilcox out of the water and onto the ice, but Fonda disappeared.

Although out of the water, both Wilcox and Spurgeon were now extremely hypothermic. Wilcox was unable to move or speak. Spurgeon realized that the only hope they had for survival was for him to try to make it to the cabin and return with sleeping bags. He was soaked to the skin and no longer had his skis. Somehow he managed to use his ski pole to lean forward into the snow so that he would not sink as deep, and made it to the cabin. Barely able to move he started up the wood stove to warm up, and as soon as he was physically able, gathered up a sleeping bag and returned to the river bank. But despite Spurgeon's heroic efforts, Wilcox had expired.

I once read a story by long-time Yellowstone Ranger Jerry Mernin regarding this incident, and how critical it is that rangers always leave backcountry patrol cabins in excellent condition for the next user. One essential duty is to lay a "one-match fire" in the wood stove. This is accomplished by preparing a pile of wax paper, wood shavings and slivers of dry kindling in the wood stove. I can only imagine the condition Spurgeon must have been in when he reached that cabin, soaked to the bone in below-zero temperatures. Just getting a key in the lock and opening the door must have been a major feat. Anything less than a one-match fire laid in the wood stove would probably have doomed Spurgeon.

The next day Jim and I paddled along the west shore of Jackson Lake. Motorboats are allowed on Jackson Lake, but very few venture all the way across the lake to the west shore. Even the road several miles across the lake to the east was all but invisible. As far as we were concerned we were deep in the wilderness as we paddled along a shoreline filled with meadows of wildflowers, grazing elk and moose, and tumbling streams cascading down from the craggy peaks of the Tetons almost directly overhead.

After leaving Webb Canyon we passed the mouth of Colter Canyon, and then stopped at the mouth of Waterfalls Canyon for lunch. Here, we hiked up the canyon to see several of the falls for which this canyon is appropriately named. At this point in the trip a front moved in, and the weather quickly deteriorated. Normally, July is the most dependable weather month, but winter can return to the Yellowstone country on any day. The cold rain soon turned to snow, so we donned our parkas, and pulled on our paddling gloves. By the time we paddled deep into Moran Bay, we realized that we were now well over a dozen miles from any roads beyond the east shore of the lake. Gazing up at the majestic 12,608' Mount Moran overhead, we realized that this bay was perhaps the highlight of our trip. We beached our canoe and climbed up to the porch of the patrol cabin here to eat our lunch away from the steady stream of wet snow flakes. We had reserved a backcountry campsite on Little Grassy Island, which contains a wonderful, small protected bay, and a fine isthmus from which stunning views of the Tetons may be enjoyed. Perhaps due to the weather, it appeared that we were the only humans out on Jackson Lake.

We managed to pitch our tents under the canopy of some large trees to escape the snow and enjoy our evening campfire. The next morning the snow continued to fall, but we were relieved to see that it was not sticking in the forest, since we had portages to make from Jackson Lake over to Leigh Lake. After breakfast we headed for Bearpaw Bay. We had never tried this particular portage before, and frankly did not know what to expect. The snow was in some respects a blessing, because the cold air felt refreshing as we carried and pulled our canoe through the forest over to Bearpaw Lake. Along the way we enjoyed picking and consuming scrumptious huckleberries that were just beginning to ripen in the lower elevations. There was no trail connecting the two lakes, and we did not see any evidence that anyone had recently attempted this portage, which really did not turn out to be that difficult.

We paddled across Bearpaw Lake, and then portaged the relatively short distance along a maintained trail over to the north shore of Leigh Lake. From here, we paddled to the west end of the lake, and the mouth of Leigh Canyon. This early in the summer the snow melt in the higher elevations of the Tetons was still in full force, so the loud noise of Leigh Creek tumbling down the canyon drowned out all other sounds at our campsite. At times, we could actually hear boulders moving within the streambed.

By sunset the snow had stopped falling, but the temperature was dropping. One of the nice aspects of backcountry campsites on Jackson and Leigh Lakes is the fact that metal fire grates are provided, and campfires are allowed. On this night Jim and I enjoyed a hearty one to keep warm. We traded stories about some of our other memorable trips into Leigh Lake, coming in the much easier way from String Lake. The one story that stood out involved a trip in mid-May in which most of the campsites on Leigh Lake were still covered with snow. On this trip Jim and I had come in with John Dirksen, and we had set up camp on the east shore. At the time John's wife, Deb, had been working in Boise, Idaho during the week, and she had planned to drive over after she got off work on Friday afternoon. John and I had planned to paddle out to String Lake to pick up Deb, and transport her to our camp on Leigh Lake. She was due in at String Lake at just about sunset. Jim was to be in charge of keeping the fire going, which was not easy since all of the wood we were burning had to be dug out of the snow. Constant fanning of the fire was required, otherwise the flames would quickly subside.

Earlier that afternoon on our way in I had soloed in one canoe, and John and Jim had paddled tandem in another. As we paddled along John and I would occasionally make conversation back and forth between our two canoes. Now John has a deep voice that is very easy to hear. On our way to our campsite we passed a fellow paddling solo in a canoe, who appeared to be out for a day trip perhaps to fish. We thought that he was headed for the portage back over to String Lake, and since he was alone, John offered to help him portage his canoe. The man's response shocked us: "I can carry my own canoe, thank you, and I'm tired of hearing your incessant chattering; you obviously have no idea how your voice carries over this entire lake!"

John and I just looked at each other in disbelief. For one thing, I guess I did not realize that we had disturbed anyone, but I was also surprised that a man by himself would feel so emboldened as to verbally attack three other adult men. I thought to myself that it was a good thing all three of us were peace loving folks. There are probably others who might have reacted with "canoe rage." At the time we assumed that the man was on his way out from Leigh Lake. However, we were wrong. He must have rounded the bend, and headed down toward the remote west end of the lake to seek complete solitude, where John's voice could not possibly reach him.

Late that afternoon John and I paddled over to meet Deb. We portaged our canoe from Leigh Lake over to String Lake, then paddled its full length to the launch site and parking area on the south end of the lake where Deb was supposed to meet us. We had hoped that Deb would arrive well before sunset, but soon it became rather dark, and we accepted the fact that she was running late, and our canoe trip back to camp would have to be made in the dark. We had pulled our canoe out of the water, and were simply lounging at the launch site, when suddenly out of the dusky light a canoe approached. It was the man who had been so irate earlier that afternoon! The fellow pulled his canoe out of the water, and then he looked up to see John and me leaning against the guard rails along the launch path. We had wondered earlier how big this fellow was since it is hard to tell when you are down on your knees paddling. However, now that the man was out of his canoe it was obvious that he was rather small in physical stature.

John and I were frankly not interested in making conversation after we had endured his harsh words earlier that day, so we continued to lean against the rail, and watched him gather up his equipment. Suddenly I realized that to this fellow, it probably appeared that John and I were waiting there to exact our revenge. The poor guy certainly assumed this because when he approached us, he emitted the most pitiful, high-pitched squeal of a little scared voice, in which he managed to squeak out a trembling "Hi!" John and I just smiled and said hello back, as the man practically ran to his vehicle. He obviously had thought we were there to waylay him and teach him a good lesson. When Deb finally arrived, John and I had great fun on our paddle back to camp, telling her the story of the lion that turned into a mouse. When we arrived there was Jim, still waving at the fire, keeping some small flames going.

Ah, the stories we enjoy telling around campfires! Two other trips into Leigh Lake proved to be good campfire fodder on this last evening of our trip. Once when our kids were small, Margaret and I had paddled toward the west end of the lake. As we rounded a point we came upon an entire family—husband, wife and three kids—all cavorting about in the nude! I can still see my little girls' eyes bugged out as Margaret tried to block their view. On another trip when Jim was struggling to carry his rather heavy cooler at the portage, his manhood was practically destroyed when he turned around to see a young lady—a very *strong* young lady--carrying his canoe for him. She had felt sorry for Jim and wanted to help out!

The next morning the skies were clear, which was a relief after spending the previous three days in snow showers with some sleet. The cool weather had slowed the snow melt as evidenced by the decrease in the volume of water in Leigh Creek. Jim and I paddled our canoe over to the portage trail that connects Leigh and String Lakes, and after three days of solitude, we had found the multitudes. Lots of people enjoy the short hike or paddle to Leigh Lake, so it came as no surprise to find crowds here on a July Fourth weekend. However, it only accentuated the enjoyment we had achieved from three days of paddling through some of the most spectacular mountain wilderness to be found in North America.

Fringed gentian, a common wildflower in Yellowstone's meadows

The Smith—Finally!

After my years 1968 through 1970 in Yellowstone and Glacier, I was pretty familiar with southwest and northwest Montana. However, upon arriving in 1971 at Malmstrom AFB in Great Falls, I found many new blank areas on the map begging to be explored. In fact, almost immediately after arriving I had a rather interesting experience. Newcomers at the Base were paired up with a sponsor, and mine was Leonard Walker from Arkansas. When he learned of my interest in the outdoors, he could not wait to introduce me to his favorite fishing location at a remote spot northwest of Great Falls called Snowbank Lake.

When we arrived Leonard pulled out his two-man raft, and we paddled out to the middle of the small lake. Each of us cast out our baited hooks and almost immediately we caught a rainbow trout. In fact, we each caught our limit of ten rainbow trout within half an hour! The fish were 10 to 12 inches in length, just perfect for frying up in a pan. When I got home I could not hold back my enthusiasm. I had enjoyed some decent trout fishing during my two summers in Yellowstone, but *nothing* like this! "Margaret," I exclaimed, "I always knew Montana was wild country with lots of great fishing, but I never dreamed it would be *this* good!"

Within a few weeks I had become friends with Larry Welton, one of my colleagues on the base. When I learned that Larry had an interest in fishing, I knew where I would be taking him—Snowbank Lake! I attempted to repeat the same routine Leonard had taken me through, including taking along a small rubber raft. We paddled out in the middle of the lake, and pulled out our fishing gear. "Larry," I said. "Hold on to that fishing rod and get ready to haul in a boat load of trout!" I expected to repeat the same success Leonard and I had enjoyed. I expected to catch a fish on my first cast, and have our limit within a half hour. However, after *one hour* neither of us had received a single bite! "Butch," Larry grunted, "I thought you said the fishing here would be outstanding. I don't think there is a single fish in this lake!" "I just can't understand it, Larry," I moaned. "I promise you the fish were practically jumping in our raft only a few weeks ago!"

I'm not the most patient angler so after about two hours of fishing and paddling all over the small lake with nary a single nibble, I called it quits. We glumly loaded up our gear and headed out the dirt road back towards Lincoln. I wanted some answers though. How could Snowbank Lake be a hotbed for fishing one day and only a few weeks later seem barren? Larry and I had used the same baits, techniques, and we fished at the same time of day. When we drove into Lincoln I noticed a small U.S. Forest Service Ranger Station, so I pulled in seeking some information.

When the ranger came out to the desk, I told him my story of two starkly different fishing experiences at Snowbank Lake. "When did you catch all those fish there?" he asked. "Oh, it was about three weeks ago," I replied. "How did you know?" the ranger asked. "Know what?" I replied. "How did you find out the date of our annual stocking of rainbow trout back there? That is supposed to be a closely guarded secret, and I want to know who let the cat out of the bag!" the ranger said, visibly disturbed. "I don't know what you are talking about," I replied. "My friend brought me up here to Snowbank Lake three weeks ago, and we caught our limit in thirty minutes. He never said he knew anything about the lake being stocked. We just assumed those were native wild trout we were catching." "Oh no, those are stocked trout you caught," explained the ranger, appearing relieved that top secret information was not being leaked. "Apparently you guys just got lucky and showed up only hours after our annual summer stocking," the ranger explained. "For the first couple of days the stocked trout swim around in a tight cluster before dispersing throughout the lake. Your raft was probably parked right over a big school of them. That's why we try to keep the stocking date a secret. No wonder you were having such success!" I never again enjoyed such fishing success. Luck trumps skill when it comes to my fishing experiences.

Larry and I had enjoyed the day however, and over the next couple of years we tried our hands at floating and fishing several of the area streams, especially the upper Missouri River and the Dearborn River. We had some success catching fish, but the real joy was floating through relatively remote country. Yet, I wanted even wilder, *more* remote country to float through. Over the next winter I spent considerable time looking at maps, and there was one big blank spot with a river running through it that caught my attention. The river was called the Smith, and it rises from streams gurgling down from the remote White Castle Mountains southeast of White Sulfur Springs, Montana, and then flows over 100 miles before emptying into the Missouri near Ulm, Montana. *Sixty* of those river miles flow through wild remote canyons between Camp Baker and Eden with practically no road access.

It was difficult to obtain much information about this wild river since almost all of its length passed through privately owned ranch land. This might be a significant problem in many states, but in Montana floaters and anglers have a legal right to access streams from any public road, as long as they stay within the "high water mark" once they get on the stream. About all I could learn was that the river had a seasonal flow, and once the snow melt had subsided, it was no longer accessible in a rubber raft, which is what we planned to use. The ideal dates for running the Smith seemed to be from mid-May through early July. We figured we would need about five days to complete the float taking into account the very difficult logistics of getting to the put-in, and then getting picked up at the take-out. Of course, good weather makes all the difference on a river float, but when you have to schedule your leave in advance, luck plays a big role regarding weather and trip enjoyment. We were about to find that out the hard way!

Larry offered to make the trip in his Volkswagen van, so we had it packed and ready to go as soon as we got off duty on a Thursday afternoon in late May. We had planned to simply drive the long dirt road to the put-in at Camp Baker, and leave the van parked there. Margaret would pick us up at the take out at the Eden bridge near Ulm five days later, and we would then drive back to get Larry's van. Larry and I were both extremely excited as we headed west out of Great Falls. Neither one of us had ever even *seen* the Smith River, much less floated it. We had only seen photos and read about it. We had no idea how the fishing would turn out but we didn't care. Just the thought of spending the next five days in the wilderness floating through wild canyons was exhilarating.

As we headed out of town the weather was pretty typical for late May—cool, overcast with a light drizzle falling. We had packed excellent rain gear along with dry bags, so we felt adequately prepared. Obviously, we hoped that we would not encounter a cold rain for the next five days. We knew that could be pretty miserable, and once we launched our raft there could be no turning back. We would be committed for the next *sixty* miles. We had hoped to at least make it to Camp Baker before it got dark. We planned to camp there and begin our float early the next morning.

By the time we turned up the dirt road leading to Fort Logan 60 miles away, the light drizzle had turned to a light snow. Pretty soon the light snow turned into a *heavy* snow, and the muddy road became completely covered in white. Then the bottom dropped out. The snow was coming down in huge, wet flakes rapidly accumulating on the already slippery dirt road. Our progress slowed considerably, and by an hour later it was dark, and we found ourselves pushing through eight inches of wet snow. We soon reached the brink of a rather long downhill section of the snow-covered dirt road. With the snow dumping and the headlights almost useless we could not see the bottom of what was probably a significant drainage, but we knew the road would probably climb back up another steep hill on the other side. "Larry," I nervously asked, "is this van going to be able to climb that hill?" "Gosh, I don't know," he replied, "normally this VW van gets great traction in the snow since the weight of the engine is directly over the drive train, but this snow is as slippery as greased owl shit!" I didn't know whether to chuckle at Larry's apt description of the snow conditions or gnash my teeth over the predicament we were in!

After a few anxious minutes studying the situation Larry announced his decision: "Well, let's give it a try. There's nothing for us here on top of this wind-blown hill!" I had to agree that I did not like the idea of attempting to pitch a tent out in the cold, wet snow on top of the barren hill, but I still had my doubts. "I'd better get some good torque up on the way down so we'll make it up the other side," Larry said. He revved the old VW up and got the rpms going as we sped down the hill. The snow only seemed deeper though as we bumped along the bottom of the ravine and headed up the other side. The van began to slow as the top of the hill neared. It was clear. We were not going to make it. Despite the weight of the engine over the drive train, the tires were spinning in the wet snow. Larry put the van in reverse and attempted to back the van up the other side to no avail. Soon we were simply stuck down at the bottom of the ravine. We could not make it up either side going forward or in reverse.

We now faced a tough decision. Here we were stuck out in the middle of *nowhere* on a remote road that was rarely used by locals in *good* weather! Larry's van was a complete mess. It was stuffed with equipment and gear, and really did not lend itself to sleeping in like some VW vans allow. We could try to sleep in the car seats, but that wasn't going to get us out of our predicament. Then we remembered. About three miles back, we had barely noticed a faint utility light through the snow off in the distance. I remember Larry commenting, "Well, at least *someone* lives out here!" Even though it was now dark the night was still young, plus the heavy snow had diminished somewhat, and was now only lightly snowing. "Larry, why don't we grab our packs and sleeping bags, and hike back to where we saw that utility light?" I suggested. "I'll bet we can find a barn or some type of out building to spend the night in. Then maybe we can find someone with a four-wheel drive who can help us in the morning." Larry agreed. After all, our options at this point were extremely limited.

We consumed a few snacks then gathered up our gear and began the three mile hike through the snow. Since we had the tracks from the van to walk in we were at least not having to post-hole through the snow. By now the temperature had dropped, which was actually a blessing, as we preferred the lighter drier snow to the wet stuff that tends to soak in. The hike was not really bad, and after about an hour and a half, we reached the point where we could see the light off in the distance. The snow had about subsided, and you could now make out some buildings. We turned off a side road which had not been travelled at all since the snowstorm, and sure enough, we soon reached some out buildings on a remote ranch. The first building appeared to be an old barn. The main house appeared to be several hundred yards further down the road. By now it was 9:30 p.m. and the lights in the main house appeared to be out. "Well," Larry yawned, "we might as well spend the night in this barn, and then we'll head over early in the morning to see if we can find some hospitable folks who might be willing to help us out." That sounded good to me. Between the anxious energy of driving through the snowstorm and the physical exertion of our hike through the snow, I was beat. When we opened the door to the barn we could not have hoped for a more welcome sight. There on the floor of the barn were layers of hay strewn about. Not only were we out of the cold, windy night, but we had a soft, dry place to stretch out our sleeping bags. Needless to say, we slept like babies that night.

The next morning I opened the barn door to find clear skies. Looking out over the snow-covered landscape, I felt as though it was February 26 instead of May 26, but hey, this is Montana, I reminded myself. We downed some granola bars and headed over to the ranch house, where we had no idea what kind of reception we would receive. I knocked on the door and soon a young man who looked like he had just stepped out of a Western movie set greeted us. As Larry was describing our predicament with his van, I looked past the cowboy and noticed what appeared to be several ranch hands gathered around a big table for breakfast. It was obvious they had not finished their meal. "Tell you what," the young fellow told us, "give us a few minutes and we'll be right out with our four-wheel drive truck. I know exactly where you are stuck and we'll pull you out of there."

We could not have asked for a nicer group of folks. Once they pulled Larry's van up the steep hill, we were able to get good traction again on the relatively level road. After giving the guys a hearty thanks we knew that our planned float trip down the Smith River was not going to happen. The sudden change in weather that transformed us from spring back into winter had doomed the trip for now. Vacation days were scarce so the Smith River would have to wait for another day. Unfortunately, that day never came. Due to budget cuts my Air Force tour of duty ended six months early, which cut out another summer in Great Falls. Soon I was in graduate school at Auburn University and any thoughts of floating the wild Smith River disappeared.

Thirty-two years later that changed when Margaret and I moved to Bozeman, Montana in the spring of 2006. However, I quickly learned that the Smith River I knew about in 1974 had changed. The "secret" was out. It seemed that *everyone* knew about the Smith, and many more people wanted to float it than the river could handle. As a result the Montana Fish, Wildlife and Parks (FWP) Department had stepped up to manage this wonderful resource. One of the first positive things FWP did was to take steps to reduce the conflicts that I had heard often occurred between floaters and landowners. Back when Larry and I were making plans to float the Smith, we had been issued a warning by the one person I actually knew that had floated it, Jim Quirk. "Keep an eye out for barbed wire fences stretched across the river just below the water line," he had warned. It seemed that some landowners did not like floaters camping on their land along the river.

Montana FWP had done a superb job of acquiring sections of land along the river, and designating them as campsites. That removed the floater-landowner conflict problem, but you still had way more floaters than there were campsites. To solve that problem the state instituted an annual lottery system. For a fee of $10 (non-refundable) you could apply for a chance for your name to be drawn that entitled you to pay another $25 fee to actually float the Smith (I'm not complaining—all paid fees are used by Montana FWP to manage the Smith River, including hiring rangers who patrol the river, especially at the put-in at Camp Baker). By the time I arrived back on the Montana scene in 2006 I learned that for every seven people who applied, only one would be successful.

For the next three years I applied for a permit but never received one. I've never been too lucky in such "contests," so I just figured that I was not destined to float the Smith. However, it was sheer luck that finally got me on the Smith River. It was mid-September of 2010 and the last thing on my mind was a float trip, since the float season had long since passed. However, Margaret was taking a short hike with friend Carolyn Hopper, when they ran into Alan Kesselheim, a noted author and paddler. Carolyn had taken a writing course taught by Alan, and somehow the subject of the Smith River came up (Margaret and I had recently had dinner with Carolyn and her husband in which I had shared my frustration with obtaining a permit to float the Smith). Alan announced that due to a wet spring and summer, the Smith was actually floatable and that he was headed out to do just that. Margaret shared this good news with me and encouraged me to go.

When I finished my seasonal work for the National Park Service at Old Faithful on September 30, I called the Montana Fish, Wildlife and Parks office in Helena to see if permits were available, and was told that practically no one floats the Smith in October. "Just go," the lady said. "You can register and pay at the put-in at Camp Baker." I started scouting around for someone to go with me. The logical choice was my old friend Tom Gerrity who lived in Great Falls. Tom and I dated back to my days in the Air Force in the early 70s and we had made numerous trips together in Yellowstone over the years. Ironically, despite his many years living in Great Falls, Tom had never floated the Smith either. However, when I asked him he balked because of some pain he was experiencing in his hip. "Find someone else," he told me.

I spent the next day making calls with no success. The unseasonably mild weather we were enjoying was just giving me fits, plus I knew that the Smith's flow was headed down. If I was going to begin this trip it had to be right away. After another day of fruitless searching for a companion I called Tom back and told him that I was going to attempt it solo. I thought that he might be able to assist me with the logistics. Tom wisely told me that it would be foolish to float through such a wild and remote place by myself, so he surprised me and told me that he would not only go with me, but recruit his brother-in-law to help us with the shuttle, which is a fierce challenge for pulling this trip off. Tom, his wife Nora, and Nora's brother-in-law Jim met me on Sunday, Oct. 3 at Camp Baker, 25 miles down a dirt road from White Sulphur Springs. Nora would drive their car back to Great Falls, and Jim would drive my truck. Tom and I planned to paddle the 60 miles in three days, so Jim would drive my truck out to the Eden Bridge at the take-out on Tuesday morning. Thus, the very complicated shuttle problem was solved.

At the Camp Baker put-in we made three observations: first, the weather was simply fantastic for so late in the fall; second, the river appeared to have a healthy flow; and third, according to the register, no one had put in ahead of us for three days. We knew that we would have the river completely to ourselves, and have our choice of the designated campsites along the way. Tom and I had decided to take the trip in my old Spearcraft ABS whitewater canoe. This fine old canoe has been everywhere, from the Everglades, to Yellowstone, and many places between. Also, this was the type of water craft we had to use, since the Smith was flowing at a low rate of 200 cubic feet per second (cfs), an adequate flow for a canoe, but way too low for a rubber raft, which required a minimum flow of 350 cfs. Most folks who floated the Smith during the main float season of spring and summer opted for a rubber raft, since they are more forgiving in negotiating rapids (they bounce off boulders and canyon walls lots easier than does a canoe!)

The first thing that Tom and I had to do was pare down and consolidate our supplies to prevent the canoe from being overloaded. We only had one six pack of beer for three days (that was a hell of a sacrifice!), and one tent. As we left Nora and Jim behind, I quickly noted just how wild and remote our setting was. We launched our canoe around 12:30 and enjoyed a swift flow with few obstructions. The stream soon entered a deep canyon and the wild and scenic surroundings exceeded my expectations. I was simply not prepared for the incredible beauty of the sheer limestone cliffs on both sides of the river.

As we floated along we noted that all of the campsites were very aesthetic and accessible from the river. Montana FWP has done a great job in securing dozens of outstanding campsites. Each has a fire ring and a latrine nearby. We had planned to cover 12 miles on our first day, which was easy to do thanks to the excellent river flow. We reached our campsite by 4:30 p.m. which allowed for plenty of time to set up camp, relax, fish, gather firewood, and cook our meal. The evening skies were completely clear, so we did not even cover our tent with a rain fly.

The next morning we were on the river by 9:30. We paddled until 4:00, with about a 40 minute lunch break. We covered about 25 river miles, but given the glorious weather and scenery, we hardly noticed. On this day Tom and I had to constantly dodge submerged boulders in the fast moving river. Our wildlife sightings included five bald eagles, dippers, raccoons and numerous white-tailed deer. The fall colors were at a peak with large golden cottonwoods lining the stream, backed by enormous limestone cliffs. We stopped for our second evening at upper Parker flat campsite at mile marker 37.5. The site was particularly beautiful, as it sits on a bend of the river, which permits views of the steep canyon walls up and downstream, as well as directly across the river.

Also, there was a fine meadow behind our camp. The Smith River is renowned for its trout fishing, but the only spots we wet a hook were from our campsites where the fishing holes were not ideal and we had no luck. Due to scheduling difficulties we had opted for a three day trip, which was fine for covering the entire 60 miles, but we did not have extra time for leisurely activities such as fishing along the way. I had brought along some fresh corn from our garden, and on this night we had roasted corn on the cob and grilled steaks for dinner! As much as I love backpacking, I have to say that wilderness canoe trips do provide quite the advantage when it comes to bringing along a higher grade of food and drink! After dinner we gathered around our campfire, cracked open a couple of beers, and toasted this wonderful and spectacular place called the Smith River!

We knew that the weather was due to change on our third day. A front was predicted to move through with a chance of rain, so we didn't take a chance and put up our rain fly on this night. It was a good thing we did, because around 4:00 a.m. the rain started. Our stretch of fabulous clear Indian summer weather had come to an end. At least so we thought. In fact, our third day would consist of a cool, steady rain throughout the day, but the next day would revert back to sunny conditions. If we had only known this, we would have hunkered down in our camp, and continued our canoe trip on the *fourth* day. For all we knew though, this front had settled in for the long term. So after a quick granola bar breakfast we packed up our wet gear, and launched our canoe into the steady rain. I had on a stocking hat, parka and rain pants, so I felt well prepared. But when you paddle all day in a cold rain, eventually your feet and hands get cold. Now, instead of deep blue skies with golden cottonwoods providing a neat contrast against the canyon wall, we experienced an ethereal setting with clouds draped over the canyon walls. I have taken many canoe trips over the years, and my paddling friends like to joke about how I never turn over in a canoe. Part of that is skill I suppose, but I think it is mainly due to the design of my trusty old Spearcraft ABS canoe, made in Mount Juliet, Tennessee.

They don't make these anymore, which is too bad, because the thing is wide and very stable—really tough to turn over. However, just before our planned lunch break, Tom and I hit a rock sideways, the gunwale dipped below the waterline, and before we knew it the canoe filled up with water. Our gear started floating away. Tom did a great job of grabbing much of the gear and transporting it over to shore, while I used the bail bucket to get the water out. We did manage to retrieve all of our gear except one cup and bowl. If we were cool before, now we were downright cold. With everything pretty soaked, we didn't even stop for lunch and simply paddled all afternoon. Eventually, we had to stop to stretch our legs and bail the rainwater out of the canoe. We still had ten miles to paddle.

The afternoon of the third day was like three trips in one. Soon we emerged from the steep canyon walls into extremely remote country with high, green rolling hills. Then, the last five miles of our trip moved through river bottom lands with dense cottonwoods lining the riverbanks. Toward the end of the trip, the river channel splits. At lower flows the historic channel runs too low to float, so we had to contend with very tight turns amid cottonwoods almost blocking the channel. Finally, we saw a bridge in the distance and we knew that we had arrived at the Eden take-out. We pulled the canoe over, walked up on the bank, and sure enough, there was my Ford Ranger pick-up that Jim had driven over from Great Falls earlier that morning.

Finally, I had completed a paddle down the Smith River, and it indeed had exceeded my expectations. However, as beautiful and remote as the Smith River is today, I fear it faces an uncertain future, because almost all of the river traverses land that is privately owned, and is therefore not permanently protected from development. Ideally, the Smith River would be protected under the Wild and Scenic Rivers Act, but given today's political climate, most Montanans do not want the federal government placing restrictions on what they can and cannot do with their land. Already, there are threats encroaching on the wilderness qualities of the river. There is one section along the way that features rental cabins with a little golf course. Energy companies are chomping at the bit to drill for oil and gas in the vicinity, and recently an extremely serious new threat has emerged—a proposed copper mine near the headwaters of the Smith. Given Montana's track record with mining companies polluting rivers with acid wastes, Trout Unlimited is one of many organizations fighting this mine. The Montana Environmental Information Center (MEIC) is another. Their basic tenet is that the river is simply too fabulous of a resource to gamble with.   Updated information can be found on their websites: meic.org and saveoursmith.org. Also, there are very wealthy and powerful individuals, mostly from out of state, who are waging a legal war against Montana's outstanding stream access law (see "Journey Down Lost Paddle Creek.")

There is no question that the Smith River is one of the finest float streams anywhere in the western U.S. The Montana Fish, Wildlife and Parks Department is doing a magnificent job of managing the spectacular Smith River. I wish that so many people did not want to float it, but once you have paddled the Smith, it is easy to understand why they do. To me, the increased demand by so many people to float the Smith is one more example of why we need to preserve and protect every acre of wild country that we have left in the Rocky Mountain West.

A Sinking Feeling on Yellowstone Lake

I have taken many canoe trips on Yellowstone Lake, and have had some misadventures as noted in my first volume. At least I have learned the importance along the way of always staying very close to shore when paddling a canoe out on the ice-cold waters of Yellowstone Lake. This turned out to be a good thing because in the summer of 2008 my worst fears came true: my canoe actually sank! I was on what I like to call a "surf and turf" or "combo" trip, where we combine a backpacking trip with a canoe trip.

My sinking canoe trip turned out to be a rather strange wilderness outing. The trip included my youngest daughter Alison, and my friends John and Deb Dirksen, Hank Barnett and Al Duff. Al now lives in Nebraska and is an expert paddler who has taken over two dozen fall wilderness canoe trips in the Boundary Waters of northern Minnesota and Canada, a place I finally made it to in 2014. During his many trips Al became convinced that he needed to purchase a little Honda two horsepower motor for his canoe to transport him across some of the long stretches of lake on his way to the wilderness area. He told me the motor was a four-stroke engine, was relatively quiet, and used very little gasoline. We decided to give the little motor a try for our trip.

At present most of the length of the arms of Yellowstone Lake allow motors, but the speed limit is only five mph. The tips of the arms are designated as hand-propelled only. For our annual "big" summer trip in 2008 my friends and I wanted to take a "combo" trip, and John and Deb volunteered to make it happen. John mounted the little motor on his 17' Coleman canoe, and towed my 15 foot Coleman canoe down to the end of the 5 mph zone near the outlet of Columbine Creek in the Southeast Arm. There are three reasons we use Coleman canoes on Yellowstone Lake: first, they are relatively inexpensive; two, they are quite durable; and three, they have a nice keel which is necessary for lake paddling. I am first and foremost a whitewater enthusiast, so I have a couple of canoes designed for whitewater trips. Such canoes do not have a keel and also have some rocker (giving the bottom of the canoe a slight arc which allows for easier turns in whitewater). You would want neither of these features out on a lake! You need a good keel to allow the canoe to track across the lake in a straight line and not get blown sideways by the wind.

After John and Deb had stashed the canoes toward the end of the Southeast Arm, they backpacked north along the east shore and we met them at Sedge Bay, where we left one vehicle. We then drove to Eleanor Lake, and began our off-trail adventure. We climbed 1200' up to the crest of the Absaroka Mountain Range, which runs north and south along Yellowstone's east boundary. We planned to camp just over the boundary in Shoshone National Forest, and eventually make our way down to the tip of the Southeast Arm. We figured we had the perfect trip: several days up in the high country in alpine settings, and then a few more days paddling along the beautiful shore of Yellowstone Lake. As you walk along the crest you find yourself on the backside of Top Notch Peak, which usually has snowfields well into late summer or even fall. There is a large meadow at the base of the mountain that has the appearance of a hanging garden. The meadow collects quite a bit of moisture and then gives rise to a stream that tumbles over the edge of a cliff. I've always wondered if there was a hidden waterfall somewhere down there, but I had never taken the time to look. In fact, it is difficult to get a view, but after climbing down the ridge a ways I actually did find a spot that provided a view back, and presto, there was the beautiful waterfall I had hoped for. I estimated its height to be around 75'. I certainly don't claim to have "discovered" this falls. I'm sure someone has seen it before, but maybe it has never been documented. In any case, if anyone ever decided to give the falls a name, I think "Hanging Garden Falls" would be appropriate.

Our plan was to stay high up on the crest along the park boundary, and eventually descend to the Southeast Arm via Beaverdam Creek. That's what Al and I had done in 1975. However, we were just a tad younger then, and by the time we reached the saddle above Rocky Creek we stopped for lunch and studied the route high on the crest. We knew there was some hard work yet to be done, especially carrying full backpacks. As we enjoyed our lunch we noticed a black bear topping another saddle and descending the slopes that led to Rocky Creek. "Good thing we aren't going that way," someone said. But we were all looking at each other as though everyone wanted someone to go first and say it: "Why don't *we* go that way!" Finally, someone did say, "You know, that is our destination down there. It sure looks like an interesting and easier alternative than staying up on top of these mountains!" It was at this point that John mused, "If the going gets tough, the tough change plans!" This has become a rather routine aphorism for our group as we get older, and I even have a chapter in this book devoted to it. I guess we were all just a bit fatigued plus the weather had been rather warm, even way up high. So after lunch we began our slow descent down into Rocky Creek.

We had to sidehill on a steep slope for quite a ways over to another saddle to reach our preferred route, and that was a real foot-busting, blister producing segment. Once we reached Rocky Creek though we found the going rather easy as the area had not burned in a long time so there was not that much deadfall to contend with. As we hiked along the creek we suddenly encountered a tree with all of its bark freshly peeled off from the base of the tree up to about five feet. There were many years of hiking experience in our group but that was the first such tree that any of us had ever seen in the park or anywhere else for that matter. We saw what appeared to be tooth or claw marks, so naturally we assumed that a bear had done this. The further we hiked the more we saw, until eventually we counted over two dozen such trees! Were these from one bear? Several bears? After our trip I found some drawings of such trees in *A Field Guide to Animal Tracks* by Olaus J. Murie. According to Murie, bears sometimes like to peel off the bark of pine trees and eat the sap as though it were candy. The question was, why had we never seen such trees before? Ironically, after this trip, I started to observe similar trees on other trips in Yellowstone. With changing food availability such as the steep decline of spawning cutthroat trout and the demise of whitebark pine nuts, had black and grizzly bears only recently discovered this delicacy in the park? A mystery to us all for sure!

As we neared the shore of Yellowstone Lake, we came to the Thorofare trail which runs north and south along the east side of the lake. John led us to the spot where he had hidden the two canoes in a dense patch of timber well away from the shore or the trail. In fact, it was so well hidden, that I was surprised *he* could even find it. We made camp at Terrace Point a day earlier than we had originally planned. No one else was at the site so it worked out in our favor. The next day we planned to make our way up to Park Point, a gorgeous campsite on the shore of the lake which provides a spectacular spot to watch the sun set. We had previously planned how everyone would reach Park Point, which would be our last camp of the trip. John, Deb and Hank would go first with the 17' canoe and motor, and tow Al and me in my 15'. Alison, who enjoyed hiking and running more than riding a slow canoe on bumpy waters, had agreed to hike the trail with her friend and meet us at Park Point. We would carry the bulk of their gear in our boat. Though they didn't know it at the time, their hike up to Park Point would prove to be much less eventful and stressful than our canoe trip up there!

Shortly after we launched our canoes, a rather stiff breeze came up, which is not at all uncommon on the lake. However, handling choppy conditions and waves when you are paddling is a completely different ballgame than from being towed. I have negotiated many a canoe trip on Yellowstone Lake with rough waters. It is a matter of you and your partner both kneeling to lower the canoe's center of gravity, and just getting your body movements and paddle strokes in sync with the choppy/wavy conditions. Looking back, this was the first time I had ever been towed in a canoe, and I was simply not prepared as to what to expect or what precautions to take. John, was in the stern, Hank was in the bow, and Deb was in the middle of the 17 foot canoe that had the motor. As soon as the conditions got rough, they were completely zoned in to their own craft, and navigating through the rough waters. After all, their situation was tougher than what Al and I had to face in our 15' canoe. Not only did they have the weight of *three* adults in their canoe, but they also had the weight of the motor clamped on the side of the stern. One thing is for certain, we at least should have gotten out on the water earlier than we did. As we were finding out the hard way, the canoe motor worked just fine when the water was placid, but in rougher conditions it was a royal pain.

By the time we had been on the water for a couple of hours, the waves and choppy conditions had just about reached the point where I would've considered getting off the lake paddling my own canoe. It was almost impossible for us to communicate with John ahead of us given the rough waters, howling wind and noise of the motor, plus the fact that he never looked back given the challenges he faced in handling his own canoe. The biggest mistake Al and I made involved the tow line. The previous evening we had discussed how we needed to tie a quick release knot in the event we needed to suddenly disconnect, but somehow we had failed to do that. By now waves were beginning to sweep over the bow into Al's lap. I knew we were in trouble, but as I glanced over toward shore, I could see that we were in a horrible place to attempt to beach our canoe. The shoreline was basically a continuous wall of cliffs with no visible sandy spot to land. I could see a rocky point protruding into the lake and I felt sure that John was hoping to get around that point in anticipation of finding a suitable place to reach shore. However, when I looked at how fast our canoe was filling up with water, I knew that we would never make it around the point.

"Butch," Al yelled back to me, "We have to get to shore. *Now!*" Al had tried to untie the knot but it was tied tight as a drum. As the ice cold water was pouring into our canoe, I yelled at the top of my voice, "*John, John!*" We needed for John to turn closer to shore, and to untie or cut the line on their end. Both Al and I were now shouting at the top of our lungs, "*John, John, John!*" No one could hear us and besides John was clearly in the midst of his own problems. I looked down. Water was now covering my legs. We were sinking. "*Al*," I screamed, "We are sinking! Cut the damn line!" In what seemed an eternity, Al rummaged through his gear until he finally came up with his Swiss Army knife and cut the line, disconnecting us from John's tow.

As I tried to turn our canoe to the right toward the wall of cliffs where the waves were crashing, I realized that we were basically paddling a submerged canoe. Our gear was tied in so nothing was floating away, but the biggest danger was simply tipping over. It was a delicate balancing act to keep our submerged canoe from rolling over and dumping us both into the lake. "Al," I screamed. "Stay steady! No sudden movements! We can't turn over!" Al would later say that he thought I had gone into shock. I don't think that was the case at all, but I will admit that I was scared "shitless," as my friend Jim Lenertz used to say during some of our own canoe adventures out on Yellowstone Lake! At least we had the good sense not to be very far from shore, but we still faced what appeared to be a continuous wall of cliffs and boulders with no possible place to land our canoe.

To this point Al and I had somehow managed to keep our submerged canoe from turning over. How I don't know, since I felt as though we were attempting to paddle a submerged tree log! As we approached the cliffs with the icy waves crashing against them, our situation appeared rather hopeless. We had on our life jackets, but people don't tend to drown on Yellowstone Lake; rather, the cold gets you. Once we reached these vertical walls, what could we do?

But then just as we prepared to crash up against the cliff there appeared a tiny cove, barely the size of our canoe. It was *just* large enough to jump out and beach the water-filled canoe. We quickly untied and retrieved all of our dry bags that contained our gear, and tossed them up on some rocks above the water line. Then we began the slow and tedious process of bailing out the canoe with our bailers (plastic Clorox bottles with the bottoms cut out). Now that we were out of the icy water and were involved in strenuous physical activity, we were not too chilled. With my feet safely on terra firma, I looked back out on the lake and briefly saw John still gripping the motor handle and trying to keep his own craft from turning over. He disappeared around the corner of the rocky point. It appeared that he still had not noticed that we were no longer behind him.

Just because we had found this tiny landing spot did not mean Al and I were out of the woods. We were barely out of the water with waves constantly crashing in and spraying us. Clearly, we had to get out of this spot and there was only one way—straight up! I grabbed a long rope and managed to scale the steep wall. Once on top, Al tied the rope onto the first of the several gear bags that we hauled up and over the edge of the cliff. Up on top the landscape was a bit more level and hospitable. Finally, Al attached the rope to our canoe and he climbed up to join me. We both then hauled the canoe up the cliff. On the one hand I felt immense relief at not only surviving the ordeal, but also not losing any of our gear. On the other hand, we both worried about the other canoe. After all the darn thing contained three people, a motor and lots of gear, and they were having to contend with the same rough waters we had to deal with. Would there be a place for them to land *their* canoe around the rocky point? We could only hope!

Al and I slowly hauled the canoe and our gear along the top of the cliffs looking for a suitable spot where we could carry them back down to re-launch. After about an hour of hauling the canoe and our gear we spotted a decent-sized inlet below where we could at least fit our canoe, our gear and the two of us. This cove was not that difficult to access from above. First we carried the canoe over and lowered it down a steep slope to the beach. Then, as we turned to go back up and get the rest of our gear, I looked up and here came John solo paddling his 17 foot canoe! John sometimes likes to think of himself as the Harrison Ford character in Raiders of the Lost Ark, when he tosses his hat across the river and rescues someone. That was the appearance he exuded as he rounded that rocky point and headed our way. He had managed to land their canoe in a safe place, and obviously was concerned about what had happened to us. As soon as he had unloaded Deb, Hank, the gear, and the motor, he headed back in search of us.

After John pulled his canoe ashore I asked him, "John, didn't you hear us yelling?" "I didn't hear a thing," he replied. "We were taking on water and I was trying to find a place where we could land. That motor hanging over the side of my stern makes a big difference in rough waters." Then he chastised us about having to cut our line, "why didn't you tie a quick release knot?" He was of course right about that. We thanked him for coming back for us, and then we loaded up some of our gear in his boat since he was solo. John led us around to where he landed, and we were re-united with Deb and Hank. After swapping stories about how fast the wind had come up and the difficulty of keeping waves from sweeping into the canoes, we all agreed on two things: first, the dynamics of handling a canoe with a motor and one in tow are completely different from what we were used to with simple paddling, and second, we were very happy that we had stayed close to shore!

After a rather brief period the wind had let up and the waters appeared to be calming down. We re-launched our canoes, this time making sure that we had a quick release knot just in case Al and I needed to part ways in a hurry. When we reached Park Point, Alison and her friend were already there. That didn't surprise me. Paddling is really not faster than backpacking. It's just that with a canoe you don't have that load to carry on your back, plus you can carry along that cooler! Park Point, with its long, grassy meadows leading down to the shore of the lake, has always been one of my very favorite backcountry campsites. As sunset approached we all dipped into our coolers, and headed out to watch the sun slowly set across Yellowstone Lake. Later that evening we enjoyed sitting around our campfire swapping stories, mostly true, about past trips.

We decided to head out very early in the morning to decrease the chance of encountering rough waters. Our first trip using the little Honda canoe motor had been a learning experience. The main lesson learned was the motor works just fine, but *only* if the lake waters are calm. The majority of the time Yellowstone Lake is anything *but* calm. Therefore, I really would not recommend using a canoe motor on Yellowstone Lake, unless you have a lot of time and flexibility to respond to changing conditions.

Journey to the Everglades or
"Ma'am, I'm Afraid I Have Bad News"

    Rod Busby was my first hiking and backpacking buddy in Yellowstone when we both worked for the Yellowstone Park Company in 1968 and 1969. We headed in separate directions—Rod to Slidell, Louisiana, and I ended up in East Tennessee, and we had not seen each other for fifteen years. Then, in the fall of 1985 I got the bright idea for another adventure: a wilderness canoe trip in Everglades National Park.
    My good friend and teaching colleague, Hank Barnett had a former student, Tom Chandler, free to take the canoe trip, so we needed one more participant. I knew that Rod and his wife Kathy lived a busy life now and wondered if he had the time and inclination to join us on this trip. I decided to give him a call. When I described the planned canoe trip Rod did not hesitate. "Count me in!" he enthusiastically stated.
    At the time my college was on the quarter system, and classes ended in early December, a perfect time to head to the southern tip of Florida to explore Everglades National Park. Our plan was to rendezvous at Oleno State Park in Florida, since it is near the junction of I-75, which Hank, Tom and I would be traveling south on from East Tennessee, and I-10, which Rod would be traveling west on from Slidell. After we met and exchanged greetings, Rod walked into the Ranger Station at the state park. He asked the ranger on duty if it would be okay for him to park his little Ford Escort there for a week, while the four of us traveled down to the Everglades in my trusty 1978 red Dodge extended-cab pickup, affectionately referred to as "Big Red." The ranger gave Rod permission to leave his car and wished us well.
    We arrived at Everglades National Park rather late the next day, and decided to camp at Lone Pine Key just inside the north entrance station. Having spent many nights out in the backcountry with Rod, I warned Hank about his loud snoring, so we decided to pair him up with Tom. Tom was a young guy and could sleep through anything. However, our little plan did not pan out. Along about midnight, Hank and I were awakened by what sounded like a herd of bison bellowing in the campground. Despite the fact that our tents were at least 25 yards apart, the loud snoring was overwhelming. Since our tent was a self-standing dome type, we opted to pick it up and move it a safe distance away from the source of our problem. The next morning I was surprised at how angry Rod reacted to our strategic maneuver. "Come on Rod," I kidded. "This is not the first time your snoring has kept me awake. At least this time I could do something about it!" However, Rod was not amused. Over the years I have noted that Rod is normally a mild-mannered fellow, but we had not been out on a backcountry trip for well over a decade. Lots of water had flowed down the stream for both of us, including stints in the military, and now the pressures

of our current careers. "Maybe this week out in the wilderness is just the tonic that we all truly need," I thought to myself. But Rod's little outburst was nothing compared to what would come the next day.

The next morning we obtained a backcountry permit to launch our canoes at Flamingo, and paddle out into Florida Bay in the Gulf of Mexico, Atlantic Ocean for a five day wilderness expedition. During the planning phase of our trip, we had seriously considered a canoe trip on the famous 99 mile-long Wilderness Waterway that extends from Flamingo to Chokoloskee, but we felt that we simply did not have sufficient time, plus we really liked the idea of a "combo trip," that would include miles within the swamp, as well as along the coastal beaches. Therefore, we planned a loop trip that would take us along the coast and around Cape Sable, then back to Flamingo via inland canals through Lake Ingraham and the swamps, prairies and mangroves.

Before heading out I stopped by to visit my former boss in Yellowstone, Al Mebane, who had just transferred from the position of Chief of Interpretation in Yellowstone to the same position in Everglades. Al had some good advice for us before we headed out. "Fresh water is very scarce along the coast," he told us. "Be sure to secure your water containers in a safe place lest the raccoons empty them for you during the middle of the night." "Al," I asked, "is it safe to take a swim out in the Gulf?" Al frowned. "There are lots of barracuda close to shore. I wouldn't recommend it," he said. His answer disappointed me. We had not brought along any fishing gear, but I had anticipated enjoying a swim in the Gulf. On the other hand, without any fresh water available, I wasn't sure how comfortable I would sleep, not being able to wash off the sticky salt water from my body. "And one other thing," Al added. "The mosquitoes and no see-ums are horrendous. Go prepared." The latter warning came as somewhat of a surprise. Since our trip was occurring in December, I had assumed that mosquitoes and their pestiferous brethren would not be much of a problem. I based that assumption on my many canoe trips to the Okefenokee Swamp along the Florida-Georgia border during the months of December as well as March. But we were much further south. I should have known we were in trouble when I saw all of the "I Gave Blood at Flamingo" bumper stickers for sale at the gift shop, one of which I stuck on my canoe and is still there to this day.

We pushed off from Flamingo and began our paddle along the beach headed for the campsite on the point of East Cape. The day was bright, sunny and simply gorgeous. This was not the first time I had paddled along the beach in the Gulf of Mexico. One of my favorite paddling destinations is the Okefenokee Swamp, and I have taken quite a few trips there during March, which is the prime season to visit when the swamp is teeming with wildlife activity and sounds, yet the bugs are really not too bad yet. But poor Hank could never join us, since his CPA work as a tax accountant always had him covered up with the drudgery of completing tax returns for his clients. So a couple of years earlier I put together a canoe trip into the Okefenokee in December that Hank and his friend John Fox could make. However, the swamp in December seemed dead compared to March, save a few sand hill crane sightings. Alligators, normally very commonly sighted, were not out. The exciting sounds from frogs and gators at night were completely missing. So after spending one night out at Big Water Lake, we revised our trip plans. We decided to leave the swamp and head over to two wonderful coastal state parks in Florida, St. Joseph Peninsula and St. George Island. Both parks feature miles of primitive gorgeous white sand beaches. On the way over we stopped in Apalachicola to purchase some fresh shrimp, shrimp boil seasoning, and cocktail sauce. We were determined to cook up our own "seafood feast" while camped on the wilderness beaches of these two great parks.

We arrived at St. George Island just before the ranger station closed, and requested a "backcountry" camping permit. This is the term we use in Yellowstone for camping in the wilderness away from any roads. But after seeing the confused look on the ranger's face I remembered that the Florida Park Service called such sites "primitive camping." We launched our canoes and once past the surf and waves I began singing one of my favorite Jimmy Buffet songs, "Mother, Mother Ocean." It seemed appropriate here. I had never paddled a canoe out into the ocean before and it simply felt wonderful. We made it to our campsite just in time for sunset, and then boiled up the best shrimp I have ever tasted, and in the most spectacular setting possible! We downed a few pounds of shrimp, as we watched the dolphins cruising by just offshore. It was this trip that led Hank and I to begin thinking about camping on the beaches along Cape Sable in the Everglades.

Paddling a canoe in Florida Bay felt totally different from my trip along the primitive beaches of St. George and St Joseph. Virtually all of Florida Bay's some 1000 square miles are contained within Everglades National Park. Here the coastline consists more of crushed shells than sugary sand, and without the rolling white sand dunes dotted with sea oats. Also, the bay is not deep. It has been said that if a man was ten feet tall, he could walk throughout Florida Bay with his head above water, as the average water depth is only three feet. We did not experience rolling waves here like we did off the coast of St. Joseph. Rather, we encountered choppy conditions. The marine life was more abundant given the shallow waters. Occasionally I would stir up a stingray with my paddle, and at times we would be showered with fish jumping out of the water attempting to flee a larger predator, such as a shark or barracuda. More than once we had several fish that landed right in our laps.

After paddling about seven miles we beached our canoes at Clubhouse Beach for a lunch break. After stretching out under a palm tree to seek shade on this warm day, we quickly realized that we had not yet ventured far enough to escape day visitors in powerboats. With miles of unoccupied beach in both directions, we were rather surprised when a powerboat pulled up right next to our canoes. A couple disembarked with a large, frisky dog that quickly headed straight for Rod, who was enjoying his lunch. When the dog practically jumped into his lap in pursuit of his sandwich, Rod exploded. He screamed in a fit of anger for the couple to get the dog, and his exhortations included several expletives. Fortunately, we did not end up with a "boat rage" incident, but it was still unnerving. "Wow," I thought to myself, "Rod has really acquired quite a temper—one that I don't recall from our many trips over the years."

After lunch we continued our paddle on our way to our planned campsite at East Cape, which marked 11 miles for the day—not bad considering the windy and choppy conditions we faced throughout most of the day. For this trip, alas, we had no fresh shrimp to boil up; rather, we had the standard canoe camping fare of cans of beef stew, etc. Once we set up our tents we eased back under the shade of coconut palms. I was tempted to shimmy up one to gather a few, but decided I did not possess the adequate skills for climbing a tall, leaning palm tree. Since our trip was taking place in December, the days were very short. Therefore, we did not even bother to keep time. We based our day's activities around the available daylight. We retired to our tents shortly after darkness descended upon us, and arose the next morning at first light. A highlight of camping on the beach was viewing the incredible sunsets. As we watched the sun disappear behind a myriad of willowy pink puffy clouds, I could not help but think about how close we were to Cuba. After all, here along the beaches of Cape Sable, we were at the southernmost tip of the U.S. mainland. Cuba was a mere 150 miles directly to the south from us.

The next morning we saw the evidence of Al Mebane's warning about storing our fresh water. There were raccoon tracks all over our campsite. We had tightly secured our water containers in the bow and stern of the canoes, then turned them upside down on the beach to protect them from being tampered with. On this day we would paddle nine miles along the coast to our most remote campsite of the trip, located at Northwest Cape. Here, over 20 miles from Flamingo, we were apparently beyond the "play zone" of recreational motor boaters, because we enjoyed two days of complete solitude. By the end of the first day I felt hot and sticky and in dire need of a bath. However, with no fresh water available my only option for gaining some measure of relief from the heat and humidity was to spurn Al's advice and take a dip in the Gulf. We had indeed observed sharks and barracudas cruising along the shore the previous evening, but I decided a quick dip in the clear waters was worth the risk. No one else but me took the plunge, but I was glad I did. Yes, this was salt water and I knew I would still have a sticky feeling, but the swim in the cool waters of the Gulf was very refreshing.

After two days of blissful relaxing under palm trees at Northwest Cape, we turned back to the south. This portion of our trip would be completely different, as we entered the brackish waters of Lake Ingraham via the Middle Cape Canal. We knew this route provided us with a good chance to see Florida crocodiles, which have a more narrow snout than the alligator, and also is a greenish-gray color as opposed to the black color of a gator. Al Mebane had also told us this was a good birding trail, especially for the colorful roseate spoonbill. By leaving the Gulf behind and entering Lake Ingraham, we were now subject to the significant variation of the tides. With our canoes this was not so much a problem for us, but we had been warned about powerboats that race through Lake Ingraham attempting to get out before getting stuck due to the receding tides. Sure enough, later in the afternoon with the tide going out, we spotted a powerboat headed straight for us. Apparently they had either ignored or terribly misjudged the water levels in the canal and low tide, and were making a desperate run to make it back out into the Gulf before they became mired in the mud and sand for hours. It was obvious they were not going to slow down for us, and there was not sufficient room for both the powerboat and our canoes in the canal. So, as it approached at a high speed, we decided not to play a losing game of chicken. We paddled over to the banks of the canal, and quickly pulled our canoes out of the water just before the guy zoomed past us. He did not even bother to wave at us for moving out of his way.

As we ventured deeper into the inland waters we did indeed begin to observe the colorful spoonbill wading in the shallow waters. Spooners have been referred to as "fish vacuum cleaners," and their populations have fluctuated wildly over the decades, mainly due to the follies of mismanaged water resources. However, we did not spot any crocs. We eventually paddled through the East Cape Canal, and worked our way over to East Cape for our final evening in the wilderness. We again pitched our tents above the high water mark of high tide and relaxed around camp as the last soft rays of daylight faded away. If there is a more soothing experience than relaxing along a wild beach to the calming sounds of a gentle breaking surf, I haven't found it yet.

Our final morning again broke clear and beautiful, and after breakfast, we loaded up our canoes and sadly headed back toward civilization. However, this day was to be quite different. Rather than paddle back along the coast, we decided we wanted to venture into the swamps and mangroves to experience the "real Everglades." What we found were a zillion bloodthirsty mosquitoes. I simply could not believe the thick black clouds that descended upon us. We were on a narrow canoe trail that was basically a tunnel through the mangroves, so there was no breeze at all. Our only measure of relief was to don our rain parkas, tightly secure the drawstring of the hood at our necks, and paddle our canoes just as fast as possible. In this manner we at least generated a bit of a "breeze" as we attempted to outrun the little beggars. The only problem with this strategy was we could not miss a paddle stroke in either the bow or stern. Just a slight variation of a paddle stroke caused our canoe to plunge straight into the mangroves. This happened several times and the mosquitoes feasted on us while we straightened our canoe back out into the narrow channel. Suffice to say that this portion of the trip did not allow for much leisurely enjoyment of the surrounding scenery! I have been inundated by mosquitoes at Shoshone Lake and the Bechler country of Yellowstone in mid-July, but I have never seen thicker mosquitoes than this December jaunt through the mangroves in the Everglades.

The canoe trail we paddled through the mangroves to get back to Flamingo has apparently been altered over the years due to hurricanes passing through the vicinity. Maps now show much of the route to be impassable. Based on our experience perhaps this is not such a bad thing. When we finally reached our takeout at Flamingo, we experienced feelings of both relief and sadness. Relief that we were finally free from the blood suckers, and sadness that our wilderness adventure in Everglades had come to an end. However, in some respects, the most interesting aspect of our adventure was yet to come.

After a week in the hot and sticky Everglades we decided to spring for a motel so we could get cleaned up, and also a fine restaurant to sample something other than camp food. The following day I pulled "Big Red" up to the entrance station at Oleno State Park. When the gate ranger came over to collect the entrance fee I told him that was not necessary. "We just need to take my friend over to that little white car in the parking lot," I told him. "Does that car belong to one of you?" the ranger asked, raising his voice. "Yes," I answered, "we left..." That was as far as I got before the ranger barked, "Pull your truck over there and come into my office!" As Rod headed for the office the ranger went off, "Do you realize we have been looking for your body all week?"

Rod turned to the three of us and said, "Stay in the truck. It's my car. There's no sense in all of us going through this!" The ranger led Rod into a little room and we watched through a window in horror as the ranger sat Rod down in a corner and began screaming at him. "You can't imagine the grief and work you have caused our staff by leaving your car here without our permission!" the ranger screamed. "When we couldn't find any trace of you, we obviously assumed that you had headed out into the woods and committed suicide! There is simply no excuse for being so irresponsible! We should bill you for every hour we have been searching the woods!" Despite the fact that we were outside the air-conditioned building looking through a closed window, we could hear practically every word that the ranger was shouting. Normally, I would have found this "keystone cop" episode to be quite humorous, but all I could think about was Rod's temper tantrums, first when we moved our tent in the middle of the night, but *especially* when the dog jumped in Rod's lap on the beach. "Oh my gosh Hank," I moaned. "I can't believe that guy! Rod is going to haul off and slug him at any moment, and then we'll all get thrown into jail!"

However, as the dressing down continued to progress we were absolutely amazed that Rod simply sat there and calmly took the verbal assault, occasionally offering a few comments but only when asked. After a while I was almost angry that Rod did not appear to be defending himself. After all, he had done nothing wrong. He had asked and received permission from the ranger to leave his car in this parking lot! *Finally* we saw Rod get up and walk out of the building, and we all moved over to my truck before any of us said anything. "Rod," I began, why did you just sit there and take it? Why didn't you stand up for yourself?" "Did you not see and hear that guy?" Rod responded. "If I had verbally fought back I have no question that he would have confiscated my car and maybe even arrested me! Now, go get in your truck and let's get the hell out of this park before that guy changes his mind!"

As we drove out of the park I realized that Rod's judgement was absolutely correct. We stopped at a Dairy Queen at the junction of I-75 and I-10 before we headed in separate directions. We had a few belly laughs as Rod recounted some of the dressing down that we had missed from our vantage point outside the ranger's office. "Unfortunately the ranger who gave me permission to leave my car in the lot went on leave the next day, and forgot to leave a note for the next ranger coming on duty." Rod explained. "Then to make matters worse, the week before we arrived, someone drove into the same parking space I was in and disappeared into the woods. It took the rangers several days to find him. He had committed suicide. Then only today they sent Louisiana State Troopers to my home in Slidell. It was only after Kathy explained to them that I had left the car here for our canoe trip that they realized there was not another body out in the woods of Oleno State Park!" We managed to gulp down some milk shakes in between guffawing over the entire incident.

Rod and I have continued to stay in touch over the years, though I have not taken any recent backcountry trips with him. When we get together we still laugh over how our Everglades trip ended. Kathy perhaps had the best story when she described what happened the afternoon that she greeted the two state troopers on her doorstep. She said they began with, "Ma'am, I'm afraid we have bad news." Before anything else was said, Kathy said that her thoughts immediately went to Rod's life insurance policy. She was that certain that Rod had perished! Then when the troopers provided details, she broke out into laughter. I had been wrong about Rod. He had not developed an uncontrollable temper after all. In fact, as I reflected on our week in the wilderness of the Everglades, I realized that we had all calmed down and relaxed as we escaped the pressures and stress of modern living. As Sigurd Olson once said,

"Wilderness to the people of America is a spiritual necessity, an antidote to the high pressure of modern life, a means of regaining serenity and equilibrium."

A cow moose with her calf along the Snake River

Troubles on the Snake

The Snake River and I—we have had a pretty rocky relationship over the years. I will never forget the first time that I floated the Snake River through Grand Teton National Park in the summer of 1968. After spending most of my first paycheck purchasing a two-man rubber raft, I quickly lost it in a mishap on the Clark's Fork of the Yellowstone River (see "Clark's Fork Fury" in my first volume.) I had learned some valuable lessons in that experience, and my love for floating down rivers had only been enhanced. I truly wanted to replace my lost raft with a larger model, but I could not in good conscious spend any more of my earnings on leisure items. I was saving every dollar to help pay for my last year of college; however, later that summer Lady Luck prevailed.

The Canyon Village Lodge had somehow managed to arrange the live telecast of the Republican National Convention in Miami. It was common knowledge that Richard Nixon was a shoo-in to receive the nomination for president once the polling of states started. Nevertheless, there was a visitor in attendance that evening from Texas who was absolutely *certain* that Nelson Rockefeller was going to win the nomination. The fellow had all the appearances of a "high roller." He appeared to be in his mid-fifties with slightly graying temples, wore cowboy boots, a cowboy hat and was constantly chomping on a cigar.

As the voting was about to begin the man stood up and proclaimed to all in attendance, "I'll bet any amount to anybody that Nelson Rockefeller is going to win the nomination!" At first I thought the man was joking but when no one stepped forward, he repeated his offer with great passion. If the Texan was drunk he certainly did not act like it. Most of the people in the room were actually employees of the concession, the Yellowstone Park Company, including my friend Rod Busby and me. Rod, who was sitting next to me, was a political science major at Washington State University, and we often had discussions about politics. "Rod," I whispered, "I think this guy is rich and he is just a showboat. If he wants to throw us some free money, I sure would like to bet enough to buy another raft!" "How much cash do you have on you?" Rod asked. I opened my wallet to find $40.00—just the amount to purchase that four-man raft I had been drooling over.

One of the restaurant managers by the name of Stan walked around the room collecting cash and writing down the amounts bet on a ledger. You could only bet the amount that you could put up in cash. Those were the rules put down by the Texan. No credit was allowed. After a lot of cash was collected Stan walked over and placed the money in a safe. We then watched the roll call. Needless to say, there were cheers rolling across the room as Nixon came out on top. To this day, I find it very hard to believe that the Texan really believed

Rockefeller was going to win. I think he just wanted to be a big shot, and draw attention to himself. All I know is, thanks to him, I was able to purchase my four-man raft!

I knew exactly where my friends and I would be heading on our next day off. I had been yearning to float the Snake River all summer. We now had the means to do it. Margaret, Rod, Rich Marchand, and I headed down to Jackson Hole in my old Chevy II to our beginning point at Pacific Creek. From here we would float 20 miles to our takeout destination at Moose. We found the clear river water flowing at a nice level, unlike the disastrous flooded Clarks Fork, where I had lost my raft back in early June. We had no life jackets and no money to purchase any, so our friends who worked at the Yellowstone Park Service Station loaned us some inflated car inner tubes to wear around our waists.

On this my maiden voyage, I managed to transport the four of us safely down river. The Snake is rather infamous for its many braided channels, but I managed to skillfully make our way through them all. It only took us a little over four hours to make the twenty mile journey. There are few rapids between Pacific Creek and Moose, other than some nice standing waves below Deadman's Bar, but the main challenge is avoiding trees across the channels knows as "strainers." The trip was simply mesmerizing to all four of us. Amazingly, we saw almost no one else on the river during our trip, a feat almost impossible to replicate today. The constantly changing views of the Tetons towering over us were awe-inspiring, and we honestly felt like we had gone back in time. We observed moose feeding along the river, and bald eagles in their nests overhead. As far as we were concerned, we might as well have been 200 miles deep in the wilderness.

I only had one problem. I did not have a hat or sunglasses, and for most of the trip it seemed that I was squinting directly into the sun. By the end of our float I had developed a splitting headache. For some reason when I was young, my headaches would often turn into nausea and an upset stomach. After taking out at Moose, Rich quickly caught a ride back to my car, while the rest of us deflated the raft, our inner tube "life jackets," and packed up the rest of our gear. All the while my headache was getting worse.

When Rich returned with my car we loaded up the gear and headed into Jackson to find a suitable place to eat. After a long day on the river everyone was starved except for me. By now my headache was starting to produce an upset stomach, yet I was determined to fight through it and try to enjoy dinner. There have always been very expensive places to eat in Jackson, but we found a unique spot with reasonable prices. The place was called "The Happy Hound Chalet," and was located in an A-framed building. By the time we took our seat inside the restaurant, I was feeling miserable. Margaret was fully aware of my problem with headaches turning into upset stomachs. "Honey," she suggested, "Why don't you just order some soup and crackers?" So while everyone else was chowing down on big juicy cheeseburgers, I was trying to force down some vegetable soup and crackers to take it easy on my stomach. It did not work.

As the horrible feeling of nausea welled up in my stomach and chest I raced out the front door but only made it to the front lawn of the restaurant. There on my hands and knees I upchucked my dinner, just as a bunch of patrons were getting out of their cars headed for the restaurant's front door. Needless to say, after watching my antics, they quickly retreated to their cars and drove away. The next time we drove down to Jackson later that summer I noticed that the Happy Hound Chalet had gone out of business. I'm sure I didn't help its business on that particular day! The Snake River trip had been a great success, but dinner had not. In future years I learned to wear sunglasses and a hat, and I think I managed my dinners okay, but I can't say the same about the Snake.

The Snake and I have enjoyed many intimate moments together. During my years working at Old Faithful, Margaret would often drop me off at Dead Man's Bar and pick me up later that day at Schwabacher's Landing. When friends would visit us in Yellowstone, I would almost always take them down the Snake. Once my sister Alice visited and we had a great trip that included an encounter with a bull moose. I had maneuvered the raft over into a small side channel, and we came around a bend to see a moose standing right in the middle of the stream. I had read numerous accounts of dog sledders in Alaska who had endured terrible encounters with moose along their backcountry trips. In many cases the moose simply stood its ground, then charged the dogsled team when it approached. Such was my fear as we floated toward the moose. For a few seconds I thought we were going to float right under its belly, but at the last moment the moose stepped up on the gravel bank, and allowed us a clear route and safe passage. The moose encounter was the highlight of our float as far as Alice was concerned. It was yet another great float down the Snake—then my unlucky streak kicked in.

My good friend Al Duff came down from Great Falls with his friend Clyde, and we headed for a relaxing float down the Snake. Al had his own raft which was identical to mine—the typical economical four-man raft available at most discount stores. On this particular trip the river was flowing rather high and was slightly out of its banks. Nevertheless, we had a rather uneventful trip right up to the end. Then during the last half mile of our trip the first of my several unpleasant incidents on the Snake occurred. My raft had developed a slow leak somewhere along the way. I always carry along a hand pump, but due to the swift flow on this day I was having difficulty keeping the raft inflated. As a result I was having a bit of a problem obtaining good purchase with my aluminum oars. The oars were fine, they were just too short.

We suddenly encountered a sharp bend in a side channel where beavers had recently felled a couple of big cottonwood trees that were blocking most of the channel. With the swift current I knew we were in trouble. Al was in front of me, and he barely made it past the downed trees, scraping right past them. I dug in as hard as I could with my oars to move my raft to the other side of the channel, but with my raft slightly deflated I simply fell short. With each stroke, it became obvious that I was not going to make it, and I braced myself as the river swept me into the tree. I managed to grab a branch and pull myself up on top of the tree as my raft was swept under the tree, and emerged on the other side. Al immediately paddled over to retrieve my empty raft and pull it to shore.

Now I was in a predicament. I was tempted to just jump into the water and float down toward Al, but the river here was extremely angry, and out of its banks. I wasn't certain that I could clear all of the debris around me. I had read stories of paddlers getting caught in strainers like this and drowning, so I decided I did not want to take a chance. When Al realized that I was not going to jump in, he sent Clyde to go get help since we were almost to our takeout at Moose, near the visitor center. The tree was big enough, and I was pretty secure, so I had no problem waiting for help. Al, a former collegiate swimmer at West Virginia University, kept encouraging me to grab hold of a rope he would throw from shore and then jump into the river. Looking back, it would've probably worked, but I was still haunted by my near drowning on the Clark's Fork of the Yellowstone in 1968. So I stubbornly refused his suggestion.

I didn't have to wait long. Within fifteen minutes I saw a river ranger from shore motioning to me that he would paddle his raft directly under the tree. He directed me to jump in at that time. The ranger then pulled his raft upstream, launched it and headed right for me. However, at the last second the swift current pulled him off course and I did not feel comfortable jumping toward the raft. I was afraid I would miss and end up in the submerged branches of the tree. I could see the ranger mumbling to himself as he pulled his raft over and dragged it back up to try again. I sensed that he was angry at me for not diving into his raft as he paddled by. This time he nailed it and maneuvered his raft almost directly under me. I jumped in and the rescue was complete.

I immediately apologized for getting myself into this predicament, and also for not jumping in on his initial pass. I prepared myself for a good scolding. Instead I got just the opposite. First, *he* apologized for not doing a better job on centering the raft the first time through and second, he dismissed my apology. "Don't worry about it," he said. "This river is running high today. You had a tough challenge in this channel and you did the right thing getting up on that tree and waiting for rescue. The worst thing you could have done would have been to jump in and risk getting sucked into that submerged debris." "Well," I countered, "I'm just sorry you had to come out here and deal with this." "That's what we are here for," he said. "Stuff happens out here. Heck, I even lost my portable radio in this river last week."

I couldn't bring myself to tell him that I also worked for the NPS up in Yellowstone. I knew that I had good skills at paddling a raft, but I had committed three big mistakes that led to this accident. First, the river was high. No, it wasn't in flood stage like the Clark's Fork had been, but it was high enough to be a stiff challenge. When a river is flowing at a high volume, it is "less forgiving," which means if you make a mistake, you often can't recover. At lower flows, you can often err without serious consequences. Second, I knew that my raft had a slow leak. I had assumed that I could keep it good and taut with my occasional pumping. However, the slow leak, cold water and swift flow combined to prevent me from achieving this. Third, and this is really what nailed me, my oars were simply too short for this raft. I needed good long oars, like Al possessed.

The first two problems were corrected. I made sure I didn't get on the Snake again at such a high flow rate, and I adequately patched up my raft so that I could gain good purchase with my oar strokes. However, I didn't have the best strategy to correct my third problem. Rather than simply going out and buying two long sturdy oars, I decided to "jury rig" my oars by inserting and taping some bamboo poles to lengthen my aluminum oars. The bamboo poles had come from my parent's back yard in Montgomery, Alabama and, I had been using them for hiking staffs. The plan worked fine for several more Snake trips, then my ill-fated trip with Margaret and Alison occurred where I encountered a cottonwood tree in a narrow channel just felled by a beaver. When I dug the oars in to avoid the tree, the bamboo snapped and I found myself again perched up on a tree while Margaret and Alison were truly "up a creek without a paddle!" This embarrassing story was described in detail in my first volume.

Needless to say I headed straight for the nearest sporting goods store, and purchased two long sturdy raft oars. I had to cringe at the price but I figured it would be a long-term investment. Well, not exactly. By now no one would get in my raft with me. If I was going to float the Snake it would have to be a solo trip. So rather than bother Margaret with the shuttle, one day I simply locked my old beat-up but very light Lambert road bike at Schwabacher Landing, and drove my truck to my put-in at Dead Man's Bar. My float was going great as the long oars were a wonderful tool indeed for negotiating the tight channels along the way. As I neared my takeout I decided to pull my raft up on an island, take a snack break, and simply soak in the spectacular surroundings with the majestic Teton Range catching the late evening sun's rays. I once again felt "in tune" with my beloved Snake River. After meditating for about a half hour I headed over to my raft for the final short jaunt to Schwabacher's. As I reached over to board my raft, I could hardly believe my eyes. Only one of my brand new oars was still on board! Apparently, the wave action of the currents had dislodged one oar from its oar lock, and it had slipped into the river and floated away without my noticing it! I simply could not believe it! Here I was in trouble on the Snake again!! However, this time my brain bailed me out. I love to paddle whitewater canoes, so I just figured that I would straddle the raft, get on my knees, and use one oar just like I use a T-grip paddle when I'm in a canoe! It worked to perfection and I ended my trip successfully, but rather frustrated. The Snake had gotten the best of me again!

I think this trip was the last time that I ever rafted the Snake River. I did make it in a canoe on several occasions, and I still think a float down the Snake can be a great experience if you go early or late in the day. As I mentioned in my first volume, I do think the number of floaters on the Snake occasionally exceeds the river's carrying capacity in terms of enjoying a truly quality wild river experience.

Despite all of my problems with the Snake River over the years, they pale in comparison to what I consider to be the biggest misadventure to ever occur on the Snake in which the participants lived to tell about it. I'm speaking of the ill-fated Doane Expedition of 1876. U.S. Army Lieutenant Gustavus C. Doane may have been an important member of the Washburn Expedition of 1870 into Yellowstone, but he embarked on one of the most stupid, insane expeditions in the history of the West when he and his men attempted to float a wooden boat down the Snake River in December of 1876. Doane thought the expedition would gain him the fame he was looking for, but the poor man encountered below zero temperatures, deep snow and ice, crashed his boat, and just about starved to death along the way.

Lieutenant Doane and eight troops left Fort Ellis near present-day Bozeman, Montana on October 11 hauling a large wooden boat. On October 27 Doane launched his boat in cold, wintry conditions on Yellowstone Lake. Incredibly, he intended to float his boat down to the West Thumb of Yellowstone Lake, then haul it overland to Heart Lake. From there he had planned to float the Heart River into the Snake River, then float the Snake all the way to Fort Hall in present-day Idaho! That far upstream both the Heart River and the Snake were way too low to support a boat, so the men had to continue lugging it along the streambanks for many miles.

Such an expedition would have been challenging enough in the summer, but to attempt a float of the Snake as winter approached bordered on suicidal. The Doane party encountered snow and below zero temperatures, and constantly had to chip away layers of ice on the boats. If not for a grizzled old trapper by the name of John Pierce the party might have starved to death if they didn't first die from freezing. Pierce simply could not believe that anyone would be crazy enough to attempt floating down the Snake River in winter, but did provide some life-saving meat and essential supplies to the expedition. Toward the end of the hapless mission when Doane realized he had lost his journal notes documenting the miseries of the early portion of the trip, he actually ordered his luckless crew to turn around in the ice and snow, and haul the boats *back up* to where they had begun, and repeat the trip all over again, so he could replace his journal notes. Fortunately for Doane and all of his men, word of this ill-fated trip had reached Fort Ellis, and Doane was promptly ordered back to the fort, eventually arriving in February. Doane never ventured out onto the Yellowstone Plateau again.

The Snake River winds through Jackson Hole below the Teton Range

The Northern Lights

From the mid-1970s through the late 1980s, Yellowstone National Park enjoyed the services of two wonderful elderly gentlemen, John Railey and Herb Warren, who volunteered as "geyser gazers" out in the Upper Geyser Basin, which includes Old Faithful Geyser. As former Park Geologist Rick Hutchinson called them, "they are our eyes out in the geyser basins." Herb would take the early shift, heading out into the cold morning air at 5:00 a.m., while John would walk out to the benches at Old Faithful after the visitor center closed, and record eruptions up until midnight. He would typically be back out in the basin by mid-morning the next day observing Grand Geyser from his comfortable spot on the bench beneath an old lodgepole pine. Occasionally when I arrived at Grand while on roving duty, John would begin his conversation with, "Butch, you should've been out in the basin last night, the Northern Lights were magnificent!"

Usually by 11:00 p.m. the Bach family was in the bed. However, his frequent observations of shooting stars and the Aurora Borealis made me envious. During the summer months when the days are so long, I rarely enjoyed spending too much time looking at the dark night skies. I wondered if I would ever see the magnificence of the Northern Lights while in Yellowstone.

The moment finally came in the early 1990s. My teaching colleague and backpacking friend, Hank Barnett, had accompanied me on many backcountry trips in Yellowstone, and finally he "caught the bug." Despite the fact that Hank was a practicing CPA and taught Accounting at Walters State Community College in Morristown, Tennessee, he wanted to be a park ranger. Since Hank did not have the necessary academic background to qualify as an interpretive ranger, he decided to pursue the career of a NPS law enforcement ranger. Hank graduated from the National Ranger Training Institute at Hocking College in Ohio. His first assignment was as a seasonal backcountry ranger in Crater Lake National Park in Oregon.

I missed having Hank come out to visit me in Yellowstone to join me on a couple of backcountry trips on my days off, but I was thrilled that he had successfully landed a job doing what he truly desired. It was in late August of 1991 that ironically Hank and I would both see the Northern Lights, but under much different circumstances. My old backcountry companion, Jim Lenertz, and I were on a canoe trip down the Southeast Arm of Yellowstone Lake. Jim had worked for two decades as an interpretive ranger in Yellowstone before suffering a debilitating stroke in 1987. He returned the next year to serve as a volunteer. The stroke severely limited Jim's backpacking trips, but really did not alter our canoe trips much. He was still a strong paddler in the bow of my canoe.

Typically my lieu days were Friday – Saturday, and my duty ended at 4:00 p.m. on Thursday, and started back up at 2:00 p.m. on Sunday. Therefore, we would usually head out on the lake late on Thursday, and plan to come back very early on Sunday morning. Paddling on Yellowstone Lake is always challenging, and you simply have to take what the lake gives you. Though storms and/or windy conditions can arise at any time, the lake normally begins to calm down by around 7:00 p.m. Therefore, we would often push off at Sedge Bay at that time, and begin our 15 mile long paddle down to the tip of the Southeast Arm. Paddling a canoe through placid waters as the sun sets and the stars come out is a tremendous play on the senses.

Jim and I were on our way to meeting John and Deb Dirksen in the vicinity of Beaverdam Creek, and with optimum paddling conditions, we decided to push on even though we knew that we would not arrive at our destination until after midnight. As we neared our campsite I was the first to see them. "Jim, look up!" I exclaimed. There above us etched across the pitch black sky were radiating streaks of green and red! We were so excited that our incessant chatter brought John and Deb away from their late evening campfire as we neared their camp. We were all beaming over the incredible nighttime skies, and frankly could not even think about setting up our camp quite yet. We all gathered round the fire and reflected on the wildness of our setting, and the thrill of what we had just experienced. Eventually, our excitement ebbed along with the embers of our campfire. Suddenly the soreness of four hours straight paddling crept back into our bodies, and we retired for the evening.

A couple of weeks later after I had returned home to Morristown, Tennessee and was gearing up for the first day of classes, I bumped into Hank. I sat down in his office and we both could not help but reminisce a bit about our summers—his at Crater Lake, and mine at Yellowstone—before we each headed to class. "Hank," I boasted, "I think the highlight of my summer was finally getting to view the Northern Lights over Yellowstone Lake on my last canoe trip!" Hank suddenly sat up in his chair. "When did you take that trip?" he asked. "About two weeks ago—the third weekend in August," I replied. "Dang," Hank exclaimed. "I saw those Northern Lights around midnight on the same evening you did, but under *much* less pleasant circumstances!" Hank proceeded to tell me a tragic story of how late one evening a young lady and her child had been standing on the rim of one of the overlooks to Crater Lake, when suddenly the child slipped and began falling over the edge. The mother dove to rescue the child from falling, but in doing so plunged head first over a cliff and tumbled all the way down to the bottom of the cliff at lake's edge.

Hank was dispatched to rappel down the side of the canyon wall to check the woman and found her dead. He had to stay with the body for hours to protect it from any scavenging wildlife, while arrangements were made for a boat to travel across the lake to retrieve the body. As midnight approached the boat finally arrived and Hank, weary from the long wait, loaded the deceased woman into the boat. As he climbed into the boat, he looked up to see a sky that he had never seen before. Suddenly the pitch dark of the starry night was transformed into streaks and bands of multi-colored hues ranging from green to red to purple. As sad as Hank's experience had been on this evening, he could not help but marvel at the skies overhead, as the boat slowly made its way across Crater Lake.

Two completely different lakes, in two different national parks, but the same nighttime display of the Northern Lights! At the same time Jim and I were looking up from Yellowstone Lake, Hank was looking up from Crater Lake. To this day I have never had this experience again. I thought for sure when I moved to Bozeman, Montana full time in 2006 that I would get to see the Northern Lights, especially during the winter. However, it turns out that unless you head "way up north" it really is not that common of an occurrence. Every night that I'm out in the backcountry, no matter the season of year, I always enjoy marveling at the night skies. But the one night on Yellowstone Lake when I observed the Northern Lights remains the most special—at least to this point!

Backcountry Companions
and the "BC Syndrome"

President Theodore Roosevelt once said that you really don't get to know someone until you have spent time around a campfire with them. Friends you can count on to accompany you into the wild backcountry are priceless. I mention several of mine in this volume as well as my previous book, *Tracking the Spirit of Yellowstone*. There is a certain etiquette involved with backcountry companions. My friends and I have standard pat rules when it comes to making plans to travel in wild country. For example, we typically have four to seven of us in our group on each trip, and we operate as a team. Each individual has different duties, such as gathering firewood, clearing out spots for tents, getting a cook stove going, preparing dinner, washing dishes, etc. We also have "unwritten rules," especially when it comes to practical jokes. In grizzly country, we simply do not do anything that would frighten another person in camp. There is nothing funny about tricking a camp member into believing that a grizzly has entered camp during the evening, such as making growling noises, or screaming, "Here comes a grizzly!"

I will never forget a trip that Margaret and I took up the Slough Creek Valley in Yellowstone during the 1980s with our friends Terry and Becky Holcomb and their two kids. Becky was scared to death of grizzly bears and during the evening she had to go visit "Mrs. Murphy" (or "the bushes") before retiring for the evening. Neither Terry, Margaret nor I had any idea that the kids were hiding out behind a tree to play a "joke" on Becky. As she passed by the tree the kids jumped out and growled. Poor Becky was so upset that she just about became hysterical.

Perhaps the most important attribute for any backcountry companion is to simply be dependable when it comes to arranging a wilderness trip. Is there anything more maddening than planning an extensive trip into the backcountry with a "friend," only to have them back out with some lame excuse at the very last moment? I call such behavior the "BC Syndrome," derived from a very unpleasant experience I once had regarding a planned trip on the Sipsey River in northwest Alabama.

After two wonderful summers working in Yellowstone as concession employees, Margaret and I returned for my final year of college at Auburn University in 1970 prior to my entering the Air Force. Spring Break was approaching and with the backwoods bug instilled in me from those two summers, I was hungry for wilderness. As someone once said, some folks need wilderness as much as food and water. I fall into that group. I had recently become friends with a fellow I will call "BC," who was in my Air Force ROTC detachment. One evening when Margaret and I were having dinner with BC and his wife at their apartment, we began talking about backcountry excursions.

BC was a country boy but he had never taken a true backpacking or canoe adventure into the wilderness. He said that he very much wanted to take such a trip with me, but being in Auburn, Alabama in the eastern part of the state, we didn't exactly have a ton of possibilities to choose from. The only wild country I was familiar with was a long way off up in the Great Smoky Mountains of Tennessee and North Carolina. But then we came across an intriguing article in an Alabama outdoor magazine.

The article detailed a fabulous forty mile canoe trip taken by two fellows down the wild Sipsey River through canyons in the Bankhead National Forest in northwest Alabama. It was a section of the state I had never visited, and late March was usually an ideal time to take the trip. Spring break was still a month away, so I located an excellent national forest map that provided good visual details of the put-in and take-out for the trip. We would cross few roads for the entire forty miles through this wilderness paradise. Margaret and I had BC and his wife over for dinner one evening, and after dessert we started poring over the map. BC eagerly shared my enthusiasm as we extensively planned our four day trip, from the logistics, to campsite locations, to exactly what our meals would consist of.

There was only one small hitch in our plans. Neither BC nor I had ever paddled a canoe! However, we had checked out books on canoeing from the library, and studied paddling techniques for two in a canoe. From what we had read about the Sipsey River, there were no rapids, only occasional turns that we had to negotiate. After reading the detailed article again, I was confident we could successfully navigate this river. What an adventure awaited us!

I was going to supply the vehicle to drive the 300 mile roundtrip distance, and BC was going to provide a Grumman aluminum canoe owned by his uncle. I knew that my cousin, Spencer Bach, who lived a short distance from my parents' home in Montgomery, also had a Grumman canoe, so I called to see if he wanted to join us. It would be great to have someone with us who actually had considerable experience paddling a canoe on a river. Spencer told me he had other commitments and could not go with us, but that we were more than welcome to borrow his canoe if we needed it. "Spencer," I told him, "thanks but my friend already has one lined up, but if anything goes wrong with those plans, I'll give you a call."

BC and I saw each other just about every other day on campus since we had classes together, and as Spring Break grew closer the excitement about our trip was building. "Hey BC," I would exclaim after our class, "only ten more days to our big wilderness adventure!" After experiencing the great adventure of two summers of hiking and backpacking in Yellowstone, I had the bug. Experts in outdoor recreation often say that such trips actually consist of four phases: the planning phase, the anticipation phase, the activity itself, and then the recollection phase. Presently, I was deriving enormous pleasure from both the planning and anticipation phases. I think part of the excitement was due to the fact that I had always wanted to travel through the wilderness in a canoe, and this was going to be my initial voyage. After all, every kid grew up reading all about the exploits of Tom Sawyer and Huckleberry Finn. We weren't going to be paddling down the Mississippi on a log raft like Tom and Huck, but to me, this was about the next best thing to it!

Finally the day of our adventure arrived! The plan was for BC to meet me at my parents' home in Montgomery, and we would head north from there. I had my trusty Chevy II all packed up with the necessary gear—tent, sleeping bag, proper clothing, food, even all of the tie downs we would need to transport the canoe atop my car. BC lived nearby and was due to meet me at 7:30 a.m., and we would be on our way. By 8:00 a.m. I was really becoming concerned that BC had run into a problem. Perhaps his vehicle had malfunctioned on his way to my home. Of course, this was the age before cell phones. I decided to call his home to see if he had left. After three rings I heard, "Hello?" It was BC. "BC, why haven't you left?" I asked. "We need to get on up the road if we are going to make our first planned campsite tonight!" "Oh, uh, gosh, I meant to call you last night," he answered. "Call me about what?" I asked. "Well, uh, I've run into a problem with the trip," he replied. "What problem is that?" I asked. "Well, uh, well, my uncle said the canoe had a leak in it, and, uh, I won't be able to go," BC replied.

My immediate thought was of pure relief. I was so amped up for this trip that all I could think about was my cousin Spencer offering his canoe to me. Before I opened my mouth my brain was saying, "thank goodness, no problem, a minor inconvenience, we will soon be on our way!" At the time I was 23 years old. Perhaps I was the most naïve young man in the entire state of Alabama. At this point it had not even *occurred* to me that BC had no intention of making this trip with me. I didn't even catch the hint with all of his stuttering to come up with an excuse. I didn't even question the fact that he had not bothered to call me the previous evening that he had a problem with the canoe. Someone once said that you can count all of your really true friends on one hand. Well, I only had a few good friends and to this point in my life, I had never experienced such a betrayal by a friend. So I guess you could say I was completely unprepared for what was about to happen.

"BC," I said, "hey that's too bad about your uncle's canoe, but we're okay man! I didn't tell you that my cousin lives just down the street, and he has a Grumman that he said we can borrow for the trip!" Well, this statement caught poor BC completely off-guard. He had absolutely no idea that I had a backup canoe. BC thought he had a good excuse for not going on the trip, though he still stammered his way through it. BC's response was pathetically lame. "Uh, well, uh, you know, I guess I better help my uncle patch up the leak in his canoe, and stay around the house during the break." It was right then and there that it hit me like a ton of bricks. BC had never, *ever* intended to go on this canoe trip! I didn't scream at BC. I didn't call him any names. Reality had now completely sunk in. As far as I was concerned, as of this moment BC was "off my list." He was not someone I would ever again consider a friend who could be counted on for *anything*, much less as a key companion for a backcountry camping trip.

After I hung up the phone I felt a terrible hurt in my chest, as though I had just been kicked in the stomach. I could not believe that a so-called friend could do something like this. Surely BC knew that the previous evening I was at my parents' house packing everything up to go on this trip. Why had he led me on the way he did? Why did he show such fake enthusiasm for going on this trip when he obviously never planned to go? Only BC can answer those questions. However, after the hurt passed I was absolutely determined to still go forward with my plans to paddle down the Sipsey River. I knew that I was incapable of paddling Spencer's 16' canoe by myself, but surely I could handle an inflatable kayak! I had recently seen one on sale at a nearby retail store called Service Merchandise.

I told my wife and parents what had happened and that I planned to go purchase the inflatable, and I think they felt the hurt of my friend's betrayal as much as me, and encouraged me to go ahead with my plans. After purchasing the inflatable I didn't even take the time to pump it up, but rather threw it into the trunk and hit the road. With the delayed start I knew that I did not stand a chance of getting started on the river on this day, but I figured I would simply camp somewhere near the river and get started early the next morning.

When I reached the Bankhead Forest late that afternoon, I was impressed with its beauty. The lush forest reminded me of the Great Smoky Mountains that I had visited a few times with my family. I gathered up all of my gear and packed it down a trail to the edge of the Sipsey River near a place called "Bee Branch," an area that was eventually included in the Sipsey Wilderness.

Even though I was not yet on the river, my soul was now at rest. The sights and sounds of wilderness surrounded me as I prepared my meal, relaxed next to my campfire, and eventually retired to my tent for the evening. The next morning it was time to pack up and launch my craft on the water, and begin my 40 mile solo journey. I inflated the rubber kayak and decided to practice paddling it around this rather calm stretch of the river before loading my gear into it. I eased myself into the kayak, and began attempting to maneuver the craft with my solo dual blade paddle. Nothing I tried worked. All I did was spin around in the water like a beach ball floating in a swimming pool. This was *nothing* like I had expected paddling a canoe to be like, and in fact, the book training I had received was worthless. Paddling this toy rubber boat bore no resemblance to actually paddling a *real* canoe.

As I was hopelessly spinning around in the river, another couple approached the river with their fine two person canoe. As they began to unpack their gear for their own wilderness adventure, they observed the troubles I was having in my little toy boat. "Say," the man said, "If you are new to this river, we would be happy to have you tag along with us as we go down river." What a nice offer! If I had actually had in my possession an authentic canoe I think I would have taken them up on their offer. However, by now I was convinced that this inflatable kayak was suitable only for paddling around a swimming pool, a pond, or perhaps along a beach somewhere. I had no confidence that it would transport me 40 miles down this river, or for that matter that I was capable of maneuvering it even if the thing could hold up for such a distance. "That's mighty nice of you," I answered, "but I don't think this inflatable kayak is really what I need. In fact, I'm going to take it back and hopefully invest in a nice canoe like you folks have."

The man agreed that my boat was indeed substandard, and wished me well as he and his wife pushed off to head down the wilderness of the Sipsey River that I had dreamed about for weeks. As for me, I packed up my gear and hiked it up to my car. I figured that I had enjoyed one great evening in this wilderness, and that I needed to focus on obtaining a decent canoe for any future paddling adventures. The inflatable kayak did not have a scratch on it, and as soon as I got home I returned it to the store and received a full refund.

I learned two valuable lessons from this experience. First, I learned the importance of acquiring a quality canoe or raft before embarking on a wilderness river trip. A few years later I managed to do that (see "Wild Times on Wild Waters.") Second, I learned the significance of only heading out into the backcountry with a friend who is truly trustworthy, responsible and reliable. After all, in wild country your life could depend on your friend having such virtues.

Of course the "BC Syndrome" became an adopted term among my family, hiking, paddling, and backpacking buddies. We try our best to never, *ever* succumb to the "BC Syndrome." When we commit to going on an extended excursion into the backcountry with friends, only some type of authentic health problem or family emergency should come in the way of making the trip. Over the years I have to say that I have been truly blessed with good friends who have gone the extra mile to keep me from experiencing the dreaded "BC Syndrome!"

Abrams Creek—A Secret Wilderness Paddle in the Smokies

Guidebooks can serve a very useful purpose for paddlers and backpackers, but there is nothing like the sense of discovery one feels when exploring "uncharted territory." In Yellowstone, that usually means venturing off-trail, which can be very rewarding and adventurous, but it also adds an element of danger. When it comes to paddling a canoe, just about every navigable stream has been written up either in guidebooks or by canoe clubs. However, in the spring of 1995, I discovered a secret wilderness that produced a feeling of discovery that must have been common a century earlier.

I have always loved poring over topographic maps, and I had come across a corner of Great Smoky Mountains National Park that truly intrigued me. Abrams Creek is a famous stream that flows through the beautiful and heavily-visited Cades Cove, then tumbles 20 feet over Abrams Falls. The stream was named for old Chief Abrams of the Cherokee Nation. A trail parallels Abrams Creek downstream from Cades Cove to the remote Abrams Creek campground, which has a few primitive campsites. I had collected most of the topo maps for the Smokies, and I took great interest in the eight-mile stretch of Abrams Creek between the primitive campground, and where it eventually emptied into Chilhowee Lake. There were no roads or trails along this section of the creek. According to the map the stream flowed through a remote and deep canyon all the way to the lake.

Abrams Creek certainly appeared to be large enough for a canoe, and for several weeks during the winter and early spring the water volume was sufficient for travel. Why was this wild and scenic stream inside Great Smoky Mountains National Park not mentioned in any guidebooks or by any paddling clubs? Perhaps there were sections of the creek choked with boulders and severe rapids. From the primitive campground to the lake, I computed that the stream dropped at a rate of 38 feet per mile, which is a fairly steep decline. There were bound to be some significant rapids along the way. Of course, the rate of drop of a stream is only part of the analysis as to whether the stream is runnable in an open canoe. Some streams are "ledge-pool," with long stretches of calm water. A drop of 38 feet per mile would most likely present very hazardous conditions on such a stream. On the other hand, if the stream's descent was continuous from start to finish, a drop of 38' per mile might be navigable.

I knew from experience that the well-known Nantahala River in North Carolina had a drop of 33' per mile and was continuous. I had successfully paddled it before. Finally I talked myself into giving Abrams Creek a try. I then convinced my friend and teaching colleague at Walters State Community College, Hank Barnett, into taking this voyage of discovery. We both had good

ABS canoes capable of bending and sliding over rocks—mine a 16' Spearcraft model, and Hank's a 16' Mohawk.

At the time I had a student, Kenneth Winter, who had joined me on several river excursions. He owned a fiberglass canoe. When Kenneth learned of our upcoming adventure on Abrams Creek, he begged me to include him on the trip. I thought that he possessed adequate paddling skills but I was concerned about his fiberglass canoe. Against my better judgment I agreed to let him join the expedition; that was my first mistake.

I guess the second mistake I made was deciding to take the trip on a Friday afternoon rather than simply allocating a full Saturday. Typically, an eight-mile paddle down a fast-moving whitewater stream should take no more than a couple of hours. Perhaps Hank or I had a conflict on Saturday, I don't recall. At least we didn't make a serious error regarding the river flow. The only way we had to gauge the stream flow was to check the cubic feet per second (cfs) flow of nearby Little River in the Smokies about ten air miles away. I had floated Little River on numerous occasions, and had a good feel for what an optimum cfs flow was there.

Also, having worked in the Smokies during the summers of 1987-88, I still knew some of the rangers on staff. However, no one really could provide any useful information other than the obvious. I was told that the canyon was very remote and inaccessible. There were no trails in to gain access to the river and canyon. It was critical that we did not head in there with the river too high or too low, or we would not make it out. I knew better than to tackle this isolated river after a heavy rain or during extended dry conditions. Nearby Little River was typically runnable only during the winter and spring months, and/or after significant rain events. Therefore, when a nice Friday in late April approached and the Little River gauge was favorable, we headed out.

We took off in two vehicles from Morristown, Tennessee at noon and were at our put-in destination at Abrams Creek primitive campground by 3:00 p.m. This allowed for five hours of daylight for our trip. The stream empties into Chilhowee Lake (a reservoir on the Little Tennessee River), so we left our other vehicle there. When we saw the stream at our put-in, we were encouraged by its appearance. The level and flow appeared to be about right. We had planned to paddle solo in each of our three canoes with only a minimum of gear to allow for maximum maneuverability in rapids.

As we shoved off I immediately felt a chill up my spine. No, this was not the Lewis and Clark Corps of Discovery, but hey, this was high adventure as far as we were concerned. We were after all in one of the most remote corners of the lush wilderness within the 500,000 acres of wilderness in Great Smoky Mountains National Park. The first couple of miles were simply spectacular. There were lots of flowering trees, shrubs and plants along the stream bank and up the steep ridges. Spring was truly bursting out upon the landscape, the water

Abrams Creek—a Secret Wilderness 164

was running crystal clear, and we had a bluebird day deep in the wilderness. What could be better than this? Furthermore, the rate of drop was just about perfect. We were in constant Class II rapids with a few IIIs thrown in from time to time to keep things interesting.

Abrams Creek is a narrow and twisting stream through this canyon, so it was a good thing we were running solo canoes. We were amazed to find evidence of old water mills where early settlers had lived in the early 1900s, especially since today there are no roads or trails that provide access to these sites. Our first hour of paddling was utterly delightful, but things soon began to change. The canyon narrowed up with blind turns and the rapids became more numerous and severe. We found ourselves having to scout rapids on these blind turns, which took up more time than we had allocated. Soon we came to a very difficult Class IV rapid that we did not want to attempt given the remoteness of our location, so we had to portage taking up more precious time.

Even though I had a detailed topographic map with me (before GPS technology), it was difficult to locate landmarks to help us determine how far down the stream we had come. Everything pretty much looked the same. Then disaster struck. Kenneth hit a submerged boulder head-on and knocked a big hole in the bottom of his fiberglass canoe. Really, this is pretty much par for the course with a fiberglass canoe in whitewater. Again, I should have never allowed Kenneth to take this canoe on a trip like this. The canoe was repairable so Kenneth did not want to abandon it.

We knew that we only had about one hour of daylight left. We weren't sure of our location, but we felt like we were within three miles of our destination. We huddled up to discuss our options. The last thing we wanted to do was to not make it out before nightfall and bivouac for the night. If we did not show up back at our homes, we knew our wives would assume the worst and call out the park's search and rescue. We certainly did not want that to take place so we came up with a plan. Hank volunteered to put Kenneth in his canoe, and place the fiberglass canoe upside down across his canoe in a perpendicular fashion. My job was to bang down the stream just as fast as possible in an attempt to make it out before nightfall, so I could at least notify our wives that we were OK. If I made it out but Hank and Kenneth did not, they were prepared to make an emergency bivouac camp for the night.

Paddling alone can be a very dangerous proposition so I was not going to take any chances. I would scout any tough rapids and portage if I had any doubt about my ability to negotiate the rapid. I have found over the years that when rapids become challenging I tend to transform my mind from the normal relaxed, soothing state that results from wafting through the wilderness to more of an attack mode. In fact, I often growl when I'm aggressively paddling through a tough rapid. My friends often joke that over three decades of whitewater paddling, they have never seen me turn over in a canoe. However, even though I consider my paddling skills to be superior, I was determined to use good judgment in this situation, and not take any undue risks above what we already had!

After only twenty minutes of "growling" through one tough Class III rapid after another, I emerged into the backwaters of Chilhowee Lake, and a tremendous feeling of relief swept over me. I now knew that Hank and Kenneth had ample time to make it out before dark, and I was confident in Hank's ability to negotiate the rapids I had just come through, even with the additional cargo. Sure enough, about twenty minutes later here came what appeared to be a giant red and yellow cross bouncing through the rapids and sliding over the last drop into Chilhowee Lake. Hank wiped his brow with a symbolic look of relief. We now had over a mile to paddle in this remote section of lake before reaching our vehicle. Hank has often ridiculed his paddling ability in whitewater, but every time the pressure has been on in difficult rapids, he has risen to the occasion. Oddly enough, I have seen him flip on a few occasions in rather minor rapids. However, in the tough stuff he always comes through and such was the case with Abrams Creek.

Over the next decade I made many more memorable floats down Abrams Creek. In fact, even with such notable nearby whitewater streams as Clear Creek and the Obed River in the Obed Wild and Scenic River system, the Big South Fork and the French Broad River, Abrams Creek became my favorite wilderness whitewater paddle. I never saw another person when paddling this stream, which is truly amazing when you factor in that the city of Knoxville with a population of over 180,000, was only 40 air miles away. While we were in the deep lush gorge of Abrams Creek we felt as though we were hundreds of miles away from any civilization.

A couple of years after our initial float down Abrams Creek, Hank and I had the adventure bug strike us once more. We decided to paddle the eight mile section of Abrams Creek from the south end of Cades Cove down to the Abrams Creek primitive campground. We had never heard of anyone attempting this section, especially since it included a drop over the 20-foot high Abrams Falls. Unlike the lower section though, this stretch of Abrams Creek did have a hiking trail alongside the stream. As we approached the lip of Abrams Falls, we passed several anglers who looked at us in disbelief. We paddled right up to the brink of the falls, and used ropes to lower our canoes down to the pool at the base of the falls.

As we were placing our gear back in our canoes an amazing coincidence occurred. There at the falls was my oldest daughter Caroline with some of her friends. They had taken the very popular 2.5 mile hike to the falls. At the time Caroline was attending the University of Tennessee, and did not even know that Hank and I were making this trip! After some hugs and conversation, Hank and I continued our paddle further down the stream. We soon discovered to our disappointment that this section of Abrams Creek bore little resemblance to the lower section that we had enjoyed. Here, the stream was more narrow and tumbled through tight chutes constricted with boulders. We had to perform many tortuous portages through "rhododendron hells," a term used by the early pioneers to describe the ordeal of having to crawl through dense tangles of the native vegetation. However, this time Hank and I had prepared for an overnight camp. We had hoped to make it down to Abrams Creek primitive campground where Hank's wife Nancy would pick us up the next day.

As had happened with our initial voyage of the lower section a couple of years earlier, Hank and I were uncertain as to our location, even with topo maps in hand. We were actually spending more time portaging around boulder-constricted rapids than we were paddling down the stream. Each portage became more difficult until finally darkness was at hand. We managed to find an open spot in the tangle of laurel and rhododendron that barely allowed for a tent, and there we spent a rather uncomfortable evening. During the night I had already concluded that we would simply have to leave our canoe on the banks of the stream, and hopefully we could manage to find the trail that paralleled the creek. I hoped that we could manage to hike our canoes out along that trail.

The next morning we placed our craft back in the stream expecting another portage, but amazingly around the next bend in the creek, there was Abrams Creek campground! We were safe. Hank and I and our canoes had survived the adventure, but needless to say, we never had any desire to paddle/portage this section of Abrams Creek ever again. There was a good reason why no one ever paddled this section! However, as far as I was concerned, the lower section from the primitive campground to Chilhowee Lake was a wilderness paddler's paradise.

Over the years I never observed Abrams Creek showing up in any paddling guidebooks or on any canoe club trips and very few paddlers made the trip. We always figured that the main reason for this was the paddling season on Abrams was tightly limited to only a few weeks each spring or after a significant rain. We had figured out how to use the Little River gauge to help us make our trips. You could not simply plan a date in the future to paddle Abrams Creek; rather, you had to take it when the flow was there, and you had to be careful to not attempt it when it was too high. After a big rain it would take several days before the flow reached an acceptable level that allowed for a relatively safe trip through this remote wilderness gorge.

Also, the fact that the last mile of the trip consisted of paddling through the placid waters of Chilhowee Lake probably did not appeal to the whitewater clubs. Furthermore, this stream did not contain the really big rapids that you find on nearby whitewater streams such as the Tellico River, Clear Creek and the Obed River. Abrams Creek was heaven for anyone who wanted a wilderness whitewater adventure with outstanding fishing to boot.

One day I was surprised to see that an outdoor writer with the Knoxville News-Sentinel had featured the Abrams Creek float as a great "fishing trip." I had learned over the years that the National Park Service had rescued paddlers on this stream who ventured down the remote canyon when the stream was running too high or too low. I wrote a letter to this writer and asked him if he had ever actually floated Abrams Creek or had contacted NPS rangers in the park prior to writing the article. I never received a reply.

Soon after the article appeared I was not surprised to learn of a close call with some "floater fishermen" who ventured down into the canyon at high water. The men were missing and I could not help but think of that Class IV rapid deep in the canyon, and what it could do to unsuspecting paddlers. Thankfully, the paddlers were rescued the next day after spending a fitful night huddled under a hemlock tree.

Just before I moved from East Tennessee to Southwest Montana in May, 2006, I took one more paddle down my beloved Abrams Creek with good friends Hank Barnett and Ron Gibson. This time I took along a video camera to film snippets of some of the more outstanding portions of the spectacular scenery. Recent rains had allowed us to take the float during the peak of spring, with mountain laurel, magnolia trees, grantsy greybeard, and many other flowering trees and shrubs in full bloom. Given the fact that the paddling season on Abrams Creek was so brief and the opportunities arose so quickly, I wondered when or if I would ever make this trip again. After all, once I moved out of the area I could no longer take a quick trip right after a good rain. Sadly, only five years later, the opportunity to paddle this secret and gorgeous wilderness stream would disappear.

In May of 2011 an F4 tornado churned across Chilhowee Lake and entered the mouth of Abrams Creek canyon. The narrow canyon channeled the twister for several miles upstream and in its path left thousands of uprooted trees lodged in Abrams Creek, thus rendering the stream impossible to float for probably decades. My good friends and paddling brothers Steve Hixson and Nelson Ross continued to at least make the one-mile paddle across Chilhowee Lake to the outlet of Abrams Creek, then hike up the valley to fish. As recently as 2013 they informed me that while much of the vegetation had healed over from the destructive tornado, the stream is still completely choked with trees blown across and into the stream from that storm.

I'm certain that I will never again experience the secret whitewater wilderness that was such a paradise. Perhaps many decades from now the thousands of logs stacked in Abrams Creek will eventually break loose and decompose, and one day other paddlers will discover this secret wilderness hidden in a remote corner of Great Smoky Mountains National Park.

Entering Devil's Jump Rapid, Big South Fork Cumberland River

The Yellowstone of the East

Some of my most memorable paddling adventures (and misadventures) have occurred on the Big South Fork Cumberland River, at one time called the "Yellowstone of the East." The Big South Fork flows north through a very scenic and remote gorge from Tennessee into Kentucky, and is not to be confused with the legendary Yellowstone River, which at 770 miles in length is America's last remaining free-flowing, undammed major river. Today, if you Google "the Yellowstone of the East" all you will find are references to the east side of Yellowstone National Park, so where did this slogan originate?

The Big South Fork National River and Recreation Area (BSFNRRA) was established by Congress in 1974, though the land acquisition and development of facilities such as visitor centers and campgrounds took quite a few more years, extending well into the next two decades. It was during the late '80s on an October day that I was in Oneida, Tennessee about to embark on my annual weekend fall canoe trip from Leatherwood Ford to Blue Heron Mine, a distance just under thirty river miles. My paddling partners and I walked into a visitor center to check the river stream flow, and I noticed a new color brochure on the counter titled "The Yellowstone of the East." The pamphlet was a marketing attempt by local business interests to put the Big South Fork "on the map" in order to attract more tourists and their money into this rather poor region of Appalachia. I had to chuckle—for three reasons. First, having worked in the Yellowstone country since 1968, I recognized that the attempt to make a comparison between two such different areas was rather silly; second, the Big South Fork was a natural treasure in its own right and didn't need to be "piggybacked" to another national park, and third, the folks from the vicinity around Oneida, Tennessee were not always so concerned about taking good care of their river.

The "Yellowstone of the East" lacked the thermal features, snowcapped peaks, big waterfalls and abundant wildlife found out West; however, the Big South Fork River gorge is absolutely spectacular. Ironically, this river and gorge almost met a watery death at the hands of the U.S. Army Corps of Engineers who wanted to build the "Devil's Jump Dam," near the present location of the Blue Heron Mine Visitor Center where most paddlers end their canoe trip. In fact, many of the locals supported the dam. Fortunately, efforts by conservation groups, most notably Tennessee Citizens for Wilderness Planning (TCWP), stopped the dam by proving that the stream's flow was insufficient to produce the revenues that the Corps had projected.

When I first paddled the Big South Fork in 1977, though Congress had authorized the BSFNRRA as a 125,000 acre multi-recreation unit to be administered by the National Park Service, the work had not yet begun and the place looked beat up and neglected. The river itself was horribly polluted from years of coal mining, some of which occurred right along the river banks and even within the streambed. In fact, the river was close to being devoid of any aquatic life. The color of the river was a sickening grayish-green, when in fact it should have been clear. ATVs and jeeps tore trails all through the scenic gorge and along the ridge tops. However, the surrounding scenery through the gorge was so stunning, especially with the fall colors from the surrounding deciduous forest, that we simply tried to overlook the poor water quality during our canoe trips.

As has so often been the case, many of the locals were extremely upset about the "Feds" coming in and possibly limiting their free rein use of this remote region on the Cumberland Plateau. We've seen this play out in many national park stories in America, from Grand Teton to Alaska, though in the end, almost all of the so-called "locals" are eventually converted and come to appreciate having a national park in "their backyard." Such was not yet the case in the late 1970s, however.

Once, while attending a whitewater camp organized by the Tennessee Scenic Rivers Association, some locals during the middle of the night drove by our camp at Leatherwood Ford and shot their rifles just over the tops of our tents. Every paddling enthusiast I enjoyed going out with had seen the famous 1972 movie *Deliverance*, starring Burt Reynolds, John Voight, Ned Beatty and Ronny Cox. For one thing, the movie featured some outstanding whitewater paddling scenes filmed on Georgia's Chattooga River. However, it was the heinous misdeeds perpetrated by local backwoods characters on the innocent paddlers that served to haunt us all. Paddle much around Appalachia and you will eventually see someone wearing a tee shirt that reads, "Paddle Faster—I hear Banjo Music!"

I lived in East Tennessee for over thirty years and I always considered the region to be a mecca for whitewater paddling in wild places. From the French Broad, to the Obed, to Clear Creek, to the Big South Fork, my partners and I always had that movie in the back of our minds as we paddled down wild streams in very remote parts of Appalachia. Finally, in the fall of 1991, our "Deliverance Moment" arrived and it occurred on the Big South Fork.

One of my favorite colleagues in Yellowstone was fellow Interpretive Ranger Bill Millar, who possessed an amazing sense of humor. During the time that Bill and I worked summers together at Old Faithful, he lived and taught college in Indiana. He had joined me for a wonderful trip down Clear Creek, a part of the Obed Wild and Scenic River, (located only about one hour away from the Big South Fork) in the spring, and now I had talked him into joining me for a paddle down the Big South Fork in the fall. Most of my favorite whitewater streams were best paddled going solo in the canoe, but not the Big South Fork, which is a classic "ledge-pool" stream with long stretches of calm water between the rapids. Given the length of the trip and the long stretches of calm water, it is best to go tandem—two to a canoe.

Our other paddling friends on this trip were Wesley Haun and his friend Doug from Illinois. Wesley and I had known each other for years from attending church in Morristown, Tennessee, and he now lived and worked in Illinois. Doug was a colleague of Wesley's from work. Paddlers had long learned not to leave vehicles unattended at the remote put-in or take-out sites. If you did so it was practically guaranteed that your vehicle would be stolen or vandalized. Many of the locals resented "city folk" coming into this rural area for canoe trips. Much of the support for the new national park status was not from the immediate area, but rather from nearby cities such as Knoxville, Oak Ridge and Nashville, where canoe clubs flourished.

I had found a very nice local gentleman by the name of Junior to be a reliable person to provide a shuttle service for us. We would park our vehicles at his humble abode on the outskirts of Oneida, Tennessee, and Junior would transport our group—usually four of us, and our canoes to the put-in at Leatherwood Ford on Friday afternoon, and meet us at the take-out at Blue Heron late on Sunday afternoon. Junior, who drove a school bus each day, had lived here his entire life, and enjoyed hunting and fishing in the area. However, he told me he had never floated down the river.

The fall canoe trip on the Big South Fork was always one of the highlights of the autumn season and was eagerly anticipated; however, the two biggest obstacles to making the trip were always the weather and the river flow. It seemed as though we would often have too much water or too little water. For example, no one wants to paddle for three days in pouring rain, not to mention the hazardous rapids in high water. By the same token, if the river's stream flow, measured as cubic feet per second (cfs), was too low, the trip simply could not be taken.

In late October of 1991 the weather forecast was looking decent, but the stream flow was anemic. From our many trips we knew that a cfs reading of 150 on the Stearns river gauge was considered to be the minimum flow, though we had once managed to take a very "scrapey" trip at a flow of 100. On the Friday that we departed for our trip the gauge read 81 cfs, not good! Wesley and I had taken the trip together several times, but this was to be the first time on this river for both Bill and Doug. We so wanted them to see this country that against our better judgment we convinced ourselves that we could manage to get down the river at this low flow.

When Junior transported us to Leatherwood Ford, we walked down to the banks of the river and simply shook our heads at just how low the water level was. There are numerous rapids in the first few miles downstream from Leatherwood, and we knew that at these levels each would have to be portaged. We prided ourselves with eating and drinking well on these canoe trips, so portaging was not something we relished doing. Even though I had never driven it, I knew that there was a primitive dirt road that descended into the gorge at a spot called Station Camp, eight miles downstream from Leatherwood. In fact, it was the only road access to the thirty miles of river between Leatherwood and Blue Heron. We decided to have Junior take us there for our starting point as it would cut off a tough eight miles of paddling and portaging through numerous rapids. We hated to do this since those river miles are some of the most spectacular on the river, especially in the vicinity of Angel Falls, but we knew we had to get off the river by Sunday as work loomed for all of us Monday morning.

We traveled down a long, winding narrow road that eventually brought us deep into the gorge at river's edge at Station Camp around 5:00 p.m. The area was eerily quiet. There was not another person or vehicle in sight. Given the lateness of the day plus some rather ominous clouds that were beginning to boil up overhead, we knew we had to make camp fast. On all my previous canoe trips, possibly because of "Deliverance Paranoia," I had abided by a cardinal rule: When paddling and camping along rivers in remote areas, never, *ever* make camp next to a road, where you are vulnerable to strangers causing trouble in the middle of the night. I thought about the trouble makers who shot over our whitewater camp at Leatherwood a few years back. "Junior," I asked, "do you think if we camp right here at the end of this road that anyone will bother us this evening?" "Heck no," he answered. "I bring my family down here to camp and fish pretty often and I doubt you'll even see anyone here tonight."

Against my better judgment I took Junior's advice to heart and we all agreed to camp in this beautiful spot. We bid good bye to Junior and watched as he drove my sturdy old Dodge pickup up out of the canyon. From past experience we knew that the reliable Junior would have that truck waiting for us at Blue Heron on Sunday afternoon. If only Junior's prediction about quiet solitude had been as reliable! After setting up camp and gathering firewood for the evening, we enjoyed our traditional first night's meal fare of beef stew. The char-broiled steaks and potatoes would come on Saturday night.

After dinner I sat around the campfire sipping a beer and marveling at the beauty and solitude of this place called Station Camp. Even the storm that we had feared earlier failed to materialize. "Guys, we'll have to remember this site for future trips when the stream flow is down," I proudly stated. We had a fairly decent supply of firewood for the evening, but Bill came wandering in with one more load just as darkness settled into the forest. He had gathered some fine limbs that had recently broken off a beech tree, but as he finished sawing them up into about eight logs I closely examined the wood. "Bill," I asked, "didn't you notice that this wood is green? There's no way this will ever burn." "Guess not," he replied. "Well, that's okay, I think we have an ample supply," I told him.

At about 10:30 p.m. our complete solitude disappeared. High up through the pitch darkness of the canyon we could make them out—one pair of headlights after another as if in a caravan, slowly traveling down the narrow winding road to the bottom of the gorge, and eventually right past our camp. About fifteen vehicles of all makes and sizes made their way to the end of the road about 100 yards past our camp. Watching this strange late-night procession, I told the guys about my friend and teaching colleague, Hank Barnett, who had worked as a backcountry ranger on the North Carolina side of Great Smoky Mountains National Park. Hank would often tell me his adventures in dealing with "mountain people"—folks who would basically sleep all day and then party out in the woods all night.

Before long these folks were partying. We could hear the shrieks, loud voices, laughter and music playing from the vehicles. This was certainly not what I had in mind for a quiet wilderness camp! But there was nothing we could do about it now. Our camp was completely set up, the canoes pulled up on shore, and it was late and dark. Moving our camp now was out of the question. "Well," I mused, "let's just hope that Junior is right and these folks stay to themselves and don't bother us."

We stayed up until midnight, at which time our firewood supply had dwindled down to the eight sappy beech logs that Bill had cut. It was pretty obvious these party goers were in for a long evening, so we retired to our two tents. Lying in my sleeping bag I could not sleep. I kept thinking about how vulnerable we were and the hard feelings that so many of these local rural folks had against the "elitists" from the big city who showed up to paddle their river. Bill, on the other hand, went to sleep right away as evidenced by his snoring. About 1:00 a.m. I was still not sound asleep when I noticed headlights from a big truck approaching our tent. I sat up to look out our tent window. Bill continued to snore away. The pickup truck was jacked up with over-sized tires for high clearance—perfect for the backwoods jeep trails in and around the gorge that the locals deeply resented losing access to due to new National Park Service restrictions in the gorge.

Our campfire still had some embers glowing, and I watched as a shadowy figure got out of the truck, walked over to our campfire, and gathered up all eight of the logs Bill had cut. This was alarming. I woke Bill up and told him what had just happened. "Well," he yawned, "they must not have noticed either that the wood was green. Serves them right." "Maybe so," I replied, "but the act of coming right into our camp and stealing our firewood was pretty provocative. What else are they going to do tonight?" I didn't want to ponder the possibilities. There was no place we could go. We had no weapons. I just wanted it to be morning. Really, all we could do was say a little prayer and try to go back to sleep. I guess that worked because I soon dozed off.

Later in the night something awakened me. At first I thought a full moon had come out and was shining through the tent, but then I awakened more fully and realized that the big, jacked-up truck was back. This time it had pulled to within about ten yards of our tents, and had its bright lights on. Then loud music began to blare from the truck. "Bill," I spoke in a low voice, "wake up, we've got trouble." Bill didn't say a word. He just got out of his sleeping bag and started pulling on his infamous old houndstooth camp pants. "What are you doing?" I asked. "Well," he replied, "If I'm going to have to get into a fight, I don't want to do it in my underwear." Vintage Bill Millar humor. I wished that I had felt like laughing but I didn't.

The truck just sat there with the bright lights illuminating our tents with the music blasting. All I could see were bright lights. I could not tell how many people were in the truck. For all I knew there was a gang of six guys with guns and clubs. "Guess they didn't like your green firewood," I mused. Bill didn't laugh. Our tent had a front door and a back door. Like Bill I got dressed as well. It was a fairly cool night so the jeans and flannel shirt felt good. I told Bill that I was going to ease out the back door of our tent and sneak over to see if Wesley and Doug had any thoughts as to what we should do. I had my own idea. For all we knew these guys had guns, and they could start firing at any moment.

Our two tents were only about ten yards apart, and with the back door, I didn't think the guys in the truck could see me as I eased over to the other tent. As I came up to their back door, I noticed both Doug and Wesley had also gotten dressed and were gazing out their tent window. "Guys," I said. It looks like they really mean trouble. I think we need to get out of our tents as quickly as possible, and head over into the woods." Wesley was quiet but Doug quickly responded, "That's exactly what they are waiting for us to do," he said. "As soon as we leave they are going to come in here and steal everything we have, including our canoes."

I immediately knew that Doug was right and our canoes would be the easiest and most valuable items for them to quickly make off with. "Doug, I agree. But what should we do?" I asked. "Well, if it's a fight they want," Doug answered, "I think we need to all get out of our tents, stand in front of the truck, and show them what they have to deal with. After all, we aren't exactly a bunch of weaklings here. Plus, if I lean on my hiking staff just the right way, I think I can make it look just like a rifle."

I quickly realized that Doug was right. I was quite scared because we had absolutely no idea of what we were up against—how many guys, how many and what type of weapons, nothing. But what else could we do? Furthermore, Doug had a point and I really had not even considered it. We were all decent sized guys, especially Doug. Doug had played linebacker for Southern Illinois University, stood six-four, and weighed 240 pounds. Bill, Wesley and I were all about six feet tall with varying weights—Wesley the lightest and Bill the heaviest. "Okay," I replied to Doug. "Let me go back and tell Bill the plan, then you guys come on around and the four of us will confront them."

I eased back in the tent and told Bill of our plan. He completely agreed with Doug. "Bill," I said, "If any words are spoken, whatever you do, keep your mouth shut! I'm afraid that your accent will only get us into further trouble with these mountain people." Wesley and I have mild southern accents and Doug's was sort of southern to mid—western. Michigan-born Bill, however, sounded like, as the locals like to say, "You ain't from around here, are you?"

The four of us emerged from out tents and lined up in front of the bright lights of the pickup. We folded our arms and basically glared at them with the meanest looks our frightened hearts could muster. I noticed that Doug did indeed appear to be leaning on the barrel of a rifle. The "standoff" lasted about one long minute. Then the truck backed up, turned, and drove back over to the party site about 100 yards away. We returned to our tents and after my heart rate had returned to close to normal, I said my prayer again and dozed off.

When we woke up the next morning we emerged from our tents to find the same quiet and solitude that we had found when we had arrived the previous afternoon. There was not a single vehicle or person in sight. I walked over to the party site and found a campfire ring with a bunch of beer cans and whiskey bottles. I looked around me at all of the natural beauty and thanked the Good Lord for looking out for us. I also vowed that I would never, *ever*, camp near a road on a canoe trip again. To this day, I still haven't.

Other than having a "Deliverance Experience," the other thing to avoid when paddling rivers such as the Big South Fork, is to not get "trapped" by a sudden change in the weather. I had subscribed to canoe club newsletters when I lived in East Tennessee and recalled reading many a story of paddlers getting halfway through a canoe trip when sudden rain storms would cause the river to rise to an unsafe level. The paddlers would have to stash their canoes and somehow manage to hike out from the bottom of the canyon in an attempt to find civilization. Thus, the importance of carefully studying and analyzing weather forecasts, the stream's current flow, and understanding how much rain it would take to bring the river too high for safe travel. In over thirty years of paddling East Tennessee, Western North Carolina, and Southern Kentucky, I had managed to avoid this misadventure except for two notable exceptions, one on the French Broad in Western North Carolina (see "Wild Times on Wild Waters") and the other on the Big South Fork in late October of 2012.

Our fall adventure this time would only include me and Steve Hixson, who lives in Knoxville and usually comes out each summer for our annual backpacking adventure in Yellowstone. We had planned our trip to begin on

Monday morning at Leatherwood with a take-out at Blue Heron Wednesday afternoon. On the Sunday evening prior to our trip we watched the weather report carefully. We noticed that a cold front was racing through the area with a strong, but narrow line of storms that eventually died out before reaching Knoxville. We could tell that the Big South Fork vicinity received some rain, but we could not determine exactly how much. Before we left on Monday, we called park headquarters. The ranger on duty told us, "We didn't get much, I doubt that the river gauges will move."

Our good friend Nelson Ross transported us to Leatherwood Ford on a gorgeous bluebird day with fall colors at a peak. When we arrived at Leatherwood around 1:30 p.m., we found the river clear and relatively low. The conditions appeared to be perfect, with the Stearns gauge running at 190 cfs. Steve and I waved good bye to Nelson as we pushed off in a sixteen foot red Dagger ABS canoe. Right away the rust stained brown sheer walls of the canyon towered over us, as we made our way downstream to Angel Falls, a Class IV rapid. The relatively low water level made for an easy portage around the falls.

There are some wonderful campsites near Angel Falls, but we decided to paddle for another couple of hours. However, I had forgotten just how consistently rugged the terrain along the river is. We really did not find a suitable spot until we reached, you guessed it, Station Camp! It was now getting late and I knew this was probably our last acceptable campsite before darkness overtook us. After my previous experience here, I told Steve that we would camp river left where there was no road access, and furthermore, we would find a secluded camp site well away from view.

We looked across the river and noted that there was not a single vehicle or individual in sight. Since this was a Monday night I really didn't expect a party to develop, and given our location across the river, frankly, I was not concerned this time around. Prior to setting up camp we walked up a hill from the river, and discovered a trail with a sign that stated, "Charit Creek Lodge – 4 miles." This backcountry lodge is operated by the same outfit that runs LeConte Lodge atop Mount LeConte in Great Smoky Mountains National Park. Twice, I had stayed at LeConte Lodge, but I had never visited the lodge at Charit Creek. We were carrying a fairly detailed map of the BSFNRRA, but we noted that this trail was not on our map. The discovery of this trail would turn out to be rather significant later.

Fortunately, there would be no repeat of the unpleasant events experienced the last time I spent an evening at Station Camp. No, this time we would have a different type of misfortune. After chowing down a couple of cans of beef stew heated up over an oak wood campfire, we enjoyed conversation and the ambiance of the quiet solitude that had eluded me the last time I had spent an evening here. Naturally, I told Steve a blow by blow account of that scary evening. I was still on Mountain Time and Steve on Eastern Time, so a little after 9:00 p.m. he retired to his tent. I decided to keep the fire company until at least 10:00. When Steve entered his tent he said, "Butch, don't forget to tie up the canoe."

Is there anything more soothing than simply relaxing next to a campfire in the wilderness? Just before turning in I walked down to the river's edge and marveled at the peacefulness of our setting. I glanced across the river where we had our unpleasant evening years before. All was dark and quiet on this evening. Then I looked at our canoe. Earlier, we had pulled it up on the bank about five yards from the water and lodged it behind a big log. As I looked at it, for some reason I decided to ignore Steve's request and break a cardinal rule of river canoeing; I failed to tie the canoe to a tree. The canoe appeared to be quite safe and snug up on the bank behind that log.

After a peaceful night of rest I heard Steve breaking sticks getting the morning's campfire going. I knew he would be up earlier than me, and chuckled to myself knowing that by the time I emerged from my warm cocoon, the fire would be roaring. But then the mood of the camp changed. Steve walked over to my tent and said, "Butch, we're in trouble! The river came up last night and our canoe is *gone!*" From the tone of Steve's voice I knew he was not joking, but I had to see it to fully believe it. I emerged from my tent, walked down to the river, and was shocked at how much the river had risen overnight. Apparently the weather front that missed us must have poured buckets upstream. The big log that we had pulled the canoe across was now well under water. The river had come up several feet, and we learned later that the Stearns gauge had jumped from 190 cfs to 1090! Steve had reminded me to tie up the canoe not because we anticipated this, but because it is the normal protocol *in case* such an event occurs. The fact that Steve displayed no anger at me for not tying up the canoe was a reflection of his demeanor and the fact that we are such good friends.

Over the years I had read about canoe parties getting stranded due to rising rivers, but at least they were able to stash their canoes. Were we actually up a creek without a canoe? Steve and I spent the next two hours thrashing through the briars and reeds along the river bank gazing downstream in a futile effort to locate our red canoe. The first two miles below Station Camp were placid, but the canoe was nowhere to be seen. After we probed those two miles all the way down to rapids, we finally accepted the fact that our canoe had been swept downstream. How far, we had no idea. By now it was 9:30 a.m. and we realized we had to come up with a plan. No one had ever showed up at Station Camp the previous evening, and so far on this Tuesday morning there was nary a person or vehicle in sight. We had cell phones, but there was no cell service down in the bottom of the canyon.

We took out our map of the Big South Fork and studied its trail system. While we had paddled eight river miles from our put-in at Leatherwood Ford, it appeared to be at least a rugged 14 mile hike back via the trail system. Then we remembered the trail sign to Charit Creek Lodge. "Butch, surely the lodge will have some type of communications in case of an emergency with its guests," Steve offered. I agreed. At first we thought about both of us hiking up to the lodge, but then I remembered how fast Steve had ascended the steep trails along the Teton Crest two months earlier on our eight day backpack trip. He was after all ten years younger than me. "Steve," I suggested, "Why don't you take off right now for the lodge, and I'll clean and pack up our camp." Our plan was to first see if there were any canoes the National Park Service might allow us to borrow. Plan B was to contact a nearby canoe shuttle service, and third, as a last resort, Steve would call poor Nelson to drive back up and bring us another canoe. Neither one of us came prepared for a hiking trip. All we had were sandals and camp booties. Steve grabbed a cup of coffee and some granola bars and headed off at 9:40 a.m. in his river sandals.

With a total of eight miles to hike, I figured at best Steve in those canoe shoes would take about 3 ½ hours, which would put him back in camp around 1:00 p.m. for a late lunch. The camp was the usual mess, so I took my time cleaning and packing it up. I had two of everything to pack up—tents, sleeping bags, dry bags, etc. Meanwhile, Steve was discovering that this "trail" was actually an old jeep road, replete with undulations, mud holes, rocky terrain, stream crossings and a steady climb. The trail was fairly well-signed until he came to a deep creek crossing at about the three mile mark. Steve had no idea which fork to take. But just before flipping a coin, almost as by divine intervention, a solo backpacker appeared. The fellow was an older gentleman by the name of Ronnie, who said he was from Nashville, and was out in the woods for a week long trek. Ronnie said that he had hiked past the lodge and Steve needed to take the left fork through the creek.

He arrived at the lodge at 10:40 a.m. and with instructions from an employee found that there was one place you could stand to get cell phone reception. First Steve called park headquarters to tell them what had happened and that we were okay in case someone reported an empty red canoe floating through the rapids. He asked if there was any possibility of borrowing a canoe but was told that nothing was available. He then tried plan B by calling the only canoe rental and shuttle business in the area. Being a Tuesday, no one was available to drive over with a canoe the rest of the day. So Steve went to plan C: he called our good friend Nelson Ross who lived about 30 miles east of Knoxville. Nelson had originally planned to go with us on our trip, but had a sore knee and had graciously volunteered to take us to the put-in at Leatherwood on Monday then pick us up at Blue Heron on Wednesday afternoon. The drive from Nelson's house to Leatherwood is about 2 ½ hours, so Steve hated to make the call. Nelson probably wished he had never answered his phone.

Steve started back down the trail at 11:00 a.m. An hour later just as I was sitting down for lunch, I saw both Steve and Ronnie walk into camp. Steve was walking so fast (about four miles per hour) that he actually caught up with Ronnie about the time both of them reached the river. He now had two bad blisters on each foot. We knew it would be at least two hours before Nelson showed up, so we sat down and tried to enjoy our gorgeous surroundings. I was having a tough time appreciating it. For one thing, I felt terrible about Nelson having to drive all the way back up, plus I figured there was a good chance I might have to buy a new canoe to replace the one Nelson had let us borrow. Two things helped the time go by. One was listening to Ronnie, a true wilderness wanderer. He had no plan for the week, other than spending time out on the trail in this beautiful area. Second, horse parties were now beginning to show up where they typically faced a relatively easy stream crossing. But with a stream flow of 1090 cfs the stream crossing was anything but easy, and some of the horses simply refused to make it and turned back.

At 3:15 we saw Nelson's truck making its way down into the canyon. He waved at us then unloaded the canoe, and paddled over to our camp. After an embarrassing apology, I told him that we needed to get him back across the river so he could head back home. Steve and I would take off and we still held out hope that we would come across the lost canoe. If we did we would paddle each canoe solo the rest of the way. Even though we had lost most of a day on the river, we figured that the high river flow would help us make up time and we could still make it out by late the next afternoon.

As Nelson and I were paddling back across the river to his truck I looked downstream and noticed a glimpse of red. "Nelson", I exclaimed, "Hold on, I see something downstream in a cove." We turned the canoe and headed downstream around an island, and sure enough, there hidden behind a logjam was our red canoe. Somehow when the water level had risen the current had pulled our canoe all the way across to the other side of the river past an island, and into this little hidden cove. There was no way we could have ever seen it from our side of the river. In fact, we were darn lucky that we noticed it now! It was barely visible from the river's main channel.

We bid Nelson good bye (for the second time) and by 3:50 were on the river. With the new, higher river level, and fast flow we were able to make great time. Gone were the exposed rocks that we sometimes hung up on. Most of the technical rapids which normally require careful maneuvering were now simply standing wave trains that actually helped us gain more speed. Years ago I had found a beautiful sandy beach with a very fragrant bush called "spicebush," named by the pioneers who would actually brew a nutritious tea from the twigs when the "cow went dry." Due to the increased flow, we reached this spot in only two hours. Unfortunately we found that this beautiful campsite had been trashed by a previous party who appeared to have hiked in. There were numerous cans and bottles littering the site. We burned what we could in our campfire, and placed the rest of it in our large mesh garbage bag that we carry for just such uses. At least in a national park area we knew we would not face actual garbage dumps, such as we once found on the Cumberland River in Kentucky upstream from Cumberland Falls, where locals had actually dumped old stoves, cars and refrigerators into the otherwise beautiful river. We enjoyed a meal of Chili Mac and a nice evening fire. Needless to say, before retiring we completely secured our canoe by pulling it into our camp and tying it to a tree.

We hit the river the next morning before 10:00 a.m. We wanted to be sure to arrive at Blue Heron early so that Nelson would not have to wait at all for us. As we paddled downstream we gave thanks that we had stopped at "Spicebush camp" for the night, because campsites were almost nonexistent due to the steep canyon walls extending down close to the river's edge. We noted the names of the tributaries that flow into the Big South Fork along this stretch: Troublesome Creek, No Business Creek and Difficulty Creek. Hopefully these names originated from the tough times the pioneers had in scratching out a living here rather than the rapids ahead.

I knew from past trips that we had two major named rapids ahead: "Bertha's Bump," and "Devil's Jump." We always scouted both and would normally run each one solo. We would typically portage our gear around the rapid, and then have one person take the canoe through. I have always found that paddling a canoe solo is the way to go in difficult rapids, since you have more maneuverability and with the lighter load and more freeboard, you are less likely to take on water. However, I had never floated the Big South at such a high flow, and we blew over Bertha's Bump without even knowing it, and then portaged around Devil's Jump without recognizing it. Only when we saw the takeout at Blue Heron did we realize the "mystery rapid" that we had just portaged was Devil's Jump!

We were now way ahead of schedule so we simply relaxed, and took a seat on a bench high up on the old coal tipple and gazed out at the spectacular setting here. I thought back to my first float here in 1977. The Blue Heron mine site then was an ugly eyesore accessible only by a jeep road replete with deep pits. During rainy weather a four wheel drive vehicle was required to even access the river here. Trash and old abandoned mine equipment was scattered about. As I looked down at the river below I realized that today the Big South Fork represents one of our nation's finest conservation success stories in recent decades. The former polluted river that was almost devoid of aquatic life now runs crystal clear and supports a healthy population of fish, mussels, and other species. There is now a visitor center at Blue Heron and the old train track supports a locomotive that transports visitors along a very scenic sixteen mile roundtrip route to Stearns, Kentucky.

Elk have been restored nearby and black bears, which were hunted to extinction in the area, have also been reintroduced. Abusive use by ATVs and jeeps in the gorge no longer occurs. Most of those old jeep roads have been converted to use by horses, mountain bikers and hikers as part of an elaborate network of 180 miles of trails throughout the park. There are fine campgrounds and visitor centers available to the over 700,000 annual visitors. As so often happens, the local communities, once skeptical, now embrace "their park," and are proud to have it in their backyard.

The slogan, "The Yellowstone of the East," a cheap gimmick to attract tourists, was abandoned years ago. The Big South Fork National River and Recreation Area now has its own identity and reputation that the folks of this corner of Appalachia are truly proud of. As I sat there high on that coal tipple, I felt a deep sense of gratification for what conservation groups and federal land agencies had accomplished. It is wild country to be revered and to be respected, which includes always tying up your canoe!

Wild Times on Wild Waters

Growing up in the capital city of Montgomery in central Alabama, I had no exposure to a running stream. The closest thing I could find was the "Three Mile Branch," which was basically a glorified manmade sewer/channel that accommodated the runoff when heavy rains occurred in the city. Parts of the branch did indeed run through large, long, concrete pipes, but other sections meandered through a beautiful shady forest environment. Even though the branch was littered with bottles and cans (I once stepped on a broken pop bottle submerged in the mud which required several stitches), the branch was my world of adventure when I was a kid. My Dad occasionally took me fishing on some of the ponds around the area, but not camping. Then one day he literally changed my life when he proposed a fishing/camping trip on Jordan Lake, a dam controlled reservoir about 30 miles from Montgomery. "Butch," he began, "How would you like to go campout on an island? We'll sleep on cots and set out a trot line to catch fish!" To my nine-year old mind at the time, it was like my Dad was proposing a trip to the darkest reaches of the Amazon. Not only was I going to experience sleeping out under the stars in a wild setting for the first time in my life, but after several years of frolicking in basically a polluted ditch, I was going to encounter a true natural free-flowing stream!

I thought I was simply heading out on a fishing trip with my Dad and Granddad, but this trip would turn out to be quite the adventure. Dad had an old seven horsepower Evinrude outboard motor that he would mount on one of the wooden boats available for rent at Joe's Fish Camp, located at the end of a winding dirt road with overhanging dogwood trees and wisteria vines. However, on our way to the fish camp, Dad pulled the old gray 1951 Plymouth over to the side of the road and pronounced, "Here is where we get our minnows." I had just assumed that Dad would stop at a tackle shop to buy some minnows, which we would put on our trot line that we would set out, but instead he had a different plan. He pulled out a lightweight seine and his minnow bucket, and said "follow me." We walked about 200 yards down a steep embankment, and as we neared the bottom of the ravine, I could not believe my eyes. Here was a sparkling, crystal clear stream tumbling across rocks and boulders through the forest. Dad carefully cast his net out across the stream then pulled it in, and it was full of wiggling minnows. There would be no need to visit the bait shop on this fishing trip! We had an ample supply. However, I was mesmerized by the clear stream. All I had ever seen in my limited travels in Alabama was muddy water ranging in color from red to brown. I suddenly realized that my favorite color was clear, as in a free-flowing stream. No, this stream was not large enough to float, but just seeing clear, clean, unpolluted water flowing in a natural setting had a profound impact on me.

The rest of the trip was glorious. We set out our trot line, cooked over a campfire, slept on cots under the stars, caught fish, and reveled in all of God's natural glory out in this corner of what was then wilderness. From that trip on I was hooked. I loved the out of doors, camping, fishing, sleeping out under the stars or in a tent, cooking over a fire, and simply relishing the wildness of such surroundings. Later, when I was old enough to drive, I would gather my friends and head for Joe's fish camp, rent an old boat, and head for that same wonderful island for more good times. By the time I was in college, Jordan Lake was rapidly changing. Soon the lake was lined with lavish cottages with power boats on every pier. Joe's Fish Camp and the winding dirt roads that led to secret wild peninsulas disappeared. It was time to look for wild country elsewhere, and I found it during the summer of 1968 in Yellowstone.

Just as I had marveled at that little clear stream where Dad had collected minnows, so did I marvel at the *large* clear streams I found out West in Yellowstone and Grand Teton. Soon I was rafting the Snake River, but more than anything else, I longed for a canoe. During the early 1970s most canoes were either fiberglass or aluminum. My budget was limited and I could not afford the top of the line Grumman or Alumacraft aluminum canoes which were durable, and great for either lakes or rivers. Instead, I was looking around for a used fiberglass canoe, which was great on lakes, but I knew could be problematic on a bumpy, rock-strewn river.

One summer's day while working at Old Faithful, I biked over to the Upper Hamilton's General Store (now operated by Delaware North) to pick up some groceries, and I noted an old van parked in front with a blue fiberglass canoe perched on top with a "for sale" sign. There were two guys in the van preparing lunch, so I peeked in to inquire about the canoe. The two guys said they had just completed a fabulous week long canoe trip into Shoshone Lake via the Lewis River Channel. They gushed over their time out in the Yellowstone wilderness, exploring the Shoshone Geyser Basin, and every inch of shoreline along the lake. However, they said they were now "dead broke" and had to sell the canoe to hopefully raise enough money to return to their homes in northern California. "How much do you want for it?" I asked. From what I could tell the canoe was rather old, but it appeared solid with no visible cracks. "150 dollars," came the answer. I thought that was reasonable but wondered if I should negotiate with them. Before I could make a counter offer something on the floor of the van caught my eye. It was a beautiful wood carving of an eagle that appeared to be sculpted right out of a lodgepole pine log measuring about ten inches in diameter. "What's this?" I asked. One of the young fellows said that he had carved it out of a log during their stay out on Shoshone Lake. I simply could not believe the perfection of the wood carving of an eagle perched on a limb, not to mention that it had been carved out of a green lodgepole pine log. I wasn't certain what type of wood most wood carvers used, but I felt sure it was not lodgepole. I didn't hesitate. "Tell you what," I said. "Throw that eagle carving in and you have a deal!" The wood carver appeared to be rather sad, but stood up and shook my hand and said, "Deal."

I hastily biked back over to my government quarters to get some money and excitedly told Margaret that I had finally found a canoe that I could afford and exclaimed, "And wait till you see what I got with it!" When I drove my truck over to get it the young fellow took me aside. "Now this wood is green. You will need to soak it in linseed oil frequently; otherwise cracks in the wood will appear once it begins to dry out." I was so proud of the carving that I immediately purchased a bottle of linseed oil and faithfully treated it just about every day. Given the craftsmanship of this excellent wood carving, I find it hard to believe that I did not think to ask the young man to sign his name on his piece of original work. For all I know this fellow may be a famous artist today, and the carving would be worth a small fortune, though I would never sell it.

That blue fiberglass canoe opened up a new world of wilderness for me. I used it to ply the waters of Shoshone Lake, the Snake River, and Jackson Lake. Lugging the canoe back and forth from Tennessee to Yellowstone was a pain, and soon my dear friend, Park Geologist Rick Hutchinson, told me that I was always welcome to use either of his two canoes—one a green fiberglass model similar to mine, and the other a fine Grumman aluminum model that I had so coveted. Of course, Rick did not have two daughters to raise like we did, so his budget for such items was larger than mine. Many fabulous trips on Jackson Lake, Shoshone Lake, and *especially* Yellowstone Lake were made in Rick's Grumman canoe. My blue fiberglass canoe stayed put at my Morristown, Tennessee home, right in the middle of some of the finest whitewater canoeing in the country. It was time to sample the mountain streams around East Tennessee and Western North Carolina.

It did not take long for me to realize that while fiberglass canoes are fine on lakes, they are simply no match for rocky whitewater streams. I found myself frequently patching cracks after each run down my favorite whitewater stream, the mighty French Broad which runs from western North Carolina into East Tennessee. The last two trips I ever took in it, both on the French Broad, convinced me it was time to move away from fiberglass. First, I made a run on the Class III-IV stretch from Walnut to Hot Springs, North Carolina with my friend and teaching colleague Jim Brown in which we just about tore out the hull of the canoe right before we took out at Stackhouse. Second, Jim and I just about "bought the farm" on the French Broad below Hot Springs when we became hypothermic after the darn canoe wedged between two boulders on a cold November day. Hypothermia has been called the "Unexpected Killer," and after our experience it was easy to see why. The day was overcast and blustery with temperatures in the 40s. The water temperature at the time was probably also in the high 40s—not a good combination. As we attempted to paddle between two boulders the canoe became stuck in the middle of the river. Jim and I each got out of the canoe, and standing in waist-deep water spent perhaps twenty minutes trying to pry the boat loose. Just as it finally came loose I suddenly realized that my hands, arms and legs were completely numb! Both Jim and I were having serious trouble communicating with each other over the roar of the rapids. Our speech was slurred. I realized we were both in the throes of this insidious killer trying to sneak up on us. "*JIM,* "I screamed at the top of my lungs. "We've got to get out of here, let go of the canoe and swim for the bank!" The closest bank would have required swimming through boulders and rapids, so we opted for the far bank which required a lengthy swim through deep but calm water.

By now I had absolutely no feeling in my extremities. All I could do was lie on my back and allow my PFD (personal flotation device) to do all of the work regarding keeping me afloat, while I clumsily flailed my numb arms and kicked my "dead-feeling" legs in an attempt to propel me to shore. Jim and I were both in the same fix, and fortunately we each had just enough muscle power left to make it to shore. There is absolutely no question in my mind that had we not both been wearing our PFDs, we would have perished in the deep waters of the French Broad River on that cold November day. I remember how "warm" I felt when I emerged from the cold water into the cool air. We both stood up and began running in place to generate some body heat, then we jogged along the shore until we reached the point where the canoe had beached. We built a fire and after regaining our strength and warmth, finished the trip without any further mishap. After this trip I put the canoe up for sale, but I emphasized to the buyer that it was appropriate to only use on placid lake waters, *not* whitewater streams! I sold it for the same $150 to a fellow who simply wanted to use it for fishing along the shores of Cherokee Lake near Morristown. I now began my search for a river canoe—one capable of handling rocky streams and technical whitewater.

A new type of canoe had appeared on the market and taken the whitewater paddling sector by storm. A material manufactured by Uniroyal called "Royalex" or "ABS" consisted of a very light weight but extremely durable material that featured a foam core that not only provided flotation, but contained a "memory" for regaining its original shape if you bent the canoe on a rock. The old standard Grumman aluminum canoe, strong as it was, did not match up to this new pliable ABS material. Not only was the canoe quite flexible for easing over and around rocks and boulders, but it did so quietly, unlike the rigid and noisy aluminum. However, the ABS canoes were quite expensive, and I was still on a tight budget, again on the lookout for a good *used* ABS canoe, hopefully one that contained only *cosmetic* damage. I wanted to find a sound but ugly canoe covered in dents and scratches that would hopefully bring down the asking price.

A canoe enthusiast by the name of Bob Lantz had started the Blue Hole Canoe Company in Sunbright, Tennessee up on the Cumberland Plateau north of Knoxville. The Plateau was home to some of the finest whitewater canoeing to be found anywhere in the country, so that's why he headquartered in Sunbright. I quickly found out that the Blue Hole canoe was in high demand. Not only were the new canoes very expensive, but there simply were no used canoes on the market. Folks who bought Blue Holes were true blue whitewater paddlers, and they were not going to get rid of their fine craft just because of some "love marks" left while paddling the great streams of the Plateau, such as the Obed, Clear Creek, Daddy's Creek, and the Big South Fork, just to mention a few. I finally located an outfitter on the Hiwassee River near Cleveland, Tennessee who rented out ABS canoes manufactured by the Spearcraft Canoe Company in Mount Juliet, Tennessee. My paddling friend and teaching colleague, Nicky Hamilton, had seen them while on a river trip there. "Those Spearcrafts are like a tank," he told me. "You won't believe how sturdy and well-built they are!" I knew the paddling season was nearing an end as summer was over and the cool days of autumn had arrived, so I traveled down to the Hiwassee, and found the rental company named the "Hiwassee Float Service." Sure enough, they had several used canoes for sale, but they were indeed beat up and dented from a long summer's use and abuse by novice paddlers running into rocks and boulders on the Hiwassee River. I settled on a green one that looked almost new save a really deep dent along one side. Apparently the "memory" foam core sort of forgets about its original shape if the collision and resulting dent is particularly severe. Never the less, I did not think the deep dent would impact the canoe's handling, and I forked over $260, and proudly headed home with my whitewater prize. A new Blue Hole would have set me back for $900, so I felt that I had accomplished my goal.

The next spring my green Spearcraft lasted two trips, both made on the Little River within the boundaries of Great Smoky Mountains National Park. Nicky (who had a Blue Hole) and I paddled a tight, technical three mile stretch above "The Y" on Little River on a Spring Saturday, and my Spearcraft handled and responded beautifully. Against my better judgment, the next Saturday I suggested that we start further upstream in much rougher water. This turned out to be a fatal error for my new prized possession. Nicky and I brought along one of our students who was riding in my canoe. We came to a very treacherous rapid that we wisely decided to portage. Nicky lined his canoe around the rapid, and I moved in position to ease my canoe around a large boulder. I shouted to my student friend Gary to hold on to the stern painter tightly while I moved around the boulder where I could grab the bow painter. When I emerged on the other side of the boulder, there stood Gary with a sheepish look on his face with the canoe nowhere in sight. The rope had slipped out of his hand, and the canoe had plunged down into a hole where the force of the rapids had it pinned against a boulder in the river. Try as we might by pulling on the rope tied to the bow, we could not budge the canoe off of the boulder.

Since we were close to the road, Nicky drove his Volkswagen van to a pullout above the river, and we tied my thick throw rope onto the bow plate of the canoe. When Nicky put his foot to the gas the canoe did not budge. Rather, the thick aluminum bow plate tore loose from the canoe! I realized that the only way I was going to retrieve my canoe was to wait for the water level in Little River to drop, thus relieving the pressure being exerted against the boat against that submerged boulder. Fortunately, one of my former students, Jimmy Tritt, was now a Seasonal Ranger in the Smokies, so I called him and asked him to check on my canoe, and the river's water level on a daily basis. The next Monday morning, only two days after the incident, Jimmy called. "Mr. Bach," he said, "I'm afraid I have bad news. I drove along that spot on Little River today, and your canoe is gone, someone else must have pulled it out." "Oh well," I replied. "Finders, Keepers!"

I had learned two things from the experience. First, not to float the upper section of Little River, and second, I needed to find another Spearcraft! The next Saturday I again traveled to the Hiwassee Float Service, and fortunately the fellow who ran the business still had one used red model he was willing to sell me. This one was *really* dented, scratched, beat-up, and just downright ugly. However, there were no truly deep dents like the last one had, and the canoe appeared to be fundamentally and structurally sound. I forked out $240 for it. The year was 1982 and that wonderful canoe has transported me through waters from the Everglades, to the Okefenokee, to many streams throughout East Tennessee, Western North Carolina, and southern Kentucky, to Yellowstone Lake, to Montana's Smith River! Unfortunately, not only did the Spearcraft Canoe Company fold, but so did the Blue Hole Company in Sunbright. I guess the competition from larger manufacturers such as Old Town, Mohawk and Mad River was the reason. Interestingly enough, as of this writing, Royalex is no longer even manufactured, thus creating a scramble by today's canoe makers to find a suitable substitute. I am still the proud owner of that red Spearcraft canoe, and I hope to continue to use it on many more wild, clear tumbling streams in the Montana backcountry!

Since moving to Montana in 2006 I have been fortunate to continue my paddling adventures near my old home base in East Tennessee. Each fall, after completing my work schedule in Yellowstone, I typically travel back for my annual medical exam with my Urologist in Knoxville, who has performed surgery on me twice. As he once quipped, "I've probably examined more bladders here than there are in the entire state of Montana." While that might be an exaggeration, I find comfort in his experience and expertise, plus it gives me a good excuse to take an annual fall canoe trip with my old East Tennessee paddling buddies. My good friend and conservation hero, Nelson Ross, had acquired several ABS Dagger canoes in conjunction with the Izaak Walton Clean Water Center to remove trash on area streams, so we would take along mesh bags with us on our trips for such duty. Over the years I had participated in quite a few myself, since so many folks who live in Appalachia tend to use wild mountain streams as their garbage disposal, rather than for floating and fishing. During periods of high water, all sorts of trash, especially plastic jugs and other various containers, unfortunately find their way into rivers. We had hauled out many canoe loads of trash from area streams.

The one river that we could usually count on floating in the fall was the wonderful French Broad River that flows from western North Carolina into East Tennessee. The river is rated Class II-IV as it tumbles through the mountains, and fortunately much of the land on either side of the river is protected as public land in national forests and/or state wildlife management areas. Even during autumn dry spells the river would channel up sufficiently to still allow canoeing. There are no roads along much of the river, only a railroad, which frankly has never bothered us. There's something rather romantic and nostalgic to experience the sights and sounds of a train slowly moving through the mountains, especially at night.

My friends and I have had many wonderful canoe camping trips on the French Broad, and it is truly one of my absolute favorite wild places. However, as you might imagine, my two most *memorable* canoe trips there were misadventures. On a Friday afternoon in October of 2004 Nelson Ross, Ron Gibson, Hank Barnett and I launched from Stackhouse for a leisurely overnight paddle down to Hot Springs, North Carolina. The morning had been rainy, but by the time we put in at 4:00 p.m. the rain had dissipated to a drizzle. The setting was ethereal—foggy with low clouds hanging in the mountains. The river appeared to be rather high for this time of year, but we made it down to our favorite island with no problems. The weather forecast had predicted a few more showers in the evening followed by clearing and sunny conditions for Saturday. After getting a nice campfire going we set up a tarp, in addition to our tents. As darkness settled in the rain did start back up, but with our tarp we managed quite well. We were able to sit under the tarp and enjoy our dinner as well as the nearby campfire. It didn't seem to be raining very hard at all. I was the last to go to bed around 11:30 p.m., and we had retired in good spirits. After all, the rain had stopped just as predicted, and a brisk breeze had come up. However, I noted that the sound of the rapids seemed to be getting louder from my tent before I eventually dozed off.

Ron is the early riser in our group, and the next morning I heard him snapping twigs to start our campfire, then he said the words I did not want to hear, "Guys, the river has come up two feet and it is still rising!" I pulled on my clothes, emerged from my tent and walked down to the river bank. What I saw was alarming to say the least. All of the little islands out in the river that were normally visible were covered up. The river was out of its banks, and had an angry brown, muddy, foamy appearance. When I walked down to the canoe to retrieve some gear, I could not believe how much water was in it. Had it really rained this much? Did it rain all night and we just didn't hear it? Had the weather forecast been completely wrong?

It was very difficult to enjoy the morning because all we could think about was the big rapid we knew we had to face just downstream. Being on the island we felt trapped. However, we knew that it could take many days for the river to drop to a comfortable level, so after much discussion, we decided to take on the big rapids just downstream. The big one was the infamous "Railroad Rapid," also known as "Frank Bell Rapid," named for an early paddler who almost died running this Class IV rapid. After the deluge the rapid's rating was probably off the charts, as it appeared to consist of a series of unrunnable waterfalls. However, we noticed a cheat chute just to the left of the huge rapid that did not even exist at lower flows.

Our plan was to carefully approach a point that separated the deadly rapid to the right from the cheat chute on river left. I headed out first followed by Ron, then Hank and finally Nelson. Suddenly, Hank tipped over. I looked back and saw Hank swimming and trying to grab hold of his submerged canoe, but it was like trying to grab onto a submerged log. Finally, he swam toward the bank cursing with every stroke, while his canoe and gear were on their way to the waterfalls. I saw Nelson pick up Hank and then I quickly paddled out into the river with Ron in an attempt to retrieve Hank's canoe. There were no painters on either end, as Hank had used all the rope to tie in his gear, so there was nothing to grab. I tried to tie my canoe onto his but it was like hitching onto a great tree floating down the river.

As the entrance to Frank Bell Rapid on the right loomed ever closer I told Ron to abandon the canoe. However, Ron just kept trying. "Ron, Ron," I screamed, "Let it go!" It appeared hopeless to me but Ron would not give up. Suddenly, I noticed that the river was beginning to move the submerged canoe to the left. In the distance was the point of a tiny island just to the left of Frank Bell. It appeared that we had a chance to prevent Hank's canoe from being smashed in the series of waterfalls ahead. I shouted for Ron to hold onto the canoe. He tied on to my canoe and the two of us paddled for all we were worth. "Ron," I shouted above the roar of the approaching falls, "be ready to bail out if we can't make the point!" Somehow we managed to beach right on the point of the little island with not a foot to spare! All of Hank's gear was tied up so nothing was lost. Soon Nelson and Hank arrived behind us and we began bailing out the canoe, all the while staring downstream at what we now faced.

After thorough scouting and discussion we picked our route through the big rapids. Ron volunteered to go first. The river tossed him about in a sickening fashion, and then he simply disappeared into a huge hole. Just as I thought all was lost he emerged back into view, and made it through the long set of rapids without flipping. Hank volunteered to go next. "Hank," I said as my heart was racing, "Whatever you do, stay out of that hole that Ron dropped into!" I held my breath as I watched Hank head out into the waves and to my horror he *also* disappeared from view into the hole. But like Ron he re-emerged and though the river tossed him about terribly, he also made it through! The interesting thing about Hank in whitewater is he often flips in a Class II rapid, but sails right through difficult rapids, and this rapid was definitely a Class IV+. Go figure! After watching Ron and Hank go through, I vowed that I would avoid that deep hole that had tossed them about so violently.

My heart was racing and my mouth felt like cotton had been stuffed in it. I knew that this was a very long rapid with no recovery pool in sight. Ron and Hank were now way downstream out of sight. There was no way they could help me if I flipped. I was proud they had both made it, but now the pressure was on. As I eased out into the maelstrom I suddenly understood why both Ron and Hank had disappeared into the hole. There was simply no other way to go with huge rocks on both sides. All I could do was lower my center of gravity and gut it out. At times like this I tend to emit guttural growls, because I truly feel as though I am in a life or death fight. I thought for sure that I was a goner but somehow I also made it through! Now it was time for the grand old master Nelson, and he rode the same roller coaster through without flipping. We had survived the worst thing that can happen to paddlers on a river—an overnight storm that transforms your pleasant canoe trip into simply trying to survive and make it out alive.

I found out a few years later that there is even a *worse* thing that can happen on a canoe trip, and it occurred in October of 2011 on the French Broad. Nelson Ross, Ron Gibson, Steve Hixson, Jim Wilson, and I launched our canoes at Stackhouse for our usual favorite fall overnight canoe trip. The river was a bit high but nothing to compare to the trip described above. As you head downstream from Stackhouse there is a fork in the river. The right fork has the deeper more treacherous water with some large boulders, so we typically take the left fork, though it tends to be shallow in the fall. The river tries to pull you to the right so we always emphasize the need to plant some strong draw strokes to pull your canoe left. I went first and after making it through the shallow channel I looked backed to see Steve, Ron and Nelson but no Jim! We assumed that the river had pulled Jim into the dangerous right fork. Once we all reached the bottom of the channel, we paddled our canoes over to the other side of the river below the fork, but there was no sign of Jim anywhere!

As much as I wanted to resist the thought, there was no getting around it. Jim had apparently been pulled beneath the big boulder and was drowned. I knew that large undercut boulders in swift current could trap and hold a canoe on the bottom of the riverbed. Our hearts were sick. It was the worst feeling in the world! All I could think about was how we were going to present this news to Jim's wife, Karen. Even though we had no hope of finding him we searched up and down both river banks. I even hiked along the adjacent railroad track. Finally we did what we had to do. We climbed to a high point right at the launch site at Stackhouse, and managed to get one bar on Nelson's cell phone. Nelson then dialed 911 to let Search and Rescue (SAR) know of the situation. I continued to walk up and down the railroad track hoping for a miracle. About an hour later the SAR team arrived in a pickup, and Nelson went over to meet them. I was on the railroad track at the time and for some reason came up with a weird idea. I pulled out my cell phone and noticed that I also had one bar. I dialed Jim's cell number. What a dumb thing to do, because for one thing there is no cell signal below Stackhouse. Nevertheless I listened as the phone rang. Suddenly I heard, "Hello?" "Jim?" I exclaimed. "Is that you?" "Yeah, where are you guys?" came the reply. I shouted at the top of my lungs, *"Hallelujah!"* Nelson, Ron, Steve and the SAR team all looked my way. "Jim's *alive!"* I screamed. I returned to my phone and eventually found out that for some inane reason Jim had selected a *third* channel to go down—a channel where the water was so low he had to drag his canoe over the rocks. None of us had ever even attempted to check out this channel for that very reason—it was always too low!

Jim was way down the river. He had gone a mile or two past the island where we usually camped. It was now almost dark. There was no way we could get to him or for him to paddle back upstream. He would have to spend the night there by himself. Talk about relief! Our emotions had run the gamut, from agony to ecstasy. We headed back to our campsite for the night, sans Jim, and I pulled out my cell phone. No service. The next morning when we reached Jim I asked him to check his cell phone. No service. Then how did my call get through the night before? What if we had not reached him? We would've spent the night with the SAR team dragging the river where we thought he had drowned. We would've put poor Karen through hell with the news. Perhaps this story would have been suitable to include in the chapter on "Angels." Ever since this incident, we have referred to Jim as "Lazarus," and the "Lazarus trip," which by the way marked my last time on a river with Nelson.

In the spring of 2015 Nelson called to tell me that he was going into the hospital for heart surgery. Nelson was such a strong and vibrant outdoorsman that at his age of 78 none of his paddling brethren were too concerned. However, Jim called to give me the devastating news that Nelson had died. All of our East Tennessee paddling brothers—Hank, Steve, Jim, Ron, Martin, and I, gathered at the funeral service in Jefferson City, Nelson's home. We told stories about Nelson, and cried together over the loss of this great man. He was a wonderful husband, father, and champion of the outdoor world. To us he was our paddling brother, having spent so many wonderful days and nights along rivers he loved—from the Big South Fork, Big Pigeon, Little Pigeon, French Broad, Abrams Creek, Little River, and the Nolichucky, to the wilderness of Okefenokee Swamp. Wild times on wild waters indeed!

Canoeing near Breeze Point, Yellowstone Lake

Call of the Loon

One of the greatest sounds heard in the wilderness is the call of the loon. It is a sound I have rarely heard in Yellowstone. Over the years I had briefly seen and heard loons around Peale Island in the South Arm of Yellowstone Lake, the Narrows on Shoshone Lake, and appropriately at Loon Lake in the Bechler country. But in the fall of 2014 I took a fabulous wilderness canoe journey into a place where the loon and its enchanting call would be our constant companion. It was a destination I had dreamed of visiting for many years--the Boundary Waters Canoe Area Wilderness (BWCAW) in northern Minnesota along the U.S.-Canada border.

Al Duff and I had taken many backpacking, canoe and rafting trips, mostly in and around the Yellowstone country. But each fall he would urge me to join him on his annual paddle deep into the maze of some 1175 lakes containing over 1200 miles of canoe routes spread over one million acres of magnificent wilderness in the Boundary Waters (*two* million if you include the wilderness to the north in Canada). Such a fall trip was not possible for me given my teaching schedule. Even after I retired from teaching I was typically working during September at Old Faithful. Then in mid-September of 2014 my work schedule was clear and the trip was on. Al would be paired up with his trusty paddling companion Rick Knoll from Minneapolis, and my paddling partner would be my good friend and former teaching colleague, Hank Barnett of Dandridge, Tennessee. The four of us had teamed up a few years earlier for a spring canoe journey down the Green River. Hank had missed my summer backpack trip in the Teton Wilderness ("To the Headwaters,") but had somehow cleared his schedule for this fall trip. We all met up in Minneapolis. Al drove up from Omaha, and Hank and I flew in. Al and Rick were practically our outfitters, providing the ground transportation, the canoes, paddles, life jackets, and the bulky Duluth bags used for hauling our gear at the many portages between lakes. Hank and I packed our tents, sleeping bags, pads, and some food and personal gear.

Al and Rick picked us up at the airport and we drove north for 6 hours until the road ended at Trails End, about 40 miles north of Grand Marais, Minnesota near the U.S.-Canada border. We stayed in a rustic bunkhouse at the Way of the Wilderness Outfitters. Al and Rick were already packed and ready to go for the canoe trip, but Hank and I had to take everything out of our luggage bags, and arrange and repack our food and gear into our dry bags. Considering that we were within 100 yards of our put-in, our rustic surroundings, and that our bunkhouse had little heat, I felt as though our wilderness journey was already underway.

We had hoped to have breakfast the next morning at "The Way of the Wilderness Cafe," but when we awoke to gray skies and windy conditions, and learned that the cafe did not open until 9:00 a.m., we decided to grab a snack and get on the water. So we started out our blustery morning without even a hot beverage—not the way I like to begin a big trip! Right off the bat we had a disaster. Al had brought his little Honda 2 horsepower motor to use to propel both canoes the first eight miles to American Point, where the wilderness zone begins, and motors are prohibited. Al had planned to stash the motor on an island, and retrieve it on our return trip. The two canoes were Wenonahs, constructed of Kevlar and very sleek and lightweight—perfect for slicing through the water and carrying during portages. The canoes are rather narrow and a bit tippier than river canoes that I am accustomed to. After Al had mounted the motor and loaded all the gear, Hank and I prepared to push the craft out into the water. However, as Rick took his seat in the bow he stumbled backward, which with the weight of the motor on the side of the stern, caused the canoe to quickly tilt over, dumping Al, Rick, the motor, and all the gear into the cold waters of Gull Lake. It all happened so quickly that Hank and I could only watch in disbelief at the scene unfolding before our eyes. I expected to hear some strong words spewing forth, but Al and Rick calmly retrieved their soaked gear and motor, and pulled the canoe back on shore where we tipped it over to empty out the water. Al immediately drained the gas from the motor, put in some fresh gas, and amazingly it started up. He then promptly announced that the canoe was too unstable with the motor. Our trip would be 100% hand-propelled, and that was fine with all of us. Apparently on previous trips to American Point, Al had used a wider, heavier and more stable Old Town Tripper canoe on which to mount the motor.

After a change of clothes, Al and Rick loaded their canoe sans motor and we were underway. As we paddled through the narrow channel of the Seagull River, which connects Gull Lake with the huge Saganaga Lake, we immediately began to notice loons in the water, identified by their regally patterned black and white markings. Some would swim close to our canoes then disappear underwater. Unlike most birds, loons have solid bones that make them less buoyant and suitable for diving and swimming underwater.

We paddled four miles before emerging from our narrow channel into the large expanse of Saganaga Lake. We hugged the shoreline as much as possible and after three more miles of paddling on this very cool and windy day, we began looking for a campsite. We were all in need of a warm campfire. There are over 2100 campsites scattered throughout the BWCAW, and they are available on a first-come, first-served basis. We pulled into a site on the south tip of Long Island, situated between Englishman and Gold Islands, and west of—yes, Loon Island. Al checked it out while we waited in our canoes. After a few minutes he returned and pronounced, "This is our home for the night!" Though we were still about one mile from the wilderness boundary, there was little evidence of motorboats in the vicinity, probably due to the very blustery conditions. Once on land our camp chores were numerous. For one thing

Rick's hip was acting up and he and Al had made the decision to make this campsite on Long Island their "base camp" for the next week, while Hank and I embarked on our loop trip around a portion of the BWCAW. Rick's wife, Kathe, a master quilter and seamstress, had pieced together an amazing four-sided tarp with numerous tie-downs. The creation was affectionately called "The Taj," (short for Taj Mahal) and was designed to provide protection in the event of inclement weather. While Rick and Al were erecting the "Taj," Hank and I pitched our tents, collected firewood, and located a stout tree limb on which to hoist our food to protect it from critters, especially the smaller variety. Though black bears and wolves are found in the BWCAW, we did not see either during our trip, though I did see some bear droppings along one of our portages. Rick and Al had brought along steaks packed in dry ice for the first two nights. No metal cans or glass containers are allowed in the BWCAW, and regular coolers are simply not practical due to the many portages required.

After a fine dinner of steaks and garlic potatoes cooked over the fire grate, which is provided at all campsites by the U.S. Forest Service, we enjoyed telling stories around the campfire and sipping some *cabernet sauvignon* from our wine box. Shortly after we retired to our tents around 10:00 p.m., the weather took a turn for the worse, as fierce winds blew in that sounded like a tornado had parked over the densely forested island, and rain began to patter on our tents. I have always enjoyed spending the night in my tent during a rain, but this storm concerned me. Al had suggested a fabulous loop trip for Hank and me, but we needed to get an early start the next morning to make it through Monument Portage and secure a campsite. When I awoke around 6:00 a.m. the rain and strong winds had not abated. It sounded as though "The Taj" would be put to good use and our loop trip was in jeopardy. We all slept in until around 8:00 a.m., and then lazily gathered under The Taj to consume our meals of coffee, cocoa, granola and oatmeal. "Looks like you guys will not be going anywhere today," Al said, "but don't worry, you can make the loop just fine as long as you leave early tomorrow." Al, a very strong paddler, had more confidence in our ability to complete the lengthy loop trip with many portages on schedule than Hank and I did.

By 11:00 a.m. the rain had stopped but there was still a rather stiff southwest wind present, which would be directly in our faces. Nevertheless, Hank and I conferred and we agreed that we needed to get going. When we told Al of our plans he seemed surprised but we felt that the extra half-day would provide us with an important cushion to completing our loop trip on schedule. Rick felt bad about his hip problem and expressed concern. "I don't like it," he said. "What if one of you gets hurt out there? Those portages are tough. If anyone breaks an ankle or leg, or if you bust a hole in the canoe on a rock, there is no one out there to help you and no cell service." "Rick," I replied, "I really appreciate your concern, and Hank and I will be super careful on those portages." While I was confident that Hank and I could successfully negotiate the maze of lakes and portages, I certainly agreed with his assessment. "Mess up out here and you may be dead," I thought to myself.

Al and Rick helped push us off and waved farewell as we headed into the stiff wind toward American Point. If all went well we would paddle over 50 miles through 14 lakes, traverse 12 portages, and loop back to the base camp on Long Island over the next five days. We would then need to paddle back to our vehicles at Gull Lake, and drive to Minneapolis to make our flight connections. Once Hank and I rounded American Point, we lost what little protection we had enjoyed from the strong southwest winds. "Fetch" is a term that sailors and paddlers use to describe the distance traveled by wind or waves across open water. The longer the stretch of open water, or "fetch," the worse the wind could whip up rough waters. At present our fetch was resulting in whitecap conditions. "Hell Hank," I shouted from my position in the stern of the canoe, "we might as well be crossing open water on Yellowstone Lake!" "You got that right," Hank shouted back over his shoulder. The good news was Hank and I had paddled through white caps on Yellowstone Lake on numerous occasions (but usually not far from shore), so we had the experience and skill to handle such conditions. The bad news was, that skill and experience was now having to be put to intense use!

We soon noticed three canoes ahead of us, and one fellow was paddling his solo. The wind was blowing the poor guy all over the place, and as we pulled even, they headed for shore to seek shelter and wait for the wind to hopefully subside. We finally entered a long and narrow channel, but the strong wind and a long fetch continued to slow our progress. By now we were traveling right along the U.S.-Canada border. The BWCAW is a unique area in that it extends nearly 150 miles along the International Boundary adjacent to Canada's Quetico and La Verendrye Provincial Parks to the north, and is bordered on the west by Voyageurs National Park. We were actually travelling along the "Voyageurs Great Water Highway," that extended 3000 miles from Montreal to the Pacific, and was used by Indians, traders and explorers in "North" canoes, which were 26' long and four to five' wide, as far back as the 17th century. Hank and I pulled over to the north shore at what we called "the Canada Cafe" for our lunch break for the next two days.

Before heading back out in our canoe, Hank and I studied our topo map. We had hoped to make it through the difficult 80 rod Monument Portage before we made camp (a rod is the measurement unit used in the BWCAW, and one rod equals the approximate length of a canoe—16.5'.) Due to the rugged terrain along both shores, there was only *one* campsite in the next eight miles. There were a couple on the Canada side of Ottertrack Lake, but we did not have a permit to camp in Canada. We therefore hoped we would find the campsite just prior to our first short portage leading to Swamp Lake unoccupied. As we rounded the last point in Saganaga Lake, we held our breath in anticipation, then found to our relief that the campsite was indeed vacant.

As we began setting up our camp, we felt good about our decision to stop. The rugged Monument Portage would be tackled the next morning. Our camp setting was quite beautiful. Impressive rock formations make up much of the terrain in the BWCAW, due to the great glaciers that carved out rugged cliffs, canyons, gentle rolling hills, and sandy beaches. The forests include a variety of evergreens, but unlike Yellowstone, the ubiquitous cedar and birch. Our campsite had everything we could ask for. We had large but smooth rock formations to wander about on, level grassy spots for our tents, and lush vegetation all around. However, the most spectacular aspect of our camp was the presence of the Common Loon. There were several visible not far from shore, and their loud and varied calls frequently pierced the quiet, still evening in this great wilderness. The different calls of a loon include the tremelo, a wavering call given when a loon is alarmed or to announce its presence at a lake. The yodel is the male loon's territorial claim. Each male has his own signature yodel. If a male moves to a different territory, he will change his yodel. The wail is the haunting call that loons give back and forth to figure out each other's location. It was this call by the loon that sent chills up and down my spine, and almost reminded me of the lonely late night howls of coyotes or wolves heard in the backcountry of Yellowstone.

After a fine dinner of steaks and green beans, Hank and I gathered around our campfire to sip some wine, and enjoy the solitude of the evening. During our trip we discovered one of the great traditions still in place here—leaving an adequate supply of kindling and firewood for the next canoe party. We found this to be the case, some better than others, at each campsite we occupied, and we planned to do the same. As darkness enveloped the forest, the skies cleared and a brilliant starry sky was revealed, quite the contrast from the previous night! We retired to our light-weight solo tents, mine a Eureka Spitfire, and Hank's a Big Agnes, around 10:00 p.m. I now use an inflatable thermarest, and have found that if you fully blow it up, lie down, then slowly let air out until just before your rear end touches the ground, you attain the perfect setting. I have never enjoyed a more comfortable wilderness bed in all my years of backcountry travel. My Kelty down bag felt cozy as the temperature plunged toward the freezing mark with the clear night skies. The wailing calls of the loons eventually lulled me to sleep.

We awoke the next morning to clear, cold, and windy conditions. We immediately faced a short five rod portage (or what Al would describe as a "lift over") into Swamp Lake. We had excellent topo maps, but reading the landscape from a lake, with its myriad of islands, bays, points, jagged shoreline, and peninsulas, is a different ballgame from reading terrain in a mountainous setting such as Yellowstone. For this reason Hank brought along a GPS with a map chip of the BWCAW. For most of our trip, the GPS was simply a backup to our maps, but every now and then it really came in handy, and rescued us from paddling down a "dead end." Such was the case on this morning, as we misread the map, and headed to the wrong bay in search of our portage.

Once we located the lift over, we entered Swamp Lake, and soon found ourselves at the beginning of the 80 rod Monument Portage, so named for the several brass monuments that mark the U.S.-Canada border. The portage was much tougher than I had expected, as the trail was very rocky and rugged, and climbed up and over a steep hill. No wonder Rick had expressed concern over falling and breaking an ankle! This being our first lengthy portage of the trip, Hank and I did not get it quite right. We loaded lots of our gear into the bulky Duluth bags, but we left too much gear in the canoe. Therefore, the hardest part of the portage was lugging the canoe, especially for the person in the rear whose visibility of the rocky trail was impaired. With much difficulty we finally safely completed Monument Portage, but swore to do better on all future portages. We would pack *all* of our gear into the Duluth bags for our first pass, and then carry an empty canoe on the second pass.

We now entered the long narrow waters of Ottertrack Lake, and continued to face the problem of stiff headwinds and a long fetch. Along the way Hank spotted what he thought was an odd square-shaped rock on the Canada side of the narrow lake, so we paddled over to take a closer look. In fact, it was a stone plaque with a man's face engraved on it, and the inscription "Ben Ambrose." After our trip I did a bit of research and according to Minnesota History Magazine, Benny Ambrose was a legend in the north woods along the U.S.-Canada border for many decades. He was a hardy and colorful woodsman who trapped, prospected, guided, and basically lived off of the land in this remote wilderness. He built a cabin on a point of Ottertrack Lake, and lived here year-round from 1931 until his death in 1982. Ambrose never found the "lost gold mine" of his dreams, but he was rich in other ways. The wilderness provided everything he needed from berries, to fish, to pelts, to fresh meat. He even hauled in organic muck from beaver ponds, so he could have a fine garden that produced such crops as carrots, radishes, potatoes, lettuce, and raspberry bushes. The U.S. Forest Service allowed him to stay on after the region had been designated as a wilderness, by officially making him a volunteer. He lived there until the end of his life, when he apparently died of a heart attack. After his death his cabin was razed by the Forest Service, and a stone memorial was erected on the site. Hank and I probably paddled right by the spot without knowing it.

Ben Ambrose was not the only pioneer who spent many decades living in solitude in the wilderness of the Boundary Waters. After five miles of tough paddling, we completed two portages, and entered Knife Lake, which was the home of Dorothy Molter from 1930 until her death at the age of 79 in 1986.

Dorothy, who was also known as "Knife Lake Dorothy," and "Root Beer Lady," for the home-made root beer she made and sold to wilderness paddlers, lived in a small cabin on an island named Isle of the Pines. She had no electricity, telephone or utilities, and her cabin, which was located only a few yards from the border with Canada, was heated by wood. Like Ambrose, Dorothy Molter was designated as a volunteer with the U.S. Forest Service so she could remain living on public land designated as a wilderness area. After Molter's death, her cabin was dismantled and moved to Ely, Minnesota, where there is now a museum to preserve the legacy of this amazing pioneer.

Hank and I continued to battle headwinds for four more miles, then I steered the canoe over for a brief rest in a protected cove. "Hank," I moaned, "I don't know about you, but I think I prefer portaging to a shortcut rather than continuing to battle these winds." Hank heartily agreed and we each studied our maps, which we kept in waterproof plastic bags tied to the canoe thwarts directly in front of us. We had originally planned to continue west until we rounded Thunder Point, but we were ready to find a different route that allowed us to turn away from the persistent westerly head winds. We opted for a shortcut that would require a 30 rod portage from Knife Lake into the South Arm of Knife Lake.

It felt wonderful to turn south and eventually east, thus escaping tough head winds. However, this day was by far our longest. We had targeted an island in the South Arm of Knife Lake as our destination to keep our trip on schedule. We finally reached it, but not until just before sunset. As a result once we set up camp and gathered firewood, we had to prepare our meals in the dark. With the steaks now gone we turned to our "MREs," (Meals Ready to Eat.) Al and Rick are both retired from the U.S. Air Force, so they have shopping privileges at the base exchange, which offers these packaged meals for sale—the same meals our soldiers consume in combat. In fact, each packaged MRE contains this statement: "Warfighter Recommended. Warfighter Tested. Warfighter Approved." Over the years I have heard soldiers joke about these meals, but I have to say that they are quite tasty—much better than freeze-dried backpacking meals. Of course, these meals are not dried so their weight would render them impractical for backpacking, but they are ideal for canoe trips. The meals are packaged in plastic rather than cans, and are easily heated up by placing in a pot of water on a camp stove. We consumed such culinary delights as spaghetti and meatballs, lasagna, chile, Mexican chile con carne, and beef stew. After dinner we again enjoyed our campfire, and listening to loons serenade us with their wilderness music. The skies were again starry, and we even observed a beaver cruising by.

The theme for our next day was "portage, baby, portage!" We traversed from the South Arm of Knife Lake, to Eddy Lake, to Jenny Lake, to Annie Lake, and finally to Ogishkemuncie Lake. But we loved every inch of it. By now we had the art of portaging mastered. Thanks to our Duluth bags and the light-weight Wenonah canoe, we easily accomplished each portage with two passes. Also, the portages provided a wonderful variety to our overall trip experience. It was almost like a combo canoe-backpack trip. The portage trails were gorgeous as they were lined with birch trees and deciduous vegetation tinged with fall colors, and often paralleled roaring streams containing waterfalls. This day was much more relaxing as we reached our campsite three hours earlier than the previous day. Our camp was located on a small island that provided a long view down Ogishkemuncie Lake, but the *real* view was from a large and tall rock outcropping on the island next to us. After we set up our tents we paddled the 100 yards over to this island to collect firewood, and also to climb up to the top of the rock bluffs to enjoy a great view down the lake. While relaxing on top we watched four people in two canoes pass below us. We had met them earlier in the day as they were out on a day trip. One couple was from Minnesota and they had invited another couple from Colorado on their trip. We watched the Minnesota couple paddle their canoe in a perfect straight line toward the east end of the lake, but the poor couple from Colorado zigzagged all over the place. Apparently the fellow in the stern had not yet mastered the J-stroke!

Hank just about did me in at dinner time. We had brought along some dried vegetable soup, and I had complained the night before about how bland it tasted. Hank dumped a full pack of red pepper from one of the MREs into the soup, causing it to taste like liquid fire. I was very hungry and determined to eat the soup anyway, but I had to swallow a slug of cold water after each spoonful of soup! Hank on the other hand, just gulped his down. It must be nice to have an asbestos-lined throat!

Our next morning started out with light rain, which would continue on an intermittent basis throughout the day. The theme for this day was "burn, baby, burn." As soon as we portaged into Kingfisher Lake, we noted that the large trees and old growth forest were missing. Huge fires had swept through this area, and judging from the size and limb structure of the emerging forest, the burn had occurred about 15 years ago. When we portaged into Jasper Lake the forest landscape did not change. There were almost *no* large trees in sight around the lake. The scene all around us reminded me of what many areas in Yellowstone looked like as it recovered from the massive 1988 fires, and served as a reminder that fire is indeed part of the natural cycle in a wild ecosystem.

Despite the lack of large trees we enjoyed the cascading waterfalls along our portage trails. Our goal on this day was to find a good campsite near the east end of Alpine Lake, which was beyond the big burn area and thus contained old growth forest. With its many islands, bays and narrow peninsulas, this lake presented the most difficult navigating of the trip, and our GPS came in handy more than once. There are absolutely *no* signs or markings of any kind in the

BWCAW, which frankly, I found refreshing. You are *on your own* here when it comes to following canoe routes, finding portage trail entry points, and finding campsites!

As we neared the portage trail to Red Rock Lake, we came upon what turned out to be the primo campsite for the entire trip. We parked our canoe against a protected rock wall, then climbed up large, smooth boulders to find a bit of paradise. This campsite indeed had it all—level grassy spots for our tents, large trees for protection and shade, house-sized boulders to wander up on for fabulous views, and an ample supply of firewood, which would be sorely needed on this very cool fall evening. The only thing lacking was the fire laid by the previous party, which consisted of four large, green logs and no kindling.

After another dinner of MREs we enjoyed the largest campfire of the trip. The key to a successful fall trip in the BWCAW is dressing in layers, and on this night I layered up to the max, which included my wool shirt, stocking cap and parka. For the most part we had escaped rain, but we were starting to joke that the BWCAW should be nicknamed "The Land of No Sun!" However, our sprits soared as we were treated to a gorgeous burnt orange sunset.

The next morning we awoke to actually find blue skies and sun-dappled shadows skipping across the lichen covered boulders in our campsite. The loons, which had mysteriously disappeared in the burn area, were now back with us, welcoming us to a rare sunny day. We enjoyed our portage along a sunny trail over to Red Rock Lake. It felt great to be back among the stately monarchs in the old growth forest. We had not seen a soul since watching the zigzag canoe on Ogishkemuncie Lake, and now Red Rock Lake was devoid of any human activity as well. After watching a bald eagle soar overhead we paddled up to the perfect lunch stop—a narrow, rock-covered island with a couple of large trees in case we needed shade. The takeout however was tricky. Hank managed to pull himself up on a boulder, then he turned to lift out the Duluth bag that contained our food. Normally when my canoe partner in the bow is exiting the canoe, I plant my paddle to provide stability, but here the water was too deep. Hank slipped into the water dropping the heavy Duluth bag onto the canoe's gunwale, causing the canoe to tip over. Before I knew what was happening I was completely submerged under the overturned canoe. I had wondered why Al had not muttered a single cross word when *he* went under, but now I knew why. The water was so cold I was gasping for breath as I flailed around under the canoe. I had my heavy hiking boots on for the portaging so my kicking was rather ineffective. It was a darn good thing I was wearing my PFD, because that is what kept my head above water. Only when I pulled myself on shore and secured the canoe and gear did I allow a few words to fly, as did Hank. However, the anger quickly passed, and I actually began laughing. After all, I knew that we were prepared. We both had a change of dry clothes in our dry bags, and though the day was very cool, the sun was finally shining. Besides, I had needed a bath!

We changed, wrung out our wet clothes, hung them out on tree limbs to begin drying, and sat down to enjoy lunch in this spectacular spot. As my old Yellowstone friend and NPS colleague, Sam Holbrook, said more than once, "I never got anything wet that didn't eventually dry out!" Nevertheless, the incident served to remind us of two things: 1) be more careful in picking a suitable spot to disembark from your canoe, and 2) *always* use dry bags on a canoe trip! Also, thankfully my camera was secured in a zip lock bag.

We soon completed our last full portage of the trip over to Red Rock Bay in Saganaga Lake, and completed our loop trip by making it back to our "base camp" on Long Island around 3:00 p.m. We promptly informed Al and Rick of our accident as we hung out our gear to continue drying. We all enjoyed a great evening around the campfire—our last in the wilderness. We dipped into Rick's famous "medicine bag" more than once, marveled at the starry skies, and prepared for an early departure the next morning. Trouble is, "Mother/Father Nature" had different plans!

Soon after entering my tent around 10:00 p.m., it sounded like a tornado had again parked over our heads. The howling winds blew *all night long!* We had planned to depart no later than 8:30 a.m., but when I walked over to "The Taj," at 7:00 a.m., trip leader Al Duff was gazing out at the raging white caps. "We aren't going anywhere!" he firmly proclaimed. The blustery cold winds were howling directly into our camp area, so I retreated to the warmth of my tent and sleeping bag.

About an hour later I got back up, pulled on layers of clothing, and returned to "The Taj" to crank up my stove to prepare some coffee and oatmeal. Al, a former weather officer at one point in his Air Force career, continued to study the layered cloud formations. By 11:00 a.m. he thought we had a window of opportunity, but first we would need to haul all of our gear around to the lee side of the island. Launching these fully-loaded skinny canoes directly into the waves was out of the question. We moved our gear about 40 rods to a protected cove around a point on the north side of the island. Then Al and I each soloed empty canoes through the windblown waves around to the cove. After loading the gear in our canoes we carefully eased our way out into open water. We had to cross a distance of one mile from our island over to the main shoreline, where we would have protection from the wind.

To this point the only significant rain that had fallen had occurred at night while we were in our tents. But now a cold driving rain began to pelt us as we braced ourselves against the wind and waves. We all knew we had twenty minutes of hard, concentrated paddling to reach the relative safety along the ragged shoreline. Mentally we had to carefully select our paddling strokes to match the peaks and valleys of the waves, while maintaining our balance and stability. One mistake during this crossing of open frigid water would indeed spell a true disaster, but we rose to the occasion. We then endured seven more miles of paddling directly into a cold, driving rainstorm. Even though I had on my boots and rain gear, I was soaked and cold. There would be no stopping now. The intense physical activity of paddling was the only thing that was barely keeping us warm.

Finally with Gull Lake in sight, as if on cue, first, several mergansers met us in a narrow channel known as the Gravel Bar, followed by two loons who gleefully escorted us along the way while voicing their eerie calls. This was indeed weather suited for waterfowl! It was only appropriate that we were ending a week's journey into one of North America's wildest places to the call of the loon. With two million acres of wilderness to explore, Hank and I knew we had only scratched the surface. We vowed to return.

Common loon, Boundary Waters Canoe Area Wilderness

A Napali Coast Wild Adventure—
The Flea on the Dog

Whenever a visitor asks me to explain the track of the Yellowstone Hotspot, I first ask them if they have ever visited the Hawaiian Islands. It is surprising how many of Yellowstone's visitors have. I then proceed to explain to them that the Yellowstone Hotspot is pretty much identical to what has happened in Hawaii. Over millions of years tectonic plates have slowly shifted to the southwest. So Yellowstone at one time was located in what is now the Snake River Plain in Idaho, and one of these days it will be over what is present day Billings, Montana.

In Hawaii the tectonic plates have done the same thing. At one time the volcano was oozing lava out and building the island of Kauai. Over time as the plates shifted, the islands of Maui, Oahu and finally the Big Island of Hawaii were formed by the erupting volcano. Kauai is the oldest of the islands and today there is no volcanic activity there. Much of the lava rock has eroded and now supports dense vegetation, and for that reason Kauai is called "the Garden Island." On the other hand the Big Island is the newest, and eruptions continue to form the island. So the track of the hotspot can easily be seen on a map as you move from the oldest island of Kauai to the newest island of Hawaii (the Big Island,) just as the track of the hot spot can be seen moving up the Snake River Plain in Idaho to southwest Montana.

When I first visited the islands of Hawaii I was fascinated by the volcanic activity on the Big Island, and its similarity to Yellowstone. But I soon discovered another parallel to Yellowstone while visiting the island of Kauai—wilderness adventure! The northern coast of Kauai is so rugged and lined with sheer cliffs and mountains, that it was impossible to build any roads here. The almost vertical cliffs rise some 4000 feet from the ocean, and this vicinity of the island receives abundant rainfall, so the cliffs are covered in thick, verdant vegetation. With no roads here much of the area is managed as a wilderness by the Hawaii State Park Service. The famous Kalalau Trail skirts this wild and rugged coast for part of the way, but it reaches a dead end after 11 miles. Beyond that the wild coastline, sans roads or trails, extends for another seven miles, until finally a primitive dirt road can be found at Polihale Beach State Park.

I had hiked the beginning mile of the Kalalau Trail once, and could only dream of taking a wilderness trip there. Since the craggy trail dead-ended after 11 miles, I wondered if a kayak trip would be the best way to truly experience this wilderness. The trip entered my "bucket list," but I really did not hold high hopes of ever making it. Then in the fall of 2014 I got a call from my youngest daughter, Alison. "Dad," she excitedly began, "Christoph (her husband) and I have received a wilderness permit for a three day backpack trip on the Kalalau

Trail in mid-May, and we made room for you!" I was extremely excited to receive that news, but I knew those dates might conflict with my spring work schedule at the Old Faithful Visitor Center. I was finishing up the last two weeks of the winter season, and ran the dates by my supervisors. Rich Jehle, the South District Naturalist, left me a voicemail, "OK, we'll be in the middle of training while you are off hanging ten in Hawaii!" Rich knew I had always been there in the past and managed to juggle the schedule to allow me to make the trip. I had the green light!

Next I asked Alison if she and Christoph would consider taking the trip by kayak rather than by backpack. She hesitated and said, "Dad, you know we all have lots of experience backpacking, but none of us has ever been on a kayak in the ocean." However, she agreed that we could conduct some research on the trip to see what was involved. She was certainly correct. I had never kayaked in the ocean, and I knew that not only would this be a new experience for me, but it would offer up risks that I had never encountered. As my good friend and wilderness explorer Roger Jenkins of Bozeman once told me, "kayaking in the ocean is serious shit," which was his way of emphatically letting me know the inherent dangers involved. Roger had been sharing his experience of once kayaking coastal waters in Alaska. At least in Kauai we would not have to concern ourselves with icy waters and hypothermic conditions.

I had taken many canoe trips on Yellowstone Lake, which at times can resemble the ocean, and also the Broken Group Islands in the Pacific Ocean, but there the 125 islands provide shelter from the raging waves and swells of the Pacific. Kayaking along a wild, rugged, vertical coast of the Pacific Ocean would be an altogether different experience for all of us.

We knew that we would have to rent top rate equipment, and that the shuttle was a nightmare, literally requiring a drive from one end of the island to the other. It seemed that Alison was more interested in sticking with the plan to backpack the Kalalau Trail *until* she came across some images of the so-called "Crawler's Ledge" portion of the trip. As we studied photos of hikers on all fours edging along what appeared to be a foot-wide trail along a sheer rocky cliff 1000 feet above the ocean, our interest in ocean kayaking suddenly cranked up a few notches. I'm certain the photos made this segment of the trail at approximately milepost 7 look worse than it really is, but nevertheless, we now had an increased interest in kayaking! Also, I was reading a hiker's guide book on trails in Kauai, and I was intrigued by the author's analogy of exploring the Napali Coast to a "flea on a dog." The author actually *discouraged* visitors from hiking the trail. First, she made the point that most visitors to Kauai have a rather limited time span to explore the island, and hiking the full length of the Kalalau Trail required quite an investment of time. Second, she emphasized just what a difficult trail this was to hike, with an elevation gain of over 5000,' with the same amount of elevation lost (ironically, she did not even mention "Crawler's Ledge" as a reason not to make the hike.) And third, she asked the rhetorical question, "Would you rather *look* at a beautiful dog, or be a flea *on* that dog?" She made the point that to truly appreciate the beauty of the Napali Coast, you need to be out in the ocean, preferably just offshore in a kayak, because for much of the hike along the trail, you are a speck hugging the sheer cliffs, and therefore cannot even see the incredible 4000' mountains that rise vertically from the ocean. Rather, many of the views consist of looking down and out at the Pacific Ocean. After reading this author, I was convinced, I knew that my first choice was to kayak the Napali Coast.

We had no gear or expertise in ocean kayaking, so we would need help. I found just the guys at Napali Kayak, located in Hanalea. One evening after I got off work at Old Faithful, I placed a call and left a voice message. Later that evening the co-owners, Ivan Slack and Josh Comstock, called me back. These two guys grilled me as to our backcountry experience, especially in the ocean. They made it clear that this trip was not for everyone, and was extremely physically demanding; however, they thought we could make it, and could help us make it happen, but only with their plan of attack. They would provide all of the gear—kayaks, paddles, dry bags, life vests, waterproof maps, inflatable coolers, and most important of all, an experienced guide. The guide would accompany us the first day to Kalalau Beach, which in their opinion was the toughest part of the journey. To reach Kalalau Beach was 11 miles by trail, but 7 miles by kayak. If we made this portion of the trip okay, then the guide would leave us on our own for the duration of our trip. Our permit was for a three-day, two-night trip, so the company would pick us up on the afternoon of our third day, when we reached Polehale Beach State Park. Although all of this was "new territory" for Alison, Christoph and me, we decided to give it a try!

The morning before our trip I drove up to meet with Josh and Ivan to pick up dry bags, coolers, etc., and get everything in order so we could begin our trip at 6:00 a.m. the next morning. Alison and Christoph were flying in later that afternoon, so I gathered everything we needed for the three of us. I told the guys that we had a permit to camp one night at Kalalau Beach, and one night at Milolee Beach. Josh pulled me over to the side and offered a suggestion: "I really recommend that you stay at Milolee Beach, and don't attempt a landing at Kalalau Beach. The waves there are quite rough," he said. While I appreciated his advice, to me, Kalalau Beach was the highlight of the entire trip. "Surely we can safely land and launch our kayaks from there," I thought to myself. I would find out later the hard way, that Josh absolutely had good reasons for his advice!

After picking up Alison and Christoph at the Lihue airport, we had dinner at Duke's, then headed to our motel in Kapaa to get our dry bags completely packed so we would be ready to roll. We had to leave by 5:30 a.m. to arrive in

Hanalea by 6:00 a.m. Once we arrived we met our guide Ben, who coincidentally had lived in Bozeman for eight years. He was now a chef on the island of Kauai, and worked part-time as a guide for Napali Kayak. There was one other kayak in our group that consisted of two guys who had a permit to spend only one night, and it would be at Milolee Beach, not Kalalau Beach. We hauled our kayaks down to the water at our launching point, Haena Beach State Park. Here the bay provided protection and the waves were minimal. Ben helped us secure our dry bags on the kayaks, and also gave us some instruction on how to use these unique ocean kayaks. I had once spent some time in an ocean kayak on Yellowstone Lake, but it was nothing like the models we were using here. Since we would be in warm waters these kayaks were "self-bailing." In other words, unlike the sea kayak I had paddled on Yellowstone Lake, I did not have to worry about water filling up the craft. The kayak almost reminded me of a long, floating surf board with holes in it. The thing floated no matter how much water washed over you, and it felt very stable. The craft had a rudder which was steered with your feet.

Josh and Ivan had warned me the previous day to take Dramamine to avoid getting seasick, so I had purchased enough for the three of us to use. We downed the pills with our breakfast sandwich. Alison and Christoph would be going tandem, and I would be in a solo kayak. Ben explained that once we launched we would be in a two mile "shakedown" portion of the journey. Once we headed out we would be out on the open ocean for two miles before we passed Ke'e Beach, which would be the last opportunity to "bail out." After Ke'e Beach, the last road access, it would be 18 miles before another landing near a road was possible. Although there would only be three kayaks plus Ben in our group, we were launching at the same time with the "day trip," which was being led by a couple of other guides. That trip went the *entire* distance of 18 miles in only one day! Though they had less gear on board, I did not envy such a long daytrip, and was glad we were planning to spread our trip out over three days. Once we got out on the open ocean it took us a few minutes to get the hang of using our feet to steer the rudder, but we soon felt comfortable. As my kayak began to ride up and down the swells, I was glad we had taken their advice on avoiding seasickness. As I looked around at the incredible beauty of our setting on this beautiful morning, I almost had to pinch myself to believe this trip was actually underway.

After two miles of paddling we neared Ke'e Beach. Ben asked the five of us how we were doing. Everyone was grinning from ear to ear. "This trip is a go!" I shouted to Alison and Christoph. However, Ben said that two members of the day group had already gotten sick and were pulling in. Since the day trip had lighter gear, they gradually pulled away from the five of us, which was fine with me. As we approached the famous Hanakapiai Beach, I was surprised at just how rough the seas had become compared to the conditions at our launch site at Haena Beach. We were now experiencing five foot swells. At one moment Alison and Christoph would be high above me on the peak of a swell, while I was down in a trough; then moments later the situation would be reversed. Despite the rough conditions I was in a pure state of ecstasy for three good reasons. First, the magnificent jagged cliffs rising above the ocean were simply breathtaking. I was so happy we were not fleas on the dog! Second, with my history of so many hair-raising canoe trips on the ocean-like and ice-cold Yellowstone Lake, it was so wonderful not to worry about our craft taking on water. The water splashing over my lap was delightfully warm. And third, while we may not have gotten sick anyway, I was tickled that we had taken the precaution of swigging down a few Dramamine tablets. None of us felt sick at all in the big waves.

Ben led us over close to shore where we could get a closer look at some waterfalls and sea caves. He asked us to stay put as he paddled right up to the entrance of a sea cave. Josh and Ivan had mentioned these unique sea caves. However, as I watched the waves crashing against shore, I was doubtful that Ben would wave us in. I was right—Ben paddled back out to us and said that given the rough seas it would be too risky. He got no argument from us. We had been out on the water for a couple of hours, and I realized that nature was calling. "Hey Ben," I asked, "What do we do if we have to pee?" As soon as the words left my mouth I felt rather dumb, but Ben quickly answered my question. "You just ease into the water then climb back up on your kayak." The reason I felt dumb was I was already sitting in a puddle of warm water in my boat. I was pretty much soaked from my chest down, so why in the world would I climb off my kayak to urinate? On the other hand, ladies being ladies, Alison opted to do just that. Ben gave them instructions on how to pull it off. "When you get back in the boat, be sure to swivel your hips to ease back into your seat. Don't try to climb up on top of the boat and *then* rotate around to get in your seat. If you do that you'll turn over. And if you *do* turn over, no problem. You each need to simply reach across the boat and pull it toward you righting the ship. Then, you each climb up on top using the swivel hip to ease back into your seats." Alison and Christoph then proceeded to perfectly demonstrate how to turn the kayak over, turn it back up, the swivel into their seats. It was a job well done and I appreciated the demonstration.

We had hoped to reach Kalalau Beach by lunchtime, and by noon we had reached our destination. The spectacular setting before us was almost otherworldly, as we looked out at the blue waters of the Pacific Ocean rolling into a broad sandy beach with vertical, jagged green slopes rising 4000' above. However, as I gazed at the size of the waves rolling in, I thought back to Josh's urgings that we not attempt to land here. I was about to attempt something I had never tried before—landing a kayak on an ocean beach with big waves.

The closest thing I had done to this was attempting to land a Grumman aluminum canoe with my friend Al Duff on the coast of Florida near Cape Canaveral National Seashore. I was in the bow as we attempted to "surf" about a three foot wave into shore. Al, who had recently been transferred to nearby Patrick Air Force Base, had told me he had tried it and it was great fun. All I know is, once we "caught" the wave my bow dug straight down into the ocean, and out of the corner of my eye I could see Al above me as he was in the process of being "pole-vaulted" over me. It was quite the maneuver—one that we probably could not have pulled off if we had tried. We had succeeded in pitch-poling the canoe, stern over the bow. Naturally, I went crashing down into the surf, and got a face-full of that glorious white sand that makes the Florida beaches so famous. The canoe slammed onto my back as I rolled around in the surf, taking in a couple of gulps of fresh, salty Atlantic ocean to help wash down that sand. It was *not* an enjoyable experience to say the least!

As I watched the big six foot waves rolling under me as they headed crashing into the shore, I wondered if I was about to duplicate my Florida pitchpole maneuver. Ben looked at the size of the waves and I could tell by the expression on his face that he was concerned. Of course, he had his hands full. Not only did he need to see us get safely to shore at Kalalau, but then he would still have to accompany the other two guys in their kayak another five miles down to Milolii Beach. Those two guys had become an enigma. They were both muscular and looked quite fit, but as the seas had gotten rough, it seems that their coordination in paddling the kayak had gone south. Twice they had turned over and slowed our progress. Once Ben delivered them into Milolii he would still need to paddle another five miles to Polihale to complete his 20 mile day. I did not envy him, or for that matter, the day trippers. Personally, given the rough seas, I was tired and hungry and ready to get on land, make camp, and have lunch. Alison and Christoph felt the same way.

Ben told the two guys to stay put safely offshore, and he paddled with us just outside where the waves were breaking. "Okay," he shouted over the din of the crashing surf, "Here's what we're going to do. I want Christoph and Alison to go first. I'm going to line you up straight into the beach so the waves will come directly behind you. I want you both to look straight ahead and be ready to paddle on my command. When I yell *GO* start paddling like hell! Now, if you flip, *get away from the boat!* You don't want the boat crashing into you." Ben waited for what seemed like an eternity, though it was probably only one minute, then shouted *GO!"* As soon as Alison and Christoph took off I knew they were in big trouble. I could see a big wave rolling toward their back, and it was slightly at an angle to their kayak. Sure enough the wave picked them up and rolled them over. It was like the proverbial garage sale on the ski slopes—the kayak going in one direction, and Alison and Christoph in the other. Thankfully, the dry bags were tightly bungeed down so nothing came loose. There were quite a few folks sitting on the shore observing our attempt to land. As I would find out later there are folks who actually illegally *live* back in the valley of Kalalau, but more on that later. In any event, whenever kayakers are approaching, it apparently makes for some excellent entertainment, so these folks bring their folding chairs to watch the action. But they are also very helpful. Once their kayak flipped some of these folks immediately assisted Alison and Christoph by helping them to drag their kayak to shore. Now it was my turn. Needless to say, what I had just observed did not exactly increase my confidence level!

Ben put me through the same drill and when he shouted *GO* I began to dig my paddle into the water. I didn't make it far, as I was apparently more off-angle than Alison and Christoph had been. It was like the pitchpole incident with Al all over again, except this time with bigger waves and deeper water. The big wave picked me and my kayak up and flipped it over, the full force of the wave crushing me deep into the ocean and underneath the kayak. When I tried to swim back up to the surface, I bumped right into the kayak. In my mind I tried not to panic, although I had really never experienced anything quite like this. First of all, I knew that the kayak was not exactly a huge raft, so I told myself to just keep holding my breath until I could work my way around the boat. When I finally made it to the surface, I took a big gulp of air, then I was surprised to see that the kayak was washing onto the beach where Alison and Christoph could grab it, yet I was still quite aways off shore. I was far enough in that when the big waves would come through, I would not ride up and over them. Rather they were crashing down right on top of my head. I leaned over to my side and began a scissors kick, which has always been my most effective swimming stroke. But kick as I might, I noticed that not only was I not making any progress toward shore, I was actually being pulled farther out! Again, in my mind I tried not to panic. "Just lean back on your side and kick. The water is warm, you will be fine," I said to myself. But I was not fine.

I knew that I was caught in a rip current that was taking me out to sea, but my biggest problem had to do with my life jacket, which I had neglected to really cinch down. The PFD was riding up around my neck, so each time a wave would crash over my head, I would go under and inevitably take in a gulp of sea water. To make matters worse, I could see that the currents were moving me to the north end of the beach, where the sand abruptly transitioned into boulders and cliffs. All along I had felt so safe thanks to the warmness of the water, but now I realized I was in big trouble. I squeaked out a "help," but I doubt if anyone could hear me over the crashing waves. However, Alison and Christoph were watching the whole thing unfold, and they could see I was in trouble, especially when one of the locals standing next to them confirmed that I was caught in a rip tide. Alison immediately began to motion to Ben that he needed to kayak in to get me. Ben probably was already on his way, but her frantic arm movements probably sped up his paddling.

When Ben reached me I was so thankful that I had something to hold on to keep my head above the water. Ben had a very nervous look on his face. "You need to come around and straddle the back of my kayak," he said. "Be careful, if we turn over in these waves, we'll *both* be in big trouble!" Since Ben had the big job of escorting kayakers into camps then making the entire paddle in one day, he had a much different kayak from his clients. While my kayak was rather blunt-nosed and wide for stability, Ben's was narrow and sleek, built for speed, not for extra stability. Once I straddled his kayak Ben somehow rode the wave in and delivered me safely to shore. He then turned on a dime and headed back out to sea, whereupon a wave promptly flipped him. He did a quick self-rescue, and made it past the breaking waves, only to find to his consternation that the other two guys had disappeared, apparently deciding to head down the coast on their own! After the three of us gathered up our gear, we headed to the far west end of the beach, where we were delighted to find a wonderful tent site under a shady tree adjacent to a grassy meadow that led to a sandy beach. Nearby was a waterfall for obtaining fresh water as well as rinsing off the salt water from our bodies.

After lunch we took a dayhike up the Kalalau Valley trail, where we marveled at the remnants of past and present residents. As many as 1900 native Hawaiians lived here until the early 1900s, when they decided to abandon the valley. More recently the valley has served as a refuge for a motley mix of folks who attempt to "live in paradise," while dodging officials from the Hawaii Park Service. We found terraced gardens, swings from trees, and a few other amenities, such as old hammocks, folding chairs, etc. After our hike we enjoyed a rinse under the waterfall, then headed out onto the beach to watch the awesome sight of the late evening sun lighting up the 4000' vertical cliffs in a golden glow. After dinner we relaxed by our tents for a while watching some of the locals surf and frolic in the waves. We noticed several of these locals chose to go au natural while out on the beach, but Alison had warned me of this, so it came as no surprise. Just after dark we were surprised to see someone on a jet ski approach shore, then zoom through the waves and up onto the beach. Quite a few of the locals came down for what appeared to be an enthusiastic greeting. It appeared to us that this guy was making a "supply run" for these folks who live in the valley—probably bringing them some food, drink, and who knows what else. These local folks really did not bother me, as they kept to themselves well away from the beach for the most part. Frankly, even though they were located in paradise, I really did not envy their lifestyles. I could only imagine what it must be like to live out of a tent day after day during the rainy winter season.

As night fell and we eased into our tents, I realized that we had enjoyed an incredible day at one of the most gorgeous and special places on planet earth. However, throughout the day, always in the back of our minds, we knew we had to contend with launching our kayaks into those waves the next morning, and this time without Ben around to assist us. In fact, the last glimpse we had of Ben was of him getting smashed and flipped over in the surf, though he made a quick self-rescue and recovery. "Will we be able to do that if we get flipped?" I wondered, as I drifted off to sleep.

We were up at first light, heated up some coffee, choked down some granola bars, and headed down to the beach in hopes of finding calmer waters than we had encountered the previous day. The size of the waves was still of concern, but we had no choice. Some of the locals were already out swimming and surfing. As we pulled our kayaks to the ocean's edge, one of the surfers came over to us and said, "you don't want to launch there, you'll run right into bad waves. You need to come over to the channel—don't you see how the water is choppy in there with less waves?" Ironically, it was the exact spot where Ben had directed me to land, so I guess Ben was also focused on the channel. However, to my untrained eyes, the waves where we had planned to launch appeared to be rather smooth compared to the rough chop in the channel. But before I could express my concern the surfer had grabbed Alison's and Christoph's kayak. "Come on, I'll help you launch," he said. I didn't object. I figured the fellow knew what he was talking about, since he "lived" here. He did not hesitate and wait for any particular wave as Ben had. As soon as he got them pointed straight he yelled, "Now paddle like hell!" After crashing through two big waves, they emerged safely out away from the breaking surf. Cheers erupted from the crowd of locals already down at the beach. Now it was my turn.

I swallowed hard as the surfer pointed me into the waves. "Now go!" he shouted. I gave it all I had but I immediately noticed a very large wave coming straight for me. I was determined to hit it straight on and not at an angle as I had coming in the previous day. I knew if I did that again I would be toast. The wave crashed right over me, hitting me square in the face, but I just kept paddling straight ahead. I managed to reach the next wave just before it broke, and after that I was home free. Again the crowd behind me cheered. Alison and Christoph held up their paddles in celebration. It was a feeling of complete joy. We continued to paddle hard further out into the ocean to avoid any possibility of getting flipped by a wave. In retrospect, we really screwed up. We were so focused on not getting flipped in the waves, that we paddled way too far out to truly enjoy the Honapu Beach, Arch, and waterfall, purported to be the most beautiful beach in the world. No one is allowed to land any type of craft on the beach—not even a surf board, but we had hoped to paddle close to it. By the time we realized our mistake the currents had taken us around the bend. It was about at this point that I began to realize that I would hopefully get to paddle this stretch again. One time just was not going to be sufficient.

Our five mile paddle to Milolii Beach went by rapidly, and the approach here was through a channel that was well-protected. No wonder Josh, the co-owner of Napali Kayak, had advised me to land here instead of Kalalau. It was a piece of cake, but I would not take anything for our camping experience at Kalalau Beach. Milolii was completely different from Kalalau. Instead of a long beach with a valley behind it, there were instead sheer vertical walls rising straight up from the rather limited level terrain. There appeared to only be one other party camping here, quite a change from the busy Kalalau. Coconut palms provided shade for Alison to stretch out and relax, while Christoph managed to knock loose a couple. Once he cracked one open he took a gulp with a huge smile on his face. The milk tasted rather bland to me, but hey, how often did I get to drink coconut milk on a wild beach in Hawaii?

We soon noticed a couple loading up their kayak getting ready to launch, so we walked over to see why they were not going to stay the night. We found that this couple was with another outfitter and they carried a radio, which we did not have. "We just got a call on our radio," the young lady said. "They told us that high winds and big swells are headed our way, and that we need to launch and head out immediately." "You have a permit to spend the night here and you are going to leave?" I asked incredulously. "Yes, we aren't taking any chances," she said, and with that the couple pushed off. Now, instead of relaxing we were on the verge of being stressed out again. "Dad," Alison began, "maybe we need to leave too. I don't want to get caught in bad waves." I looked out at the calm channel and it was hard for me to imagine this was going to change so quickly. Our weather forecast had mentioned building seas, but not until the day *after* we finished our trip. "Tell you what," I said. "Let's just relax and enjoy ourselves, and when the day trippers arrive for lunch, we'll see if they have an update on the weather forecast."

After an early lunch we studied our map and decided to try hiking up a narrow canyon that appeared to be accessible just around the point from our camp. We followed a small stream that had cut deep into a canyon. The going was hot, dry and rocky—no lush, dense vegetation here! Therefore, it came as a shock after hiking about 45 minutes to come upon a clear, ice-cold spring bubbling up next to the little stream. The spring was not shown on our maps. We filled our water bottles and did not bother to filter it. As we continued up the canyon we suddenly noticed a huge waterfall in the distance which became our destination. However, we reached a sheer wall about six feet high that blocked our progress, at least for me and Alison. Christoph scaled it and he made it to the foot of the falls, while we relaxed in the shade of the alcove.

We arrived back at our camp and waited for the day trippers. However, before they arrived a fishing boat pulled up, and two locals hopped out to fish the rocky shoals around the point from which we had just returned. I walked over to them and after exchanging greetings, I asked, "Have you heard anything about the seas getting rough today?" One of the young men replied, "Swells are due to increase but not until late tomorrow afternoon." "That's what I thought," I commented, then told him about the kayaking party getting the call from their outfitter. The young man just shrugged and said, "As long as you leave out of here early in the morning you will be just fine."

By 2:00 pm we watched the exhausted day paddlers arrive for their lunch break. By the time they reached Milolii the kayakers had been paddling for over seven hours without a break. Several just fell out of their kayaks and stretched out on the beach, not interested in eating. I was thankful we had three days rather than just one to cover the 20 miles! I walked over to the guide and asked her about the weather forecast, and her report matched ours. Of course, they were with the same company we were using. After the group left peace and solitude returned to the beach. Later that afternoon I walked past an old Hawaii Park Service cabin, and was surprised to find an outdoor shower that worked! Our day gradually transitioned into evening, and we enjoyed another magnificent sunset over the ocean and a fine dinner, this time without the worry of getting flipped by a wave the next morning. As I looked out over this wild, spectacular, peaceful beach, I had to again pinch myself to realize I was not dreaming of this trip. I was actually here.

The next morning the seas were calm and we eased out into the ocean and headed for Polihale Beach state park. I could not help but feel sorry for the couple who had been needlessly called away from this gorgeous place. The guide for the day trippers on the previous day had warned us that we would probably have a long, hot wait for our shuttle. "There is cell service at Polihale so call as soon as you arrive. It will take them 2.5 hours to get there. They normally don't get there until around 2:00 p.m. If I were you, I would hang out here at Milolii Beach for as long as I could. Man, Polihale is hot!" she had warned us. However, we did not want to take any chances with the sea conditions. For one thing, while things were very easy at Milolii Beach, we had no idea what the landing at Polihale would be like. Sure enough, when we reached Polihale we had some significant swells to deal with, with waves reaching four to five feet. We were all stressed out as we lined ourselves up to surf our way in. This time there would be no one shouting for us to go. Rather, we would line ourselves up square to the waves and take off. This we did with precision and we both made perfect landings to shouts of celebration. We also found that the guide's description of the beach had been way off. It was spectacular with vertical cliffs and plenty of shade. In fact, I found myself wishing that we were camping here for one more night! But alas, our shuttle was on the way. What a feeling of joy and accomplishment as we pulled our kayaks up on the beach and relaxed in the shade of this beautiful beach.

The predicted swells did indeed arrive as predicted a day later. In fact, on our last few days on the island, we made several day hikes including one down the Kalalau Trail for four miles. We passed a backpacker along the way and made some small conversation with him. A few days later as I was about to catch my plane in Lihue for the return trip to Montana, I saw the young fellow in the airport terminal. When I asked him about his trip he told us that we had timed it well. He described a group of kayakers that came in during the rough seas, and just got pounded to bits trying to land. They were unable to launch the next day and a rescue boat had to be called in for them. These kayakers were on their own, as the outfitters never run in rough seas, which apparently lasted for several more days. We had been so very fortunate to safely complete our kayak trip along the twenty miles of wild Napali Coast of Kauai—undeniably an incredible world treasure. The volcanic comparison between Hawaii and Yellowstone was real; however, this was a new type of wilderness experience for me that will forever be ingrained in my memory.

Bob Kistart with his Old Town Discovery on "Lost Paddle Creek"

Journey Down "Lost Paddle Creek"— Montana's Stream Access Law

I suppose I have always had a bit of Tom Sawyer and Huck Finn in my blood. No matter where I travel, whenever I cross a free flowing stream that appears to disappear into wild country, I have the strong urge to pull over, lower my canoe into that stream and start paddling. I was fortunate to spend 31 years of my life in East Tennessee, which is a mecca for whitewater streams that course through remote valleys and canyons. During summers in Yellowstone I attempted to explore every nook and cranny of the far reaches of Yellowstone Lake, Shoshone Lake, Jackson Lake and area streams such as the Madison, Jefferson, Yellowstone, Gallatin and Big Hole. When I moved to Montana full-time in 2006, I came across an interesting article by writer and expedition canoeist Alan Kesselheim in *Outside Bozeman,* in which he described floating small streams that flow completely through private property. Alan stated that the East Gallatin River was his favorite.

The state of Montana is quite unique among Western states and states in general regarding its Stream Access Law, which legally allows recreational use of any stream, as long as the user stays within the "high water mark" in the streambed. The law allows access to the stream from any public road at the bridge that crosses the stream. The law does not allow access by trespassing over privately-owned property to reach the stream. Given the fact that the East Gallatin River flows only a few miles north of the city of Bozeman, I was surprised that Alan listed it as one of his favorite streams to float in southwestern Montana, especially given the proximity of so many other well-known rivers. I decided to give it a try in my 15 foot ABS Mohawk Odyssey whitewater canoe, which if paddled solo, is perfect for negotiating small streams with tight, technical turns. The trip exceeded my wildest expectations, as I enjoyed continuous rotating views of the Bridger Mountain Range, as well as an assortment of flora and fauna. This little stream became a favorite for me as well, and I now enjoy taking my grandson on this trip each June when the streamflow is sufficient, and we usually see white-tail deer, sand hill crane, beaver, bald eagles, hawks, and herons.

I soon began studying maps of Montana to see if there were other small streams that might provide paddling adventures, except I wanted something on a larger scale. I began poring over topo maps, studying large roadless areas of Montana that contained streams flowing through them. Montana is a huge state. In fact, at 147,000 square miles, it is the fourth largest state in the nation, behind only Alaska, Texas and California. I found several possibilities, but one particular stream truly intrigued me. The stream flowed over sixty miles through a remote stretch and appeared to only have one primitive road that crossed it. As I studied topo maps it appeared that the stream flowed through some significant narrow canyons, and dropped at the rate of about 25 feet per mile. From my past extensive experience paddling small streams in East Tennessee, I knew that this was a significant drop and could pose problems. It all depended on the nature of the drop. If the drop was continuous from beginning to end, the rapids would probably be mostly navigable. On the other hand, if the stream was a "ledge-pool" stream, where you have long stretches of calm water and then a series of short abrupt drops, then the paddler might find those sections unrunnable. The reason why this was so important was because almost all of the stream coursed through private property. From a legal standpoint, the paddler had to stay below the high water line, and sometimes that is not possible when having to portage rapids.

Since this stream flowed through remote country all on private property, there was absolutely no information available anywhere, not even on the internet. The more I studied topo maps and Google Earth, the more I realized that a huge adventure was brewing—one that reminded me of the first descent that Hank Barnett and I made on Abrams Creek in Great Smoky Mountains National Park.

I floated the idea of running this stream to several of my friends and most just laughed at me. "What are you going to do if you get several miles downstream in that remote country and you get bouldered out?" was a typical question asked of me. I found no takers and I was not going to try it solo. Then one day while working at Old Faithful, I was talking to Seasonal Ranger Bob Kistart, who runs the Backcountry Office at Old Faithful, about canoe trips. Bob and I shared a passion for paddling wild country, and he always brought his 16 foot Old Town Discovery ABS whitewater canoe with him to the park, and often enjoyed running streams north of the park in Montana on his days off or at the beginning or end of his work season. Just for fun I pulled out a map and showed him the stream I was interested in. Unlike my other friends Bob immediately expressed an interest to give it a try. He said he had a good friend, Norm Miller, who lived up in Livingston, Montana, who paddled streams all over Montana, the Northwest, and even up in Canada. "I'll bring this up to Norm and see what he thinks," Bob said.

I knew that this trip was full of risks. Short of renting an airplane or helicopter, which I was not going to do, there was simply no way to discern if the trip was even possible. If the stream was not runnable then we would be stuck in the middle of nowhere with no way out. The fact that the land was so remote and privately owned presented a huge problem for us. My friend Lou Regnerus has lived in Montana for over fifty years, and has hiked, backpacked, paddled, fished and hunted from one end of the state to the other—north to south and east to west. Lou was familiar with a few of the landowners in this region and advised us that they did not allow access to any recreational use, including fishing and hunting. "If you get stuck back there and have to walk out across their land, you may have hell to pay," Lou advised me. So Bob and I continued to discuss the trip but talk is all we did. No plans were made to give it a try. Then while working at Old Faithful during the early spring of 2015 the situation changed.

I had been on the job for a couple of weeks when Bob rolled in for his season of work, which typically extends from mid-May through late September. During the winters Bob works for the National Park Service at Bent's Old Fort in Colorado. It is always a joy to see Bob's trusty Dodge truck with his Old Town canoe perched on top arrive at Old Faithful. Bob almost reminds me of Buffalo Bill Cody. He is a big man with long flowing whitish-blonde hair, mustache and goatee. With his wide-brimmed bangora western hat, Bob is easy to spot in a crowd. After Bob had settled into his quarters that evening we met at the Bearpit Lounge in the Old Faithful Inn to catch up on each other's activities. Of course the topic of our proposed canoe adventure came up, but this time there was a significant new twist. Bob had recently talked to Norm who had some important new information. By chance Norm had run into a couple of young fellows who *claimed* that they had run the lower 20 mile stretch of this stream without any great difficulty. Since Norm did not really know these guys we did not place a great deal of stock in their report, but it was just enough to tip us over the edge. We were now willing to give the trip a try. Given the small size of the stream we knew we had a small window of opportunity for floating it before the water level was too low. We decided to pick the third week in June for our adventure. Given the severe logistics involved we decided to utilize three boats and three vehicles. I would solo in my 15' Mohawk Odyssey, Bob and Norm would go tandem in Bob's 16' Old Town Discovery, and Norm's friend Kris would go solo in her kayak.

Due to the long shuttle, we staged for the trip the night before and began the vehicle shuttle at first light. We hoped to make the trip in two days, camping one night on a sand bar below the high water mark along the way. One thing in our favor in case we ran into difficulties in negotiating the stream was the fact that we were making the trip at the summer solstice, so we basically had sufficient daylight for paddling from 5:30 a.m. until after 9:00 p.m. On a gorgeous June morning, we drove to the put-in at the one bridge that crossed the stream along the primitive dirt road. There was a very small area to park and "NO TRESPASSING" signs were posted. We all walked out to the bridge to gaze at the small stream. We had agreed ahead of time that we were not going to try anything stupid. If the stream looked too rough or the water level too low, we would make alternate plans and go float a larger more proven river somewhere else in the region. It appeared to us that there was a sufficient flow of water, but one problem that concerned me was the fact that there were lots of jagged rocks at the put-in. We would have to lower our boats down a steep bank over these rocks then launch in a shallow rocky section of stream.

Whitewater ABS canoes always leave behind color on the rocks. As I studied the rocks leading down to the stream and in the water, I could not find a smidgeon of color on any rocks. "Had these guys Norm ran into really floated this stream?" I wondered to myself. On the other hand, the stream did appear to have sufficient flow and at least in this beginning stretch we could see no rapids of any great difficulty. So we nervously unanimously decided to give it our best try.

We left Norm there with our three boats and gear. Bob, Kris and I drove all three vehicles to the takeout site at the next road access some 20 miles downstream. Here we left my truck along with Bob's, then we traveled back to our put-in site in Kris' truck. It was a good thing that we had met and staged near the area the night before, because we began our shuttle at 6:00 a.m. and did not get in the water until after 11:00 a.m. That's how remote the country was we were traveling through. Near the put-in we received a pretty good idea of how the landowners felt about trespassing when we came across a large hand-painted sign that read, "Prayer is the Best Way to Meet the Lord, but Trespassing is Faster!"

After almost four hours of negotiating narrow primitive dirt roads, we arrived back at the put-in site in Kris' truck, and immediately were concerned by the pained expression we saw on Norm's face. Norm told us that a landowner had come by and lectured him for twenty minutes. He told Norm that this stream was classified as "un-navigable" and that we had better not end up trespassing. He also shared with Norm the many trespassing incidents that he had encountered, where anglers and hunters brazenly walk across his land without even asking for permission. Of course, these types of "slob" hunters and anglers do not help the cause of access in the state. Legally, an angler could walk down into the stream from the bridge and begin fishing below the high water mark thanks to Montana's Stream Access Law. However, the law does *not* allow access to the stream by trespassing across private land to reach it. The landowner was quite stern in warning Norm that we would have to access the stream via the steep rocky bank with the jagged rocks. Initially we had hoped to walk down a gentler grassy slope a few yards away to reach the stream, but the landowner ruled that out.

It took us a good thirty minutes to take our loaded boats down the steep, rocky bank but by 11:00 a.m. we were all in the water. It was decided that I would lead since I had the smallest, most maneuverable canoe, plus I had the most experience paddling small technical streams. Lots of the paddling that Bob, Norm and Kris did were on larger rivers and lakes. As I led out and gazed downstream at the first of many large canyons that we would have to negotiate, my heart began to race. "Just what the hell are we getting ourselves into?" I quietly muttered to myself. On the other hand, the feeling of stress associated with embarking on a great adventure was rather exhilarating. It is one thing to hike a trail or paddle a stream that had copious amounts of information in guidebooks, but it is altogether a different experience to head out off-trail, or *especially* off the grid when it comes to running a whitewater stream! I really did not know what to expect. Anytime I travel in remote wild country, I find it extremely rewarding, whether I'm in the mountains, deserts, swamps, coastal waters, or canyons. It doesn't matter. However, as our stream entered our first canyon, I was awestruck by the beauty of the sheer colorful canyon walls and overhanging cottonwood trees.

Bob had printed out a detailed set of topo maps so we were able to pinpoint our location as the stream made its many tight, meandering turns through one canyon after another. The further we floated the more optimistic I became that those two young guys Norm had run into had indeed been truthful. Despite the fact that I still was not seeing any color left behind on rocks as evidence that someone had canoed this stream before us, it appeared to me that the rate of descent was continuous. If this continued we had a great chance that we would not run into formidable rapids or big drops in rock gardens. We could not have picked a better time to be on this stream, as the flow was sufficient, at least for me, and the water was crystal clear. Bob is a big guy and he and Norm and their camping gear in one boat caused them to occasionally hang up on the rocks in sections that I negotiated with ease since I was in a smaller and lighter boat. Kris' kayak was actually designed more for lake paddling than river running, but she was proficient in skillfully maneuvering through the tight turns. In fact, on several rapids Kris and I would blaze right through but then have to wait for Bob and Norm, who had to walk around some boulders in midstream.

By 2:00 p.m. we reached a gorgeous sand bar at the bend of the stream. Looming overhead was the sheer wall of a canyon with wonderful views of wild country in all directions. There was no sign of civilization in sight. We figured that we had covered about six miles and decided to take our lunch break in the shade of the canyon wall. This spot would've made a spectacular campsite but we knew we needed to put more miles behind us, especially since we knew that we could face obstacles to our progress at any time. Although we knew we were only four miles from the halfway point of our trip, we had unanimously decided to paddle until about 5:30 p.m. before starting to look for a campsite. After a nice break we reluctantly left this ideal campsite behind and continued downstream.

We paddled two more miles through colorful canyons with few obstacles in the stream. My biggest fear had been that we would encounter steep drops in a narrow canyon choked with boulders, but this had not been the case. However, our first serious obstacle was about to be met and since I was the lead paddler, I would be the one to get the unpleasant surprise. I entered a strong class II rapid with a blind turn to the right. Blind turns in a rapid on a new stream are unnerving, but given the consistent nature of the streambed so far I decided not to pull over. That turned out to be a mistake, because as soon as I rounded the turn, immediately ahead was a barbed wire fence that stretched completely across the stream. I dug my paddle into the water and just barely managed to make it to the right bank in time to avoid being swept into the fence. I jumped out of my boat and ran back along the shore to signal to Bob, Norm and Kris to pull over. The fence extended all the way down into the water, and if I had been swept into it, it would have been a life-threatening situation. After getting word to the other three to pull over upstream, I have to admit that my next reaction was that of pure anger. The fence reminded me of my time in Great Falls, Montana during the 1970s when I had unsuccessfully attempted to float the majestic and now famous Smith River (see "Finally—the Smith!"). That river also traverses private property and during the 1970s I had read that one of the biggest hazards to floating the Smith had been barbed wire fences that landowners strung across the river, sometimes intentionally placed right at the water line so as to puncture rubber rafts.

    I taught Principles of Economics at the college sophomore level for 35 years, and I fully appreciated the importance of private property as an institution of the free market system; however, my views had gradually shifted over the years. I have always respected the old saying that "we don't own the land; rather, we only borrow it from our grandchildren." Even back in the 1970s, I had a hard time understanding why large landowners would resort to such drastic measures as stretching barbed wire fences across the Smith River. Did those landowners think they owned the river in addition to the land? Apparently so. Then, after I moved to Montana full-time in 2006, I observed that the "old" Montana was changing. Billionaires, who made their fortunes elsewhere, were now moving into the state buying up huge parcels of land. Folks who had previously been able to receive permission to hunt or fish on private lands were no longer being allowed access. Some of the landowners were attempting to block access not only to rivers, but also to public lands in our national forests. Sometimes these landowners would successfully lock up access to surrounding public lands, then charge exorbitant fees to enter via private property so that only the wealthy could hunt or fish in the area—not a bad business model. As I now stared at the barbed wire fence that had almost engulfed me, I said out loud, as if the landowner was standing there on the bank, "mister, you may own all of this land, but you *do not* own this beautiful free-flowing stream!"

    Of course, my statement was only valid because of Montana's magnificent Stream Access Law, which, incidentally, wealthy and powerful interests continually attempt to dismantle, but more on that later. Our immediate concern now was, how were we going to get around this fence, which extended all the way down steep banks on both sides of the stream? There was no way we could get our boats and gear over or under the fence on land, so it appeared that our best chance was to pry the wire up from the stream, and slip our boats and ourselves under, which we managed to do but not without great difficulty.

To this point we had not observed any cattle, but we assumed this fence was in place to prevent cattle from crossing the stream later in the summer when the water level is much lower. As we prepared to push off I could not find my paddle. During the stress of bailing out I could not remember where I had left it. Did I carry it with me when I ran around the bend to warn the others of the hazard? Had I stuck it in the sand on the beach where I bailed out? After several minutes of searching with no success, we finally assumed that I had inadvertently knocked it into the stream while working our boats under the fence. However, as we continued downstream several hundred yards in slow moving water, it eventually became obvious that the paddle must have been lost somewhere around that fence. I vowed to conduct a much more thorough search the next time I floated this stream. The paddle was not just any paddle. It was the paddle that my colleagues had presented me at my retirement at Walters State Community College in May of 2006. It is for this incident that I call this stream "Lost Paddle Creek," because I would never want to encourage anyone to attempt this particular trip. The dangers are many as I will summarize at the end. Besides, this book is a book of stories, and is not intended to be a guidebook.

Thankfully, I had a good backup paddle, or I would have literally been "up the creek without a paddle!" I concentrated on keeping a good grip on my only remaining paddle as I maneuvered through the rapids. My close encounter with the barbed wire fence caused me to sharpen my focus as I gazed downstream. I would not allow myself to be surprised again. Before our trip was over we would encounter about ten more fences, but there were no more close calls. A few times it was very difficult to see the fence, especially if there were no vertical posts on the wire. In each case we were able to pry the bottom strands of wire high enough to slip our boats under.

As planned, at around 5:30 p.m. we began looking for campsites, and by 6:00 p.m., we found a nice sand bar on the bend of the stream, and pronounced it home for the night. At this point, we figured we had covered about 14 miles in seven hours of paddling. Here, the character of the stream changed dramatically. We were now completely away from any canyons, and green, rolling country extended away from us as far as the eye could see. I often rate campsites on a scale of ten, and the one where we had taken our lunch break was perhaps about an 8. Our selected site was about a 6.5, mainly because there were no trees or shade, but this did not concern us this late in the day. In fact, as it turned out we enjoyed a spectacular sunset later that evening. As the evening approached and the temperature dropped, Bob built a small campfire out on the sandy beach. We toasted our trip to this point, enjoyed dinner, then it was time for stories. I'm usually the story teller, but these guys had me beat. Since Bob performs living history programs at Bent's Old Fort, I enjoyed listening to his stories about trappers and mountain men. Norm and Kris have traveled extensively by canoe to retrace the routes of early explorers, especially Lewis and Clark, so it was great to listen to them share their adventures, experiences and knowledge of early pioneer exploration in the West. Prior to sunset the surrounding hills were bathed in gold light. There was not another soul in sight. For all practical purposes, we *were* those early explorers, except our boats were ABS not birch bark. We had encountered numerous beaver and their sign, so it was easy to speculate just how many early trappers had traveled this country back in the early 1800s. Later that evening clouds obscured the view of the stars, but the soothing sound of running water made it easy to drift off to sleep inside my small dome tent.

The next morning Bob was up at 5:30 a.m. and had a nice campfire going to warm up next to and enjoy coffee. We marveled at the changing light conditions as the sun gradually lifted above the horizon to the east. A shower had passed over during the evening, so we attempted to dry things out before packing up and getting back on the river. With six miles to go we figured we had perhaps three more hours of paddling, and from our surroundings it appeared that it would be through mostly open country. We were wrong on both counts. We were soon back in deep canyons. Along with the magnificent scenery one of the highlights on our second day was when we rounded a bend in the stream to see a huge eagle nest in a cottonwood tree overhanging the bank. We saw first a mature bald eagle but then noted that perched on a branch right along the shore was an immature yet large eagle. We floated right past him without making any paddling strokes. The eagle made eye contact with us and did not budge from his perch as our three boats floated past. It was truly a moving experience for all of us.

As we neared the end of our trip I was amazed that other than having to deal with the fences across the stream, neither Kris in her kayak nor I in my canoe had needed to make a single portage! Bob and Norm had lined their canoe a few times given the weight they carried. We had encountered a large cottonwood tree that had fallen across the stream, but it was high enough for us all to pass underneath; however, my streak was about to end. Our stream entered yet another narrow section of canyon and we all heard a loud roar ahead. From our vantage point it appeared that the stream made quite a drop ahead. I pulled over, climbed up the bank, and sure enough, we had about a four foot waterfall dead ahead. From past experiences on other rivers, I knew we were looking at about a one hour portage to get around this waterfall. In this narrow canyon we basically had two choices: carry our boats and gear around the waterfall, or portage the gear and attempt to run the boats over the falls. After much discussion we finally decided on the latter. After we carried the gear down below the falls, Norm, Bob and Kris positioned themselves along the streambank with a throw rope, and I returned to run both boats through. I had no trouble going over the falls solo in Bob's Old Town; however, my 15 Mohawk Odyssey was smaller than Bob's Discovery and not as stable. I entered the top of the falls exactly where I wanted to, but as I paddled out over the brink I somehow leaned the wrong way and over I went! Norm quickly had the throw rope out to me, plus the water was not that deep. We bailed out the water and I was completely soaked, but it was not a cold day plus everything I had on was synthetic and fast drying.

After the excitement of negotiating the falls we continued our paddle, and soon could see the bridge where our vehicles were parked. For two days and over 20 miles, we had not seen a single soul once we left our put-in. I was thankful for Montana's Stream Access Law. Without it there is no way that we could have enjoyed our great adventure on "Lost Paddle" Creek. However, given the wealthy and powerful interests with connections in the Montana State legislature, the law will require constant vigilance. There is one organization in particular that dedicates itself to protecting the law, and that is the Public Land/Water Access Association Inc. or PLWA, a citizen group organized and operated under the Montana nonprofit corporation act. If you care about continued access to streams and public lands in the state of Montana, you should consider joining this outstanding group. Annual membership dues are only $20.00, and much more information as well as their current newsletter can be found at their website: pwla.org.

The law has made it possible for me to enjoy day paddles with my grandson on streams such as the East Gallatin River, and to search topo maps for adventures such as the one described here. Finally, the reason I did not reveal its location is because the stream flows over twenty miles through wild, inaccessible country. If you found yourself on the stream at a water level that is too high, the dozen or so barbed wire fences would be deadly hazards. On the other hand, if you traveled the stream when flows were too low, you would find yourself stranded on rugged private land many miles from any road. Nevertheless, the opportunity for such a paddling adventure is present in Montana, not to mention anglers being able to access streams for fishing. Montana's last two governors, Brian Schweitzer and current governor Steve Bullock, are strong supporters of the stream access law. Schweitzer once told the New York Times, "If you want to buy a big ranch, and you want to have a river and you want privacy, don't buy in Montana. The rivers belong to the people of Montana." It will take this type of leadership and political courage in the future for Montana to successfully ward off attacks by wealthy and powerful special interests. Montana's stream access law is a wonderful statute that the vast majority of Montanans enthusiastically support.

Part III

Through the Seasons

Grizzly bear tracks along the Cache Creek Trail

Autumn

Way Down in the Fall in "Bear Valley"

During the 1970s some of my greatest Yellowstone backpacking adventures were in early to mid-September. Those trips through Thorofare, across Big Game Ridge, up the Bechler Canyon, along the Absaroka high country, and on Yellowstone Lake led me to realize that fall was the wildest and best time of year to explore Yellowstone's backcountry. The meadows are tinted gold, the days are short with brisk if not downright cold evenings, the pesky bugs are gone, the elk are bugling, and the bears are getting serious about finding food. However, after I moved to Bozeman in 2006 and began to venture out in mid to late October, I found that another layer of wildness was added to the fall adventure. Because when you go out way down in the fall, winter can descend onto the landscape at any moment, and I don't mean one of those quick snow showers that melts off in a few days.

In mid-October of 2006 I had a great backpacking trip set up with my friends Jim Horan and George Heinz. Jim was a former backcountry ranger and I had met George as a colleague while working at Old Faithful. Our plan was to make a three day, two night semi-loop trip in the northeastern section of the park. We would begin at The Thunderer trailhead, climb up and over the pass just east of The Thunderer, descend down to Upper Cache Creek patrol cabin for the first night, then continue down the Cache Creek Valley, until we had to ford it and head up the Lamar River until we reached Calfee Creek patrol cabin. On the third day we would hike out via the Lamar River trail, and we hoped we could hitch a ride the six miles back up the road to The Thunderer trailhead.

Yellowstone's patrol cabins are primarily used by backcountry rangers on patrol. Personally, for most of the summer hiking season I would rather camp in a tent than use a cabin. It takes quite a bit of time and work to open up and then properly close down a patrol cabin. It's much easier to roll up your tent and hit the trail. However, during winter or cold, wet conditions, a patrol cabin is a godsend. In order for an interpretive ranger to use a patrol cabin, permission must be obtained from the subdistrict ranger who has jurisdiction for the cabin(s). Over the years most of the subdistrict rangers I have known in the park have been willing to grant that permission as long as you take a radio, and follow protocol such as filing a trip plan with the Communications Center, checking in for messages, wearing an official uniform, taking in needed supplies, completing a backcountry patrol report (which documents visitor contacts, wildlife sightings, and cabin needed maintenance/supplies,) and properly caring for and closing down the cabin. When I use a cabin on my days off, I have always felt that the Park Service is basically getting a "free" backcountry patrol. If I run into someone in trouble or witness a violation of park regulations, I can immediately notify a law enforcement patrol ranger (this has been the case several times.) Also, occasional use of a cabin keeps the critters, such as mice from taking over.

My plans were to depart Bozeman very early, pick up Jim at his home in Livingston, and meet George in Mammoth, where both he and his wife Megan worked. George and Megan both commuted to work each day from their home about 25 miles north of Mammoth. George was off for several days, and had planned to ride with his wife to Mammoth, where we would pick him up. However, when I woke up on the morning of our trip, I thought I had been transplanted to Alabama, such was the ferocity of the downpour I heard outside my window. Worse yet, the temperature was not much above freezing. I knew that the heavy rain in Bozeman would be falling as heavy wet snow in Yellowstone. I discussed the situation with Margaret and she urged me to call Jim and George and postpone the trip. "No one will enjoy themselves in this type of weather," she said. "This trip was your idea so you need to be the one to speak up." I knew she was right. We had lots of miles to cover on this trip, and I have always considered cold rain, sleet or wet snow the most miserable and dangerous weather conditions for backcountry travel.

First I called Jim over in Livingston and asked what he thought about postponing the trip until the next weekend. Jim is one tough dude. He was fine to head out in the miserable conditions, but said he was also fine to wait a week. Then I called George at his home north of Gardiner. Despite the early hour of 6:00 a.m. there was no answer. "Surely Megan has not already left for work," I thought. I decided to call Megan's office in Mammoth not expecting an answer. "Computer Support, Megan" came the answer. "Megan, this is Butch, what are you doing working this early?" I asked. "Oh, I have the early shift today," she answered. "And I suppose George is there waiting for us?" I sheepishly asked. "Yes, he's so excited about the trip, and he's outside in front of the visitor center, expecting you soon," was her reply. "Megan, how is the weather down there this morning?" I asked. "It's a very nice morning," came the unexpected reply.

At this point I apologized and asked her to tell George that based on the horrible weather in Bozeman, we had decided to postpone the trip a week. That night I called George expecting to get chewed out, but he said that he had salvaged the day and not to worry about it. When I asked him if it had rained or snowed at all during the day, he told me that it had not. I felt like a complete fool and vowed to go the next weekend no matter what. Of course, now we were getting on into late October—way down in the fall in these parts!

The following week we had a clear forecast, at least for the first part of the trip, but then a winter front was due to blow in, bringing with it snow and frigid temperatures. If we were lucky we would be ending the trip at the Lamar River trailhead late Sunday afternoon, just as the front arrived. As the next Friday approached, George called to say that a conflict had come up, and he would not be able to go. Naturally, I felt terrible. The following week I picked up Jim in Livingston, and we headed south through Paradise Valley. When we entered through the north gate and drove over to Tower, and then through Lamar Valley, the park seemed absolutely deserted. There were no vehicles to be seen. "Jim," I asked, "does this lack of traffic concern you? What if we can't hitch a ride?" "Oh, someone is always heading up to Cooke City," he assured me. "It may just take longer than usual."

All the way down through Paradise Valley and Lamar Valley, we had noticed that the mountains were white from the previous week's precipitation, but we could not determine if it was just a dusting of snow or more substantial amounts. We arrived at The Thunderer trailhead, parked my truck, and hoisted our packs for the trip ahead. Right away, our first order of business was an icy ford of Soda Butte Creek, followed by a long steady climb up to the saddle just to the east of The Thunderer. As we gained elevation we started to encounter more and more snow, until finally at the top of the pass, we found it a foot to 18 inches deep. "Jim," I said, "maybe it didn't rain in Mammoth last week, but it was obviously dumping wet snow here. I think we made the right decision in postponing our trip after all." Jim agreed with me. We had hoped the snow depth would lessen as we topped the saddle, and began our descent into upper Cache Creek, but if anything the snow was deeper on this side of the mountain. For all appearances we were traveling through a winter landscape. This no longer felt like a fall trip at all.

As we approached Cache Creek patrol cabin, we noted that rangers Mike Ross and Brian Chan were just leaving the cabin on horseback. They had brought in some supplies for late fall and winter patrols. We stopped for a nice chat about the changing weather conditions. Brian was aware of the approaching winter storm, and urged us to keep tabs of it via the weather channel on my portable park radio. The entire landscape around the cabin was wintry. The cabin roof and porch were covered with snow. On this evening the old wood stove would certainly be a comfort compared to crawling inside a tent pitched on top of the snow. Patrol cabins are stocked with canned food and blankets and sleeping bags, but I always carry my own food and my own bedding. After checking in with the Comm Center via my radio, we cooked up our dinner, and then sat around the wood stove telling stories of past trips. Jim had many tales to tell.

Before retiring for the evening I turned on my radio as Brian had suggested to listen to the latest weather forecast. The NOAA station out of Riverton, Wyoming was now issuing a severe winter weather warning. A frigid air mass with strong winds was on the way to northwest Wyoming. It did not sound as though that much snow was forecast to accumulate, but the drop in temperature, accompanied by strong winds, was expected to produce severe wind chill readings of below zero. Such conditions would be ripe for hypothermia and frostbite, and the storm was now forecast to blow in a day earlier on Saturday evening while we were at Calfee Creek patrol cabin, which meant we would face an 8 mile hike into the teeth of the tempest on Sunday. Hiking in such conditions did not worry me as much as whether we would be able to catch a ride back to my truck!

The following morning was *very* cold, the thermometer reading in the single digits. On this day we had 16 miles to cover, and we were somewhat discouraged to head out in such cold, wintry conditions. However, as we gradually followed Cache Creek downstream and lost elevation, we finally emerged from the snow cover into gorgeous deep golden meadows. But just as we were about to begin enjoying the fall scenery, we looked down at the trail. All we could see going up and down our trail were bear tracks. Bear tracks of all sizes—little tracks, big tracks, huge tracks, and going in both directions. The hair stood up on my neck. I looked above me and about 100 yards away up on the hill grazing was a large grizzly bear. It had not seen us. We quietly continued down "bear trail" until soon we saw something below us in Cache Creek. It appeared to be a bison laying down in the creek. I pulled out my binoculars and discovered that it was a bison alright, a *dead* one, and laying right on top of the bison was one of the biggest grizzlies I have ever seen in Yellowstone.

The big bear apparently had been feeding on the bison for some time, and had taken a nap laying right on top of it, perhaps to keep other predators and scavengers away. Then, all of a sudden, we noticed a coyote approaching the bison carcass and the bear from upstream. The bear charged the coyote, running if off, and returned to the bison. The coyote came back and the bear charged again, this time chasing him farther away. Then the coyote circled around the bison and bear, and approached from the downstream side—the same side of the creek Jim and I were on. The huge bear appeared infuriated at the pesky coyote, and this time chased him about 30 yards before turning back. I looked at the coyote and this time noticed a gulley that led directly up to our trail that Jim and I were standing on. We were only about 100 yards up the hill from where all this action was taking place. "Jim," I whispered, "if that bear gets serious about going after that coyote, he will probably chase him right up that gulley to where we are standing on this trail!" "You are absolutely right," Jim whispered back to me, "let's get the hell outta here!"

We quickly and quietly walked as fast as we could down the trail, and rounded a bend several hundred yards away. The trail had now moved away from where we could obtain a view of where the bear had been. "Jim," I asked, "do you want to ease over to the edge of the hill to see where that bear is?" "Hell no!" Jim exclaimed, let's keep hiking, and put distance between us and that bear!" Of course, I knew Jim was right. I would have loved to ease around that ridge that was blocking our view, and enjoy watching the bear and coyote from what would have probably been a safe viewing point. But what if we eased over the ridge and came nose to nose with the bear? It definitely was not worth the risk, so we continued our brisk hike down the trail. There were still bear tracks everywhere. I took several photos of the muddy trail covered in bear tracks, and have enjoyed using the images in my evening interpretive programs in recent years. Once more, we looked above us and saw yet *another* grizzly grazing high up on the grassy slopes. This late in the fall there were no other people around—just us and the bears it seemed.

Finally the tracks disappeared from the trail. Why those bears were concentrated in that particular portion of the valley and what they were feeding on, other than that one bison carcass, I will never know. But I was glad to emerge from this corner of "bear valley!" By now the scenery was more to our liking. We were walking through wonderful groves of aspen, though the golden leaves had long since tumbled to the ground. The golden grasses and the white barks of the aspen provided a beautiful contrast against the deep blue skies. The snow that we now observed was up high on the mountains, where it belonged in the fall!

We had certainly not expected to see another soul this late in the fall, but as we approached the junction of the Lamar and Cache Creek trails, we saw a person standing out in the middle of Cache Creek. He was making extremely slow progress in getting to the south side, where we noticed his partner was waiting, having already completed the ford. Jim and I had been dreading this ford most of the afternoon, but as cool as the day was, the sun felt good. In fact, the day had turned out just gorgeous! We had gone from winter to late fall on this single day, and from the weather forecast, winter would return sometime in the middle of the night. We tied our boots around our necks, rolled up our pants, slipped on our Crocs, and completed the ford in short order. Our hiking sticks, which served as our "third legs," were essential.

When we made it over to the south side of Cache Creek, I looked up and was surprised to see that the fellow was still in the creek. He had made it about three-quarters of the way across, but his progress had slowed significantly. After pulling on my boots I walked over to his partner to ask if they needed any help. "No," the young 30ish looking fellow said, "he is just very slow at fording streams. And actually, he would probably do better if you two guys leave. When he saw you two coming down the trail he was just furious. He was 100% certain that we would make this trip and never see another human being." "Where are you guys from, and where are you headed?" I asked. "We drove up yesterday from Salt Lake City and we have a campsite a couple of miles past Calfee Creek," he said. "Then we plan to hike on down to Cold Creek Junction to camp, before we start heading back." "Have you heard about the severe winter weather warning that is out?" I asked. "Frigid air and strong winds are forecast for later this evening." "No, but we are prepared. We'll be fine," he confidently answered. "Well, I'm an off-duty ranger and my friend and I will be staying the evening at Calfee Creek patrol cabin," I said. "The trail goes right past it. Why don't you guys stop in to warm up and have some hot cocoa?" "Well, I think my friend wants to just get down the trail, but thanks," the fellow said. Although Jim and I had not seen any more bears on Lower Cache Creek, I still shared our numerous sightings and urged them to be extra cautious.

I looked back at his friend still barely making progress across the creek and could not help but worry a bit about just how prepared they really were. It may have been my imagination, but I swear that he was glaring at us as though he was waiting for us to leave. I turned to Jim and suggested that we ease on down the trail to a point where we could get a view back. When we reached the viewpoint we looked back to confirm that the fellow had finally made it across Cache Creek, and was pulling on his boots.

Jim and I reached Calfee Creek just before dark. It had been a long day, and it felt good to get out of our boots, stretch out, and prepare our dinner next to the warmth of the wood stove. We had hot water on for cocoa, but the two fellows from Utah never showed up. Before retiring for the evening I again checked the weather forecast, and it was identical to what we heard the previous night. Sure enough, around 2:00 a.m. the predicted winds began to shake the little cabin. Then we heard ice pellets pelting the windows of our cabin. As I lay there in my warm sleeping bag, I wished the fellows headed for Cold Creek well, because I did not think the next couple of days were going to exactly be conducive to comfortable backpacking and tent camping.

The next morning after putting the coffee on, I stepped out on the porch of the cabin. Everything was white, there was a sideways snow spitting, and it was *cold*! After a hot cup of coffee and a quick breakfast, we closed down the cabin and hit the trail. I had properly prepared for cold weather with one exception. Heeding the adage, "cotton kills," I had opted for nylon hiking pants. However, I had no liner or thermal underwear. Normally, in cold weather, my legs are the last part of my body to get cold, but on this trip they were freezing. Jim and I hiked as fast as we could straight into the fierce, frigid north wind and spitting snow. The ford of Cache Creek was brutal. After we made it across and pulled on our boots, my worries turned to hitching a ride up to our truck. "Jim," I said, "you can hike much faster than me. Why don't you charge ahead, get to the trailhead as soon as possible, and start trying to hitch a ride?"

Jim left me like I was standing still. I was walking as fast as I could go, but I could not believe the distance Jim put between us, as he streaked across the open sagebrush flats on his way to the trailhead. He was but a speck in the distance, when I saw him arrive at the road. I finally made it to the trailhead an embarrassing 45 minutes after Jim, but his speed was to no avail given the complete absence of traffic. Another thirty minutes passed. It had now been well over one hour without a single vehicle. I was freezing, especially my legs, as the wind chill dipped close to zero. *Finally*, we saw a vehicle approaching. I decided to step out into the road and wave my arms, rather than just stick out my thumb. A pickup truck with Montana plates stopped, and when a young fellow rolled down his window, we told him of our situation, and that we could certainly use a lift up the road. "Sure," the young fellow said, "hop in." It turns out that this young man was from Montana, but had an athletic scholarship to attend Northwest College in Powell, Wyoming, not far from Cody. He had decided at the last instant to drive the "picturesque route from Montana" by going through the park, and then taking the Chief Joseph Scenic Highway from Cooke City eventually over to Cody and then Powell.

When the young fellow dropped us off, we thanked him profusely, and then hopped inside the truck and cranked up the heater to warm up. As we headed back north in deteriorating weather to our homes in Livingston and Bozeman, we reflected on our late fall adventure—the snow, the bears, the frigid front that blew in, the two fellows from Utah, who we were *still* wondering about, though we never heard of any trouble they had. It had been a great trip. One thing we definitely agreed on—heading out into the Yellowstone backcountry this late in the season adds to the adventure. September is great, but heading out into the woods *way down in the fall* creates an extra spring in your step!

Of Wolves and People—Encounter at Cougar Creek

In 2011 the Museum of the Rockies in Bozeman (a world class museum) sponsored an exhibit titled "From Wolf to Woof." The exhibit revealed that all dogs evolved from wolves, which is amazing considering how so many folks in the three states surrounding Yellowstone absolutely love dogs but hate wolves! I moved to Bozeman, Montana full-time in 2006, ten years after the reintroduction of wolves to Yellowstone, and immediately began to appreciate the wide chasm that existed between those who supported the return of this keystone predator, and those who detest wolves. While working in the park I have rarely encountered wolf haters. Most visitors strongly supported the return of the wolf, and were excited to see them in the wild. I also observed that whenever a member of our staff gave an evening program on the topic of wolves, the auditorium was usually packed.

I even occasionally ran into ranchers who supported the return of wolves. One day I had an interesting conversation with a rancher from the Madison Valley near Ennis, Montana. He said that prior to the return of wolves, he would often have a serious problem during the winter with elk "camping out" on his property, and consuming the hay that was intended for his cattle. However, once wolves began showing up in the area, he said that the elk dispersed, and no longer congregated in his fields and eating up his hay. So here was a rancher who actually reported benefits from wolves returning, though I feel certain he would fall in the minority if all ranchers were polled.

Since their reintroduction in 1995 wolves have been a popular topic of discussion among park visitors, and it has been rewarding to discuss the key role that this predator plays in the Greater Yellowstone Ecosystem. For example, biologists are beginning to see changes that are most likely directly attributable to wolves once again roaming the Yellowstone Plateau. The great American conservationist John Muir once made this profound statement: "When we try to pick out anything by itself, we find it hitched to everything else in the Universe." Wolves have reduced the number of coyotes, which has resulted in an increase in foxes; with less coyotes, we see more snowshoe hares which has led to more lynx sightings; wolves have been a contributing factor in the decline of the elk population, which has resulted in an increase in deciduous shrubs and trees such as aspen, cottonwood and willow. This has resulted in an increase in beaver, which has resulted in more beaver dams and wetlands, all of which have benefited songbirds. Grizzly bears have seen their consumption of meat increase since they frequently displace wolves from kills. Biologists are confirming that John Muir had it correct. Things *are* connected and Yellowstone is a great place to observe these natural processes.

However, when I am not working in the park and am tooling around Southwest Montana, the intense negative attitude regarding wolves is often encountered. There are lots of enthusiastic elk hunters in Southwest Montana, and many of them look at Yellowstone as some type of elk farm that should produce lots of elk for them to hunt when they migrate out of the park. Such hunters simply view the wolf as an undesirable competitor. One evening Margaret and I were attending a potluck at our church and a group of my friends who hunt elk were over in the corner just lambasting wolves. I walked over to them and said, "You know, the Good Lord included wolves on our planet, do you think He made a mistake?" Boy that sure put an end to that conversation!

Sometimes I would read statements about wolves from some of our state legislators in our local newspaper that I knew were outlandishly in error. I once called up the state representative from my voting district west of Bozeman, and quizzed him about his extreme anti-wolf statements. Try as I might I found it impossible to logically discuss wolves with him. He basically had the attitude that wolves were going to take over the state, eat up all the elk, then come after our children waiting at school bus stops! Of course, such politicians are merely reflecting the attitudes of many of their rural constituents who harbor strong negative feelings regarding wolves. Local politicians even attempted to remove "wolves" as the long-held official mascot for Three Forks High School! Ranching and elk hunting are huge parts of Montana's economy, but so is tourism and many visitors come to the Yellowstone with the hope of seeing wolves in the wild. Politicians are certainly entitled to their views, even when they border on what many people refer to as "barstool biology." However, it is discouraging when views not based on sound science begin to turn into policy. The Montana state legislature occasionally introduces and even passes legislation that is based on emotion rather than science.

Montana's Department of Fish, Wildlife and Parks is responsible for managing wildlife, including wolves, in the state beyond the Yellowstone National Park Boundary, even though most of those lands are in our national forests—public lands owned by *all* Americans, not just those from Montana. When the agency authorized a hunting season for wolves in late fall of 2012, several collared wolves were legally shot just north of the park's boundary. Yellowstone's biologists had GPS tracking records from those collars for the past several years that showed those wolves had rarely ever ventured outside the park's boundary, and had never taken any domestic livestock. One of the wolves killed was known locally as a "rock star" wolf, given its proclivity to make itself highly visible to visitors and photographers in Lamar Valley. This raises another point: such wolves were accustomed to visitors staring at them through spotting scopes, and had never been hunted. Shooting at such wolves violates the "fair chase" principle as defined by the Boone and Crockett Club as "the ethical, sportsmanlike, and lawful pursuit and taking of any free-ranging, wild, native North American big game animal in a manner that does not give the hunter an improper advantage over such animals."

Some of the big strong wolves that were shot were instrumental in teaching younger wolves in their packs how to take down bison instead of elk. Wolves have to use a completely different technique in taking down bison as compared to elk. Once a wolf pack identifies a weakened elk, the pack can take it down within a matter of hours. However, a rather long waiting game is often used on bison that might take a week or more.

Each winter I ski up the Slough Creek valley not far from the park's northern boundary. In recent years I have noted just how intensely wolves had followed along with the bison herds, constantly observing and looking for a weaker specimen to single out and then play the "waiting game" to eventually take it down. I found wolf tracks even up on top of granite rock outcroppings that provided a "bird's eye view" of the bison. However, when I took my ski trip in February, 2013, after several key wolves were shot along the park's northern border, I once again observed plenty of bison, but I could not find a single wolf track anywhere. I thought it ironic that the politicians who wanted to kill wolves so they wouldn't compete with hunters killing elk, had apparently now helped turn a wolf pack from hunting bison back to hunting elk.

The loss of collared wolves serves to cripple the important data being collected on an animal that was once almost hunted, trapped and poisoned to extinction. The placement of collars on wolves is not only a very dangerous operation that requires the use of helicopters very close to the surface, but many private individuals and organizations have contributed significant sums of money to fund the research. While the killing of such wolves right on the park boundary probably would not have a significant effect on the park's overall wolf population, it would have a profound impact on the park's ecosystem and research. The Montana Fish, Wildlife and Parks Commission apparently recognized that there was a problem, and attempted to close the region just north of the park to further wolf hunting. However, politicians intervened— politicians with no training in wildlife management or biology. Of course, some political observers have noted that biologists for the agency are afraid to speak out strongly for scientific management of wolves near the park, lest the state legislature transfer the management of wolves to the state's department of livestock, as has already happened with wild bison.

So just how much of a threat are wolves in the wild to humans? Should we really be concerned about wolves running down our children at school bus stops in towns around Yellowstone? I live in a subdivision about halfway between Bozeman and Belgrade, Montana, and I frequently enjoy walking (or skiing during the winter) a two mile loop through open spaces around my neighborhood. Each time I do that though, I am amazed at the ferocious barking and growling from dogs located in neighbors' backyards, which are fortunately secured behind fences. With bared teeth and raised hair on their necks, it appeared to me that the fences were the only thing saving me from a vicious attack. If these domestic pets could appear so savage, I sometimes wondered how a wolf in the wild, that might weigh up to 150 pounds, would react if a hiker surprised one out in the backcountry. In the late fall of 2009 I would find out!

Over the years fall has become my favorite time of year to head out into Yellowstone's backcountry. For one thing it is so relaxing to not have to deal with mosquitoes, buffalo gnats, deer flies, horse flies, and any other of their pestiferous brethren! The meadows are tinted golden, fresh snow appears on the mountaintops, and the elk are bugling. Grizzlies are also quite active during the fall, so it is always a good idea to hike with a group of three or more and carry bear spray. However, despite my best efforts I could not find a hiking companion, so I decided to set out on my own. I had planned an overnight trip along the Gneiss Creek trail, which begins from Seven-Mile Bridge located halfway between Madison and the West Entrance, and eventually make my way to Cougar Creek patrol cabin for the night. This particular trail features grand meadows with the Gallatin and Madison Ranges serving as majestic backdrops.

I left the trailhead at 2:00 p.m. on a cool, late October day, with a temperature of 33 degrees and light snow falling. The trail traverses through willow flats, stream bottoms, and deep grassy meadows, all of which provide great habitat for moose, elk, and bison, and, of course, grizzlies. I had my canister of bear spray secured on my shoulder strap, and anytime that my visibility was limited, especially in the willow flats, I was careful to make noise. I have found that breaking sticks, banging a hiking stick on a log, and clapping hands, along with the obvious, "Hey bear, here I come," tend to work well. Actually, I think the clacking of sticks on logs carries better through dense vegetation than does the human voice.

After hiking about four miles I had crossed Cougar Creek, travelled through some dense willows, and finally emerged out into an open grassy meadow tinted a beautiful golden-brown hue. I could now easily see hundreds of yards in all directions, so I was able to relax and let my guard down somewhat regarding being alert for surprising a bear. However, I soon noticed that the grass was deeper than normal for the fall; in fact, it was waist deep in places. As I continued I suddenly noticed movement to my right only about 25 yards away! A large gray-colored wolf stood up out of the deep grass. It was almost like an apparition—one second there was nothing there, then, poof, there stood a big wolf just off to my right. I had observed wolves on several occasions before in the backcountry, but usually at quite a distance with binoculars. This wolf was way too close for comfort. Before I could even collect my thoughts as to what I should do, *another* gray-colored wolf stood up to my left. And then came the real shocker: *five* black-colored wolves all stood up right in front of me. This wolf pack had been bedded down in this meadow, and it appeared that I had interrupted their nap! I now had seven wolves standing in a semi-circle around me, all *staring* at me from a very uncomfortably close distance!

Here I was all concerned about surprising a grizzly bear along the way, but I had never considered that I would jump an entire pack of wolves. During the seconds that followed all sorts of thoughts raced through my mind. First, I thought about my canister of bear spray. I had carefully prepared my mind regarding how I would use bear spray if I ever needed to, but that was with a single bear. What do I do against *seven* large wild wolves? I couldn't help but think of all of the letters to the editor in local newspapers regarding how it was just a matter of time before wolves would attack and tear to shreds some poor unsuspecting hiker. Was I going to be that hiker? I immediately thought of those dogs in my neighborhood that charged back and forth against the fence with fangs bared, viciously growling and barking. As I looked at the sheer size of these wolves a chill came over me and the hair stood up on my neck.

But then as my trembling hands rested on my single canister of bear spray, I began to look at the face of each wolf. I noticed that not a single wolf was growling or barking. No fangs were bared. No hair on the ruff of their necks was standing. In fact, these wolves did not even appear to be peeved at me in the least! Here I had come along and disrupted what must have been a rather nice fall nap in the deep grass, but the expressions on their faces revealed not an ounce of anger with this human who had wandered way too close into their space. The expressions on their faces actually seemed to exude boredom.

I had already decided that I was going to let these wolves make the first move. I really couldn't just "back away" because they pretty much had me surrounded! The wolves did make the first move. One by one they walked away from me, eventually gathering on a ridge about 100 yards to the north of me. As they walked away from me, and I realized that an attack was not forthcoming, I quickly snapped a couple of photos. One finally raised its head and howled, then they all disappeared into the forest to the north.

I walked over to a log by the stream and sat down. The hair was still standing on my neck, and even then I was trembling. As I pondered the incredible experience I had just had I began to calm down. I realized that these animals had behaved with a dignity that I find rather consistent among wild animals in Yellowstone, whether it be elk, bison, grizzlies or wolves. I knew that these wolves could have easily torn me to shreds, and no, I don't think my bear spray would have been very effective at halting an attack by *seven* wolves! But these wolves did not growl, snarl or even bark. They simply stood up to reveal the majesty of their size and beauty, looked me over, and casually departed. As I approached the patrol cabin I again looked out over this beautiful valley. The snow had frosted the peaks to the west and north. The temperature was steadily dropping, and I knew that I would be enjoying a toasty campfire on this evening. By the next morning a light snow had coated the surface and the temperature was hovering around five degrees. After entering this rather unique wildlife encounter in the logbook, I closed down the cabin and headed back across the meadows and sagebrush valley toward the trailhead. My senses were on top alert, but there was no sign of the wolf pack.

Over the past several years I have shared this story with lots of folks and on more than one occasion have been told, "You are just lucky those wolves had full stomachs!" However, I think wolves really don't want to have anything to do with humans. Obviously, wolves are wild animals. If I had made a threatening move toward these wolves, I have a feeling that my worst fears would have materialized. Certainly it was not my intent to get so close to a wild wolf, much less *seven* of them. I would never want to get this close again, and in fact, Yellowstone has the common sense regulation that requires visitors to stay at least 100 yards away from bears and wolves, and 25 yards away from all other large animals.

Since this encounter I have observed wolves in the wild, thankfully at much greater distances, and to me it is always a thrilling experience. The wolf is a symbol of wilderness, and belongs in the Greater Yellowstone Ecosystem. However, my view is not shared by many others who live close to this ecosystem. If anything, the negative feelings toward wolves in Yellowstone have become worse since they were first reintroduced in 1995. Given the political landscape that exists in most of the Northern Rockies, I truly believe that in coming years it will be a challenge to maintain a viable and healthy population of wolves in the Greater Yellowstone Ecosystem. After the last wolf was killed in Yellowstone way back in 1926 it took six decades to restore them to their rightful place. The question now is, will they remain?

Mary Mountain and the Shutdown

Yellowstone has around 36 patrol cabins scattered throughout the park's backcountry. The oldest cabins date back to the early 1900s, when the U.S. Army ran the park, and utilized them for patrols to guard against poaching of wildlife. Early maps refer to these cabins as "snowshoe cabins," since many of those patrols were in the dead of winter. Today these cabins are still used by National Park Service staff for a variety of functions. The most important use is for backcountry patrols to assist hikers and backpackers, provide law enforcement duties when necessary, and to guard against poaching—especially during the hunting season in the fall when some hunters somehow "get lost" and wander across the park boundary in pursuit of that trophy elk. Other uses include trail crews working on trails and footbridges, wildlife research, monitoring of thermal basins, and general use by staff. Over the years I have had the opportunity to stay in almost all of the cabins, and I always feel as though I am stepping back in history. This is especially true when you read the entries made by rangers in some of the older logbooks. The rustic cabins are particularly useful during the winter months or during cold, inclement weather.

My friends John and Deb Dirksen, who volunteer each summer for the National Park Service in Yellowstone, had spent several weeks during the summer of 2013 building a new log cabin pit toilet for the Mary Mountain patrol cabin located deep in the park's Central Plateau. I had intended to go in to see them, and also visit the nearby Glen Africa thermal basin to document any changes in activity since my last visit there in 2008, especially in light of the many earthquakes that potentially can cause significant changes; however, the summer got away from me before I could make it in. John told me that they had not finished the project when they had to leave in mid-August for Deb to get back to her teaching duties at Western New Mexico University.

By late September I had completed my seasonal work and was on intermittent duty until I would report for winter training in mid-December. The weather had started its seasonal change, with cold rains and sleet sweeping across the Yellowstone Plateau. John and I always had a term for this kind of weather; we called it "patrol cabin weather." I wondered to myself if I might still make that trip into Mary Mountain cabin, which falls within the jurisdiction of the Old Faithful Subdistrict. Ranger Bob Kistart has run the Old Faithful backcountry office for many years. I knew that Bob was nearing the end of his season, and would soon be headed for Bent's Old Fort National Historic Site in Colorado, where he worked during the winter months. I stopped by his office and soon the discussion turned to Mary Mountain cabin. I was curious to get a progress report on John and Deb's work at the cabin, and I also asked if the cabin had been closed down for the season.

Bob's eyes lit up. "Say, I was planning to get back in there to close the cabin down for winter, but I have some urgent projects around here that need to be taken care of. Would you like to go in and close it down for me?" "Bob," I said, "I would love to. Just tell me what needs to be done." Bob then described the duties: I would need to cut a good supply of firewood for any winter ski patrols, turn the outside table on its side, and lean it up against a tree so the snow would not crush it, and double check that all windows and doors were tightly secured so a late season visiting grizzly could not pry its way into this cabin. This has actually happened in Yellowstone at other cabins, and needless to say, is a complete disaster for the cabin. Over the years I had read logbook entries that described the damage grizzlies had made at Calfee Creek patrol cabin in Lamar Valley and Cabin Creek patrol cabin along the Upper Yellowstone River on the Thorofare Trail. In fact, the damage to Cabin Creek was so severe the cabin had to be rebuilt.

John had also asked me to check to be sure his tools and cut logs were properly stored so that he could complete his work on the pit toilet during the summer of 2014. John and Deb had recently completed building a "log cabin" pit toilet at Cougar Creek patrol cabin.

Mary Mountain was the first park patrol cabin I ever stayed at in the summer of 1971, when Ranger Tom Griffith at Canyon asked me to go in and check on a reported break-in. The cabin is located in the middle of the Central Plateau, so the hike in is about 11 miles one-way, whether you start from the Canyon side in Hayden Valley, or the Lower Geyser Basin on the Old Faithful side. Also, the Central Plateau provides excellent habitat for grizzly bears. Grizzlies frequent the "edge effect" where large meadows meet the edge of forests, and much of this habitat is found along either trail that leads into Mary Mountain cabin. Bob Kistart typically rode horseback into the cabin; however, I would be hiking and preferred not to go solo. Therefore, I was pleased when two of my friends in Bozeman, Bruce Hoffman and Al Frank, said they could join me for the trip and help with the work.

The three of us decided to go in via the Nez Perce trail from the west side. We planned a three day, two night trip to allow sufficient time for work and exploration of the thermal basin. When our departure day of September 30 arrived we faced two complications—one was the threatening weather, the other was the impending government shutdown on October 1, 2013. A fierce weather front was moving through that threatened very high winds with sleet and snow. We figured we had the gear to handle the weather, but the possible shutdown was a different matter. Congress had a deadline to pass spending bills that funded the government, but there was a major disagreement. The Republicans insisted that no spending be approved unless the Affordable Health Care Act, which was passed by Congress and signed by the President on March 23, 2010, was repealed or defunded. The Democrats and President Obama were adamant that they would not agree to any spending bill containing that provision. If Congress did not fund a spending bill, the federal government would be out of money by October 1, which would mean that most functions of government would grind to a halt, including the National Park Service.

I called Bob to discuss the situation. "Bob," I asked, "What happens if we get down there and the park closes?" "Butch," he answered, "just be sure that you begin your trip before the park closes. If the shutdown happens after you are already in the backcountry, you should be able to exit the park with no problem when you come out."

We arrived at the trailhead at Nez Perce Creek at 10:30 a.m. on September 30, the day before the possible shutdown, so the only problem we faced on this day was the weather. It was already raining and strong winds exceeding 45 miles per hour were howling through the woods. We began our hike through a series of meadows, and along the way we passed by a group of hot springs where two rather mysterious thermal deaths involving concession employees occurred, one in 1967 and the other in 1975 (see "On Protecting Thermal Resources"). While out in the meadow the rain began to turn to sleet as gale-force winds almost blew us over. We had to lean into the wind to keep from going down. The sleet then turned into snow and began to accumulate on the trail. On the way in we observed several bison, a huge bison skull, and fresh grizzly droppings, but that's all. Bob had warned us that he had run into a grizzly along this trail when he was riding his horse out a few days earlier.

When we crossed Cowan Creek at the seven mile mark, I had to tell Bruce and Al all about the incredible story of George Cowan, whose group from Radersburg, Montana had encountered Nez Perce warriors during their flight for freedom. Cowan somehow survived numerous gunshot wounds, and managed to crawl several miles to his camp where the U.S. Army found him and provided first aid. The Nez Perce, with 2000 horses and 800 people of all ages, managed to elude General Howard and the U.S. Calvary. Historians still debate today precisely where they traveled across the Mirror Plateau in their escape. However, they were stopped by U.S. Army reinforcements in the Bear Paw Mountains just short of reaching freedom in Canada, and Chief Joseph sadly delivered his famous surrender speech: *"Hear me, my chiefs, I am tired; my heart is sick and sad. From where the sun now stands, I will fight no more forever.'"*

All three of us were damp and cold by the time we reached "heart attack hill," the common description for this section of trail that climbs 900 feet up to the top of the plateau, where the patrol cabin was located. By the time we reached the front door my hand was so numb I could hardly insert the key to the lock. Bob Kistart had been the last person to the cabin, and he had left us a fine "one match" fire, so the three of us gathered around the wood stove trying to warm our bodies after hiking eleven miles through what I consider to be the toughest of conditions—cold, windy, rain, sleet and wet snow. I would have preferred to be skiing through a powdery snow at 15 below zero!

We had envisioned sitting around a campfire after dinner, but snow and sleet continued to fall, so we stayed inside. Mary Mountain patrol cabin is one of those vintage old-style log patrol cabins that dates back many years. According to the website www.secretyellowstone.com, the cabin was first built in 1927. One of the unique aspects of this cabin is the fact that some very old notations are penciled on some of the logs inside the cabin. Typically observations are recorded in the cabin logbooks, which, once filled, are housed in the park archives. As I gazed over some of these "log entries," there were two that stood out. One was made by long-time legendary ranger Jerry Mernin: "Mernin, Hughes 18-19 FEB 1965. 60-70 inches snow. Skied from Nez Perce. Going out to Canyon via Alum." I could not help but wonder how difficult that ski trip must have been with the snow that deep and most likely not consolidated.

The entry that really amazed me though was this one: "Hughes, Coe, Reynolds. Winter Ski Patrol. Soda Butte-Frost Lake-Fishing Bridge-Mary Mountain-Nez Perce-Norris. 24 inches snow. 1/24/60 & 1/25/60." In my mind I tried to conceive of the enormity of that trip. Basically, it was a loop ski tour of most of the park during what is typically the coldest month of winter. From that entry it appeared that these intrepid rangers headed up the Lamar River staying at Calfee Creek cabin and then Cold Creek cabin. The confusion comes with Frost Lake. Cold Creek cabin sits at an elevation of 7400' near the Lamar River. Frost Lake is situated at 9600' up on the park boundary. I've been to both places. The logical route to follow would be to continue from Cold Creek cabin over Mist Creek Pass toward Pelican Springs Cabin. I can understand a patrol during the *fall* up to Frost Lake, but climbing 2200' to go up there in the frigid, snowbound month of January? And where would they go from Frost Lake? The trail continues into rugged terrain in Shoshone National Forest and eventually reaches Pahaska Tepee resort just outside the east entrance of Yellowstone.

I had never heard of a patrol cabin at Frost Lake, so why in the world would those rangers ski up there? However, that mystery was solved a couple of months later at winter training, which was held at the old Mammoth elementary school. During a break I was studying a very old map that students had constructed many decades ago, and to my surprise I noticed that it contained a symbol for a patrol cabin located at Frost Lake. Upon further research I discovered that the Frost Lake cabin had been abandoned many decades ago. At least that helped me understand why these rangers skied up to Frost Lake on their patrol!

But I still could not imagine how they negotiated that steep terrain on skis. Perhaps Hughes, Coe and Reynolds skied up to Frost Lake and returned to Cold Creek before continuing on to Pelican Valley over Mist Creek Pass. One thing is for sure, they must have had a hell of a downhill ski from Frost Lake regardless of which direction they traveled! The entry implies that they eventually made it to Pelican Springs cabin, then on to Lake Ranger Station, and from there to Mary Mountain cabin, to Nez Perce cabin, to Madison Ranger Station to Norris Ranger Station. Perhaps that is where the trip ended. Keep in mind that in 1960 there were few if any over-the-snow vehicles in the park. Such a trip seems amazing to me, but as my friend and notable photographer Tom Murphy likes to point out, it is really no big deal when you consider what the early frontiersmen such as John Colter did in their snowshoes and buffalo robes! Tom should know. He has traversed the park on skis from south to north on more than one occasion.

The next morning we peeked out the front door to see a fresh coating of snow around Mary Lake, but at least it had stopped. We decided to venture out into the valley, check out Glen Africa basin, loop back to the cabin in time for lunch, then get to work on our chores at the cabin. We followed the old Trout Creek road climbing over lots of deadfall before breaking through into the open valley. The sight before us was eerie. On this cloudy and cool day we could see Mount Washburn in the distance, undulating golden meadows, and steam rising from the basin. A couple of bison were wandering through the valley as we made our way down to upper Alum Creek. I first visited here in 1977 and returned a few years later with park geologist Rick Hutchinson. If there were any changes in the springs along the creek, I could not recognize them. We noted several elk and bison skulls, and surmised that with all of the warm thermal grounds, animals must attempt to seek warmth here in winter and/or early spring.

We walked upstream on Alum Creek to the mysterious remains of a small log cabin that had a stone fireplace. The roof was missing. From my conversations with Park Historian Lee Whittlesey, and Lake Ranger John Lounsbury, now retired, I'm not sure anyone knows the full story. It sounds as though the cabin was originally a poacher's cabin, but when the U.S. Army found it sometime around 1890, it was utilized as an early Army scout cabin. One of the key functions of the Army at that time were ski patrols to protect the few remaining bison from poachers. Perhaps the cabin was used in this manner prior to Mary Mountain cabin being built.

Knowing this was prime grizzly country, we were extra cautious as we looped back to the cabin by lunch time. It was now time to work. Bruce is the axe man so he went to work chopping firewood. Al and I split a bunch of kindling and stacked firewood on the porch. We placed the outside table on its end, and also secured John's peeled logs destined to become part of the pit toilet, which we found was almost finished. On this evening the three of us enjoyed a campfire, since the precipitation had thankfully ended. Campfires always mean great stories and we spun several.

The next morning broke cloudy and quite cool, but dry. After tightly securing the cabin, its windows and door, laying a "one-match" fire, baiting and setting mousetraps, we felt the cabin was now safe and sound for the frigid winter snows that would grip this high plateau for the next eight months. We seriously doubted that anyone would visit here again until June of 2014, though winter patrols by rangers and biologists still occur.

Our hike out was rather uneventful. We saw a number of bison but no elk or grizzlies. Descending "heart attack hill" was certainly easier and we made good time. We found my truck in good order at the trailhead, loaded up and headed out on the Old Faithful-Madison road. We noticed a large herd of bison on the west side of the road out in a meadow, but when we did not see a single person or vehicle in either direction, we immediately knew that the government shutdown had indeed happened.

On our way to the west gate we stopped to look at a big bull elk rounding up its harem. Normally, we should have seen dozens of vehicles stopped with visitors snapping photographs, but there was not a soul in sight. When we reached the west gate, sure enough, we observed that it was locked on the entrance side. The exit lane was open and we drove through, then stopped to look at the sad scene. There were dozens of cars and buses lined up staring at the sign that read "Yellowstone is closed due to government shutdown." A few rangers along with Yellowstone Association volunteers were talking to visitors, many of whom were international. I personally saw one family from Australia explaining that this was their trip of a lifetime to come see the wonders of Yellowstone.

I don't think I have ever been more embarrassed or ashamed of my country's politicians than I was on this day. Only a few months earlier Margaret and I had taken our own "trip of a lifetime" to Australia and New Zealand. What if we had been denied entry to their great wonders, such as the Great Barrier Reef, due to political squabbling? How would I have felt? When I first started working in Yellowstone in 1968, visitor use was mostly concentrated between Memorial Day and Labor Day, but that has dramatically changed. Today, visitors from the U.S. and abroad, marvel at Yellowstone's wonders from opening day at Old Faithful in mid-April, until the roads close for the winter in November.

The shutdown lasted 16 days and according to Standard and Poor's cost the U.S. economy $24 billion. About 8000 visitors were still coming into Yellowstone each day when the shutdown hit. System-wide about 715,000 visits per day were curtailed, which translated into $76 million per day in lost spending in communities near the parks, and a loss of $450,000 per day in lost revenue from fees collected at park entry stations. Seeing the hordes of visitors being turned away from Yellowstone was bad enough, but I could not help but think about all of our other national parks. I could imagine the raft trips about to begin through the Grand Canyon that were stopped, cancelled tours to view the fall foliage in the Great Smokies, and on and on.

According to Moody's the shutdown cost Montana $45 million. The Montana Congressional delegation voted along party lines, with Senators Jon Tester and Max Baucus, both Democrats, voting for funding the federal government, and Representative Steve Daines, a Republican, voting to shut it down. Frankly, I was surprised that Representative Daines voted the way he did since polls at the time showed that most Montanans opposed the government shutdown, which is not surprising since Montana is home to Glacier National Park, as well as three of the five entrances to Yellowstone National park.

During and even after the shutdown the National Park Service received quite the black eye. Some outdoor writers maintained that Yellowstone should have remained open, even with visitor centers closed and few if any rangers on duty. That sounds easy but it is not. There are so many issues that deal with visitor safety, liability, and protection of wildlife and thermal features. Most park employees I know would have preferred to keep working without pay during the shutdown to accommodate visitors; however, legally that is simply not an option.

Our trip into Mary Mountain patrol cabin had been a success. Venturing into Yellowstone's backcountry in the late fall has such a wild feel to it. It seems that you are caught on the edge between two seasons, and there is no telling which way the weather will tilt at any given time. The animals seem to sense this as grizzlies are seeking maximum caloric intake, and bull elk are bugling and aggressively rounding up harems. It is a magical time of year to visit Yellowstone, and there is simply no excuse for our nation's politicians to interfere with visitors' opportunities to enjoy the world's first national park. I truly hope I never, ever again finish a wonderful wilderness trip in Yellowstone by having to observe visitors being turned away due to what I consider to be childish political posturing.

Addendum

Two years later almost to the day I returned to Mary Mountain cabin to close it down. This time Bob Kistart and Beth Kruezer from the Old Faithful backcountry office had been snowed out from making their season-ending trip, so I again volunteered to help out. Ironically, another government shutdown was looming, but this time last minute negotiations extended the deadline by a few weeks. So at least that sad episode was not repeated.

Rather than go in from the Old Faithful side as I had done before, I decided to make a loop trip around Hayden Valley by hiking in from the Canyon side along the old Trout Creek road on the south end of Hayden Valley, then come out along the Mary Mountain trail, which travels along the north end of the huge valley. Hayden Valley is prime grizzly country with its rolling open sagebrush, grassy hills and valleys interspersed with stands of lodgepole pine. The valley is approximately seven miles long from the Canyon road extending east to west, seven miles from north to south, and covers over 50 square miles. The grizzly evolved out on the Western plains in this type of habitat and the bears seem to favor the "edge effect" found along the tree line in Hayden Valley, named for Ferdinand V. Hayden, the geologist and leader of the important 1871 expedition that was instrumental in Yellowstone becoming the world's first national park the following year.

Since grizzly attacks are almost non-existent with parties of four or more, I again arranged for three of my friends, Clyde Austin, Al Frank and Sam Haugestuen, to go with me and help with the chores. I realized that having four of us was a good idea right off the bat, as we observed our first grizzly near the Mary Mountain trailhead. About three miles in along the old Trout Creek road cut (no longer marked or maintained), we spotted a second grizzly along the tree line. After crossing Trout Creek we turned away from the faint road cut and set a compass course across the valley toward Mary Lake. Along the way we walked through a narrow, rather spooky canyon that surprisingly contained several elk skulls. Surprisingly, because this little canyon contained no thermal activity, so I would not expect to find elk here during winter and early spring. Perhaps the animals had been "ambushed" in this deep, narrow canyon. We emerged from the west end of the canyon just as a large black-colored grizzly was about to enter the canyon. He took one look at the four of us then turned around and sprinted up a hill in the opposite direction. I was amazed at his speed as well as the rippling muscles. I could not help but wonder if that grizzly's reaction would have been different if I had been hiking solo or only had one other companion. I strongly do believe in the "four or more" recommendation for hiking in grizzly country!

As I watched the grizzly run away I could not help but think about the animal's fear of us. After all, grizzlies in Yellowstone have never been hunted. Looking around at the rather dry open valley, I pondered just what these bears were finding to eat. Grasses, roots, insects and perhaps some small rodents appeared to be about all that was available. While grizzlies are potentially extremely dangerous, I was thankful that they did not seem to have a taste for humans.

The following morning we headed over to the thermal basin, and also the old soldier cabin, where we were surprised to find it completely wrapped in aluminum foil. Apparently the nearby Spruce Fire, only a couple of miles away from us to the south, had been considered a threat to this historical resource. We saw many bison in the upper end of the valley along Alum Creek and a few elk, but no grizzlies on this day. Most of the rest of the day consisted of cutting firewood. The weather for early October was extremely mild, just the opposite of what we had experienced two years earlier.

On our third day we had planned to hike out via the Mary Mountain trail. When we reached the tree line where the valley comes into view, Al and Sam, who were ahead of us, turned and motioned for quiet. About 100 yards directly ahead of us out in the golden tinted meadow was a grizzly digging. The bear had not detected our presence at all. We sat on a log, pulled out our binoculars and watched the bear digging for roots and insects. We must have watched it for 30 minutes, and even with the calm conditions, I was frankly surprised that the bear did not pick up our scent. We could not have asked for a better situation to view this majestic animal. We felt that we were at a safe distance in the forest, there were four of us, each of us had a canister of bear spray, and the bear was simply doing its thing out in the meadow. Given the beauty of the fall day with blue skies and puffy clouds, the summit of Mount Washburn rising above the horizon in the distance, and the fact that we were nine miles deep into the Central Plateau, I sensed that we were truly experiencing the epitome of wild Yellowstone!

However, we still had a long way to hike on this day, so we knew we had to continue our trek out. Each of us pulled out our bear spray and held it in our hands as we moved forward, attempting to make as wide a detour around the bear as we could. We knew that as soon as we emerged from the forest, the bear would detect our presence. Once again, I would have been extremely concerned if I had been hiking solo. But with four of us I was confident the bear would move away from us. If the bear approached us we had discussed our plan to stay close together and attempt to back away. If the bear kept approaching, each of us was prepared to discharge a cloud of bear spray. Since we had no wind whatsoever, it would not be difficult to get the spray where we wanted it. One can of bear spray would be bad enough, but I could only imagine how terrible it would be for any animal to encounter four cans of the nasty stuff.

Sure enough, once we stepped out into the meadow the big bear looked our way, stood up to take a look at us, then it ran away, just as the bear in the canyon had. Observing this magnificent animal in such wild surroundings energized all of us—our packs seemed to be lighter. We soon left the Mary Mountain trail to follow a ridge line to take advantage of the views of the many bison below, the peaks to the east, and rising blue smoke from the remnants of the Spruce Fire to the south.

When we finally neared the trailhead on this pleasant fall day, I could not help but feel a sense of wonder and privilege at having observed several grizzly bears in their natural habitat doing their own thing. It was the most bears I had viewed in Yellowstone since Jim Horan and I hiked over The Thunderer and down Cache Creek on a late October trip (see "Way Down in the Fall in Bear Valley.") I simply could not imagine a wilder setting than Hayden Valley!

When winter is winter: Three River Jct. Patrol Cabin

Winter

GP at 25 Below—Winter at Old Faithful

During the 33 years that I worked summers in Yellowstone, I would often hear a rather redundant theme from my colleagues who worked in the park year round: "Summers are nice, but you should be here in the winter!" Well, I *had* been to Yellowstone in the winter, but never to work. Rather, it was either a backcountry ski trip, or a quick in and back out visit. Frankly, I was skeptical of my friends' glowing remarks about working in the park during winter, when the thermal basins' brilliant colors would be enshrouded in snow. Plus, what about the constant noise and pollution from snowmobiles? My opinion about the park in winter was about to change.

I entered "post-retirement" with my college in 2006, which basically meant I was going to continue to teach some on-line classes for the next five years, but from Bozeman, Montana instead of Morristown, Tennessee. By this time Margaret, an artist who loves plants, was craving to have a full-time home where she could grow flowers and vegetables. The National Park Service allowed me to continue working, but rather than working all summer, I would work during the shoulder seasons of spring and fall, plus fill in several weeks during the winter.

After attending winter training, which is quite a bit different from summer seasonal training, I anxiously awaited my assignment at Old Faithful. When it arrived in January, Margaret and I loaded up our supplies on a "tow sled" behind a snowmobile, and I drove it the thirty miles from the West Gate in West Yellowstone, Montana to Old Faithful. During the winter you can drive your auto through the North Gate from Gardiner, Montana up to Mammoth Hot Springs, and on out to Tower, through Lamar Valley, and eventually out the Northeast Entrance at Cooke City, Montana. These roads are kept open year round weather permitting. However, accessing the park's "interior" is a different situation altogether. Staff at such locations as Old Faithful, Canyon, and Lake do not have the luxury of driving into their work station. The roads are allowed to cover over with snow, so the only way to reach the park's interior is by snowmobile or snow coach.

By the winter of 2007, the Park Service in Yellowstone had winter use policies in place that substantially reduced the horrendous noise and pollution problems from the unregulated use of snowmobiles, which had plagued the park through the 1980s and 1990s. Visitors could only enter the park's interior on snow coaches or guided snowmobile trips, and the snowmobiles were required to be "best available technology," or BAT for short. Such machines are four stroke rather than two-cycle, and for the most part significantly reduce the air and noise pollution that used to look and sound like a chain saw convention was taking place.

During training we were warned what to do if you approach a herd of bison walking down the middle of the road. We were instructed to pull the snowmobile over to the side of the road farthest away from where the bison were walking, get off your machine and crouch down, putting the machine between you and the herd of bison, some of which weigh a ton or more. On my very first trip into Old Faithful, I was pulling my gear on a tow sled, and Margaret had decided to take a snow coach ride in rather than bump along behind me on the rear of a snowmobile. I had not travelled even ten miles when suddenly I looked ahead of me to see a herd of about forty bison coming right for me. As instructed I dutifully pulled my sled over to the right side of the road and parked. I managed to hoist my legs weighted down with heavy pak boots up over the seat and shuffle off of the machine. With the heavy insulated snowsuit on, I felt just like the "Michelin Man." As soon as I stepped away from the machine, I sank up to my waist in deep, soft snow. "They sure didn't mention *this* at training," were the words that raced through my mind. I managed to extricate myself from my snow cave just as the big bison were approaching. Since I couldn't place myself on the other side of the machine, I did the next best thing possible—I knelt down at the rear of sled. Of course, while maybe I was hiding to some degree, there was really nothing between me and the bison as they walked by. I peeked over to my left, and there not five feet away, was a huge bison head with a baseball sized eyeball staring at me as he walked by. I just held my breath, said a little prayer, and did not move a muscle as the herd walked right past me down the middle of the road. After sinking up to my waist in soft snow, I could certainly see why these animals preferred to walk down a packed, groomed bed of snow, rather than trudge through five foot snow drifts!

When I have worked spring, summer and fall, I have always ridden my bike to work from the residence area. In the winter the mode of transportation is by ski. I have always felt that the best duty in the National Park Service has to be "geyser predict" or GP for short. Even in the summer, there are very few souls out and about at first light in the Upper Geyser Basin. I could only imagine what it would be like in the winter. After a couple of days of working in the visitor center, which included giving some interpretive programs and roving the basin, I was due for the revered duty of GP!

After Margaret and I enjoyed breakfast in our warm and cozy cabin, I glanced out at the thermometer to get an idea of how many layers to wear. The thermometer read minus 30 degrees F! "Margaret," I exclaimed, "This can't be right!" The first three days after arriving the temperature had basically ranged from highs in the 20s to lows around 0. "Well," she answered, "You had better trust the thermometer." I layered up and headed out on skis for the visitor center. It usually took me about 20 minutes to ski from our cabin to the center. At first I simply thought the thermometer was wrong. It just didn't feel all *that* cold. But that's because I was moving, there was no wind, and the humidity was low. After about ten minutes of skiing I began to realize that, yes, this is one cold morning!

When I reached the visitor center I found that my colleague Carolyn Loren had already arrived, and was busy preparing the building for opening. Of course, Carolyn was an old hand at working in cold climes. She and her husband Stu had actually homesteaded a piece of land in Alaska, and built a small cabin on it, which they still occupy for part of the year. After gathering the instruments we use to download and determine the overnight eruptions of the major geysers, I headed for the door to again don my skis. "Where do you think you are going? Carolyn asked. "What do you mean?" I replied. "Don't you remember our winter training?" she responded. "Only essential duty is allowed when it is colder than minus 25 degrees F," she reminded me.

I was so excited about heading out on my very first winter GP duty that this rule never crossed my mind. Opening the visitor center at Old Faithful was considered "essential duty." Heading out on GP was not. I looked at the thermometer just outside the visitor center window. It now read minus 28. "Three more degrees to go," I thought. As I was waiting for the thermometer to reach minus 25, the phone rang. It was my friend and colleague Marc Hanna calling from his quarters at Madison. He was scheduled to work at the Madison Warming Hut only a short distance from where he lived, but like Carolyn, knew the rule. Staffing the warming hut, just like GP duty, was not considered essential duty. "Has it reached minus 25 at Old Faithful yet?" he asked. "Look Marc," I answered, "if I can ski for twenty minutes to work at 30 below, I think you can walk across the road to the warming hut!" I looked at my thermometer, which by now had almost warmed up to minus 25. "Let's call it 25 below and get our butts to work," I proudly proclaimed. Marc was as anxious to get to his job at the Madison Warming Hut as I was to get out on GP, because he knew he would have some frigid snowmobilers on his hands shortly. He had to fire up the wood stove in the warming hut. I don't care how thick a snowmobile suit is, the wind will always cause the cold to filter through to your body.

So, at 25 below, layered up to the hilt, I headed out in the basin on skis. It was an absolute wonderland to behold. At such temperatures the trees frost up due to all of the steam emanating from the many hot springs and geysers. But the star attraction was an eruption of Old Faithful Geyser. I have witnessed Old Faithful erupting early and late in the day before, when I was the only apparent observer, but *never* at 25 below zero! On this very cold, still, clear morning the superheated water gushing out (over 200 degrees F.) created an enormous, mushrooming steam cloud that climbed straight up into the sky. Then, after a while, miniature prisms appeared all over the basin, as the tiny droplets of water had frozen, and drifted slowly back down to earth. The sun's rays caused the little ice crystals to act as colorful prisms suspended over the snow.

After watching Old Faithful all by myself, I ventured on down basin, not expecting to see another soul on this frigid morning. However, as I approached Castle Geyser, I saw one other hardy soul out on this morning. It was Terry McEneany, the park's bird biologist, who was teaching a Yellowstone Institute class. Terry was scouting out things for his class that started later in the day. He had actually been out earlier than me on this frigid morning, and was now on his way back in to meet some of his students for breakfast over at the Snow Lodge. I had to chuckle at what it must be like to enroll in a birding class that involves going out at 25 below!

As I skied over toward Grand Geyser, I crossed the Firehole River bridge, and gazed both up and downstream at this marvelous river, that never freezes— even at 25 below zero, due to the constant supply of thermal waters flowing into it. It was while I was standing on the footbridge that I first heard it: the low, slow, mournful sound of wolves howling. If there is another sound that better resonates with wilderness, I don't know what it is. The wolves sounded just like they were located on the rock outcropping above Grand Geyser. However, when I reached Grand, the howls continued, but now seemed to be further away to the northwest. I simply stopped skiing, cupped my ears, and listened to the magical harmonizing chorus of howls. There for a moment, I felt just like I was Joe Meek, or Jim Bridger, or Osborne Russell—one of those pioneer mountain men who explored this wilderness almost 200 years ago. As I looked around me I realized that I was the only human being out in the basin. I felt an incredible sense of wildness from the solitude, and hearing wolves howling. After two hours of skiing the entire loop of the basin, and downloading and observing all of the major predictable geysers, it was time to head back to the visitor center to warm up and grab a hot cup of coffee.

Despite the frigid temperatures I had stayed warm thanks to my several layers of clothing, and the constant movement on skis. Also, typically when the temperature plunges way below zero, there is almost no wind. I have never really had a problem keeping warm in cold weather unless the wind is blowing. I knew beginning around 10:30 a.m. we would begin to see lots of visitors arriving on snow coaches and snowmobiles. The visitor center remains busy until about 3:30 p.m. then things really get quiet again. As a postscript, shortly after my GP duty at minus 25 degrees, the NPS moved the "cutoff temperature" up to minus 20 degrees for ceasing the performance of non-essential duties outside. I may have been one of the last rangers to ever perform GP duty at Old Faithful in minus 25 degree weather. As the 2015-16 winter season begins the limit is now minus 15 degrees.

During that portion of the winter season that the Old Faithful Snow Lodge is open, we do tend to get folks over to the visitor center early and late in the day. Several years ago there was a wonderful documentary filmed on winter in Yellowstone titled "Christmas in Yellowstone," narrated by Linda Hunt. The film shows what it is like to visit the park in the winter, as well as some great segments showing wilderness photographer Tom Murphy out skiing and camping. The film does a good job of romanticizing winter in Yellowstone, and has motivated many older folks to visit the park in winter. The thing is, unless you enjoy cross-country skiing, there just isn't much to do at Old Faithful in the winter. Therefore, it was rather common to find lots of folks simply sitting by the fireplace in the Snow Lodge enjoying a good book, and that is a great and relaxing "activity" in and of itself.

For those who enjoy ski touring however, Old Faithful in winter is a paradise. Most of the outstanding skiing occurs right around the basin, where ski trails are actually groomed. The trail along the Firehole River to Lone Star Geyser is groomed and is a favorite. My personal choice for a fabulous cross country ski experience is Spring Creek. Each day a snow coach from the Snow Lodge drops people off at different destinations such as trailheads to Mystic Falls, Fairy Falls, Lone Star, and Spring Creek. After being dropped at the Divide Lookout trailhead, the skier enjoys a gradual downhill eight mile ski through a canyon along first Spring Creek, then the Firehole River. The forest is old growth, and is typically mantled in deep snow. The vertical rock formations along the streams are spectacular, and seem to swallow you up as your continue through the deep canyon. There are many intermittent springs that seep even during the winter, thus the name "Spring" Creek. The trail crosses Spring Creek via snow bridges many times along the way. Since you begin your ski near the continental divide at an elevation of over 8300,' the trail provides a gentle descent down to Old Faithful at an elevation of 7337,' which is one reason why this ski trip is so desirable.

However, for anyone visiting Old Faithful in the winter, the first place to head is out in the geyser basin to experience the ethereal setting that stems from the clash of cold air with hot water. The rising columns of steam, the ice crystals, the ghost trees, all laden in snow, makes for a breathtaking sight. If you don't ski, the trails around geyser hill are usually walkable with good boots with the proper ice grippers to provide traction. If you *do* ski then by all means head down the groomed ski trail that runs from Old Faithful to Morning Glory Pool. The Upper Geyser Basin in winter is a paradise to behold. No wonder my friends and colleagues told me that the winter season was the best in which to work at Old Faithful. While all four seasons are fabulous, I have to agree, winter is the best!

A Frigid, Late-Night Winter Duty

One of the nice things about working on an intermittent basis during the winter season is you have a great deal of flexibility for odd jobs. For example, during the latter part of the 2009-2010 winter, the park needed a film monitor for four consecutive days to accompany a crew filming a documentary on Yellowstone during the winter. Any organization filming in Yellowstone for commercial purposes is required to have an NPS employee to serve as a film monitor. Given the increase in commercial filming in the park, especially since the great fire season of 1988, the park has instituted this requirement to insure that filmmakers follow all park regulations, especially those that deal with wildlife and thermal basins. For example, a visitor is not allowed to get any closer than 25 yards to large ungulates, such as bison, elk and moose. For bears and wolves the distance is 100 yards. This regulation is for the safety of both visitors as well as wildlife. Also, there is no off-trail travel permitted in thermal basins, again for safety reasons as well as to protect the delicate mineral deposits.

Typically, a film monitor is needed for only one or two days, so most of the time NPS employees will offer to perform this duty during their lieu days. However, a four day job is a different story. When I read the film office's frantic emails about needing someone for this assignment, I knew they would have a tough time finding anyone. I was currently in between my working assignments at the Old Faithful Visitor Center, so I called the Public Affairs Office and offered my services. It was then that I learned of the odd circumstances regarding this film crew. The filmmakers were attempting to simulate what would happened if a super volcano, such as the one located in Yellowstone, had a catastrophic eruption, which has occurred three times at approximately 600,000 year intervals. It has been about 640,000 years since the last one, but geologists are not exactly holding their breath as to when it will blow again.

Most volcanic experts say that such an eruption would create a "nuclear winter" in parts of the world, as the ash would filter out the sun, causing temperatures to plummet and growing seasons to drastically shorten. In order to simulate these conditions, the film crew was set up to film primarily in low light conditions using infrared, "night vision" cameras.

I was instructed to drive to Mammoth and obtain a park snowmobile from the Mammoth Garage, and drive it to Norris Geyser Basin, where I would meet the crew early that afternoon. I had planned to simply drive from my home in Bozeman over to Livingston, and then down to Mammoth the same day that I was scheduled to meet the film crew. However, after dinner the evening before I was planning to depart, I observed a weather warning. A blizzard was on the way with a foot of new snow forecast overnight. I knew that there was a good chance that Interstate 90 over Bozeman Pass between Bozeman and Livingston would be closed.

I called Public Affairs to advise them of this potential problem, and I was instructed to immediately head to Mammoth, where they would put me up in the Mammoth Hotel. I started out about 8:00 p.m. and wondered if the weather forecasters would get it right. I couldn't help but think of the previous spring when we had received a winter storm warning that forecast 18 inches of snow at Old Faithful; we didn't get a flake. The storm had moved down from Canada and made it as far as Great Falls, Montana, but stalled. As soon as I left Bozeman I quickly realized that, if anything, the weather folks had *understated* the severity of this storm. Snow was dumping at a rapid rate, visibility was horrible, and by the time I reached Bozeman Pass, close to a foot of snow had accumulated. There was no way to tell where the lanes in the road were. In fact, the only way to stay on the road was to focus on the snow markers located on the side of the shoulder of the road for the benefit of the snowplows. Margaret and I had purchased a new AWD Subaru Outback when we moved to Bozeman in 2006, and it was now receiving its first test. Of course, if I veered off the road, I knew the AWD would be of little help in preventing me from getting hopelessly stuck.

I found out later that the Montana Highway Patrol closed I-90 between Bozeman and Livingston only thirty minutes after I crossed over Bozeman Pass. By the time I reached Livingston, it was obvious that I would encounter few if any other travelers on the fifty mile stretch between Livingston and the park's north entrance. This particular approach to Yellowstone goes through the appropriately named Paradise Valley. With the huge Absaroka Mountain Range soaring above the winding Yellowstone River below, this is one of the most beautiful valleys to be found anywhere. Typically, this valley does not receive all that much precipitation, but on this evening the snowstorm was raging. Snow depths on the highway were rapidly approaching a foot, and I seemed to be the only person traveling on this evening. If it had not been for the snow stakes along the shoulders of the highway, I would have never made it. There was simply no other way to identify the road other than by looking at the stakes.

I finally made it into Mammoth for the night. By the next morning the storm had passed, and the skies were now blue, but well over a foot of fresh powder had been dumped onto the surface. I headed over to the maintenance garage to check out my snowmobile and immediately realized I had a bit of a problem on my hand. I had never driven a snowmobile up the narrow trail from Mammoth to Golden Gate in the winter. During the summer this route is actually a little-known bicycle trail, which I had biked once several years ago. However, I had no idea what it was like in winter. With all of the fresh snow there were no tracks or markings on the trail. I would be the first person to travel it after the big storm. Up to this point all of my snowmobiling in Yellowstone had been along the park's major roads. However, this little service road was the only feasible way a person could ride a snowmobile up to Golden Gate, unless you used a trailer to haul it up the highway to the point where wheeled access ends and oversnow vehicle access begins. Of course, that was out of the question. I was on my own.

I packed all of my gear on the rear of the sled, and carefully picked my route up the trail until I successfully reached Golden Gate. From there I drove out into the gorgeous expanse of Swan Lake Flats, with the towering Electric Peak rising above the valley to almost 11,000.' Even though this peak is not the park's highest (Eagle Peak is the highest at 11,358' down in the southeastern corner of the park), to me it is the most impressive given its prominence. Here I took a break to make sure everything was fastened down, when I realized that my daypack was missing. The pack contained critical food and gear. I looked at my watch and wondered if I should just continue on to Norris to meet the film crew, and hope that someone else would find my pack and somehow get it to me. But then I remembered exactly what I had done. I had taken the pack off and placed it on the back seat while I bungeed in my other gear. I had fully intended to put the pack back on after I finished fastening down the gear, but in all the excitement with wondering if I was going to be able to find the trail, I had forgotten.

I made a decision right then to return to retrieve my pack. I now knew that the trail was well-tracked since I had just made the journey, and figured I could make much better time on the return trip. When I arrived back at my starting location, I found the pack had fallen off the sled exactly where I had figured. After retrieving it I did indeed make very good time going back up to Swan Lake Flats. In fact, I arrived at Norris at 1:00 p.m., a full half hour ahead of when I was supposed to meet the film crew. By now the skies were a deep blue and the temperature was a rather moderate 24 degrees, so I just leaned back on my sled and relaxed, taking in all of the beauty around me. By 2:00 p.m. the film crew had not shown up. I had no idea where the crew was working or where they needed to go. I just knew that I was supposed to meet them at Norris at 1:30. I called the Communications Center on my radio but they said that public affairs had received no updates. My instructions remained to wait at Norris.

However, at 2:30 p.m., the Comm Center called with an update: "The film crew is at the Old Faithful Snow Lodge. You are requested to be there by 3:00 p.m." I could only chuckle. "3:00 p.m.!" I exclaimed to myself, "I'll do good to make it by 3:30 p.m.!" I made the trip in about an hour and met the film crew in the lobby of the Snow Lodge. It was then that I learned that the filming would actually be done rather late in the evening, usually between 8:00 p.m.

and 10:00 p.m. I immediately realized that this was going to really be a frigid experience.

After dinner at the Snow Lodge we gathered up our gear, donned our snowmobile suits, and headed north. The assignment this evening consisted of filming elk along the Madison River about 22 miles from Old Faithful. Once at the film site I could only admire the film crew, and especially the young lady from Great Britain who was doing the narration. Everyone was having difficulty keeping warm, and I felt sorry for her since she had to memorize such long and demanding lines. She would typically walk along as she was narrating in a very animated tone.

All during the filming I simply had to stand by and watch. I tried to jump up and down in place to try to keep warm as the temperature plunged to minus 15 degrees. Once the filming was completed the true adventure began, as we had to ride our snowmobiles back to Old Faithful in the frigid night air. It is one thing to stand around when it is minus 15, but the wind chill created from riding the sled was brutal. No matter how many layers I put on or how bundled up I was, the cold would creep in around my neck and chest. Obviously, we had to proceed at a rather slow speed to reduce the wind chill effect.

The following day the film crew wanted to film in a geyser basin. It was on this day that I realized why the NPS utilizes film monitors, as I was asked outright to "look the other way" so they could film a researcher taking water samples well away from the boardwalk. I explained to the director that his film permit prohibited any travel away from established trails and boardwalks in thermal areas. Such regulations exist not only for personal safety, but also to protect the very fragile and delicate mineral deposits. However, I could envision what the film director was attempting to achieve, so I suggested that we go to Porcelain Basin at Norris, where it would be possible for the researcher to stand right over a runoff channel flowing under the boardwalk.

That evening long after the sun had set we drove our sleds the thirty miles from Old Faithful to Norris. As the crew prepared to film, I had to chuckle at the narrator's attempts to keep herself warm by jumping up and down as she rehearsed her lines. Just as we moved out into Porcelain Basin under a rising moon, a gray wolf emerged from the forest directly in front of us and lifted its head to howl. What a spectacle for us to enjoy on this frosty evening in Yellowstone's winter wilderness!

On our last evening we again rode our sleds into the Madison Valley to film elk and bison grazing. When our activities were completed later that evening we headed back to the warmth of the Old Faithful Snow Lodge, and I was thankful that we had managed to avoid any serious problems, such as mechanical issues with our sleds, during this rather unusual project.

The next morning the Public Affairs Office called to tell me there was one more film monitoring project that needed to be completed prior to my heading back to Mammoth. This film project would be much simpler, as I only had to monitor a crew filming around the Upper Geyser Basin at Old Faithful. When I met the film crew at the Snow Lodge I was surprised to learn that they were filming for a large investment banking firm. I asked the producer why his firm needed to make a film in Yellowstone. "We are promoting geothermal energy firms as some excellent investments," he replied. His answer greatly concerned me because such drilling has destroyed many of the world's geysers. Most people believe that Yellowstone's geysers are completely safe from such threats, but actually the Upper Geyser Basin is only thirteen miles as the crow flies from the park's west boundary where interest in drilling is strong. Drilling in Iceland destroyed geysers as far away as fifteen miles, so Yellowstone's geysers are vulnerable.

I explained this to the film crew and asked a pointed question, "You aren't going to photograph anything that can definitely be tied to Yellowstone National Park are you?" "Oh no," the film producer replied. "We only want to get some good photos of steam coming out of the ground, which should be easy to do in this cold weather." We spent about two hours travelling the boardwalks mostly around Old Faithful Geyser, during which time the crew took many photographs. I was then told that the project was completed. I was somewhat surprised since I had been told that the crew would spend the entire day filming.

I had originally planned to spend the night at the Snow Lodge and head back the next morning, so I called Public Affairs to let them know that the film crew had finished early. "That's great news because you need to get back to Mammoth today," came the reply. "We just found out that Maintenance is going to begin plowing the road from Mammoth first thing tomorrow morning."

While the road from the West Entrance to Old Faithful typically remains open to oversnow travel through the end of the winter season in mid-March, spring plowing can begin several days earlier from Mammoth down to Norris and Madison. However, I was not aware that it was due to begin *this* early and thanked my lucky stars that I was going to get out ahead of the plows. Since it was still early in the day I decided to stop at the Indian Creek warming hut and don my skis. I had always wanted to ski the loop trail that extends out into the gorgeous open valley along Indian Creek with the Gallatin Mountain Range towering overhead. The snow was nice and deep and I had a bluebird day. There was no one else around. Earlier in the winter the concession snow coaches bring hotel guests from Mammoth out to this warming hut for day ski trips, but since we were down to the last day, there was nothing but complete silence and solitude.

The only disadvantage to my privacy was the fact that the trail was untracked due to the recent snow. However, that didn't bother me in the least as I marveled at the beauty around me in this winter wilderness. I looked up at the named peaks above me: Quadrant Mountain and Antler Peak. They were like old friends. When I worked a summer at Mammoth in 1975 I had spent time tromping around up in that high country. Except for the gurgling of Indian Creek, the quietness was overwhelming. When I am alone in such spectacular surroundings in Yellowstone, I often fantasize that I am a mountain man wandering through this country for the first time in the early 1800s. Over the past two centuries not a whole lot has really changed here, and how wonderful that is!

As I continued my relaxing ski over gentle, undulating terrain I pondered the contrast between riding a snowmobile and skiing. To me, a snowmobile is simply a form of transportation to travel over the snow from point A to point B. I really don't get that much enjoyment from riding a sled in the park. After all, you have this big bubble helmet on your head, so you can't hear anything other than the muffled sound of the engine. Also, you really can't see much. When you are driving a sled you have to look straight ahead to pick your route in the snow among the many ruts, otherwise you can very easily lose control and end up stuck off of the road. The only way a snowmobile rider can truly appreciate his surroundings is to occasionally pull over, turn off the engine, take off the helmet and allow your senses to soak in the setting. On the other hand, while skiing, all of your senses are *continuously* in play.

I sometimes use an analogy from trips I have taken at a place a long way off from the cold snows of Yellowstone: the Okefenokee Swamp. I have taken many canoe trips in this wilderness, and just as in cross-country skiing, all of the senses are constantly being utilized. However, one spring I was in the vicinity of the Okefenokee with my sister Alice, and she had never visited the swamp. Our time was limited so I decided to drive over to the edge of the swamp just short of the wilderness designation, where you were allowed to rent small motorboats. As we headed out I quickly realized that all of the incredible sounds of the swamp typically heard while paddling were being totally obliterated by the sound of the outboard motor. Also, rather than ease around a bend to see an alligator sunning on a bank, as so often occurs while paddling a canoe, the sound of the motor caused the gators to move off into the water well ahead of our arrival. Our tour via outboard motor was pathetically devoid of the exciting experience provided from paddling a canoe in the wilderness. Riding a snowmobile to me is the same type of situation. However, that being said, when I work at the Old Faithful Visitor Education Center during the winter, I meet many visitors who seem to be enthralled with their experience of riding sleds in the park.

Late that afternoon I safely arrived back at the Mammoth Garage, and turned in my snowmobile and other gear. As I traveled back to Bozeman I noted the incredible difference a few days can make when it comes to weather. The roads were now plowed and completely clear of any snow. Several weeks later I went out to my mailbox to retrieve my morning edition of *The Wall Street Journal*. I have always enjoyed the excellent feature articles in the Journal, which for the most part are very accurate and objective (which is *not* the case for the editorial pages, of course). I was shocked to see right there on the front page a photo of Old Faithful Geyser with the caption, "Call for a prospectus on how you can profit from investing in geothermal energy!" I mumbled a few strong words under my breath, and then called Public Affairs to tell them of the discussions that had taken place on the day of the filming. I was told that at this point there was nothing that could be done. Over the years while giving walks and programs in the Upper Geyser Basin, I have tried my best to educate the public regarding just how unique, delicate, fragile, and *vulnerable* Yellowstone's geysers are. To see that photo of Old Faithful coupled with an ad on geothermal drilling in one of our nation's most widely read daily newspapers truly felt like a hard punch to the midsection.

During the years since this interesting film monitor duty I have watched for a documentary about the effects from a super volcano eruption. Either I have missed it, the film has not been released, or the project was scuttled. I certainly hope that it was not the latter. I can attest to the fact that a lot of effort went into the project, which was filmed under very harsh conditions that led to one of the more fascinating duties I have ever had the privilege of participating in during my time in Yellowstone.

A Winter Ordeal High in the Smokies

December 21st—the shortest day of the year. If you are going to be out in the backcountry with nights that are over 14 hours long, then you need to be someplace warm. If you are in cold country then you had better have a good plan for keeping warm. I have experienced the longest night at both ends of the temperature spectrum. I have twice spent Christmas Eve in a rental Forest Service patrol cabin just north of Yellowstone—once with Margaret and my two daughters, and again with my niece and her family. Each time the temperatures fell to about 20 below zero, and with such a long night, we had to take turns feeding the wood stove. But that was just one night. Twice though, I took extensive backcountry trips during the winter equinox—one a canoe trip in the warmth of the Everglades, which turned out to be a magnificent expedition (see "Journey to the Everglades"); the other in the high country of Great Smoky Mountains National Park, which to this day remains the coldest wilderness outing of my life!

After spending so much time in Yellowstone during the winter, including an eighteen day ski trip in 1973, people usually laugh when I tell them that the coldest I have ever been in my life was while on a backpacking trip in Great Smoky Mountains National Park in December of 1970. After spending three fantastic summers working in Yellowstone and Glacier National Parks, Margaret and I were about to begin a tour in the U.S. Air Force. One of the great friends we made during those summers was my backpacking pal Rod Busby. Rod was about to enter the U.S. Army. We each had one more academic term left in college before we both entered military service in mid-January, so we hooked up for one last wilderness backpacking trip.

Rod flew into Montgomery, Alabama after Christmas, and we headed to the closest big mountain wilderness, the Great Smoky Mountains along the Tennessee-North Carolina border. I had visited the Smokies with my family on a couple of occasions but had never hiked there. Rod and I had three summers of extensive hiking experience in the Northern Rockies, but that was it. Our winter experience was nil (see "A Winter Primer" in the first volume,) but the high country of the Appalachian Trail (AT) through the Smokies with its many rustic shelters was calling us.

Margaret had joined me with Rod and his fiancée Kathy on several trips in Yellowstone, but wanted no part of a December backpacking trip, which turned out to be a wise decision on her part. Rod and I drove straight to the park, and made it to Cades Cove campground just before dark. There was not another soul in the campground. We had planned to begin our trip along the AT at Davenport Gap on the east end of the park, and hike it through to the west end near Fontana Dam, a distance of 71 miles. We had hoped to make the journey in a week or less.

A Winter Ordeal High in the Smokies

We felt well-prepared for cold weather. During our last summer in Yellowstone, each of us had purchased goose-down sleeping bags rated to fifteen below zero from the Alaska Sleeping Bag Company out of Eugene, Oregon. Oddly, this firm went out of business right as the interest in backpacking skyrocketed. The sleeping bags were obviously well-made, as both Rod and I still own and use those same bags 46 years later! We would be hiking at an elevation above 6500' at times, which is some of the highest terrain in the Eastern United States. Yet, at the base of these peaks the elevation is only 1300'. It has often been said that hiking from the valleys to the higher elevations in the Smokies is equivalent to hiking from Georgia to Maine, regarding the vegetation encountered along the way.

Our first evening at Cades Cove indeed felt like we were in *south* Georgia. The temperature was downright balmy, having reached the mid-70s during the day. We pitched my canvas Coleman tent for the night, and struggled to get comfortable in our winter bags on what felt like a late spring evening, then all hell broke loose. Tremendous thunderstorms produced a solid deluge of rain throughout the night, until eventually we realized that our tent was about to float away. We had not paid much attention when selecting our campsite, and had placed the tent in a natural depression, which had now turned into a small pond. Furthermore, our down bags were now soaked—not a good thing. We moved our tent to higher ground, and then tried to sleep like wet puppies until daylight finally arrived.

We had planned to drive to Cosby, Tennessee and catch a local bus to drop us off at Davenport Gap, but now we had a major time-consuming task ahead of us—trying to somehow dry out two soaked goose-down sleeping bags! We located a laundromat in Gatlinburg, and each of us stuffed the wet bags into a heavy-duty dryer. Rod made the mistake of also tossing in a wet space blanket. There were quite a few patrons in the laundromat waiting on their wash, and they seemed quite entertained by our antics. We had the feeling that these folks had never even camped out, much less backpacked, and had no idea what we were trying to do. After a few minutes Rod opened the dryer to check on his space blanket, that was now about the size of a chewing gum wrapper. When he pulled it out and hopelessly tried to unfold it, guffaws from the patrons rolled through the laundromat.

We ignored the laughter and continued to check on our bags until we found them both to be sufficiently dry, and were they ever puffed up! My stuff sack was rather generous, but Rod had a very small one. When he sat down on a bench and commenced trying to stuff his hugely inflated bag into that tiny stuff sack, loud chuckles again broke out. Perhaps these folks were not aware of the compression qualities of goose down, but I was *certain* they were unaware of Rod's determination! Rod simply continued to doggedly knead his fist into that little sack until finally he had that entire bag reduced to a 12 X 8 inch wad. As his audience looked on in disbelief, Rod stood up, tossed the sack over his shoulder, straightened his hat, gave the crowd the once-over, and confidently strode out the front door of that laundromat.

The lengthy episode with drying our gear had caused us to miss our early ride out of Cosby, so it was not until late afternoon that we finally arrived at Davenport Gap via a rustic gravel road which skirted the park boundary. The AT that runs from Georgia to Maine crossed the primitive road at the Gap at an elevation of 1800 feet, so this would be the trailhead for our journey, and as it turned out our low point along the route. We had planned to stay in trail shelters throughout the trip, since they are located about every five to eight miles along the way; in fact, we had not even bothered to pack our tent. We began our hike in a fine forested setting consisting mostly of deciduous trees with a few scattered pines. One of the advantages to hiking in the Smokies during the winter is that you tend to get much better views with all of the leaves gone from the trees, plus there is less humidity than in summer, which helps provide clearer skies. After hiking the short mile to the shelter, darkness was already settling in even though it was only a little after 4:00 p.m. Ah, the benefits of December backpacking! I had seen photos of some of the shelters along the AT and they had appeared to be cute rustic little backcountry abodes. When we walked into the shelter itself I was very impressed as it appeared identical to the photos, with the rustic shingle roofs and fine stone fireplace and chimney. However, reality was about to set in!

We set down our backpacks and began the race against the dark to gather some firewood. We immediately found that the forest had been completely cleaned out within hundreds of yards of the shelter. There was not a loose stick to be found! At first this did not really concern us since we had brought some candle lanterns for light, plus the weather had been so balmy. But things were *rapidly* changing! The temperature, which had been in the 70s only 24 hours earlier, was now plunging toward the freezing mark. When I moved to East Tennessee in 1976, and lived there for 31 years, I learned that such weather events in the fall, winter and spring are very common. Storms roll in during warm humid weather, heavy rains fall, then it clears up and the temperature just plunges.

With no firewood the stone fireplace was useless in providing warmth. It was at this point that we discovered the next huge disadvantage of a shelter—they are three-sided, and one side is basically a fenced enclosure which you can latch shut to keep out larger animals such as black bears. But we quickly found out that the fence does *not* keep out cold air. We heated up some canned stew with our SVEA stoves, and choked it down in the cold of the shelter. With no firewood the only thing left to do at this early hour of 6:00 p.m. in the cold and dark was to retire to our sleeping bags. We then discovered the final and perhaps *worst* feature of these shelters—the bunks consisted of mesh wire, which allowed the cold air to penetrate right through your sleeping bag. We had ensolite pads, which before thermarest pads were about the best thing you could get to sleep on top of, and when placed on the ground worked pretty well. However, the pads were not thick enough to provide sufficient insulation when placed on a wire mesh bunk! Rod and I curled up and tried our best to keep warm, but we were miserable—and we had thirteen hours of darkness and cold to look forward to.

At first light we should have immediately started our day; however, during the night the temperature had continued to plunge, and was now down to ten degrees. There was simply no way to warm up. Having spent many years in both the South and the Northern Rockies, I can honestly say that ten degrees in the humid South feels the same to me as fifteen below zero feels in the dry Rockies. The hardest thing of all was stuffing our sleeping bags into our stuff sacks, which caused our hands to freeze up. Then we had to prime our cantankerous little gas stoves that we discovered don't work well at all in cold temperatures. By the time we finally finished eating, cleaning and packing up, it was nearly 10:00 a.m. It suddenly became pretty clear that our plan for making ten to twelve miles per day, and covering the entire 71 miles from Davenport to Fontana in about a week was a pipedream.

The temperature hovered around ten degrees all day as we steadily gained elevation on our way up to Cosby Knob shelter. As we neared the shelter we could see the firewood disappearing, so we collected what we could carry. As darkness approached and with clear conditions we were headed for the coldest night of the entire trip. The mercury plunged to negative ten degrees. Once we had a roaring fire in the fireplace, we learned of yet another disadvantage of these despicable shelters—the fireplace was worthless! All of the heat went straight up the chimney. Rod actually took a photo of me squatting inside the fireplace inches from the flames as I attempted to get warm. Needless to say, we endured another long and miserably cold night. I have camped out at 38 below zero at Mammoth Campground, but I can honestly say that I was colder on this night at Cosby shelter.

The next two days were spent hiking along the highest elevations around 6000,' but thanks to cloud cover the temperatures moderated during the day to around twenty degrees. It now began to snow. The mornings that we arose at Tricorner Knob and Icewater Springs shelters, we found fresh snow of up to five inches on the ground. The snow presented no problems for hiking, and was quite beautiful, as it mantled on the limbs of the deciduous forest around us. Then it cleared up and with the contrast of a gorgeous deep blue sky we headed toward Charlie's Bunion, where the views of the surrounding snow-covered peaks were spectacular.

We managed to reach Newfound Gap and U.S. 441, the only road that crosses the AT in the park, around noon on our fifth day. We had not seen another human being during our five days on the AT between Davenport Gap and Newfound Gap. But now we observed a steady stream of cars and folks playing in the snow along the road. We soon caught a ride down to Gatlinburg, and eventually to Cosby, where my 1964 Chevy II was located. Our winter backpacking ordeal had come to an end, and I had learned a valuable lesson about those AT trail shelters. Six years later I would take a teaching job only forty miles from Cosby, and Margaret and I would spend the next 31 years living in East Tennessee. I took many more hikes and backpacking trips along the AT, but I never spent another night in one of those shelters. I actually did take more winter trips in the Smokies, but found that a good four season tent with a vestibule for cooking was much preferred over a three-sided shelter!

Jim Horan on skis in upper Slough Creek Valley below Cutoff Mountain

Slough Creek Solitude

In March of 1972 I took my first overnight cross-country ski trip up the Slough Creek Valley with Steve Veltrie and Ron Bestrom. Ron and I had become good friends and hiking companions when we worked at Canyon in 1968. I had purchased some Tronderski Norwegian wooden skis with 3-pin bindings from REI, along with a pair of leather boots. Brian Severin had taught me how to apply a base wax with the use of a blow torch to my wooden skis, and also how to use various waxes based on the temperature.

Brian and I had taken several day ski trips in the area around Neihart, Montana, including a fabulous one-way eight mile trail that ran from the top of Kings Hill Pass slightly downhill along a stream to the little town of Neihart. I had cut my teeth on those outings, and established some good skills and knowledge of backcountry skiing. However, I had yet to take an extended overnight ski trip. Rod Busby and I had quite the misadventure during the winter of 1971 attempting to reach Arrow Lake in Glacier National Park on snowshoes (see "A Winter Primer," first volume). But my day trips with Brian had convinced me that skis were the preferred means of travel for an overnight trip. After all, you don't glide downhill on snowshoes!

I don't think I could have selected a more gorgeous setting for my first overnight ski adventure than the Slough Creek Valley, which is surrounded by spectacular mountains, particularly the prominent 10,638' Cutoff Mountain with its conspicuous notch "cut out" of the top. Furthermore, the valley contains gentle rolling terrain, and features the meandering Slough Creek flowing through meadows and forests consisting of aspen, spruce and fir.

In 1972 there was an old cabin (just below the actual Lower Slough Creek Patrol Cabin) that was utilized as a small bunk house, and maintained by a Boy Scout troop in Yellowstone. Back in those days Yellowstone actually had an elementary school at Mammoth, since many of the employees in the park had families with kids, and several of the boys were in this Boy Scout troop. The cabin was available for use by the public, so Steve, Ron and I had planned to utilize it for our base camp, from which we would ski up the valley to explore.

That particular trip turned out to be a magical adventure that I have since attempted to duplicate several times with no success. We took that trip in mid-March, and found a consolidated base of snow. We were able to zip up and over Transfer Hill (a 640' climb in one mile), and cover the four miles to the cabin with ease. The next day we planned to ski nine miles all the way up to the north border of the park. We had heard about the historic Silvertip Ranch located deep in the wilderness just north of the park, and wanted to check it out.

That day we again benefited from absolutely perfect snow conditions. We were gaining good traction on the gentle slopes going uphill, and enjoyed

Slough Creek Solitude

wonderful glides going downhill. The day was warm but the snow was crusty, so we were not sinking at all. After six miles we reached Elk Tongue Creek, and we noticed a patrol cabin close to where Elk Tongue Creek empties into Slough Creek. This cabin was not shown on the maps we were using, though according to the website secretyellowstone.com, it was built in 1936. The same source states that Slough Creek cabin was constructed in 1916. We skied down to the cabin, hung our backpacks under the covered porch, and continued on up to the Silvertip Ranch with daypacks. Upon arriving at the Silvertip we were surprised to find that a winter keeper was on the premises.

The young man was very friendly and invited us inside. He served us a cup of hot chocolate, then gave us a tour of the main lodge. I had read about the infamous poacher, Joseph "Frenchy" Duret, a trapper who lived in a cabin just north of the park, and was rather notorious for his poaching exploits inside the park. In the spring of 1922 Duret had found a grizzly bear in one of his traps, and he shot the bear. The enraged bear broke free from the trap and severely mauled Duret. Frenchy managed to crawl a couple of miles back to the edge of his property where he died. He is buried in "Frenchy's Meadow" a few miles north of the Silvertip Ranch. His gravestone reads "Joseph Duret, Born in France 1858, Died 1922." NPS Rangers searched for the injured bear but it was never found. Perhaps the relatives of that bear inhabit Yellowstone today. In any event, it was fascinating to see the actual newspaper clippings of those events posted on bulletin boards in the lodge. The Yellowstone superintendent then was Horace Albright, who went on to become the Director of the National Park Service.

After visiting the Silvertip we bid the winterkeeper goodbye. He had told us that we were the only people he had seen all winter, so I think he appreciated our company as much as we enjoyed his hospitality. We simply could not imagine a lonelier job as being winterkeeper at the Silvertip Ranch deep in the wilderness, but we also knew that the rewards were unique and abundant. The three of us skied back to Elk Tongue cabin, retrieved our packs, and skied back down to the Lower Slough bunk house. Once again the conditions were fantastic. We made much better time on skis than we could have made hiking. "Man, this cross-country skiing is a piece of cake," I thought to myself. Of course, the following year when I took an 18 day backcountry ski trip in Yellowstone with Brian Severin and Steve Veltrie, I learned just how variable ski conditions can truly be! (see "Ski Touring—18 Days Through Yellowstone," in the first volume.)

That evening after we had retired to our bunks we were awakened by a very loud roaring noise. "Was an avalanche tumbling down the north side of Bison Peak behind the cabin," I wondered? We were hearing an avalanche of snow alright, but it was coming from directly over our heads! The winter's full accumulation of snow on the metal roof was giving way to the heat produced from the cabin's wood stove. Despite the fact that this bunk house was available for use by the public, it appeared that we were the first ones to stay there that winter.

When Margaret and I moved to Bozeman in 2006, I could not help but think back on that ski trip up to the Silvertip Ranch 34 years earlier, and I could not wait to repeat it. Ironically, in 1997 my oldest daughter Caroline landed a job working at the Silvertip Ranch for the summer, and Margaret and I were invited to ride in on a horse-drawn wagon to attend the "shake-down dinner" prior to the arrival of the season's first guests. The ranch is actually owned by a consortium of families, and the staff that works there caters to their guests. The ranch is not typically available to the general public. Our summer experience was fabulous as we enjoyed the shake-down dinner, and rode horses up to Frenchy's Meadow to view his grave site. At this time we lived in Tennessee and were only in Yellowstone during the summer months.

I longed for the day that I could repeat my magical winter wilderness ski trip up to the Silvertip Ranch. I attempted it on a solo March trip in 2007, but when I reached Lower Slough Meadow, I found that I was sinking knee deep. Since I had no companions to break trail with me, I decided not to even try. When I reached the trailhead there was an irate visitor who was anxious to "tee off" on a uniformed NPS employee. I listened to his expressed anger about the little yellow plane that often heads out early in the morning, and flies low to track wildlife, typically wolves. He said that the park was creating a horrible intrusion on the natural scene by conducting research on animals, and that he hated to see collars on wild animals. "Why can't you just leave the animals alone!" he forcefully stated. Actually, I had heard this complaint before, and frankly the overflights have disturbed me while camping deep out in the wilderness.

Fortunately, our winter training in December had featured an outstanding presentation by Wolf Project Leader Doug Smith. Doug acknowledged the intrusion but explained the trade-off. He pointed out that the wolf reintroduction and subsequent research were unprecedented, and that the opportunity to gather data on wild wolves was critically important. The much-maligned wolf had been extirpated from almost all of its former range, and there would never be another chance to gather this type of data, which would greatly assist biologists in future decades. Thanks to Doug's eloquent report, I was able to actually help this visitor understand why it was necessary to carry out this research in the park.

In February of 2012 I skied into Slough Creek with Ranger Steve Ballou and Jim Horan. Steve was stationed at Old Faithful for the winter, and Jim had previously worked as a backcountry ranger in Bechler. The first two miles follow the primitive dirt road that leads to Slough Creek campground. In summer, the road is filled with visitors driving into the campground, or hikers and anglers headed to the trailhead to hike up Slough Creek. However, during the winter months the road is not plowed, so the distance to the Lower Slough Meadows is doubled from two miles to four miles.

On our way in we were intrigued to see numerous wolf tracks and dozens of bison. The bison migrate back and forth over Transfer Hill, which can create a frozen and bumpy trail; however, a recent snow had produced a fresh coating of five inches of powder, which made our trip up and over the ridge rather easy. When we arrived in the Lower Meadows we headed up to the patrol cabin to store our gear, then out for a day ski in the valley. We counted about 75 bison in the meadows, and decided to ski a wide loop around them. We followed a set of wolf tracks, and they eventually led us up to the top of a hill consisting of an outcropping of granite. The hill is sort of an island in the meadow, and serves as a great sentinel post for observing activity throughout the meadow below.

I had recently watched a documentary on PBS about the techniques and strategies that wolves use up in Canada to prey on bison, which are completely different from those wolves use to prey on elk. Wolves essentially carefully scout for a single weak bison, which explained all of the fresh wolf tracks on top of the granite outcropping. Once a weak animal is identified the wolves might observe it for over a week before making a move. Despite all of the evidence of wolves in our area, we did not spot one or hear one. This particular trip was more of a working trip with numerous chores to be completed at the cabin. We did not have the time to attempt to ski up to the northern boundary, but given the deep snow conditions, and temperatures near 20 below, it would have been a tough ski, certainly nothing to compare to my 1972 ski trip.

I tried again in late January of 2014. I had received reports that the snow was set up rather nicely. Bruce Hoffman and I made plans to ski up the Slough Creek valley, and hopefully venture on up to the Silvertip Ranch. I had no idea if the Silvertip still employed a winterkeeper, but we looked forward to finding out. From previous trips I knew that the trail over Transfer Hill could be icy and hard-packed due to bison continually traveling here. Therefore, when we saw a weather forecast predicting a front to move through and drop 4 to 7 inches of fresh powder, we were encouraged. But things didn't quite work out as planned. The 7 inches that were forecast had turned into 18-24 inches. We headed out on a clear, calm day with the temperature at 8 degrees F. With all of the recent snow and wind it was impossible to pick out where the road was located. Soon we encountered steep hills, and it was at this point that we really started to struggle. Because of the cold temperatures and dry snow, our "waxless" skis were simply not working. We would take two steps forward and slide one step back. Normally when I encounter a steep hill I simply use the "herringbone" technique of pointing my skis outward 15 to 20 degrees, and waddling up the hill like a penguin. However, this technique does not work so well when you are sinking deep into two feet of fresh snow with each step. What we really needed in these conditions were some "mini" or "kicker" skins. You simply loop each end on your skis and you can walk with ease up a steep hill; as a bonus they slow your speed when you have to go *down* a steep hill. Alas, Bruce and I did not possess this critical accessory, so we continued to struggle along. Once we reached the trail that leads up Transfer Hill we stopped at an old log, wiped the snow clear, put down some ensolite, and sat down for a lunch break. Our surroundings could not have been more beautiful on this clear, cold day. There was absolute silence. I could not help but think about what this spot is like in mid-summer with visitors coming and going. Now, in the middle of winter, we might as well have been twenty miles deep in the heart of Yellowstone's wilderness.

After lunch we began our steady ascent through some dense timber with Bruce leading the way, and I soon heard a "Whoa!" around the bend. Bruce had skied right up next to a big bull bison hidden down in the deep snow and the huge beast jumped up only a few feet away, then just stood in the middle of the trail. Bruce had managed to use the gate across the old wagon road as a barrier to ease past the bison, but I had no such luck.

There were steep ridges choked with blowdown on both sides of the trail, but when I realized the bison was not going to move, I decided to navigate through the tangled mess of downfall. After I managed to climb up on the slope and get engulfed in the blowdown, the bison looked at me as if to say, "Hah, now that you are miserably stuck up there, I can move on down the trail." The rascal. I managed to backtrack down the hill, and then continue my long, slow ascent of Transfer Hill.

After climbing 640' we finally topped out and enjoyed spectacular views in both directions: Mount Washburn to the south and Slough Creek Valley with Cutoff Peak in the distance to the northeast. We managed to negotiate the descent down to the valley, but we faced one more climb through the deep slippery snow up to the cabin. By the time we reached the cabin we realized that it had taken us *five hours* to ski the four miles. We had decided at lunch that there was no way we were going to attempt continuing on to Elk Tongue on this day.

We were surprised to see the very low supply of firewood on hand. Typically, firewood is cut and split each fall season, so that there is a good supply on hand for winter use. But then I realized what had probably happened. The park had experienced a three week shutdown due to the political shenanigans. Therefore, with seasonal NPS workers furloughed three weeks early during the fall season, I suspected that the traditional job of fall backcountry patrol and firewood replenishing had simply not happened.

Given the deep snow conditions and amount of work that needed to be performed at the Lower Slough patrol cabin, Bruce and I decided against attempting to ski up the valley to Elk Tongue. Instead we spent most of the next day chopping and splitting wood, and hauling it thirty yards through thigh-deep snow to the cabin. We also shoveled the deep snow off of the edges of the roof of the cabin. Late that afternoon Bruce and I headed back up Transfer Hill and on to the trailhead. A small amount of snow had fallen overnight, but our broken track made for great skiing.

Along the way we noticed fresh wolf tracks, which we had not seen the previous day on our trip in. It only took us a little over two hours to ski the four miles back out—quite a change from the five hour ski trail breaking the previous day. When we arrived at the trailhead I found wolf expert and observer extraordinaire Rick McIntyre with his scope. I told Rick about the fresh tracks we had seen, and he said that early that morning he had observed the Junction Butte Pack headed up the valley.

I still have high hopes of making it all the way up Slough Creek Valley on skis one of these days, but I think I'm going to aim for a late spring ski the next time that I give it a try! By then perhaps the snow would be more consolidated and replicate the conditions that I experienced on that magical trip of March, 1972. However, even a "bad" day of skiing into the Lower Slough Creek Meadows of Yellowstone beats just about anything else!

Addendum

In early March, 2016, I took a three day ski trip up the Slough Creek Valley with Jim Horan and Bruce Hoffman. Given the recent warm weather, the snow had repeatedly thawed out and re-frozen, thus providing a firm, consolidated surface ideal for "crust cruising." We performed work at both the Lower Slough and Elk Tongue cabins, and I even contacted a couple of backcountry campers enjoying the rather mild, spring-like weather. We made it all the way to the historic Silvertip Ranch, but there was no winter keeper on the grounds this time. There was no one around—complete solitude. Thanks to the ideal ski conditions, we were able to cover 27 miles on our weekend trip. After 46 years it felt great to finally again ski the entire length of this spectacular valley.

Several times during the trip I felt the presence of my long-ago Yellowstone buddy Ron Bestrom. A couple of days after the trip I decided to contact Ron to share my experience. I wanted him to know that skiing up the Slough Creek valley was still just as great as it was when we first made the trip in 1972. It had been over a decade since I had talked with Ron, who hailed from Colville, Washington. When I attempted to find his current whereabouts, I was stunned to learn that Ron had recently passed away due to complications from Alzheimer's Disease. Perhaps it was no accident that I felt the presence of Ron's spirit with me amidst the solitude of Upper Slough Creek valley.

Late Winter Wildlife Adventures at Old Faithful

On March 8, 2013 a rather strange thing happened at Old Faithful. I had just skied into the visitor center to prepare to go out on geyser predict duty (GP), when I heard Old Faithful Subdistrict Ranger Colleen Rawlings call over the radio that we had two dead bison right on the road just west of Old Faithful. Colleen said there were wolf tracks everywhere. Her first concern was contacting maintenance to figure out how to pull the carcasses off the road, so snowcoaches and snowmobiles could get through later in the morning.

When I headed out on GP the basin seemed a bit more vibrant. There were coyotes romping about, and ravens were flying overhead. It was almost as though the dinner bell had just been rung: "Come to breakfast!!" Later that morning I heard over the radio that maintenance had pulled one carcass out of the road into the trees, but the other one was so large, all that could be done was to roll it off the road down an embankment.

That afternoon after we closed the visitor center for the day at 5:00 p.m., my colleagues, Brian LaWatch and Tom Arnold, and I decided to take a ski up the Fern Cascades Loop, a distance of three miles. The trail climbs 500 feet up to a plateau that overlooks the entire Old Faithful area below. I have never been much of a fan of this trail during the summer months, but in the winter it is spectacular. By the time we reached the top, the glow of the late afternoon sun was casting a rich, golden tint to the forest and basin below. After a hair-raising descent on our skis down off of the plateau, we reached the groomed road and came up with a bold idea to ski down to the bison carcasses to check out the scene.

We were a bit nervous about doing this. By this time of day no one was around. The Snow Lodge had been closed for a week. Even the Geyser Grill, which is only open from 11:00 a.m. to 3:30 p.m. after the Lodge closes, was empty. It was just the three of us. Tom had a can of bear spray. So far there had been no bear activity reported in the Old Faithful area, though Ranger Mike Curtis had discovered fresh bear tracks the day before in the south-central area of the park's backcountry. Of course, we knew for certain that wolves were in the area, based on earlier reports. So the three of us proceeded to ski down the deserted road toward the Black Sand Basin area where the carcasses were reported to be.

Tom was the first to note movement ahead down the road. Something dark was running across the road, though we only got a brief glimpse. As we skied closer we saw a bison carcass on the south side of the road with a coyote running away from it. Once we were even with the carcass we looked around. Wolf tracks were everywhere, as was blood and mats of hair. It was a rather spooky feeling, though we felt pretty safe since there were three of us, plus we had good visibility in all directions. "Let's ski down and take a closer look at this thing," Tom said. "Well guys," I commented, "before we do that I have to tell you a little story I once heard from Tom Murphy." Tom is a notable photographer of the Yellowstone landscape, and gained much fame when he was featured in the PBS Nature special, "Christmas in Yellowstone." He had told this story a couple of years earlier in Bozeman at the monthly meeting of the Sacajawea Audubon Society.

Once while trekking with a friend out in Hayden Valley during the bison rut in August, they topped a knoll and discovered a bison carcass. Sometimes during the rut the big bulls inflict serious wounds during the battles, which later become infected and lead to death. Grizzlies are tuned into this ritual and with their incredibly sensitive noses are quick to find fresh kills. Tom scanned the open valley in all directions, and seeing no sign of a bear suggested that they take a closer look at the carcass. His friend had just purchased a new pair of binoculars, and was still having difficulty with the eyecup adjustment. As the two men approached the huge animal, to Tom's horror a huge bloody head emerged from the cavity of the bison. It was a grizzly! The bison cavity was so large that the big bear was completely obscured from view. Tom's friend was still searching the horizon with his binocs, trying to fit them to his eyes. "Stand still," Tom whispered to his friend. "We are about to be charged by a grizzly." "Where"? His friend asked, as he pointed his binocs in every direction, except where the grizzly was located.

Suddenly the bear backed out of the cavity of the bison, and began a full speed charge right at Tom and his friend. "Stand your ground. Don't move," Tom ordered. "What bear?" his friend answered. "I don't see anything," as he continued to overshoot the scene with his binocs. The big bear came within a few feet of Tom, stopped, shook his head, and then retreated. It was probably a good thing that his friend never saw any of the frightening event, which turned out to be a bluff charge. Other than aging a few years, Tom said he was just fine after the hair-raising incident.

After I finished telling the story to Brian and Tom, we looked again at the bison carcass below us, and concluded that this animal was only about two years old, and thus lacked the size to house a big grizzly in its cavity as had occurred with Tom Murphy. So we carefully approached the carcass. Very little had been consumed at this point. It appeared that wolves had snagged the rear leg of the bison, probably causing it to tumble to the ground, and a big strong member of the pack had gone for the throat, killing the animal. However, penetrating the substantial winter hide of a bison is no small task. Grizzlies, with their long claws are much better equipped for opening up a bison than a wolf. Even though wolf tracks were all around the carcass, we did not see or hear any sign of a wolf, and with darkness approaching, we skied back to our quarters in the government area.

I invited Tom and Brian in for a beer, and shortly thereafter we heard a knock at the door. It was Colleen Rawlings. "Are you three the ones who skied out to the carcass?" "Yes," I said. "We wanted to take a closer look at the carcass to see how the wolves managed to bring down a bison." "Well," we now have reports that bears are beginning to emerge from hibernation, so be sure to carry bear spray when you are out in the basin." We assured her that we would.

The next day my younger daughter Alison rode a snowcoach in to visit me. Even though the park's season was winding down the snow conditions for skiing were still wonderful. Alison arrived late in the afternoon, and after we closed the Old Faithful Visitor Education Center at 5:00 p.m., Alison, Brian, Tom, and I headed out to the overpass on our skis to see if any wolves were near the bison carcasses. Alison had never seen a wolf in the wild. We slowly skied within about 100 yards of the carcass, and presto, there were two large black wolves patrolling the area. When Alison saw them she turned her head to look at me, and her eyes revealed her thrill and excitement. I caught the image on my camera, and it was one of those priceless moments to treasure. We stayed back at a safe distance and watched the big wolves feeding on the carcass and prowling about the area for half an hour. It is always a thrill to see wolves in the wild, and in early March, the Old Faithful area is most definitely "in the wild" with no one else around!

The next morning Alison accompanied me on my favorite duty of all, "geyser predict" or GP. We headed out on skis early in the morning into the Upper Geyser Basin, where I had to download the Hobo loggers we have in the runoff channels at Castle, Grand, and Daisy Geysers, so we can determine the overnight eruptions, and provide some reasonably accurate predictions for folks coming into the area later in the day. We skied down to Riverside Geyser, which erupts about every six hours, and to our sheer joy it began erupting as soon as we arrived. We watched the steaming water gush out of the vent across and into the Firehole River for at least 15 minutes before heading back to the visitor center. The snow conditions for mid-March were outstanding, and we were able to ski across Geyser Hill to the backside of Old Faithful, and eventually to the visitor center.

When my days off arrived I loaded Alison on the back of a snowmobile, and we began our thirty mile drive from Old Faithful out to the West Gate. Things were going along fine until we rounded a bend to see about 40 bison walking right down the middle of the road in the same direction we were traveling. It is not that big of a problem when you have bison approaching toward you on the road. In those cases, you simply pull over and allow the big hairy beasts to pass. But it is a different story when the bison are walking in your direction of travel. I trailed the herd for 30 minutes, hoping the bison would move to one side of the road, but they were spread from one shoulder to the other. Just when it seemed hopeless, a commercial guide with clients on about six machines approached from behind me. I asked the guide, "Say, what do you do in a situation like this? We've been behind this herd for 30 minutes?" "You just have to pick an opening and ease through it," he said. "Do you mind if we tag along?" I asked. "Not at all," he said, "just follow us and stay close."

At that the guide quickly darted into an opening among the beasts. "Hold on!" I shouted to Alison. However, I guess I accelerated too slowly, because all of a sudden, instead of seeing a snowmobile in front of me, all I could see were the rumps of bison. "Dad!" Alison shouted, "Just gun it!" That I did and thankfully, the bison parted just enough to allow us to make it through.

Once we made it past Madison we thought we were home free, but then we encountered another herd of 35 to 40 bison traveling down the middle of the road, this time coming *toward* us. I told Alison that we just needed to pull over to the side of the road, and crouch alongside the machine as the huge beasts passed us. Alison did not like my plan; she wanted much more space and protection than a mere snow machine could provide, so she proceeded to wade through the thigh-deep snow over into the trees, and hide behind the trunk of a big tree.

When we finally made it out to the government area just west of the West Gate, I found that the recent snows had covered my Ford Ranger pickup in about two feet of powdery snow. When I tried to drive out into the groomed portion of the road, the truck quickly high-centered, and was going nowhere. We each pulled out a shovel and began digging out the snow from underneath the truck, and soon we were free of the deep snow, and on our way to our homes, hers at Big Sky and mine in Bozeman. It had been a magical time of bonding with my daughter in a special place for a couple of days.

When I returned to Old Faithful for the last week of the season I knew that it was just a matter of time before a grizzly emerging from its den would pick up the scent of the dead bison. On the afternoon of March 13, one of the snowcoach guides reported that he had seen a bison slip into Wall Pool, a hot spring located at Biscuit Basin, two miles to the north of Old Faithful. He said the bison managed to get out of the pool, but appeared to be terribly injured. That afternoon when we closed the visitor center, Tom, Brian and I decided to take our sleds down to Biscuit Basin to see if we could confirm if we now had a *third* bison carcass in the area. When we arrived we turned off our machines and walked over to the edge of the Firehole River. "There it is!" Tom exclaimed. About 75 yards northwest of Wall Pool was the dead bison. We walked up the boardwalk trail to get a better look. Brian had his binoculars and it was apparent that the bison was bloated, but it did not appear that any wolves or bears had found this carcass yet. Since we were in a thermal area where you are required to stay on the boardwalk, we were not able to get a closer look. I called Coleen Rawlings to let her know that we now had another carcass in the area. A grizzly bear had been observed only three miles to the north of here the previous day.

The next morning I arose at 7:00 a.m.; it was March 14, the morning before Old Faithful closed for the winter season and I would depart. Due to the rather warm weather with temperatures staying above freezing, I cracked opened my bedroom window, and immediately the low, mournful chorus of wolf howls completely filled my apartment. The howling may have *sounded* mournful, but with at least three bison carcasses in the area, the wolves were probably celebrating! Frankly, I was surprised that a grizzly bear emerging from its den had not yet followed his nose down to Old Faithful with all of this meat on the hoof available. I skied over to open up the Visitor Center. With everything closed and only two days left of the winter season, I knew that this would be a slow day, especially given the warm conditions we were experiencing.

About an hour later I heard the news crackling over the radio that I expected. It was Colleen reporting that a big grizzly bear was on the bison carcass at Biscuit Basin. She reported that the basin had been closed to any human entry. Traffic throughout the day was rather sparse, but the few snowmobile and snowcoach guides who came into the visitor center were ecstatic, having watched the grizzly from a safe distance feeding on the bison carcass.

By the time Brian, Tom and I got off work the entire area was eerily quiet. After all, it was the last evening of the winter season. We decided to hop on our sleds and head out to Biscuit Basin. When we arrived we saw that Colleen had posted closed signs, and had roped off the boardwalk at the footbridge across the Firehole River, which provides access to Biscuit Basin. But from the roadside we had a magnificent view of the majestic grizzly feeding on the carcass. It was over 100 yards away, but with our binoculars, we could see the movement of his eyes, and the rippling of muscles as it tore into the bison carcass. Here in front of us was a scene that truly represented Yellowstone at its wildest.

The next day the excitement continued as tour guide John Layshock walked into the visitor center, and graciously gave us a copy of a photo he had taken of two wolves on a fresh elk kill along the banks of the Firehole River about five miles west of Old Faithful. "You guys had better head out there when you get a chance," John said. "Some visitors are walking away from the road to the river to get photos, and even though the wolves are on the other side of the river from the road, they are getting too close—well inside the 100 yard distance visitors are required to stay back from wolves and bears."

When traffic at the visitor center lightened later in the afternoon, my supervisor, Rita Garcia, told me to go grab a snow machine and head out there to make sure visitors were staying at least 100 yards back from the wolves. I arrived just as a couple of the last snow coach tours were about to depart. It appeared that the folks on these tours had abided by the rules, but one of the tour guides pointed out tracks other visitors had made in the snow walking all the way down to the river's edge, and getting way too close to the carcass the wolves were feeding on. "Where are the wolves?" I asked one of the guides. "There are two of them and they are back in the woods with their tummies full, but I suspect they will come back out soon," came the reply. As the two groups pulled away, complete silence enveloped me. All I could hear was the gurgling of the Firehole River in front of me.

My machine was turned off and I took a seat in hopes the wolves would return. Suddenly, I saw two big mostly gray colored wolves emerge from the trees, and head back to the elk carcass, which was partially submerged along the banks of the river. Soon both wolves were at work on the carcass. In the otherwise complete silence of my surroundings, I could actually hear the tearing sounds as the wolves pulled the meat away from the bones of the elk carcass. With my binoculars I could see the eyes and teeth of the wolves as they hovered over the elk. Their facial expressions seemed peaceful, contented and relaxed, just as most of us would be sitting at the table eating our dinner in a fine restaurant. There was no aggression or ferociousness in their eyes at all. After all, the hard work had been done earlier, when I suspect there had been quite the struggle. I felt privileged to witness such a sight in the Yellowstone winter wilderness. The episode playing out before me reminded me that death is part of life, and in the wild Yellowstone ecosystem, death is not really "bad," it is simply part of the natural cycle. Nothing is wasted here. Anything that is not consumed will eventually be recycled to the soil. Even the bones are gnawed and partially consumed by various scavengers and little critters, such as chipmunks and ground squirrels. I watched the wolves for at least half an hour, during which time no one else came by this late in the day. It was an experience I will never forget.

Well, what a difference two years can make! Alison had planned to again join me at Old Faithful as I worked the last two weeks of the 2015 winter season, but with the warm temperatures and paucity of snow, she decided against it. She made a wise choice as I'm sure she would have been disappointed after having such a great visit two years earlier. The snow was largely gone from the geyser basin. There was no skiing on geyser hill; no skiing from Old Faithful down to Morning Glory Pool. In fact there was not even enough snow to ski to and from the Visitor Center from my apartment! Gone were the snowmobiles and snow coaches. The company tours coming in from West Yellowstone were driving in with wheeled vans on mostly bare roads! Still, the final two weeks were special in their own way.

The only decent ski remaining was the Fern Cascades loop, which is located behind the government housing area, and sits on a north facing slope, so it holds the snow well. I managed to take several excursions on the three-mile loop, both early before work, and late after work, and enjoyed every minute.

However, going out on geyser predict, and *walking* the basin rather than skiing it, was a first for me. Nevertheless, there is just nothing like the Upper Geyser Basin early in the morning, and in the winter, there is *no one* out there. For that matter, that is pretty much true in all seasons if you head out very early.

I headed out on March 9, and immediately heard red-wing blackbirds voicing their distinctive "welcome to spring" calls. "Way, way too early to be hearing that, especially *here,"* I thought to myself. Even though the temperature would rapidly climb to the mid-to high 40s during the warm spell, at least the mornings on GP felt crisp at around 15 degrees. I observed several bison grazing, and noted that most of them looked very healthy for this late in the winter—not good news though for the wolf, bear and coyote who depend on weakened animals this time of year to take down. As I walked down the basin, both Daisy and Grand Geysers erupted, which resulted in tiny ice crystals floating down from the clear, blue morning skies. I noticed some fairly recent wolf tracks in the basin, probably following the herd of bison around looking for a weak specimen to pick out. "Good luck," I thought. Wolves have an uncanny sense for picking out a weakened member of the herd, but I sure didn't spot any that I would classify as weak.

As I completed my two hour duty that involved making a three mile loop of the Upper Geyser Basin to observe our four primary predictable geysers—Daisy, Riverside, Grand and Castle, I was again reminded of just how special this duty is. I never cease to be amazed at the peace, the quiet, the stunning, ethereal beauty of the Upper Geyser Basin early in the morning. I'm often the only soul in the basin this early, and it is so easy to imagine what it might have been like for the first explorers to walk into this otherworldly place!

The next afternoon I was on rove, and was lucky enough to walk up to Beehive Geyser, one of the world's largest, with eruptions reaching well over 170 feet and lasting five minutes. I also observed something that has to be very strange for March 10 in Yellowstone. I observed a herd of about 40 bison, and several were lying down in the snow, even though bare, thermal-heated ground was nearby. At 48 degrees with the sun bearing down, these bison were simply trying to cool off! On March 10! At 7400' elevation in Yellowstone!

As the winter season of 2014-15 drew to a close, I realized that in this my ninth consecutive winter season of having the privilege of working at Old Faithful, that I was going to do a very rare thing. For all I know it may have been a first. Rather than ride a snowmobile, I was going to drive my truck out on roads that were now almost completely bare of snow. Spring appeared to be right around the corner, but looking at the calendar it made no sense. I wondered if the animals were as confused as me. Changes are coming to Yellowstone—and they are coming too rapidly!

A Late Season Ski and Diminishing Winters

I knew the 2014-15 winter season at Yellowstone was in trouble when I saw that Steve Ballou was on the roster. Steve is an outstanding interpretive ranger who is a good friend of mine, but it seems that when he works a winter season at Old Faithful we have a paucity of snow. Therefore we have nicknamed him "No Snow Ballou." The winters when Steve did not work at Old Faithful turned out to be cold and snowy. I was hoping against hope that we would break the "Ballou jinx" this time around, but perhaps it is more than just his jinx.

At our winter training session in December, Yellowstone NPS Climate Specialist Ann Rodman gave a presentation on "Yellowstone's Diminishing Winters." I had previously seen a similar program by Tom Oliff, when he was chief of the Yellowstone Center for Resources. Ann used graphs to depict the amazing climate change affecting the park over the past fifty years or so. For example, the growing season on the Northern Range (North Gate out through Lamar Valley) has increased by 30 days over the past 50 years based on the number of nights that now go below freezing. Since 1948 daytime highs and nighttime lows are much warmer. The winter's snow is melting more quickly. The SNOTEL site atop Parker Peak averages 25 fewer days with snow on the ground than it did 30 years ago. The Northeast Entrance at an elevation of 7349' has 35 fewer days with snow on the ground than it did 45 years ago. Since 1961, 70% of the thirty snow measurement stations in and around Yellowstone have shown significant declines in April 1 snow water equivalent readings, while 30% have shown no significant trend. No increases were detected.

However, it was Ann's last image that convinced me that I should not pick on Steve for Yellowstone's trend toward lackluster winters. Her graph revealed a frightening correlation between steeply rising global temperatures and carbon emissions since 1980. Ironically we got off to a decent start at the beginning of the winter season. By Christmas there were some nice snowstorms blowing across the Yellowstone Plateau. I snowmobiled in to work during January, and while the snow accumulation was less than in previous years, things were going along rather smoothly. The park was a winter wonderland, it was cold, and visitors were having a ball. But we had a reversal of fortunes in February, which turned out to be a record month in terms of warm temperatures and lack of snow in places like West Yellowstone and Bozeman. Record highs were being set on a daily basis, and the new highs were not just one or two degrees above the old record high, but several were six or seven degrees warmer than at any time in recorded history. The Gallatin Valley around Bozeman took on the appearance of spring time. Robins showed up in our yard in Bozeman on February 11, way ahead of schedule. Bridger Creek Golf Course, normally a Mecca for groomed cross country ski trails in February, actually opened for the golf season, and why not? There was not a flake of snow in sight.

My good friend and former Old Faithful supervisor Joe Halladay has had a home north of Belgrade since the early 1970s. I asked Joe if he could ever remember a winter so warm and snow free. "Never," Joe replied. Yellowstone was hard hit as well. Beginning on February 16, *over a month before the end of Yellowstone's winter season in the interior,* snowmobiles and snow coaches with metal tracks had to be banned from entering the park from West Yellowstone. Only wheeled and rubber mat-tracks were allowed. There was simply hardly any snow on the roads. I asked long-time Yellowstone maintenance employee Bronco Grigg at Old Faithful if he could ever remember a winter like this. "Nope," was his reply. Mike Bryers has lived in West Yellowstone and worked as a winter guide for the last 32 years. I asked Mike the same question. "I remember some winters, especially in the late 70s when it was awfully dry," Mike said, "but never have I ever seen a winter this warm." Perhaps the best confirmation came from long-time winter keeper Jeff Henry, who walked into the visitor center on March 8. Jeff and I have known each other for several decades. He is also a photographer and the author of the excellent book, "Snowshoes, Coaches, and Cross Country Skis: A Brief History of Yellowstone Winters."

More than once during the warming months of the spring season at Old Faithful, I have heard Jeff strongly express his preference of seasons when he pontificates, "Heat is an evil *thing!*" After exchanging greetings and pleasantries, I asked, "Jeff, how long have you been shoveling snow off of roofs in Yellowstone as a winter keeper?" "Thirty-eight years," came the reply. "Have you ever seen a winter like this?" I asked. "Never," Jeff immediately replied. Jeff seems to possess a photographic memory about Yellowstone winters, and like Mike, he remembered two or three back in the late 70s and early 80s that had been rather dry. "But *never* have I seen such a *warm* winter," he said. As he spoke the outside temperature was headed for 50 degrees at an elevation of just under 7400' with the bright sun bearing down. Jeff was appropriately dressed in a tee shirt. I had been scheduled to work the last two weeks of the season which ended on March 15, and was able to simply drive my Ford Ranger into Old Faithful from the West Gate. In the previous nine winter seasons that I had come into Old Faithful to work late in the season, I always had to drive in on a snowmobile. This was a first.

I could not help but think about my friend and former colleague Mike Yochim's commentary in his book, "Yellowstone and the Snowmobile," which detailed the history and controversy of Yellowstone's winter use. Mike had pointed out that with the changing climate, one of these days there might not be enough snow to support over snow travel in much of Yellowstone's interior. In fact, during the height of the controversy over the winter use plan, some people advocated for simply keeping the majority of park roads in the interior plowed all year, as is presently done on the lower elevation road from Mammoth out to Tower through Lamar Valley to the Northeast Entrance. I was personally opposed to that plan for two reasons. First, what if visitors had a winter vacation planned at Old Faithful, and a big snowstorm hit? At least with over snow travel a big snow storm is not going to prevent folks from getting into the park for their vacation, and for some it is a once in a lifetime trip. Second, I guess I'm just a romantic at heart, but there is simply something "romantic" and very special about entering Yellowstone's interior in the winter via an over snow vehicle as opposed to simply being driven in on a bus or in a van. The analogy I use has to do with visiting an island. There is just nothing special about the visit if you simply drive your vehicle over a bridge to the island. However, if there are no roads or bridges, and you have to take a boat to get to the island, then you really feel like you are in an extraordinary place. Maybe that's why I love Cumberland Island National Park off the coast of Georgia so much, but that is another chapter for another book.

It seems that during the winter of 2014-15, the Northeast U.S. was having the winter we were supposed to have. Lots of snow and cold weather continued to blow over much of the East and even the South. I had to chuckle that my friends back in East Tennessee, where we lived for 31 years, were at times experiencing a colder and snowier winter than we were having in Bozeman! I also laughed out loud when I saw on the TV news U.S. Senator Jim Inhofe, Republican from Oklahoma, toss out a snowball during a Congressional speech. Who needs science to debate the impacts of climate change as long as you can locate a snowball? I guess Senator Inhofe was not paying much attention to the heat waves and droughts plaguing so much of the Western U.S. during the winter of 2014-15.

After I arrived for the last two weeks of the season at Old Faithful, I skied into work the next morning. I was scheduled for my most revered duty of "geyser predict." But Steve had warned me the night before that I should not even attempt to ski out into the Upper Geyser Basin. There simply was too little snow, and many large bare spots due to the thermal warmth of the ground. So for the first time in nine winter seasons working at Old Faithful, I walked around the basin to collect the data from geysers such as Riverside, Daisy, Grand and Castle. It might as well have been spring or early summer. The basin was gorgeous as always, but it just didn't seem like winter.

When my first day off on March 6 rolled around, I had already observed that plowing was underway. So far that winter I had not taken a single backcountry ski trip, the first time that had happened since moving to Bozeman in 2006, so by March 6 I was ready for some backcountry skiing, even if it had to be a solo day trip.

I had not been up the steep Howard Eaton trail from Old Faithful to Lone Star since my adventurous 18 day winter ski trip back in 1973. I had been *down* the trail after a big powdery snow, and it was heavenly. Believe me, you do not want to ski down or up this trail, affectionately referred to as "the Howie" if it is hard packed or icy. On this day I basically had hard packed conditions with about an inch of recent powder on top, so I figured it would be fine. My plan was to ski up my beloved Fern Cascades trail, which being on a north-facing slope always held good snow, and cut over to the Howie, and eventually come into Lone Star Geyser about four miles up. From there I would explore around the Firehole River, then follow the trail over to the Spring Creek cutoff trail, and explore that canyon before returning to the Lone Star trail out to the main road. My loop solo ski would be about ten miles, and I was primed and pumped to go.

I left the housing area at Old Faithful at 8:45 a.m. on a textbook bluebird day with the temperature in the mid-20s. The ski conditions during the steady climb of 500' through dense lodgepole pine were perfect, and I made it to Lone Star in about two hours. The geyser was spitting water and steam continuously, but it did not appear close to erupting. Lone Star erupts to a height of about 40 feet out of its 12 foot cone fairly regularly, about every three hours. It appeared to be about midway between eruptions. Looking at the geyser, I could not help but remember my ski trip up this trail in 1973 on our first day of an 18 day trip into the Yellowstone backcountry. The snow that I observed around Lone Star on this day was nothing compared to what we experienced here on that 1973 trip. In fact, I had to take my skis off in several places where the snow had already melted out, due to a combination of low snow, warm days, and underlying thermal heat. I enjoyed a lengthy snack while sitting on a log directly in front of Lone Star's cone. I soaked in the quiet and peaceful surroundings of this corner of Yellowstone's spectacular wilderness.

I finally skied over to the trail, which leads along the Firehole River some 2.5 miles out to the main road. I had not seen another soul on this day, and did not expect to considering the time of day, and time of year. So it was a surprise to round a bend in the trail, and see two men with large backpacks headed my way. When we pulled even with each other I commented, "You guys look like you are going to be out for a while." "We are skiing all the way to Bechler, 30 miles away," came the reply. "Wow," I said, "I envy you. How many days do you plan to take?" "Five," one of the men answered. They seemed to be well-equipped and knowledgeable. I had backpacked the 30 miles between Old Faithful and Bechler several times in the summer, and had always dreamed of such a trip in the winter. Given the current weather conditions with nice relatively warm weather, they were fortunate. As I bid them so long and wished them well, one of the men said, "Oh, by the way, there are nine more coming." Sure enough, I passed nine more skiers, and these men were not exactly spring chickens. Several appeared to be in their sixties. "What a great adventure these guys are having," I thought to myself with some envy. However, my thoughts soon returned to the gorgeous day ski I was enjoying along the gurgling Firehole River, with large fluffy mounds of white snow crumpled all along its banks.

I had halfway expected to see some bear tracks, but so far only bison had traveled through. When I reached the main road there was not a snowmobile in sight. At this time of year the traffic is light anyway, and the machines coming in from the South Gate were apparently at Old Faithful waiting for an eruption. I merrily skied past Kepler Cascades, and made it back to my quarters by 1:00 p.m. I had made the ten mile ski with stops along the way in a little over four hours. The ski trip had been just the tonic I needed for my soul—even in this abbreviated winter season. However, I could not help but wonder to myself, "Were the long, frigid, snowy winters that we had always been accustomed to in Yellowstone, and taken for granted becoming a thing of the past?"

Moonlight Skiing

There is something utterly ethereal about moonlight skiing. During the 31 years I lived in Tennessee, I was often terribly frustrated by the lack of cross-country skiing opportunities, especially as we moved from the decade of the 70s to the 80s, when the amount of snowfall in East Tennessee declined significantly. My friend Nicky Hamilton and I would often find snow by heading up high into Great Smoky Mountains National Park. We lived only about an hour's drive from the entrance near Gatlinburg, and while the elevation there is only 1300,' the Newfound Gap road takes you up to an elevation of over 5000.' On more than one occasion I can recall driving through Sevierville, Tennessee with the temperatures in the high 60s, but by the time we reached Morton Overlook at 4500,' we would suddenly enter a winter wonderland with several feet of snow on the ground. I would usually call ahead to talk to Park Ranger Glen Cardwell, who was actually my supervisor at Sugarlands Visitor Center during the summers of 1987-88. "Glen," I would ask, "Any new snow fall up at Newfound Gap?" Glen had a direct line to the snow gauge there, and he would give us the most current conditions. At first we would drive up early on Saturday mornings after a new snow, but we quickly found that did not work out for us. That's because the road leading to Newfound Gap was curvy and treacherous, and would first have to be sanded prior to opening, which usually took until 11:00 a.m.

Nicky and I came up with a plan for skirting that problem. We would leave on Friday afternoon after work, and drive up to Newfound Gap. By afternoon the road had been sanded, was in decent condition, and most importantly was open! We would park at Newfound Gap, ski up the Clingman's Dome road (not plowed in winter), and spend the night in the vicinity of Collins Shelter on the Appalachian Trail (AT.) We always carried a tent to pitch nearby in the snow, because frankly it was warmer in our tent than it was in the three-sided shelter. It was on such trips that we discovered the magic of moonlight skiing. Once we set up our tent we would head out into the woods on the AT, marveling at the eerie lighting of the moon filtering through the snow-laden trees. Another advantage to moonlight skiing in the South is the fact that ski conditions are often great at night, compared to the warm sticky conditions during the day. Once after a big snowfall, we drove up to Roane Mountain State Park in upper East Tennessee, but found warm, sticky snow. However, the moonlight skiing that night was marvelous.

When I began working at Old Faithful during the winter, skiing under the moonlight was something to behold, but it could be rather tough physically. Nighttime temperatures are often twenty below, and without any comfort from the sun, you had to not only layer up, but keep moving. On one full moon evening several members of our staff headed down into the Upper Geyser Basin for a late night ski. First we watched the gushing hot water and mushrooming steam cloud arise from Old Faithful's eruption, then we skied past the Old Faithful Inn, which is eerily quiet during the winter months. Only the Snowlodge is open during the winter, since heating the huge log and stone structure of the Inn would not be practical. However, on a side note, the concession employees have a tradition, where on one night during the winter season they are given permission to enter the dark and cold Old Faithful Inn lobby, where they set up a projector and screen, and show the movie, "The Shining." The two dozen or so employees bundle up in sleeping bags and blankets on the lobby floor to watch the horror movie in the spooky setting of the Inn. I attended the showing once, but left after about thirty minutes as I was about to freeze!

The highlight of our moonlight ski was witnessing an eruption of Castle Geyser, which had a twenty minute water phase, followed by a very powerful and noisy forty minute steam phase. During the summer, if an eruption is predicted for late in the evening, I always encourage visitors to go out to experience a moonlight eruption. On a winter's full moon night with the landscape covered in white, witnessing an eruption of Castle Geyser is akin to visiting another planet. It is that otherworldly! We observed Castle's eruption until our bodies told us it was time to get moving on this cold night, so we continued down past Daisy Geyer over to Black Sand Pool. This large and deep blue pool is off the beaten path, and is overlooked by most folks walking through the geyser basin even during the summer. Few people ski to it during the winter. For the past several years this pool has been having small eruptions that involve steam explosions in its deeper cavities. These actually cause the ground on which you are standing to vibrate, giving the sense of a small earthquake. The steam explosions vary quite a bit in intensity and intervals. On this evening, we stood behind the large log railings, and experienced two such "quakes," which only added to our unearthly experience. From Black Sand we skied down the trail, which is often not possible because of the warm underlying ground. However, on this trip there was sufficient snow on top that had not yet melted out. Once we reached the road near Black Sand Basin, we had it all to ourselves as the snow coaches had finished their day's travels.

Perhaps my most memorable moonlight ski near Old Faithful actually occurred early in the spring season, when there is typically a good accumulation of snow remaining. My good friend Martin Klinghard and his daughter Mary Elizabeth were visiting from Tennessee. Martin and I have taken many wonderful canoe trips in East Tennessee, Kentucky, Western North Carolina and even the Okefenokee Swamp; however, this was their first visit to Yellowstone. When Martin told me he was coming in early May, I warned him that winter still had its grip on the high Yellowstone Plateau, and that we would not be able to do any hiking or backpacking near my duty station at Old

Faithful. Martin and I had downhill skied before, but he and Mary Elizabeth had never tried cross-country skiing. We made plans to take a ski trip under a full moon after everyone got off work at 5:00 p.m. We planned to ski three miles down the DeLacey Creek trail to the shores of Shoshone Lake. We had some extra skis and boots for both of them. I wasn't worried about Martin, but I wondered how his 15 year-old daughter would do on the undulating terrain leading through the forest down to the meadows that led to the lake.

The snow was deep and nicely consolidated, so conditions could not have been better. Mary Elizabeth quickly caught on, and before long was gliding with ease through large meadows. Soon we arrived at the edge of frozen Shoshone Lake, one of the largest backcountry lakes in the lower 48 states. The moon lit up the entire landscape, and even Mount Sheridan in the distance was easily in view. We relaxed on some logs along the snow-covered shoreline, and immersed ourselves in the wild solitude of our setting. It was difficult to pull ourselves away and retrace our tracks to the trailhead. The light of the moon continued to be our friend on this night by lighting up our route back through the forest. I simply cannot imagine a more invigorating experience than moonlight skiing in the wilderness, and the high plateau of Yellowstone provides the perfect setting.

Spring

Spring Comes to Old Faithful—Geysers, Grizzlies and Snow

Each year around mid-March the winter season comes to an end at Old Faithful, and the calendar states that spring is just around the corner; however, winter does not always give up so easily at Old Faithful, located high on the Yellowstone Plateau at an elevation of just under 7400.' The visitor center and all services shut down for a month, as crews begin plowing the roads to prepare for the re-opening in the spring. For a full month the Old Faithful area reverts to almost a wilderness setting, as only a tiny skeletal staff remains. When the roads open into Old Faithful in mid-April, the number of visitors starts out quite low. For one thing snowstorms can be frequent. In the spring of 2007 I was scheduled to begin work on opening day at Old Faithful. My supervisor, Katy Duffy, called me at my home in Bozeman to warn me that a huge snowstorm was headed for Old Faithful, and to be sure to bring my skis. I decided to drive down a day early, which turned out to be the right decision, because on opening day I awoke to find two feet of fresh snow on the ground. Instead of riding my bicycle to work, I donned my skis to get there!

It is at this time of year that grizzly bears begin emerging from their dens, and the very first place that some of them head are the thermally heated and snow-free geyser basins along the Firehole River. Along with some forage the bears might find some weak bison to prey on. This is also true for wolves. Bison will stay in these thermal areas, using nature's energy to keep warm rather than burning up their own calories. However, it is a false sense of security for some of the older, weaker bison. The shaggy animals may feel comfort from the warm ground, but unless they are finding some nutrition, they will soon be unable to move from their comfortable, warm "hot pads." Retired Yellowstone Interpretive Biologist Norm Bishop, now of Bozeman, once put it aptly: "Yellowstone is like a box of cereal to the ungulates (e.g. elk and bison); in the summer they eat the cereal, in the winter they eat the box."

When the Old Faithful area re-opens in mid-April, and access is again available for cars from Mammoth and the West Entrance, visitors are often treated to sights that just don't happen during the busy summer months. Grizzlies and wolves have had the place to themselves for a full month, and they are sometimes reluctant to move out of the area, as visitors begin trickling in. Sometimes it is a challenging balancing act that the rangers must face in attempting to keep the boardwalks open with grizzlies traveling the geyser basins. After all, folks come from all over the world to see Yellowstone's world famous geysers, such as Old Faithful, Grand, Castle and Riverside.

One spring we had a bison carcass near Grand Geyser that grizzlies were feeding on, so rangers closed the boardwalks beyond Old Faithful and the Geyser Hill area. We began receiving complaints at the Visitor Center from visitors. Grand Geyser is considered to be the world's largest predictable geyser, with eruptions reaching a height of 200,' so visitors traveling into the Upper Geyser Basin obviously wanted to see it. Our maintenance workers somehow managed to move the bison carcass away from the geyser basin, so rangers could re-open the boardwalks. Normally, the policy in Yellowstone is to allow "nature to take its course," but this proved to be an exception.

A few years ago shortly after opening for spring, a small crowd had gathered to watch the next eruption of Old Faithful. They got much more than they bargained for. A young and very weak bison was walking out near the cone of the geyser, and a grizzly bear emerged from the woods, took it down, and devoured it!

Roving the Upper Geyser Basin during this period can create some hair-raising moments. Each morning we head out to download the overnight eruptions of the major geysers, so we can begin posting the day's predictions. With grizzlies roaming the basin, you tend to have your head on a swivel as you bike and walk through the basin. That is especially true near Castle Geyser, where a line of trees extends right down to the trail from both directions. It is at this point where grizzlies often cross the trail. Once I rode up to Morning Glory Pool on my bike to see a big grizzly bear standing upright with his back against a tree, using it as a scratching post!

However, my most unusual and memorable early spring incident with a grizzly bear occurred in 2007. Our staff was utilizing a temporary modular facility for our visitor center while the new Old Faithful Visitor and Education Center was being constructed. We had just opened for the morning, and the day's first prediction of Old Faithful had been posted. A small crowd of about 15 visitors was out on the boardwalk awaiting the eruption. I had just printed off the day's weather report, and when I turned to take a copy over to Christine working in the Yellowstone Association bookstore, I was alarmed by the expression I saw on her face. Her eyes were as big as saucers, and nothing was coming out of her mouth. However, she was vigorously pointing at something behind me. I turned around, and to my shock, there was a grizzly bear standing right at the front door!

I immediately got on the radio and transmitted, "Old Faithful Patrol, Old Faithful Patrol, this is 724 Victor. We have a grizzly bear at the front door of the visitor center!" Ranger Boone Vandzura answered that he was on the way. The grizzly moved away from the door, and to our deep concern, none of the visitors out on the boardwalk waiting on Old Faithful were aware of the bear coming their way. Tom Kearney was on the desk with me, and we quickly came up with a two-pronged plan. Since the bear had taken a few steps toward the trees in front of the visitor center, Tom would inform the visitors out on the boardwalk what was going on, and I would go outside and attempt to keep the grizzly in my sights until Boone arrived. As soon as Tom walked out the door to the porch he shouted, "Grizzly Bear! Move that way! Run! Run for your lives!" At least I'm pretty sure that's what he shouted, but whatever he said worked. The small crowd turned around, and when they saw the bear, they began moving in the direction Tom had pointed, toward the Old Faithful Lodge. By now the bear was running slowly through the trees headed west toward the Old Faithful Inn parking lot. I was running along on the sidewalk parallel to the bear keeping in touch with Boone on my portable radio. I remember thinking at the time, "This is really weird—I'm taking a jog with a grizzly bear!"

Everything seemed to be going just as planned. The Old Faithful Inn was not yet open for the season, so Tom and I had hoped to "haze" the bear in that direction, then Boone could finish the job with his patrol car's horn and siren, and, if necessary, rubber pellets from a "deterrent gun." However, what we did *not* know was Tom's wife, Joanne, was walking back from her early morning geyser predict duty with several visitors accompanying her. She and her group had walked past Castle Geyser, and were approaching the vicinity near the Lower General store, when they suddenly saw the bear headed right for them coming down the paved sidewalk!

By now Boone had his bullhorn and siren going, and Tom and I were standing above the parking lot. Joanne immediately told her group to stay with her, try to look large, make some noise so the bear would be aware of their presence, and above all, not to run off. "Why is that policeman chasing that bear toward us?" one of her group demanded to know. When Boone saw the group with Joanne he took out his deterrent gun and managed to haze the bear off of the trail, and out into the meadow, away from any trails or visitors. Of course, when the group learned that one of the rangers involved in the hazing was her husband Tom, they gave Joanne a hard time about him chasing the bear toward her!

Eventually, with more visitors arriving with each passing day, the brief, magical time ends, as the bears and wolves figure that they need to move further back from the road—to thermal areas in the Firehole Bear Management Area, which is closed to any human visitation each spring from March 10 to late May to allow the bears to continue their early season feeding without being disrupted.

Mid-April to mid-May is truly a fascinating time to visit Old Faithful, but folks need to remember that even though the calendar says it is spring, for the most part winter has not released its grip on the landscape. Other than walking in the geyser basins, there are no trails suitable for hiking. However, skis or snowshoes may still come in handy. The trails to Lone Star Geyser (5 miles roundtrip) and DeLacy Creek to frozen Shoshone Lake (6 miles roundtrip) are delightful, where the snow may still be several feet deep. Visitors need to remember, it's a good idea not to travel alone and don't forget the bear spray!

A cow bison and calf struggle through an early spring snow in the geyser basin

Part IV

Geologic Wonders

One never tires of watching the eruptions of Old Faithful

Please Don't Be Critical of Old Faithful— It's Under Enough Pressure Already!

Pressure indeed! Not just within the plumbing system of Old Faithful Geyser, but among the staff at the Old Faithful Visitor Education Center. Before leaving the building, no matter how brief the time, you had better know the next prediction for Old Faithful. And if you are the one making that prediction, you had better not make a mistake in your calculations. Old Faithful—the icon of Yellowstone; in reality, for America's entire national park system.

I have always been amazed at just how "faithful" and "predictable" Old Faithful is. Geysers are, after all, natural phenomena. We are not in a "Jellystone" theme park here. Most all of Yellowstone's 300 active geysers are *not* predictable. The few that are require rather sizeable windows: plus or minus two hours or so is not uncommon. But not Old Faithful. It can be predicted within plus or minus ten minutes an amazing 90% of the time.

I always thought it rather humorous that the Washburn, Langford, Doane expedition of 1870 that first documented the geyser named it "Old Faithful." How did they know it was faithful? They were only in the Upper Geyser Basin a couple of days before they moved on. However, they could not have selected a more appropriate name. For as far as we know, Old Faithful has not missed an eruption since that expedition named it. The very unique "faithfulness" of the geyser has sort of created a monster in a way. Visitors are demanding. They expect the geyser to erupt like clockwork.

I seldom work the desk at Old Faithful that someone does not come up and say, "Old Faithful sure isn't as faithful (or predictable) as it used to be!" Or, "When I was here thirty years ago Old Faithful erupted 200' every 25 minutes!" When I explain to the visitor that I was also here thirty (or *forty*) years ago, and that is not the case, visitors sometimes become quite perturbed. "I was here and I know what I saw," they might tell me. To which I typically respond with a smile as I attempt to describe the geyser's current activity. It really isn't worth getting into an argument over, but I do find it amusing just how adamant some visitors are about Old Faithful's previous performance over the years: "It was bigger." "It was more frequent." "It was more predictable." "It erupted every hour on the hour!"

I first saw Old Faithful in 1968 and began working at the Old Faithful Visitor Center as a park ranger in 1976. Yes, Old Faithful *has* changed a little, but not much really. It is still as predictable as ever. It is still as tall as ever. In fact, we think the height has actually increased in recent years. It might actually erupt with more regularity now than it did in previous years, but the average interval has indeed increased some over the years. Of course, Old Faithful never erupted every hour on the hour. That was a popular myth.

When I arrived in 1976, Old Faithful was erupting about every 78 minutes. The formula that we used to predict Old Faithful back then was about the same as the one we use today. We simply time the length of the eruption from the first continuous splashing of water until the water goes completely to steam. So the next eruption is really a function of the how long the eruption lasts. Currently, if the water comes out less than three minutes, we give it about 65 to 68 minutes before the next eruption. If the water comes out longer than three minutes (which is typically the case), we give it about 88 to 94 minutes. The actual number is based on the geyser's current average intervals. Occasionally the geyser stops about half-way between what we consider a "short" or "long" duration. When that occurs we tend to fudge just a bit and predict its next interval to be somewhere in between a short and long, say around 75 to 84 minutes.

There are four good reasons Old Faithful deserves all of its fame as the world's most famous geyser. First, it is one of the five tallest geysers in the world. Eruption heights of 150' are not uncommon. Second, the geyser is so predictable as mentioned above. Third, the geyser erupts so *frequently*. Most big predictable geysers in Yellowstone erupt much less frequently, usually averaging anywhere from six to 12 hour intervals. And fourth, yes, the geyser has been amazingly faithful. It is the very nature of geysers to change. Their intervals may shorten or lengthen, or the geyser may simply go dormant for an indeterminate period of time. Old Faithful just keeps plugging along.

The theory behind this faithfulness is pretty simple. If you stand in front of Old Faithful out on the boardwalks you will note that there is not another significant thermal feature anywhere near it. Over across the Firehole River on Geyser Hill, there are dozens and dozens of thermal features situated in close proximity to each other. Therefore, we speculate that Old Faithful has a very deep and durable plumbing system that it does not have to share with any other nearby features. Yellowstone averages over 2000 earthquakes annually. Most of these quakes cannot be felt, but they show up on a seismograph. It is the shaking of the ground that can rearrange a geyser's plumbing system, and cause it to change its behavior. But not Old Faithful. Even the huge 7.4 Richter scale earthquake of August 17, 1959 did not radically alter Old Faithful's activity.

Now, having said all this, *all* geysers do eventually change. Even Old Faithful. In fact, when you look at Old Faithful and its surroundings, you can easily see that Old Faithful has dramatically changed over the years—just not since 1870 when it was first documented. First, you note that Old Faithful sits up on a mound. Mounds form from overflowing hot springs, not geysers. So at some time in the past, Old Faithful was an overflowing hot spring, not a geyser. The mineralized knob that sits up on the top of the mound of Old

Faithful is actually an old tree trunk that has been covered by the siliceous sinter from water erupting from the cone over hundreds of years. The silica builds up at the rate of about one inch per 50 to 100 years. Scientists once drilled into the old tree trunk to date the wood, and they were surprised to find that it was really not that old. They concluded that Old Faithful had been erupting for perhaps 800 years or so. We really should be calling the geyser "Young Faithful."

In the mid-90s some scientists received permission to plumb Old Faithful's vent right after it had concluded erupting. They lowered a tiny video camera, insulated to protect against heat, down into Old Faithful's vent. They reached about 50' before they came to boiling water; however, the major finding was the fact that 22' down, Old Faithful's vent narrowed down to only four inches! So obviously, one of these years there is bound to be a major change with Old Faithful's activity. As the constriction continues to narrow, it could stop erupting, or perhaps only the manner in which the water is expelled could change. It might come out in more of a fanned, spread out pattern. Or, rather than erupt as a giant hose, which is the case now, it might turn into a fountain geyser similar to Sawmill, Great Fountain, and Grand. A big change could occur next week, or it could be over 100 years. Who knows? That's one reason geysers are so fascinating. Their changes in behavior are impossible to predict.

I shudder to think what might happen if Old Faithful ever stops erupting. There would probably be a law passed in Congress that requires the National Park Service to "repair" the geyser, though hopefully the politicians would not prevail. As I stated earlier, the Upper Geyser Basin at Yellowstone is a natural phenomenon, not a theme park like Disneyworld. In the meantime the pressure continues, both below Old Faithful's vent and among the staff to get those predictions right. We often check each other's math. We occasionally post on our prediction board, "Remember, we predict the geysers, we don't *schedule* them! Some folks mistakenly believe that geyser eruptions are like the ocean tide tables. "Don't you have the predictions printed out for the six months?" they ask. "No," we answer, "we can only predict them one eruption at a time."

When working on the visitor center desk at Old Faithful, it is not uncommon to receive a phone call from a visitor requesting Old Faithful's predictions for the next week." We always attempt to explain the variation, and that we can only make predictions one eruption at a time. One day, however, a lady from California would not give up. After I had gone through my spiel about how we can only predict the next eruption, and that she would just need to give us a call once she arrived in the park, the lady said, "Well! I guess everything I've read about Old Faithful is untrue!" "What do you mean?" I asked. "Well, I read that Old Faithful was predictable, but obviously it is not, because you refuse to give me a prediction for the day we arrive on next week!" She was just about to hang up but I quickly asked, "What day and time do you anticipate arriving at Old Faithful next week?" "We should be there by 3:00 p.m. next Thursday," she answered. "All right then," I confidently stated, "the prediction for Old Faithful next Thursday afternoon is 3:30 p.m. plus or minus *one hour*." "Well," she said with a tinge of indignity but also satisfaction, "what took you so long to give me this information?" "That's all I wanted to know!" at which time she hung up. Of course, the only reason I could make such a prediction is due to the frequency of Old Faithful's eruptions. You could come up with *any time* and give it a plus or minus one hour, and you would be "in the window" for most all eruptions!

I guess the most upset I ever heard anyone get over not being able to obtain a prediction for Old Faithful was not from a visitor; rather, it was a fellow ranger working the South Entrance gate during the winter season. It was my first day on the job at Old Faithful in the winter season during January of 2007. My supervisor, Katy Duffy, had instructed me that the first order of duty upon arriving at the Old Faithful Visitor Center was to call the day's first prediction out to the South Entrance, where snow coaches and snowmobiles would soon be arriving, and planning their drive into Old Faithful around the time we predicted for the next eruption. When I arrived at the visitor center, Old Faithful looked quiet, and there was no one in the basin. In those cases we would playback our video recorder, which recorded all of the eruptions. However, on this frigid morning there was a heavy fog over the basin, which is common in the winter on cold mornings given all of the thermal heat being expelled. When I played the video back all I could see was gray fog. I therefore had to wait until Old Faithful erupted before I could make the day's first prediction. While waiting, I received an irate call from the South Gate ranger demanding that I give him the next prediction. He did not seem to understand why I was not able to magically give him a prediction. Perhaps I should have pulled the same trick on him that I did with the lady from California. In any event, later in the day when Katy found out I had been chewed out by the South Gate ranger, she proceeded to make a phone call to the south gate and give the ranger an earful. Katy stood behind her staff. Needless to say, it made me feel better, especially since it was my first day on the job in the winter.

So yes, the pressure is on. Both below the ground at that four inch constriction in Old Faithful's vent, and above the ground where the pressure is on to get the predictions out in a timely and accurate manner. I for one don't mind. I have observed Old Faithful probably over 10,000 times, and I revere each and every eruption that I see. The geyser is truly a marvel of nature, and while I know it must change one of these days, I certainly hope it is not on my watch!

On Protecting Thermal Resources

I'm not sure I understand the fascination with folks wanting to soak in thermal waters in Yellowstone, especially on warm summer days. Most homes these days have a bath tub that you fill with hot water that allows one to soak to your heart's content. In fact, on some of Yellowstone's coldest winter days, I have been thankful for a hot bath after skiing to my quarters in below zero temperatures. In any case, when I am working on the desk at the Old Faithful Visitor Education Center, I occasionally get asked, "where can I go soak in a hot spring?"

It is illegal to swim or bathe in any thermal feature or its runoff channel. The only place where you can legally soak in warm water is in a natural stream where warm waters enter from another source. There are two primary reasons for this regulation: safety, and the protection of the delicate and fragile thermal features. There have been 20 documented deaths due to the scalding waters in Yellowstone's thermal basins. Even if the water is not hot enough to burn you, there can be some nasty stuff contained in the water, such as bacteria that can enter your nose, ears or eyes, and be fatal. Some of the park's hot springs are more acidic than battery acid, and can eat a hole right through your jeans or shoes, so you can imagine what that might do to your skin.

Over the years I have seen some interesting changes in the park regarding "thermal bathing." During the late sixties when I began working in the park with the old Yellowstone Park Company, I really never heard any of my fellow concession employees even talk about wanting to go swimming or "hotpotting," as some call it now (though based on fatalities documented in "Death in Yellowstone" by Lee Whittlesey, the activity was certainly taking place). My first exposure to swimming in thermally heated waters came about completely by accident.

During my first two summers, Margaret, our friends, and I had a penchant for visiting waterfalls, and the park's Bechler Region, or Cascade Corner, as it is appropriately called on topo maps, was the place to go. During the summer of 1968 we traveled to Three River Junction, and came upon a backcountry ranger there by the name of Pete Thompson. As we rounded the bend in the trail, Pete had just finished swimming in a large thermal pool next to a cliff that actually had a log wedged into the rocks to serve as a diving board. He pulled on his gray National Park Service shirt, extended his hand out to greet us with a broad smile and said, "Welcome to the garden spot of Yellowstone! You guys are over 13 miles deep into the wilderness here! Isn't it fabulous?" It was my first season in Yellowstone, and Pete was the first ranger I had encountered in the park's backcountry. The man was a walking ambassador for wild country. It was obvious that Ranger Thompson was passionate about his job, about the wilderness, and striving to protect and preserve it. He wished us continued happiness on our journey, and then headed back toward his camp.

Our hike on this day had been a long one, and I decided to emulate Ranger Thompson, and take a refreshing dip in the pool. I even took a couple of dives off of the "diving log" protruding from the cliff. I didn't think of myself as taking a "thermal bath," or "hotpotting." As far as I was concerned, I was simply taking a swim in the backcountry to get rid of the day's sweat and dust, which I do on any backpacking trip in warm weather. The diving board and warm water were simply a bonus. I've taken swims in many of Yellowstone's icy lakes, so the warm water of about 85 degrees was comforting. However, while entering this pool may have been allowed in the backcountry in 1968, today this would be illegal—and for good reasons.

As backcountry use increased, concerns over visitor safety and protection of delicate thermal features led to the regulation prohibiting swimming in thermal pools. For one thing, almost all of Yellowstone's thermal features are *way* too hot (by 50 to 100 degrees!) to stick a toe in anyway. For the handful of thermal pools not too hot, such as the one near Three River Junction that I entered in 1968, the water could be quite acidic or contain the deadly above-mentioned bacteria. And even if the water was safe, imagine the damage to the delicate bacterial mats and mineral deposits by large numbers of visitors.

During July of 1971 Rod Busby and I were on a hike from Old Faithful to Bechler, and we came upon backcountry ranger Paul Miller camped out at Three River Junction. After visiting for a spell it must have become apparent to Ranger Miller that Rod and I were very enthusiastic regarding our love for the Yellowstone backcountry, especially the Bechler region in general. Miller knew that we had a permit to camp nearby, and he decided that he wanted to show us something that he said was "very special." He led us away from the trail for about one mile to a beautiful stream that actually had a hot spring bubbling up in the middle of it. "Just try that out," he proudly said. The setting was incredibly gorgeous. This stream meandered through a verdant meadow replete with an array of colorful wildflowers, and our backdrop consisted of vertical slopes covered in green vegetation.

I'm not sure that hot tubs or Jacuzzis were in common use back then, but in any case, this was my first experience in one. Unlike the thermal pool at Three River Junction, which by now was off limits to soaking or swimming, this spring was legal to soak in, since it came right up in the middle of a natural streambed of non-thermal origin. I feel certain that Ranger Miller was not the only person who knew about this feature or used it, but there was absolutely no evidence of anyone ever being here before us. There was no trail or "social path" to this feature, and it was surrounded by lush undisturbed vegetation. This feature was destined to be eventually "discovered" and unfortunately, severely degraded.

During the summer of 1976 I took a backpacking trip across the Pitchstone Plateau with my friends Rod and Kathy Busby. We traveled cross country until we dropped off the plateau down into the Ferris Fork, and followed it until we eventually passed the delightful spring that Ranger Miller had shown us five years earlier. We found the setting every bit as pristine in that summer of 1976 as we had in 1971. Unfortunately, that was soon about to change.

Rod, Kathy and I made our way down the Bechler Canyon, and eventually came out at the Bechler Ranger Station, where we ran into Ranger Dunbar Susong, who would spend many years working in the Bechler backcountry. We had planned to hitch a ride out to Ashton, Idaho, where Margaret was due to pick us up later that day. However, there was a lack of visitors in the area. It just so happened that Ranger Susong was going out to Ashton that afternoon to haul out the week's garbage in an old beat up pickup truck, so we let Kathy ride shotgun, while Rod and I squeezed in among the garbage bags.

It was during the summer of 1976 that I had the privilege of working with and getting to know the park's geologist and geothermal specialist, Rick Hutchinson. During the next few years the remarkable thermal feature along Bechler's Ferris Fork became rather well-known and a plethora of social trails were beaten into the site. Ranger Dunbar Susong apparently decided that the "secret" was out, and the many unofficial trails were causing serious resource damage, so he established a marked, maintained trail leading to the feature. At some point along the way, this feature became known as "Mr. Bubbles."

Rick Hutchinson was a stickler for monitoring Yellowstone's backcountry thermal basins, including the many hot springs along the Ferris Fork. Rick did not like the social trails anymore than Susong, but Rick expressed a strong concern that the marked trail into such a fragile thermal region would lead to serious resource damage from overuse. Unfortunately, Rick's concerns were spot on. When Rod and I visited the Ferris Fork in 1971, and again in 1976, the stream was lined with dense vegetation. There was actually a grassy island in the stream, which provided a comfortable spot from which to enter the spring, and to simply relax and take in the beautiful surroundings. Also, the spot in the stream bed from which the hot water entered was quite deep, certainly over my head. However, one summer's day in the mid-1980s Rick came over to my quarters to share with me his sad findings of some significant human-caused changes here. While on a backcountry thermal monitoring trip in the Bechler region, Rick had walked up the marked trail along the Ferris Fork, and was dismayed by what he found. The beautiful grassy island was gone. Apparently so many people had been gathering and cavorting on the island, that all the grass was worn away, leaving only rocks and dirt. Then the heavy snow resulted in large volumes of water flowing down the Ferris Fork, which caused the rocks on the once verdant grassy island to wash directly over into the hot spring. As a result, the depth of the hot water pool had been cut in half.

The irony of this is, if you hike to "Mr. Bubbles" today, you will think it is certainly a neat place. However, you should have seen it before it was really "discovered." Damage to a wild natural resource can be very insidious. Rick Hutchinson was devoted to monitoring Yellowstone's backcountry thermal basins with the main goal of protecting them from this very type of thing. It was tragic for all of us, and especially Yellowstone, when Rick perished in an avalanche while on one of his backcountry thermal monitoring trips to Heart Lake in the winter of 1996.

The most famous place to legally soak in hot water in Yellowstone without question is Boiling River, where hot waters from the Mammoth hot springs cascade down into the Gardner River. My first experience with Boiling River was in 1975, right after I had been transferred from Norris to Mammoth. Frankly, I had never even heard of Boiling River until I came to Mammoth, so on a bright and sunny morning on one of my first days off, Margaret and I gathered up our nine-month old daughter Caroline in our backpack, and hiked down to see it. We only wanted to explore the area and scout it out. We really had not even considered soaking in it ourselves. As we neared the location where warm waters tumble into the Gardner River, the trail squeezed between some large boulders. Just as we reached the "narrows," we encountered a young couple without a stitch of clothing on. As they squeezed past us they said, "Come join us."

At this time there were few restrictions at Boiling River—how you accessed, when you could swim, and of course, clothing. Apparently, unbeknownst to us, this spot had become very popular for nude bathing, especially at night. Margaret just about had a fit. In fact, she demanded to speak to the district ranger at Mammoth, so that's where we headed. We walked into the office of Ranger Craig Johnson, and Margaret began to lecture him on how indecent Boiling River was, and how terrible it was for a family to have to run into a bunch of nude people. Ranger Johnson tried his best to listen to Margaret, but her red face and hot-tempered remarks were more than he could handle. Right in the middle of her rant he erupted into rolling laughter. "I've never had the pleasure of seeing a Southern lady lose her temper," he managed to say in between his guffaws.

Today, Boiling River is tightly regulated. It is closed at night, and also when the Gardner River is too high. The many social trails down from the road were closed and rehabilitated, and now there is only one trail that provides access. And, of course, the spot is "family friendly," so nudity is prohibited. I am simply amazed at the number of people who wedge themselves into those few places where the warm water flows in. It is a busy, busy spot year round, even on the hottest days of summer. Frankly, why would you want to soak in hot water on a day when the air temperature is in the 90s?

During the mid- 1980s, a similar situation was developing closer to Old Faithful, but this time it was in the "front country," at Midway Geyser Basin. Since it was legal to swim in a natural stream, where thermal waters entered from another source, more and more folks were starting to bathe in the Firehole River at Midway Geyser Basin, where over 4000 gallons of hot water flow each minute from Excelsior Geyser Crater. By then, there were guide books on the market specializing in where to swim in natural hot springs throughout the West. The spot at Midway was almost always mentioned, since it was completely legal. The problem was, each day we would have two dozen bathers along the banks of the Firehole River, and cavorting on the delicate mineral deposits in the runoff channels. Whenever I had roving duty at Midway, I was always so dismayed to observe the swimming activity, and I took many complaints from visitors. After all, they had come here to experience one of the most exquisite and unique thermal basins in the world. Midway is home to Grand Prismatic Spring, the park's largest, and in addition to the spectacular Excelsior Geyser Crater, the very colorful Opal and Turquoise Pools. They certainly did not expect to find a swimming party a la Coney Island taking place in the midst of all of this spectacular natural beauty!

Our staff at Old Faithful continued to submit the many complaints to park headquarters, but nothing was being done. Our District Ranger at Old Faithful supported a special regulation, which would prohibit swimming in the Firehole River at Midway, but so far no action had been taken. Then one day it just so happened that I was off duty, and walking across the footbridge over the Firehole River that provided access to the boardwalks at Midway Geyser Basin. As usual, the party was on. Swimmers were frolicking on the mineral deposits along the runoff channels; several had beer cans in their hands, and were also smoking. The scene just disgusted me. Suddenly, up walked Roger Siglin, Yellowstone's Chief Ranger. Now, Yellowstone is a huge park with a large staff, and it would be rare indeed if the park's chief ranger was acquainted with all of the seasonal interpretive rangers. Certainly, Roger did not recognize me as a fellow NPS employee, since I was out of uniform.

I noticed that Ranger Siglin stopped on the bridge, and was carefully studying the swimming party below. Apparently our many complaints had worked, and he had driven the fifty miles down from park headquarters in Mammoth to see for himself what the fuss was all about. Then, ironically, Siglin walked over to me, and asked what I thought about all of this. Well, needless to say, I gave him an earful, and I figured that my comments would have more clout if I didn't volunteer that I also wore the green and gray. Did my comments make a difference? I'm sure they didn't, hurt but he probably made up his mind what needed to be done as soon as he walked out on that footbridge, and observed just what an unnatural and distasteful situation existed at Midway. Soon we were thrilled to learn that a new special regulation had been approved, which prohibited swimming in the Firehole River in the runoff below Midway Geyser Basin. A few authors of hot spring bathing guide books were not too happy at the new regulation, but today the natural beauty of Midway can be enjoyed absent the swim parties!

The other popular spot for swimming in Yellowstone is in the Firehole River Canyon, where in mid-summer the water temperature can approach 75 degrees F. or more. Again, what a change I have observed at this place over the years. I can actually remember during the late 1960s peacefully fishing in the spot that today is the "Firehole Swimming Area," which for most of the summer, is absolutely covered with visitors frolicking in the river.

I feel sure that Native Americans and early frontiersmen enjoyed soaking in the hot waters of Yellowstone. During the early years of the park, when visitation was relatively light, the park did provide rustic thermally-heated swimming pools in such places as Old Faithful. The primary source of hot water for the Old Faithful swimming pool was Solitary Geyser, and its activity changed due to the unnatural tapping of its water source. With increased visitation along with a better awareness of the fragility of thermal features, those swimming facilities were removed. Today in the modern era of four million plus annual visitation, swimming in hot water is very limited. There are basically two choices for visitors: Boiling River, which is often closed due to high water levels in the Gardner River, and the Firehole River Canyon, which is also closed for much of the summer due to high water. Both of these places are usually very crowded. Yellowstone's thermal features are rare and unique and deserve complete protection. Because of this as well as the extreme dangers involved, the primary focus for the National Park Service is the protection of thermal resources, not recreational swimming. Besides, for folks bent on swimming in thermally-heated waters, there is an abundance of commercially operated hot spring swimming pools all around Montana, Idaho and Wyoming.

Adventures at Norris Geyser Basin

My first two summers, 1968-69, in Yellowstone were spent at Canyon, where Margaret and I worked for the Yellowstone Park Company. Norris Geyser Basin was only 12 miles to the west, and we occasionally visited, especially since Steamboat Geyser, the world's tallest, was having the most active decade of eruptions in its history. But Steamboat's eruptions were completely unpredictable, and the intervals might be months apart. So at the time, Norris was a rather quiet, peaceful out of the way spot. It therefore came as a surprise when I learned that this would become my first duty assignment as a ranger with the National Park Service in the summer of 1974. In a very busy park like Yellowstone, it was the perfect place to begin.

My transition from the U.S. Air Force to that of a seasonal interpretive ranger was anything but smooth. First, we had to get moved out and have our rather meager belongings shipped to my Mom and Dad's home in Montgomery, Alabama. Then we had to separate out what we needed for our summer stay at Norris. We had a little Datsun pickup truck with a small camper on it, so we did not have much room. In addition to packing the necessary items for Margaret and me, we had to somehow fit a baby bed into the camper for our eight month old daughter Caroline. Things were going along as planned, when suddenly I found out the Air Force needed me to work one week longer than had been originally scheduled. That meant we would not be able to leave Great Falls until the evening before I was scheduled to begin work in Yellowstone. I called my supervisor, West District Naturalist John Stockert, to see if there was any flexibility regarding my arrival date. "Absolutely not," John said. "Training for all new rangers begins early Monday morning on June 10."

When you are packing up and leaving a place things always take longer than planned, and we did not arrive at Norris Geyser Basin until after midnight. John Stockert had warned me ahead of time that the only quarters available was a tiny apartment in the rustic Norris Trailside Museum, a log and stone building constructed in 1929. It was either take a job as an interpretive ranger in Yellowstone with these quarters, or take a job as a gate ranger in Glacier. I know several gate rangers who love their jobs, but I really wanted to be an interpretive ranger, so we figured we could rough it at Norris.

By 1974 Norris Geyser Basin was still a quiet spot, but that was *especially* true after midnight! We parked our little truck in the parking lot, and walked down the 100 yard trail through the pitch black night to the museum, which is situated on a hill that overlooks the Porcelain Basin below to the north, with the Back Basin located immediately to the south. There is a large breezeway that frames a great view of the Porcelain Basin. The stars were brilliant in the clear cold skies as we gazed out over the thermal basin that would be our home for the summer. The first thing we both noticed was the incredible quiet, punctuated with the howls of coyotes and the gurgles of thermal features all around us. The place just had a wild and eerie feel to it in the middle of the night. But we had little time to soak in its beauty. It was after midnight and I had been told to be ready to be picked up at 6:00 a.m. in the morning to begin two weeks of intense training required of all new interpretive rangers.

We unlocked the door and found that John Stockert had not overstated the shortcomings of our accommodations. There was a tiny bedroom, and a little wood stove for heat and cooking. Mice droppings were everywhere, as it appeared no one had been in the place all through the long winter months. I hiked back up to our truck, grabbed a couple of sleeping bags and pillows and the baby bed, and returned to our rustic abode. We were exhausted from the full day of activity, and drifted off to sleep amid the constant hissing and gurgling of thermal features. A couple of times during the night we were awakened by the loud roar of eruptions from Harding Geyser, located in a ravine only a few yards to the east.

The next morning my ride arrived at 6:00 a.m., and I was on my way to Yellowstone Lake, where we would begin our whirlwind two weeks of training. I felt so guilty leaving Margaret and little Caroline in that situation. The truck had not even been unpacked, other than the bedding for our first night. Thankfully, while I was off at training, a fine fellow by the name of Fred Longino, who worked for the division of maintenance, came by to check on Margaret, and helped unload the rest of our belongings into the apartment. Fred was a native of Arkansas, and we greatly enjoyed his friendship over the course of the summer. Fred had a penchant for playing practical jokes on the visitors. Since he spent lots of time working the trails in the basin, he encountered a lot of visitors, and did not mind "answering" their questions. One day while I was on rove Fred did not see me approaching from the rear. A visitor had just asked him to identify the elk droppings on the ground. "Ma'am," Fred said with a serious expression on his face, "those are antelope eggs. Please be careful not to step on them as they will be hatching out soon." I scolded Fred more than once for this sort of thing, but always with a smile on my face.

As soon as I returned from my two weeks of training, I was amazed at how Margaret had neatly set up and organized the apartment, but then she told me of all of her difficulties with baby Caroline in this place. With nothing but cement and linoleum floors, Margaret did not think it was safe for Caroline to crawl, since mice were present. Also, the laundry facilities were over in the government housing area, well over a mile away. Since Caroline was in cloth diapers, this alone presented quite the problem. Also, Margaret said visitors would knock on the door at all hours early and late in the day, wanting to know geyser predictions. Ironically, as soon as I returned from training, I ran into a fellow who lived in a trailer over in the government housing area who wanted to trade his quarters for mine. He had just been divorced, and his trailer only brought him bad memories. He told me that the little apartment in the Norris Museum would suit him just fine.

Thrilled with this news, I called John Stockert to see how quickly we could arrange the swap. "Can't do it," John told me over the phone. "The museum apartment belongs to the Division of Interpretation, and the trailer belongs to the Division of Maintenance." After my pleadings went nowhere, I proceeded to break an important management principle, by making an end run, not only around my own supervisor, but also by calling another division. I called Chuck Tobin, Yellowstone's Chief of Maintenance, and made my plea. I told Chuck that I had just been discharged from having authority in the Air Force over nuclear missiles, and I fully understood why we did not have any flexibility on rules in *that* critical situation. But then I described the predicament that Margaret and I were in with trying to live in that little apartment with a baby, and that surely the rule of not allowing the swaps in housing between divisions could be re-visited. Chuck listened and understood. He okayed the swap.

The next day I received a call from John Stockert. "How did you do it?" he asked. First I apologized to John for the end run I had made, but then I went on to describe how I had reasoned with Chuck. "John," I said, "I told Chuck that while I was in the Air Force dealing with hundreds of nuclear missiles, I understood why there should never be an exception to a rule; but when it comes to providing housing for government employees, I did not understand why there could not be some flexibility with the rules."

Most supervisors would have chewed me out for making an end run such as this, but John was pleased that I had been able to accomplish the task. However, except perhaps in the direst of circumstances, I can honestly say after working 43 seasons with the Park Service, I do not recommend this. The National Park Service is similar in many ways to the military regarding following a chain of command.

Once we moved into a trailer in the government housing area, life was much easier for Margaret, since we had more room, laundry facilities were close by, and the floor at least contained some carpet to go along with the linoleum. The trailer was several decades old, but at least we did not see the evidence of mice that we saw in the museum apartment. We naturally missed the sights and sounds from living right in the middle of the geyser basin. I had to ride my bike to and from work, which was not easy on those days with snow and sleet, which seemed to occur often at Norris given its elevation of 7600.'

However, on one memorable day during early summer, Margaret encountered a serious problem at the trailer. The night before we had returned from buying groceries up in Gardiner, but had not brought everything in from the truck. The next morning I got up early, and headed off on my bicycle for the workday. Margaret got up a bit later and needed something still in the truck. All she had on was her gown. As she headed out to get it, she heard the door slam behind her. She hoped the door had not locked, but alas when she tried to open it, she found it locked tight. So there she was on the front steps in her gown, and with no key. The front door had these little adjustable slats that you could barely see through, and baby Caroline would stand up and barely reach eye level at the bottom slat. When Margaret looked in she was horrified to see Caroline holding little pieces of broken linoleum in her mouth. All Margaret could think about was, "Oh no, she is going to swallow that and get choked while I'm locked out here on the porch." Margaret tried her best to coax Caroline to not put the pieces of linoleum in her mouth, but then Caroline would sit down on the floor, and Margaret could no longer see her.

Finally, Margaret walked down the gravel road to see if anyone else was home at the two or three other trailers in the little housing area. Fred Longino was on the late shift, and was still at his quarters. She sent Fred over to the geyser basin and as luck would have it, I was toward the end of my guided walk to Echinus Geyser, which meant I was a mile away at the far end of the Back Basin. Fred came running up and interrupted me, "Butch, I need your trailer key!" When he told me what had happened, I immediately tossed him the key, and he sprinted back up the steep hill. Fortunately, when Margaret got back in the trailer, little Caroline had not ingested any pieces of that broken linoleum floor. Some duplicate keys were quickly ordered after that day!

I have to say that working at Norris in 1974 was one of the greatest summers of my Park Service career. For one thing, there were so many active geysers. Granted, by 1974 Steamboat had returned to dormancy and did not erupt again until 1978. However, Echinus Geyser was easily the star of the show. Eruptions occurred about every 80 minutes, and since it was a fountain geyser that filled with water prior to the eruption, you could pretty much guess the eruption times from just looking at it. In fact the first duty I had when I arrived at the basin was to quickly walk down to take a look at Echinus, then return to the museum to post the day's first prediction. Most of our guided walks started from the museum and headed for Echinus. We would make stops along the way at such impressive features as Emerald Spring, Steamboat, of course, and Cistern Spring, but we would always time our walk so that we arrived just before Echinus would erupt.

Other geysers that were frequently active that summer included Porkchop, Bear Den, Constant, and the magnificent Ledge Geyser in the Porcelain Basin. In fact, the summer of 1974 marked the best year ever for this, the second largest geyser in the Norris Geyser Basin. That summer it erupted every 12 to 14 hours, and for a while it seemed that it would erupt at sunset each and every day. The water would burst out at a 45 degree angle with the setting sun backlighting the powerful bursts of water. What a sight it was!

Since we really did not have a visitor center at Norris, for most of the day we roved the basin, observing the activity of the geysers and springs and talking to visitors. The staff that I worked with was outstanding. T. Scott Bryan, who would later write "The Geysers of Yellowstone," was a great colleague, and I learned much from him. Park Geologist Rick Hutchinson was stationed at Old Faithful, but he loved Norris, and he spent a great deal of time there. He was always quick to invite me out into the basin and beyond, when he was performing geothermal research. Sometimes he would invite me into backcountry places where he had been many times. Places like 100 Spring Plain, with its many wonderful features, including Cinder Pool and Firecracker Spring. I was always extremely careful to follow in the exact footsteps of the expert when he took me out into those places.

The hills around Norris contained mysteries, such as sagebrush lizards, which I don't think are found anywhere else in the park, and caves that appeared to be thermally heated bear dens. Other places contained hot springs with a pH equivalent to battery acid. All in all, my first summer at Norris was an absolutely wonderful experience. I was quite sad the next summer when I learned that my duty assignment had been changed to Mammoth. However, having worked over the years at just about all locations in the park, each place is unique and spectacular in its own right.

Norris Geyser Basin has always been a very active place with changes occurring frequently. We felt earthquakes often during my summer there. I know that as our old film at Old Faithful used to say, "Yellowstone is like a living sculpture, always changing." However, when I walk around Norris today, I can't help but feel nostalgia when I stroll by Echinus, which is now dormant, and think about how we took those eruptions every 80 minutes for granted. Then I walk past Porkchop Geyser, which used to have such dynamic eruptions out of its two-inch vent. But in 1989 the tremendous pressure blew the crater apart, transforming what had been a fascinating geyser into a quiet hot spring. And when I walk down the hill into the Porcelain Basin past Ledge Geyser, now quiet, I can easily in my mind's eye envision those spectacular sunset eruptions that we enjoyed in 1974. Who knows what the future will bring at this, Yellowstone's hottest and most active geyser basin? But in 1974 it was a fabulous place for a novice seasonal ranger to begin a career in Yellowstone.

Strange Incidents at West Thumb and Old Faithful

In 43 years of working in Yellowstone, there occurred two particular incidents that to the best of my knowledge had never happened before. One happened at West Thumb Geyser Basin, and the other was at Old Faithful. During June of 2003 I had just finished giving my evening program at the Old Faithful Visitor Center, and was putting things away, when a middle-aged woman who was visibly upset walked into the auditorium, and headed straight for me. Before she said anything I noted that her blouse had several tears on the front. "I have been attacked by a bear," she managed to say in a shaken voice. I quickly escorted her over to a chair to sit down, and then asked her if she was okay. "I think so," she said, "I'm just still so upset, and wanted to report this to a ranger. You are the first one I could find." I asked her if she had any injuries, and she said that she did not think so, but I wanted to know what had happened. "I was walking the boardwalk at West Thumb Geyser Basin, and this bear just came running out of the trees toward me," she said. "It looked like it was going to attack, so I fell down and played dead. The bear pawed at me, even rolled me over, but then left me alone. I was too scared to move, but in a couple of minutes I raised up, and the bear had apparently headed back into the trees. I then got into my car and drove here."

After telling me this the lady initially refused my offer to have her checked out, but I talked her into it. Even though she did not appear to have any puncture wounds she did have some scratches. I told her that bears get into nasty stuff, and that she did not want to risk an infection. She agreed to meet with one of our Law Enforcement rangers who was trained as an Emergency Medical Technician (EMT). I knew that the proper medical protocol would be followed regarding getting treatment from the Old Faithful Clinic, but I also knew we had a bit more of a problem on our hands.

Grizzly attacks in Yellowstone are quite rare to begin with, especially in the modern era of bear management with no human feeding of bears allowed, and careful disposal of garbage (which was *not* the case prior to the early 1970s). When attacks do occur they almost always involve a hiker who accidentally surprises a bear in the backcountry. I had never before heard of a bear attack right on a boardwalk in a thermal area in the park's frontcountry! However, as soon as the lady told me her story, I realized that it could have just as easily been Margaret or me that was attacked by this bear. The previous day, close to sunset, Margaret and I had driven the short 17 miles over to West Thumb after work. We have always enjoyed the geyser basin there with its very colorful hot springs flowing directly into Yellowstone Lake, and the Absaroka Mountains serving as a beautiful backdrop to the east.

Strange Incidents at West Thumb and Old Faithful 312

During our stroll along the boardwalk, we had noticed a rather putrid odor emanating from a group of trees just south of the boardwalk. If the wind had not been drifting in our direction, we probably would not have noticed it. It smelled to us like an animal carcass, but then we weren't sure. This was, after all, a thermal area where the "rotten egg" odors of sulfur are rather common. Still, Margaret immediately expressed a concern about bears being nearby, but when we looked at the location right next to the boardwalk, and in such a heavily travelled area (also, we were less than 100 yards from the restroom and parking lot), we did not really give it much more thought. In retrospect, obviously, we should have. Certainly during the main part of the day when thousands of visitors are strolling through the geyser basin, I feel there would be little if any danger of running into a bear. However, Margaret and I were walking the basin just before sunset when few people were around. Almost exactly 24 hours later, so was the lady who was attacked. That bear was obviously on the carcass in the trees near the boardwalk.

When the law enforcement ranger arrived to provide medical care, I told him about the incident, and the possible carcass, and he quickly notified the patrol rangers at Grant along with the Bear Management office. Typically, when we have a carcass close to a trail, the trail is closed for an unspecified period of time until the carcass is "cleaned up" by predators and scavengers, and Bear Management deems it safe to re-open. However, in some cases, if the carcass is close to a popular attraction trail in the *front* country, an attempt is made to remove the carcass. I'm pretty certain this is what happened at West Thumb Geyser Basin.

The incident at West Thumb served to remind me that *all* of Yellowstone National Park is home to bears and other wildlife, and that if there is a food source close to a developed area, predators will seek it. Ever since this happened, whenever I go out into the geyser basin early or late in the day, I remind myself to be alert and observant as I hike along. And that particularly includes utilizing my nose in trying to distinguish between sulphurous thermal odors, and the rank smell of a decaying animal carcass. I am also reminded to always carry bear spray with me. As far as the woman was concerned, I'm not sure bear spray was that available in 2003, but her decision to play dead probably saved her from serious injury or even death.

The other weird incident occurred during the early afternoon on June 21, 2005, while I was on duty at the Old Faithful Visitor Center. I was on the desk with my colleague Rebecca Roland, when the skies began to darken, then I heard a weather warning announced on our park radio. The National Weather Office in Riverton, Wyoming had issued a severe thunderstorm warning for much of Yellowstone National Park, including the Old Faithful area. At the time, I was talking to a couple of my former students from Walters State Community College in Morristown, Tennessee, where I taught September through May from 1976 through 2006. Jimmy Tritt, William Hughes, and their wives and families were visiting Yellowstone for the first time, and in fact I had not seen these guys since they were students of mine in the late 1970s. Jimmy and William were East Tennessee boys, and both loved the outdoors, so I'm sure I had shared many stories with them about Yellowstone.

William and his wife Sharon were at the desk talking to me just before Old Faithful Geyser was due to erupt. Their children along with Jimmy and his wife were already out on the benches in front of the geyser eagerly awaiting the eruption. Despite the darkening skies and the weather warning, we had yet to experience any rain or lightning, but that suddenly changed. While I was in the middle of a sentence with Sharon, a bright bolt of light lit up the area accompanied by an earsplitting clap of thunder. My eyes had been on Sharon across the desk, but Rebecca looking out toward Old Faithful shouted, "Someone's been hit!" Immediately Sharon looked up and shouted, "That's my son!" Looking back there is no way on earth Sharon could have seen who got hit by lightning. From our location at the Old Faithful Visitor Center desk, we were at least 100 yards removed from the throngs of people out on the boardwalk benches. I think it was just her mother's instinct that told her what had happened.

Rebecca quickly told me that she had actually seen someone knocked up into the air by the lightning strike, and she immediately made an announcement for everyone in the visitor center to stay inside. I quickly got on the park radio and made the following call, "700, 700 this is 724 Victor with an emergency. We have had a lightning strike in front of Old Faithful Geyser, and we have people down on the boardwalk." Ranger Tim Townsend quickly answered and said that he was responding, so I grabbed a portable radio and ran out to the boardwalk. I could see that someone was performing CPR on a young victim. I learned that he was a physician, and was being assisted by a nurse, so I got on the radio and informed Tim of this. Then with ugly, black clouds roiling over us, I quickly began shouting to the crowd waiting on the benches, "Folks, we have a very dangerous storm over us! Get off the boardwalks immediately! Get inside a building. Head for the Lodge or the Visitor Center!" Not everyone had seen the people go down from the lightning strike, and while folks did start to leave, many just continued to sit on the benches. "Folks," I shouted at the top of my lungs, "people have been struck and are down, you need to get away from this open area. NOW!" With this emphasis, I noted that most everyone did begin to head east over to the Old Faithful Lodge.

I ran back to where the victim was being administered CPR, and by now Tim and his assistant were on the scene. It was at this point that I saw Sharon Hughes kneeling and sobbing next to her 12 year-old son Josh, who appeared unresponsive as the medical team continued to give him CPR. I asked Tim if there was anything I could do to help. "Just get everyone out of here!" he said.

Once I had finished clearing the boardwalks, I headed back inside the visitor center where I saw several other people who had also been hit by the lightning. Many were stunned and groggy, and several had numbness in different parts of their bodies. Up until this point I think we were under the impression that only one person, little Josh, had been struck. I shouted out to the throngs gathered in the visitor center, "If you feel that you were injured by the lightning strike, please step over to the front of the building." When I saw what appeared to be a dozen people headed my way, I got back on the park radio to let them know that more medical assistance would be needed immediately.

Eventually we found that ten other visitors had received injuries from the strike, but only one, Josh, was critically injured. After these folks received medical assistance, I headed over to the Old Faithful Clinic to check on Josh's condition. As soon as I walked in I saw William and Sharon and also Jimmy and his wife gathering together in a circle to pray. It was at this point that I learned that Josh had suffered a complete cardiac arrest. Two physicians and a nurse just happened to be sitting right next to Josh when he was struck, and immediately initiated CPR. Josh had a burn on his shoulder blade, singed hair, and also a hole had burned in his shorts where the lightning apparently exited his body.

A lightning strike victim can be resuscitated by CPR to get the heart beating again, but the big concern becomes the respiration. This was the chief concern as I walked in. While Josh was being attended to by the physician on duty, I joined in the prayer circle, and to this day I have never heard more impassioned prayers, especially from Sharon, Josh's Mom. After being placed on a ventilator, Josh was flown by helicopter to a hospital in Idaho Falls, Idaho, and later flown in a fixed wing plane equipped as an air ambulance to Salt Lake City.

Eventually, Josh completely recovered from his ordeal, though he has no memory of the lightning strike. Clearly, he was a very fortunate young man, given the fact that he was in full cardiac arrest, and there just happened to be the physician nearby who immediately started CPR and resuscitated him. In addition, he was only a few blocks from the Old Faithful Clinic. I could not help but realize if this had happened out on a trail, even in the front-country, he would have never had a chance.

A few days after this incident a gentleman came up to the front desk of the visitor center and told me that he had a video recording of the lightning strike. He played it on the small screen of his recorder, and it was incredible to watch. Basically, a bolt of lightning had come down about 15 yards out from the boardwalk where all the people were, but just before it reached the ground, it split off into three bolts. Two bolts landed harmlessly away from the boardwalk, but one landed right on the boardwalk, where visitors were seated on benches. Josh took the worst brunt of this bolt.

Later that day when I had rove out at Old Faithful Geyser, I walked out to where I thought that particular bolt had struck the boardwalk. Several years earlier the Park Service had replaced the old wooden planks with recycled plastic planks, which tend to last much longer than the wooden ones. Sure enough, I noticed a place on the plastic boardwalk that had melted from the direct strike of the lightning bolt. Looking at that video and then seeing the scar left behind on the boardwalk, I find it almost a miracle that Josh Hughes survived that direct hit from the lightning bolt. Maybe those passionate prayers that day were answered.

Following this incident, our visitor center initiated a new protocol for severe thunderstorm warnings from the National Weather Service. As soon as a warning is received over the park radio, we immediately make an announcement to all visitors in the building to stay inside, and we also go outside and request visitors to seek shelter inside a building. No, we can't "order" them to leave the Old Faithful Geyser benches, but we can strongly encourage them.

After so many years in Yellowstone, and never hearing about a lightning strike at Old Faithful, ironically only five years later in early June of 2010, it happened again. This time nine visitors were injured when they were struck by lightning while on boardwalks or walkways near Old Faithful. A small thunderstorm produced a single bolt of lightning. This time it was a 57 year old man who had to be resuscitated, and eventually flown by a helicopter to a medical center in Idaho Falls, Idaho.

Over 40 years of working in Yellowstone I have noticed a definite pattern of changing weather. Perhaps the weather is more volatile than it once was around the Yellowstone area, and as for a bear attack on a boardwalk, I have to remember that Yellowstone is a very wild ecosystem where we humans are merely the visitors.

Part V

To Leave Then Unimpaired

The Treasure of an Undeveloped Shoreline

I have always considered a natural, undeveloped shoreline a magical place, whether it is along a stream, a lake, or the coast of an ocean. Yellowstone Lake is the second largest lake in the world at such a high elevation. Its surface area consists of 134 square miles, and it contains 119 miles of shoreline, most of which borders wild, roadless country. I have paddled along every inch of it numerous times, and it is indeed a treasure, especially when you look at the congested, unplanned development that we have allowed in this nation around so many of our lakes.

What is even more unique though is a natural coastline. Having grown up in central Alabama, Margaret and I both spent lots of time along the Florida panhandle, which is home to some of the world's most beautiful white sand beaches in the Gulf of Mexico. My family would usually take the three hour drive south from Montgomery for our summer vacations, and as a kid I was always thrilled to see those rolling white sand dunes, that would begin to come into view along highway U.S. 98. During the 1950s and 1960s, much of the coast along the Florida panhandle was still undeveloped. Many of the motels consisted of the Mom and Pop variety, and were located on the opposite side of the highway from the beach, which meant that you had to walk across the road, and then meander your way through the sand dunes to eventually reach the beaches. It wasn't long before developers began to build their huge hotels on the ocean side of the road, which eliminated the sand dunes, a big mistake itself, but then the thirty-story high rise condo developments started to line the beaches. The state of Florida did nothing to stop it, and as a result, as far as I'm concerned, the gorgeous stretch of beaches along the panhandle has for the most part been destroyed.

Today, when driving along any of the roads close to the beach, it is a rare sight to spot any sand dunes, and in fact, it is difficult to even know that there is a beautiful ocean with white sand beaches nearby, since most of the views are blocked by large hotels and high rise buildings. It is one thing to build a bunch of high rise hotels on the strip of Las Vegas, but a gorgeous coastline? Where were the conservation leaders in Florida during this time? Did not *any* of Florida's politicians possess a smidgeon of foresight?

In January of 1970, just about the time that the Florida coastline was on its way to being ruined, I was on my way to Vandenberg AFB near Lompoc, California for my first duty assignment in the Air Force. Margaret and I would be stationed here for ten weeks, before heading to Malmstrom AFB in Great Falls, Montana. We had never been to California before, and like most young folks who grew up in the South during the mid-1960s watching The Wonderful World of Disney, and the Rose Bowl Parade on TV, and listening to the Beach Boys glorify California surfing, we could hardly wait to see the "Golden State."

The Treasure of an Undeveloped Shoreline 318

    I will never forget the first time that we drove Highway 1 from Santa Barbara north up to San Francisco. It was the most beautiful stretch of highway either of us had ever seen, as the constant views of the Pacific Ocean, and rugged coastline were spellbinding. For the majority of the drive there were no large hotels or high-rise developments to be seen along the coast. Furthermore, almost all of the low level hotels were located on the *other* side of the road from the ocean. There was nothing artificial to block the view of that magnificent coast. Pullouts along the way were numerous, and there were often trails that led down to the natural coastline and beaches, free from any tacky development.

    In the spring of 2013, Margaret wanted to take a trip to return to her old "stomping grounds," which included visiting the panhandle of Florida, and its coastline. To Florida's credit, they have one of the finest state park systems in America. The slogan for the Florida Park Service is appropriate, "The Real Florida." Many wonderful parks have been established that have preserved small segments of the panhandle's once glorious coast. However, the damage has been done. Today, to "old-timers" like Margaret and me, it is truly disheartening to view the wall-to-wall development along the coast, and in our mind's eye remember what it was like only about fifty years ago.

    Now that we live in Bozeman, Montana, and we want to leave the "mud season" in late March and early April, we often head for the coast of California. What is truly amazing is that for the most part, California's spectacular coastline from Santa Barbara up to San Francisco has not appreciably changed since we first saw it 46 years earlier in 1970. What little development that exists is nestled down rather low, and across the road from the ocean side. There is *none* of the unsightly high rise condo-type developments that now line the coast of Florida. This situation did not occur by accident.

    The citizens of California decided that they wanted to keep their coastline close to its splendid natural state for present and future generations. Through different types of government legislation, and its Coastal Commission, the state has largely succeeded so far in accomplishing its goal. Every now and then a Montana friend will make a comment to me deriding the state of California. The most common statement that I hear is, "I hope we never Californicate Montana!" Now I know that California is not perfect, and the state has its share of pressing problems; however, whenever I hear this statement, especially from a Montanan, I do not hesitate to tell them the story of two coastlines—the Florida Panhandle's and California's, and what happened in both places. Then, I go out of my way to scoff at the favorite slogan that Montanans love to boast, "Montana—the Last Best Place."

    Montana obviously does not have any ocean coastlines, but it does indeed have some fabulous streams and lakes. At present the state of Montana is doing very little to make sure that Montana stays "the Last Best Place." For example, big-monied interests are moving in and building "trophy homes" right along the banks of marvelous rivers, such as the Gallatin, Madison, Yellowstone, Jefferson, Missouri, and Big Hole, just to mention a few. Streams such as these are treasures when it comes to river floats and fly fishing. In fact, visitors come from all over the world simply to float and wade out to cast a fly in such a magnificent natural setting. They do not come out to float past newly constructed homes situated right on top of the river bank. Furthermore, the Gallatin and Yellowstone Rivers serve as the gateways to visitors coming to Yellowstone National Park. Bozeman's airport has become the busiest in the state, and the first impression that visitors see when driving to Yellowstone National Park are the Gallatin and Yellowstone Rivers. If they are headed for the West Entrance to the park, they travel through the spectacular Gallatin Canyon and along the Gallatin River; if they are headed for the park's north entrance, then they travel along the Yellowstone River and the suitably named Paradise Valley. Private land along both rivers is being subjected to uncontrolled, unregulated, development.

Unfortunately, the current makeup of the Montana state legislature has no interest in using any foresight at all to protect the natural scenery along Montana's grand rivers. Each time a "stream setback" bill is introduced, which would simply require the landowner to build a specified distance back from the river bank, politicians cry "property rights" and defeat the legislation. In general, there is currently very little foresight being used by Montana's state and county governments when it comes to how raw land is used and developed. In fact, the state of Montana is heading down the same exact path that Florida traveled fifty years ago. Yes, Montana is blessed with many wonderful national parks and national forests, which, by the way, did not come easy. To get an idea of just how difficult it was for President Theodore Roosevelt to establish many of the splendid national forests in Montana and the Northern Rockies, read the excellent book, *The Big Burn* by Timothy Egan.

The Montana media doesn't seem to understand the insidious threat of unregulated development either. A recent news article glamourized a newly remodeled home located along the banks of the Gallatin River. According to the story one of the final segments of the movie, "A River Runs through It," was filmed from this spot. As more and more homes pop up along the Gallatin River, the river is losing its appeal for any movie producer desiring to depict a wild and scenic river.

In years to come I'm afraid that our grandchildren and their children will see a very different Montana. I fear they will see many of Montana's cherished rivers, such as the Yellowstone and Madison, lined with development. But, to conclude on a positive note, I am optimistic that they will still be able to see the spectacular natural coastline of California, and the wild shores of Yellowstone Lake!

The Gallatin Crest—The Need for Wilderness

Over the years my backpacking trips have expanded to just about all corners of the Greater Yellowstone Ecosystem (GYE)—an area of land that comprises about 20 million acres (34,000 square miles), and is considered to be one of the largest nearly intact ecosystems in the temperate life zone on Earth. Yellowstone National Park is obviously the ecological and spiritual center of this ecosystem, and biologists universally agree that the health of the park depends on the health of the entire ecosystem. We are fortunate that the park is surrounded by several large wilderness areas on all sides. However, there is one last unprotected roadless area adjacent to Yellowstone, and that is the "Gallatin Crest," located to the north and west of the park boundary. In 1988 most of this diverse, high mountain region almost became wilderness, as a bill to protect it was supported by both of Montana's U.S. Senators and also one of its two House members. The bill passed both houses of Congress, but was then vetoed by President Ronald Reagan. Since that time the region has remained in limbo, largely unprotected.

After I moved to Bozeman in 2006, I found myself staring at the mountains south of town in "the Crest," in particular the prominent pyramid-shaped Mount Blackmore. On a glorious, clear, mid-summer's day I hiked the six mile trail to its summit at 10,154,' and found the view toward Yellowstone to the south absolutely stunning. The wild and rugged mountain scenery matched anything I had viewed anywhere in the Greater Yellowstone Ecosystem. These mountains are replete with abundant wildlife, cascading streams, and high mountain lakes. If ever a place deserved wilderness protection this was it. However, partisan politics supported by the resource extractive industries, and the thrill craft industry (ATVs, motorcycles, and snowmobiles) have so far prevented such protection.

Each year when my friends and I try to select a portion of the GYE for our annual extended summer backpack trip, I would bring up the Gallatin Crest. The closest trips to the Crest we had taken were on the Skyrim trail along Yellowstone's northwest border, which like all of the park's backcountry, is managed as wilderness. However, several in my group would balk at the idea of backpacking north of the Skyrim Trail: "I'm not going to backpack in an area where motorcycles could come screaming by me on the trail—it would absolutely destroy the very wilderness setting that we are seeking," was a common theme expressed, especially by Deb Dirksen. Nonetheless, in the summer of 2014, I was to finally venture into the high country of the Gallatin Crest. In addition to my annual "big" extended backpack trip, a few years ago we had initiated the tradition of taking a "family" backpack trip that typically lasted a long weekend. Our trips would include my two daughters, my two grandkids, my son-in-law, and a few friends. These short trips would typically be into Yellowstone, or one of the surrounding wilderness areas. However, my youngest daughter, Alison, had just returned from a hike to Windy Pass up on the Gallatin Crest. "Dad," she exclaimed, "The alpine meadows up there are carpeted with wildflowers. I can't think of a better place for our trip this summer!"

Alison and I did some research, and found that the U.S. Forest Service in the Gallatin National Forest had implemented a "shared use" program, where motor vehicles were limited to certain days of the week. So we attempted to squeeze in our trip around the dates that the trail would supposedly be closed to such use. Our trip was scheduled in mid-July, when both mosquitoes and wildflowers were normally at their peak. After negotiating an extremely rough and rocky road to reach the trailhead, our group of ten emerged from our vehicles, only to immediately be engulfed by clouds of mosquitoes. We quickly applied repellent, and began our ascent up the trail. Thankfully, by the time we reached the vast open meadows of Windy Pass, the mosquitoes disappeared. I have always maintained that a stiff wind is the backpacker's friend and the paddler's enemy, and on this day it was our friend! Alison had not exaggerated regarding the carpets of flowers—ranging from red to purple, blue and yellow. The snow-covered peaks of the Crest were gorgeous. The entire region around Windy Pass was so reminiscent of Julie Andrews' famous scene from *The Sound of Music*.

We would spend two days exploring the trail along the Crest here, and marveling at the ruggedness of these high mountains all around us, but also the spectacular views of wild country and big peaks in all directions. The Sphinx at an elevation of 10,840' to the west over in the Madison Range was especially prominent. As I gazed out over this diverse landscape I could not help but think of the many species that made these mountains their home—grizzly and black bears, wolverines, wolves, mountain lions, deer, elk and moose. And as I looked at the winding single track trail that snakes along the top of the Crest, I could not help but wonder how we had gotten so far off the track when it comes to protecting wild country. I could not even in my mind's eye *imagine* a motorized vehicle up here. Given the wild and peaceful natural setting in these mountain meadows, I simply could not think of a more inappropriate activity.

I have seen so much change regarding the use of our national forests just in my lifetime. Back in the early 1970s when I would take backpacking trips into the Bob Marshall Wilderness, I rarely even paid that much attention to where the wilderness boundary line was in the national forest. Back in those days most of the travel in the national forests was by foot or horseback. Occasionally you might see a jeep, but that was about it. ATVs had barely even been invented, and motorbikes were rarely seen. During the winter snowmobiles were mostly limited to groomed trails along old logging roads, otherwise the machines would bog down in the deep snow. However, over the past few decades the thrillcraft industry has exploded, and so has the technology of their machines. Now, snowmobiles, ATVs, and motorbikes can go just about anywhere, often tearing up the land, and shattering the serenity of the natural landscape. Plus, these industry groups have been very vocal in their push to open up more public lands to motorized use.

When you look at maps of our public lands, there is a very large amount of old logging roads and trails that are already available for motorized and mechanized use. The amount of remaining wilderness is so very small. In fact, only a little over 2% of the land in the contiguous United States is protected as wilderness. Yet the thrillcraft industry and their constituents want more access. In Montana there is an organization called "Citizens for Balanced Use" that lobbies politicians to not protect anymore public land as wilderness, and in fact, to open up more lands. Their campaign slogans include "Take Back Montana!" "Share It!" and "No More Wilderness!" However, when I look at their concept of "sharing" I am reminded of similar campaigns by smokers railing out against non-smoking ordinances. It really doesn't make much sense to demand a non-smoker to share their smoke-filled areas in a restaurant, lounge, etc. Similarly, it really doesn't make any sense for someone on a loud motorcycle to demand that you share a single-track trail in a fragile high mountain alpine meadow.

I was 18 years old when the Wilderness Act was passed by Congress in 1964. The act passed by a near unanimous vote. In the House of Representatives the vote was 434-1 in favor, with only Representative Joe Poole of Texas voting nay. President Lyndon Johnson signed the bill into law. I thought then that the idea of wilderness was a bi-partisan and universally accepted idea. President Johnson made the following statements about wilderness: "If future generations are to remember us with gratitude rather than contempt, we must leave them something more than the miracles of technology. We must leave them a glimpse of the world as it was in the beginning, not just after we got through with it. ... Once our natural splendor is destroyed, it can never be recaptured. And once man can no longer walk with beauty or wonder at nature, his spirit will wither and his sustenance be wasted." Today when I read those words, I wonder how any reasonable person could not agree. Obviously, in 1964, not only did our President believe that message, but so did almost all members of Congress, both Democrats and Republicans—which is one reason I have always considered myself an Independent when it comes to politics. I really don't care what political party a person is in; rather, I'm most concerned about what the lawmaker can do for society as a whole.

But as author Mike Yochim so eloquently details in his excellent book, *Protecting Yellowstone,* published in 2013, something changed in 1980 when Ronald Reagan was elected as President. Suddenly the federal government, which is to a large degree in charge of our nation's wild country—its national parks, wilderness areas, national forests, national wildlife refuges, environmental protection laws, etc. –was the enemy. As President Reagan put it: "Government is not the solution to our problems, government *is* the problem!" All of a sudden the idea of protecting wild country, setting aside critical wildlife habitat, protecting endangered species, clean air, and clean water legislation, became a political issue. President Reagan appointed James G. Watt to be his Secretary of Interior, a man who was devoted to the "Sagebrush Rebellion," a group which not only was opposed to adding any lands for wilderness protection, but who also supported transferring federal public lands to private or state control. James Watt's infamous quote "I don't like to paddle and I don't like to walk" spoke volumes about his views on wilderness. Since that turn of events in 1980, it seems that the concept of protecting wilderness has now become a partisan issue, and that is truly a sad turn of events for our nation.

As of 2016, protecting and preserving wild country falls under a completely different political environment than it did when I was just becoming a young adult. Today, it is a rare Republican who advocates for wilderness protection, and that includes the Gallatin Crest. At present much of the Crest falls into the category of a "Wilderness Study Area" (WSA), which means it meets the criteria necessary for establishing it as a legally protected wilderness area. As long as it remains in that category conservation groups probably have the law on their side for stopping proposed destructive activities such as new roads, mines, or logging activity within the boundaries of the WSA. However, Republicans in Congress, including some from Montana, have proposed removing public lands from the WSA category. If that happened then the Gallatin Crest could easily lose its wild character, and the strength and integrity of the entire ecosystem would be damaged.

When Yellowstone National Park was established as the world's first national park in 1872, the park was an island of wilderness surrounded by an ocean of wilderness. Today the park—the island, remains pretty much intact. About 98% of the park is managed as a wilderness, though that could change if Congress becomes successful in micromanaging our national parks (see "This Horse Should Stay in the Barn.") The health and well-being of the park—the island, depends on the health and well-being of the entire ecosystem. Two groups that are working tirelessly to protect the Gallatin Crest as a critical component of Yellowstone's ecosystem are the Montana Wilderness Association (wildmontana.org) and the Greater Yellowstone Coalition (greateryellowstone.org). Aldo Leopold's quote haunts me: "I am glad that I shall never be young without wild country to be young in." As our population continues to grow, don't we need to heed those words? As I age I truly believe in wild country more than ever for our children and grandchildren. Those of us who love wild country and care about protecting Yellowstone would be well-advised to stay in touch with these groups regarding the status of the treasure known as the Gallatin Crest.

Has Yellowstone Exceeded its Carrying Capacity?

A commonly accepted definition of "carrying capacity" is the maximum population of a particular organism (people) that a given environment can support without detrimental effects. In a national park that would refer to degradation of the resource and/or the quality of the visitor experience. Many national parks experienced record visitation in 2015, and more than a few appeared to exceed their carrying capacity. Did Yellowstone? It depends. If you were backpacking in the backcountry I would say no. That's because many years ago officials in Yellowstone implemented a tightly regulated permit system, which guarantees a quality experience to backcountry users. Also, permits are generally obtainable for most areas of the backcountry, which is certainly not the case in other popular wilderness areas. Try getting a permit to backpack the highline trail in Glacier, or if you *truly* want a challenge, try to get a multi-day permit for canoeing the Okefenokee National Wildlife Refuge in March. If you want to see a wilderness area that has exceeded its carrying capacity, take a backpack trip into Wyoming's Wind River Range along the popular trail from Elkhart to Island Lake in early August. There, the U.S. Forest Service has done nothing to limit use. No permits are required, so expect to see crowded trails, and a significant impact on the resource from overuse.

The front country in Yellowstone is a different matter compared to its backcountry. Annual visitation to Yellowstone has now surpassed 4 million, which is double the number when I first started working in the park. At the height of the summer season, it took some visitors three hours just to get through the West Gate, then another hour to simply drive the 14 miles to Madison Junction. There were times when the parking lots at Fountain Paint Pot and Midway Geyser Basin were not only full, but the traffic backed out into the main road, thus blocking traffic flow. If you arrived fifteen minutes prior to Old Faithful's predicted eruption, there were few if any places left to park, despite the huge east and west parking lots there.

During the summers of 2013 and 2014, I worked part-time for the National Park Service (NPS) by assisting/coaching commercial tour operators. I witnessed firsthand the frustration tour guides (and, likewise, visitors) had in trying to find a parking place at popular sites around the park, such as at geyser basins, and viewing points along the Grand Canyon of the Yellowstone. When I am working and living at Old Faithful, I don't always notice just how bad the situation is until I have roving duty beyond the Upper Geyser Basin, and therefore face the problem of finding a parking place.

So according to the above definition then yes, Yellowstone's carrying capacity has been exceeded in the front country, at least for several weeks during the summer. This is not a problem unique to just Yellowstone. The difference is, several of our nation's most popular national parks have tackled this problem head on by providing shuttle bus operations. These include Zion, Bryce Canyon, Yosemite, Sequoia-Kings Canyon, Denali, and Grand Canyon.

Ironically, the nation's most visited national park, Great Smoky Mountains, does not have a shuttle bus system. During the two years that I worked at Great Smoky Mountains National Park, I became acutely aware of just how serious the traffic problem is in Cades Cove. Often referred to as the "garden spot of the Smokies," the cove has an eleven mile loop road around it that is often gridlocked with traffic. The NPS proposed staging shuttle buses in the Townsend, Tennessee vicinity, similar to the way Zion stages buses in Springdale, Utah. However, local communities voiced disapproval of the plan, preferring unlimited, anytime, access to Cades Cove. So as of 2016 there is still no shuttle system in Cades Cove. If you plan to visit there expect bumper-to-bumper traffic on any day of the year, and a driving time of at least two hours for the 11 mile loop road. In my opinion, this represents a lack of leadership. The local communities should not have the final say in dictating policy in a national park. If leaders in Yellowstone had behaved in this manner, the park would still be inundated with the unlimited use of two-cycle snowmobiles, and the accompanying horrific air and noise pollution. Instead, Yellowstone park officials bit the bullet, and eventually crafted a winter use management policy that protects the natural environment, and still provides for a quality visitor experience.

It appears that the time has now come for Yellowstone to confront the overcrowding issue in the summer season. One suggestion that I have heard from some tour guides would be to emulate the Zion National Park shuttle system by treating the 16 mile road from Madison Junction to Old Faithful along the Firehole River the same way that Zion treats the Zion Canyon. In other words, a visitor could only visit the many geyser basins along the Firehole River, including the Upper Geyser Basin at Old Faithful, by taking a shuttle bus, which would logically be staged in West Yellowstone, Montana, just outside the West Gate. There is ample space for visitor parking west of town. Such a system would alleviate the horrendous parking problems at Fountain Paint Pot, Midway Geyser Basin, Biscuit Basin, Black Sand Basin, and yes, even Old Faithful.

Due to Yellowstone's sheer size there would be some inconveniences. For example, visitors entering from the South Gate would not be able to take the shortcut from West Thumb to Old Faithful. As in Zion, visitors with lodging reservations at Old Faithful would be allowed to drive to Old Faithful and park. This plan would be a start but it would not solve the overcrowding problems in other areas of the park, such as at Norris Geyser Basin.

It appears that the problem of overcrowding is only going to get worse, so the sooner park officials tackle this issue the better. Fortunately, the NPS had a great system in place for backcountry use, both in Yellowstone and Grand Teton. When folks ask me how to deal with the overcrowding issue in the front country, I offer the following two suggestions: first, plan to visit outside the peak summer period between July 1 and August 20. Second, plan to get up at *first light* to begin sightseeing along the park roads. Most folks tend to get up around 7:30 a.m., eat breakfast at 8:30 a.m. and hit the road around 9:30 a.m. On July 1 the sun rises at 5:39 a.m. so the opportunity is there for at least two hours of uncrowded sightseeing.

The Firehole River, Upper Geyser Basin

This Horse Should Stay in the Barn

When I first arrived in Yellowstone in June of 1968 to work for the Yellowstone Park Company, I was enamored with its wild country and could not wait to explore it by any means possible—by foot, horseback, raft or canoe. I soon found out that most of the streams in the park were closed to recreational floating. I really didn't question why until I started working as an Interpretive Park Ranger in Yellowstone in 1974, and that's because one day I had a visitor ask me why we had such a policy. At the time I thought that it was wrong for officials to deny paddlers access to many of the park's beautiful waterways. I think my opinion on this changed one day in the early 1980s during our seasonal training, when Roderick Nash spoke to our group of Yellowstone interpretive Rangers. Nash had quite the reputation. He was a renowned author, conservationist, wilderness enthusiast, and professor of environmental studies at the University of California, Santa Barbara. Nash also loved running rivers, especially the Grand Canyon's Colorado River, and he wasted little time in stating how wonderful he thought it would be if visitors could float the Yellowstone River through Hayden Valley.

I immediately conjured up images of trains of rafts coursing through the wild and scenic open valley with its abundance and variety of wildlife. At this point in time not only was the river closed to floating, but several sections were closed to fishing, so wildlife could feed along the river undisturbed. Of course, the natural scene of animals and waterfowl along this magnificent river, with the huge green expanse of Hayden Valley and the Washburn Mountain range serving as a spectacular backdrop, was not lost on visitors. The many pullouts along the road provided thousands each day the opportunity to view scenes reminiscent of what much of the West must have looked like 200 years ago.

Nash's comments made me think long and hard about what would happen in Yellowstone if streams such as the Yellowstone River were opened up to paddling. Over the years I had certainly enjoyed many float trips down the Snake River through Grand Teton National Park. The Snake was typically very busy, with many rafts that carry lots of visitors; however, I felt that situation was completely different from Yellowstone. For the most part, the Snake River flows away from any roads. The river may be busy with boats, but there are few pullouts where the natural viewshed is spoiled by a procession of watercraft. Also, the Snake in the Tetons does not meander through large meadows filled with bison and elk, as do so many of Yellowstone's streams. I had never given serious thought to what it would be like if watercraft were floating each day down such streams as the Yellowstone, Madison, Firehole, and Lamar Rivers, where so many visitors simply enjoy observing wildlife and the natural, undisturbed scene.

I realized on that day, over 30 years ago, that with all due respect to Roderick Nash, he was wrong when it came to this idea. In fact, it made me wonder for the first time if Grand Teton had ever conducted any type of study to ascertain just how many rafts should be allowed on the Snake River, and what type of impact rafting had on its wildlife. For example, on several occasions I had encountered lines of boats on the Snake, where it was almost impossible to escape from seeing rafts upstream and downstream during your entire float. It is one thing for an angler to wade out on a stream and cast a fly, but what about a steady procession of boats?

I was thankful that the National Park Service in Yellowstone had never allowed this horse to get out of the barn, so to speak. Whenever a park visitor approached the visitor center desk to ask about Yellowstone's policy on not allowing paddling on park streams, which was rare, I had no trouble explaining the park's position, and why it was good for both wildlife and visitors. And another point that I have always made: if you truly wanted to paddle into the wilderness in Yellowstone or Grand Teton, there were ample opportunities. After all, I was an expert on the subject, having paddled every available stream and lake in both parks. For wilderness trips in Yellowstone, one could paddle over 100 miles of shoreline on Yellowstone Lake. Another fabulous trip is to paddle along the west shore of Lewis Lake, and then up the three mile Lewis River Channel into the wild waters of Shoshone Lake. As I detail in another chapter ("A River-Lake Wilderness Combo Trip"), Jim Lenertz and I once paddled down the Snake River from Flagg Ranch near the Yellowstone's South Entrance, into Jackson Lake. We then paddled along the entire 20-plus mile length of its west shore to Bearpaw Bay, and portaged/paddled Bearpaw Lake, Leigh Lake, and String Lake. So for a paddler to somehow suggest that there are no wilderness paddling opportunities in Yellowstone and Grand Teton National Parks is to be a bit disingenuous. But I rarely received complaints about Yellowstone's paddling policy, and when I did and explained the park's position, the visitor was satisfied with the answer. I can honestly state that in 43 years as an interpretive ranger working at visitor centers at Norris, Mammoth, and mostly Old Faithful, I never received a single request from a visitor to fill out our official complaint/comment form on this subject. The vast majority of park visitors and constituents supported the park's ban on recreational floating on park streams.

So it came as quite a surprise during the winter of 2014 when I learned that Representative Cynthia Lummis (R) of Wyoming had introduced a bill, known as the "River Paddling Protection Act" in the U.S. House of Representatives. The bill would have forced Yellowstone's managers to conduct a comprehensive study regarding opening up the park's 6700 miles of streams for potentially all types of recreational use, including kayaks, canoes, inner tubes, rafts, drift boats, and anything else that can float on water.

Given my length of service as a seasonal ranger for the National Park Service, I would be the first to say the organization is not perfect. However, during these years, I have always been impressed by the quality of its employees, and their dedication to protecting and preserving park resources. I could not help but chuckle at the idea that Congress, with an approval rating that sometimes dips into the single digits, wants to manage resources in Yellowstone National Park, or any other national park for that matter.

The displacement of wildlife in such places as Hayden Valley, Lamar Valley, and along the Madison, Gibbon and Firehole Rivers, would be a huge issue, but it is not the only one. Let's consider whitewater paddling. The section of the Yellowstone River that flows from near Tower Junction until it exits the park at Gardiner, Montana, is completely inaccessible by road. There are very large and dangerous rapids here, and opening it to paddling would be a colossal mistake. The Black Canyon is very narrow, deep and remote. Any boating mishap here is going to require a very risky, and costly rescue effort by National Park Service personnel, who are already overtaxed with a plethora of duties. For example, there have been occasions when outlaw paddlers have attempted to sneak down this section, only to have serious accidents that required extremely dangerous, difficult, and costly rescues involving the use of a helicopter.

The Black Canyon is indeed a wild and beautiful place, but there are fabulous trails that hikers and backpackers can take that provide access along the river for much of the way. So, if you want to enjoy the beauty of the Black Canyon, it is very easy to do so by trail. Also, there are numerous whitewater streams available just outside the parks, such as the North Fork of the Shoshone, the Gallatin, the Yellowstone, and the Snake River south of Jackson. All of these whitewater streams are along roadways, which provide easy access in case of an accident.

"Pack-rafting" is a relatively new outdoor activity thanks to an innovative light raft that a backpacker can actually pack along into the backcountry. Some pack-rafters say they want to backpack into the backcountry, and float remote streams, such as the Upper Yellowstone River, which flows into the Southeast Arm of Yellowstone Lake. I have taken many backpacking trips along the Thorofare trail that parallels portions of the Upper Yellowstone River. That river provides critical habitat for grizzlies, moose, wolves and other species. All you have to do to understand that is to walk down to the riverbank in those sections where the trail passes a bend in the river, and simply look at the incredible abundance and variety of animal tracks. You don't have to be a seasoned wildlife biologist to understand that a train of paddlers floating down every nook and cranny of this stretch of river would displace and disturb wildlife. Can't we leave a *few* unspoiled places out in the wild where the animals come first? That's why the park limits use in certain Bear Management Areas, so that grizzly bears do not abandon critical feeding areas due to interaction with human visitation. This was actually documented by researchers from Montana State University. Presently it is possible to enjoy the wild beauty of the Upper Yellowstone by trail without disrupting wildlife, since the trail is mostly away from the river's edge; however, floaters going straight down the river here would adversely impact wildlife.

The National Park Service is on record strongly opposing this bill. They are not alone. Columnist Todd Wilkinson with the Jackson Hole News and Guide spent several weeks interviewing conservation organizations, fly fishing guides, prominent conservationists, scientists, land managers, and former park superintendents, to see how they felt about the paddling bill. Other than a few pack-rafters and whitewater enthusiasts, he could find no support—just robust disapproval. Some of the organizations voicing opposition to the bill include the Coalition of National Park Service Retirees, with 1,000 members who combined have thousands of years of expertise stewarding national parks, the Montana Council of Trout Unlimited, representing 13 chapters and 3,400 Trout Unlimited members, the National Parks Conservation Association, the Jackson Hole Conservation Alliance, the Wyoming Wilderness Association, the Cougar Fund, the Greater Yellowstone Coalition, the Natural Resources Defense Council, the Wild Foundation, the Sierra Club, Wyoming Wildlife Advocates, the Gallatin Wildlife Association, People and Carnivores, Great Old Broads for Wilderness, and 30 prominent greater Yellowstone anglers and fly shops.

The politicians who are carrying this legislation forward have some of the worst voting records in Congress, when it comes to protecting the environment according to the League of Conservation Voters. I don't pretend to understand why Congress feels the need to micromanage our national parks, but it is a slippery slope to go down. If this legislation is passed, we will probably see other special interest user groups with political connections attempt to get their favorite activities forced upon park management. Perhaps a golf course in Hayden Valley, or an ATV trail across the Mirror Plateau. As of the summer of 2016 this bill (H.R. 974—"The Yellowstone and Grand Teton Paddling Act") has passed out of the House Natural Resources Committee and is awaiting a vote in the full House.

Yellowstone is a unique and treasured resource that requires careful management. There are serious issues and threats facing the park's aquatic ecosystems, such as invasive species, drought, and critical wildlife migration routes and habitat needs. I sincerely hope that we will continue to allow the professionally trained biologists, scientists, and recreation specialists, to manage our national parks. It would be a terrible mistake to set the precedent of allowing Congress to dictate resource management in our national parks that may not be science-based. Yellowstone is more than just a pretty place to play. This horse should never leave the barn!

Memories of the Yellowstone Cutthroat Trout

When I tell visitors that I first starting working in Yellowstone National Park in 1968, I am often asked to compare the "good old days" in the park to the present. They are usually surprised to hear me boast about the park being in finer shape today than back then. That's because during the 1960s we had such things as begging bears along the roadside, park garbage dumps, roads through geyser basins, a missing keystone native predator—the gray wolf, and a plunging grizzly population, just to mention a few issues. However, there is one huge change in the ecosystem from the "early days" to the present time that is discouraging. The loss of the native cutthroat trout in Yellowstone Lake and its tributaries has indeed been an unmitigated disaster, though there is developing some hope of recovery.

I am almost embarrassed to admit that the first time I ever cast out a fly in an attempt to catch a wild Yellowstone cutthroat was from hanging over the edge of the famous (or infamous back then) Fishing Bridge. I worked at Canyon in 1968, and a friend named Bruce said he wanted to go catch some trout for dinner, and he heard they were hauling them in from the bridge only sixteen miles to the south. We both had some cheap fly rods we had purchased from the camp store along with some flies ("try this imitation mosquito," the fish and tackle clerk told us), so one afternoon after work we headed down.

As we neared the famous bridge that crosses over the Yellowstone River where it flows out from Yellowstone Lake, I will never forget the sight of anglers lined up elbow to elbow, each with a fishing pole. We parked some distance away, then walked out on the bridge which contains a protected walkway for pedestrians, and back then, the many anglers. There were dozens of poles and lines protruding out, and occasionally someone would catch a trout. That's when the real fun started. Since the lines were so close together, and occasionally tangled, it was tough to tell exactly which pole the fish belonged to. Typically, about fifteen anglers would all attempt to reel in "their" catch.

Needless to say, I did not find this very appealing, and subsequent attempts at catching cutthroat eventually took place in wild stretches along the shores of the Yellowstone River, Yellowstone Lake, and its tributaries. In those days no fishing permit was even required, and you were allowed to keep a couple of fish. Eventually, fishing was prohibited from the Fishing Bridge, since it was over a prime spawning area for the cutthroat. Hence, a more appropriate name could have been "Fish View Bridge," since visitors could observe thousands of spawning cutthroat each June, but could no longer attempt to catch them.

As recently as the mid-1990s, catching cutthroat trout in Yellowstone Lake was a rather routine and almost mundane affair. There were millions of them, and they were incredibly easy to catch. I first visited the South Arm of Yellowstone Lake in 1969, and I recall catching one cutthroat per one cast back then. Through the 1980s and early 1990s, I would typically take a canoe trip every other year down into the remote arms of Yellowstone Lake with my ranger colleague and friend Jim Lenertz, who was an avid fly fisherman. I would usually paddle along shore, while Jim hauled in and carefully released about twenty trout before he got bored and stowed his rod. Most of the cutthroat did not exceed three pounds, so why not bring in some fish that can grow to a size of over thirty pounds? After all, a fish is a fish, right? If only that person or persons who illegally introduced lake trout into Yellowstone Lake had understood the consequences of their action. The first lake trout in Yellowstone Lake was discovered in 1994. Fishery biologists estimate that they were placed into the lake sometime in the mid-1980s. The introduction of lake trout into Yellowstone Lake has been called the greatest ecological disaster to ever occur in the park. The native cutthroat allowed for a tremendous transfer of energy from the lake to the land. Since the cutthroat stayed in shallow water, and utilized streams for spawning, numerous species depended on them as a critical source of food. These included eagles, ospreys, otters, and grizzly bears. As recently as 1990, biologists were still counting over 66,000 cutthroat spawning in Clear Creek, one of the lake's tributaries where studies have been conducted over the years, but then the number dropped off a cliff, and in a few years was near zero.

The lake trout primarily lives in deeper waters, and spawns along the lake bottom, rather than streams. Commonly referred to as a "freshwater shark," the lake trout can grow to over 40 pounds, and consume over 50 cutthroat per year. Therefore, this critical source of food has practically disappeared. The grizzly no longer has this source of meat in June, and osprey nests along Yellowstone Lake have practically disappeared. With financial help from the Yellowstone Park Foundation, the National Park Service is supervising intensive efforts to reduce the lake trout population through a variety of programs. These include aggressive gill-netting operations, as well as destroying lake trout spawning beds. Transmitters placed on lake trout allow technicians to track these "snitch fish" to their spawning areas, where eggs can be removed. Close to two million lake trout have been removed from Yellowstone Lake, and biologists are beginning to see some hopeful signs that perhaps the cutthroat has turned the corner, and is starting to recover. Some small cutthroat were being found and also the spawning numbers have turned up. Obviously, the lake trout will never be eliminated from Yellowstone Lake, but the hope is that their numbers could be significantly reduced.

I had not visited the South Arm of Yellowstone Lake since Jim and I had paddled down there during the mid-1990s. In August of 2013 Hank Barnett and I launched our canoe from Grant and headed for the very tip of the South Arm, where we would meet John and Deb Dirksen for a backpacking trip over the Two Ocean Plateau. I decided to fork out $25 for a park fishing permit just to get an idea how the cutthroat were coming along deep in the South Arm. I'm not an expert angler, but it has been my experience that to catch cutthroat you don't have to be. During my previous visits here Jim and I had easily caught cutthroat. However, in 2013 I spent three hours on two separate days fishing deep in the South Arm, and I did not hook a single cutthroat. I was extremely disappointed, not for my own fishing satisfaction, but just from knowing that this native trout, once so common here, was now practically nonexistent.

Hopefully the promising reports from the lake trout eradication program will eventually produce some positive results. I realize that my two day fishing expedition was not a scientific survey; however, it sure seemed to reinforce the fact that the cutthroat are still missing from their once heavily populated status.

Paddling and fishing near Peale Island, South Arm of Yellowstone Lake

Ten Ways to Advance in the Park Service

After fifteen consecutive summers working in Yellowstone, Margaret was itching to spend a couple of summers at home, and not pack up to head across the country. We lived only forty miles from the east end of Great Smoky Mountains National Park, and had spent lots of time hiking and touring in the park. I decided this would be a great opportunity to work in the Smokies, so I applied for the job, and was thrilled to land a position working at Sugarlands Visitor Center on the Tennessee side of the park. Furthermore, I was very pleased with our quarters, which consisted of an apartment located practically on the banks of Little River near Elkmont Campground.

During our week of training for the interpretive ranger staff, I learned more about the park than I had during all the previous fifteen years I had spent hiking, skiing, and trekking around my "home park." The park's biologists, scientists, and historian did a fabulous job during training bringing our seasonal staff up to date regarding vegetation, wildlife, fisheries, air quality and human history. Our final day of training was memorable. For our last activity, we all headed for Cades Cove just before sunset, when the eleven mile loop road closed to motorized traffic for the evening. The training staff had arranged for us to be pulled around the loop on an open flatbed trailer covered with bales of hay. We marveled at the majestic mountain and valley scenery, occasionally spotting deer and bear, while the biologists filled us in on wildlife dynamics. The reintroduction of red wolves was in full swing and was a hot topic along the way. Unfortunately, competition and diseases spread from domestic dogs eventually doomed the effort, and the red wolf did not make it here.

Having previously worked fifteen summers in Yellowstone and one summer in Glacier, I was naturally comparing those two parks with the Smokies regarding how efficiently programs were administered. The week of training had been very impressive—just as good if not better than most of my week-long training sessions that I had attended in Yellowstone. For one thing, I was very impressed with bear biologist Kim DeLozier's emphasis on the importance of maintaining a wild population of black bears with zero tolerance for human feeding. The bear management program in Yellowstone was committed to absolutely no human foods getting to bears, as evidenced by the presence of wildlife rangers, bear-proof garbage cans, and warning signs. The Smokies seemed just as committed, but I was about to find out otherwise.

Only a few days after Kim DeLozier had passionately told us that a "fed bear is a dead bear," (just as we often said in Yellowstone,) I received an assignment to drive up to Chimney Picnic Area to give a bear talk at 1:00 p.m. My twenty minute talk primarily covered the life cycle of the black bear in the Smokies, along with important safety precautions and bear etiquette, such as taking all precautions to prevent bears from getting into human food. My supervisor, Glen Cardwell, reasoned that visitors would be just finishing their picnic lunches, and would welcome a brief presentation on bears. When I arrived at the picnic area I could not believe my eyes! There were four bears, each standing on different picnic tables, just chowing down on visitors' lunches! I was absolutely horrified! The visitors did not seem all that upset at losing their lunches to the bears. They were taking photos, and enjoying the "entertainment." I immediately ran into the picnic area, and instructed everyone to back away from the tables, then yelled at the bears hoping to frighten them off. Either the bears did not like my voice or my ranger flat hat, because they immediately headed off into the woods. I noted that there were trails leading from the tables up into the woods; apparently the bears' feeding frenzy here was a daily occurrence.

The drive from Chimneys to Sugarlands is a short one, and as soon as I arrived back at the visitor center I called Kim DeLozier, and told him of the incident I had just witnessed. Kim reacted exactly as I thought he would; he was equally distressed to learn of this, since he was first and foremost concerned for the safety and well-being of not only visitors, but the bears. He thanked me for the call, and said that he would take the necessary measures to insure this unnatural feeding of bears did not continue.

The following morning I had desk duty at the visitor center at Sugarlands. Our interpretive staff partially shared offices with the law enforcement (LE) staff from the Little River Ranger District. There was a long hall connecting our offices with the Supervisory Ranger for the district. As I walked into our offices, the head ranger saw me and yelled, "Hey Bach, get down here!" I walked down to his office and was told to sit down. "I was called on the carpet this morning because of you!" the District Ranger began. "Look Bach, you aren't working in Yellowstone now! We don't have grizzly bears here. It doesn't hurt a thing if folks want to throw some food out to our bears. I'd better not *ever* get called into the Chief Ranger's Office again because of you! *Do I make myself clear?*" "Yes sir," I responded. I wasn't about to argue with this guy. After all, I was just a seasonal working my first summer in this park. This man was a long-term permanent LE ranger who had lots of authority, and had worked in the Smokies for many years. I knew though, that the wishes of the bear biologist were not being followed and implemented. In only my first week of work, I developed a negative comparison between how Great Smoky Mountains National Park was run compared to Yellowstone, and it would only get worse.

I began to compare every single aspect of park operations—from the enforcement of park regulations, to communications, to interpretive programs. My very first campground evening program was at Cosby Campground on the quiet, east side of the Smokies, only forty miles from my home in Morristown, Tennessee. After walking through the campground reminding campers of my program later that evening, I headed over to get my projector and slides set up in the amphitheater. Normally about thirty minutes prior to the beginning of the program, you light the campfire. I went over to the wood box and found nothing but logs. There was no kindling of any kind. I had just assumed that each wood box at the campground amphitheaters would be set up similar to ours in Yellowstone, where we had an ample supply of not only dry kindling, but kerosene soaked sawdust, which we affectionately called "ranger juice." On many an evening at Madison Campground amphitheater in Yellowstone, I had put some of that ranger juice in some crumpled up newspaper, placed it under a stack of dry logs, lit a match to the paper, and just walked away. I would often hear a visitor on the front row remark, "Ha, he thinks that's going to burn." They didn't know about my secret ingredient. Minutes later when the logs burst into flames, visitors would approach me with the obvious question: "How did you get that fire to start so easily?" I never had the heart to reveal our secret. "Oh, we just use extra dry wood," was my typical response.

Having dry kindling and kerosene soaked sawdust was standard operating procedure in Yellowstone. Here I was only thirty minutes prior to the start of my program at Cosby, and I could not get my darn campfire to light. It rains almost every day in the Smokies, so naturally all of the little twigs I gathered up were damp. All I managed to achieve was a cloud of smoke that frequently engulfed me as I continually tried to get wet twigs to burn. Eventually I just gave up and focused on giving my program titled, "The Diversity of the Great Smokies."

The next morning I walked into our office at Sugarlands and approached one of our supervisors, Terry O'Halleron, and committed a huge mistake. Rather than make a simple suggestion about how we might supply dry kindling and kerosene soaked sawdust at the campground amphitheater wood boxes, I began my comments with, "In Yellowstone we always…" I'm afraid that I did that several times.

The following week I had my first evening program at Elkmont Campground, one of the park's largest with over 300 campsites. This time I carried a supply of dry kindling along to make sure that I could get my campfire to light. Prior to the program I led a nature walk, and also walked through the campground to remind the campers of my program later that evening. The campground was filled to capacity, so I was expecting a large turnout. We typically had turnouts of 250 or more when I gave programs at the equally large Madison Campground in Yellowstone. After giving my program over at Cosby the previous week before a rather small crowd, I was now geared up for a large audience. Our programs typically start right after sunset so that our projected images on the screen can be easily seen. When I stepped up on the stage to begin my program, I was dismayed to see that the amphitheater was less than one-fourth full. I had been expecting a crowd of over 250, and it appeared that only about forty to fifty folks were present. I didn't get it, the campground was completely full. I had walked the entire campground greeting campers and reminding them of the program. We had posters advertising our programs on bulletin boards, and in restrooms, all through the campground. Where were the people?

The next morning I walked over to Terry to express my disappointment at the low turnout and ask for an explanation. "Well Butch, you have lots of competition here," he began. "You are not the only show in town. Most of the folks camping at Elkmont head for Pigeon Forge in the evening. There, they can choose between tons of shows, trinket shops, go-cart race tracks, Goofy Golf, you name it." I had not even thought about such a thing. Yes, it was true that the tourist trap town of Pigeon Force was *loaded* with every amusement attraction imaginable. I had just assumed that folks camping in Great Smoky Mountains National Park were there to see the *natural world* of the Smokies, not the silly amusement attractions! Once again I opened my big mouth and said, "Terry, you know in Yellowstone, most of the visitors are there to see the park, and the campers really turn out at the evening programs."

A few days later I encountered yet another example of a difference between the Smokies and Yellowstone. Each morning at Sugarlands Visitor Center, it was critical that we post the day's expected filling times for the park's campgrounds, along with the weather forecast, and any important messages. In Yellowstone, we had a handy form to record this information, and it was placed in our "operations logbook" for quick reference. The Smokies had no such forms or logbooks. Once again, I began my comments to Terry with, "In Yellowstone we…" It's a wonder he didn't throw a clipboard at me.

I think the final straw occurred one morning when I was on my way to work at Sugarlands. Living in the apartment near Elkmont Campground, I had about a five mile drive to work each day. Little River ran along the spur road between the campground and the main highway, and it seemed that each morning I would count at least a half- dozen anglers illegally fishing with worms. The Smokies had pretty much the same fishing regulations that Yellowstone had, in that no organic baits were permitted. The reason for this rule was simple. Most of the fishing consisted of catch and release. Fish tend to swallow organic baits, and there is no way to release the fish alive. Thus, the rule that required the use of only artificial flies and lures. This regulation was *strictly* enforced in Yellowstone. In fact, it was common for LE rangers to actually don fishing gear, and walk the banks of the Firehole River, checking anglers' fishing permits, and also ensuring that they were following the regulations. I recalled the excellent presentation by the Smokies' fisheries biologist during training, which emphasized the importance of the "no organic bait" regulation.

When I arrived at Sugarlands Visitor Center I noted that both of my supervisors were either off, or were away for the morning. I wasn't going to wait for them to return. I went straight to the phone and called up Fred, the park's fisheries biologist. "Fred," I began, "is the regulation against using worms for bait really that important here in the Smokies?" Fred assured me that yes, it was a *critical* regulation that needed to be adhered to. He went on to explain how important it was to preserve and protect the native brook trout species in the park. "Then Fred," I continued, "can you explain to me why we don't enforce this regulation if it is so important?" I went on to describe how I encountered on a daily basis several anglers illegally fishing with worms, as I drove along Little River to and from Elkmont to Sugarlands. I also shared with him how strictly the regulation was enforced in Yellowstone. This time I was not "accosted" by the supervisory Little River District LE Ranger; however, he must have called my immediate supervisors. The following morning when I walked into our interpretive offices I was met with a big chart on the wall that contained the following narrative: "Ten Ways to Advance in the National Park Service: 1. Work in Yellowstone; 2. Work in Yellowstone; 3. Work in Yellowstone…etc. I was pretty sure that Terry had written that up for me.

It was at this point I realized that while I was simply motivated to see the Smokies "raise their bar" so to speak to what we had in Yellowstone, I was truly going about it in the wrong way. I apologized to both Terry and Glen, and promised them that they would never again hear me make a statement that began with, "In Yellowstone, we.."

Looking back on my two summers spent working in the Great Smokies in 1987 and 1988, I have to say it was two of the greatest summers of my life. I would also say that both Glen and Terry were two of the finest supervisors I have ever worked for during my many years as a seasonal ranger with the National Park Service. After Yellowstone's great fires of 1988, I yearned to return there for the summer of 1989. I wanted to see firsthand how my beloved park had been impacted and changed. Also, after spending two summers close to home in the South, Margaret was ready to head west again. I think we had both forgotten just how humid things can get during the hot summer months. As hiring season approached I called up my old Yellowstone supervisor, Joe Halladay to let him know that we wanted to come back. "Butch," Joe began, "I'm afraid it doesn't look good. Everyone we had here last summer wants to return. I guess they want to see how the park recovers from the great fires last summer. It doesn't appear that there will be a single opening for you." "Joe," I responded, "isn't there any hope at all that a position will open up for me?" "Not unless someone cancels at the last minute," Joe answered. "Right now we are completely staffed for the 1989 summer."

I knew that I had rehire status all set up in the Smokies, but I so wanted to return to Yellowstone. I decided to pay a visit to the Smokies' Chief of Interpretation, Stan Canter, who had actually previously worked in Yellowstone. Stan and I went back many years. I told Stan of my predicament, and asked him how he would feel about me if I committed to work another season in the Smokies, but then took a job in Yellowstone if something opened up at the very last minute. Stan responded just like I thought a good manager would: "We would frown on that very much." As the 1989 summer approached, I found myself moping around the house. Then we attended a special program at our church given by Evangelist David Ring. David had suffered throughout his life from cerebral palsy, but despite his many hardships had developed a very successful ministry. The title of David's sermon was, "Shine, Don't Whine!" Following his excellent sermon and testimony, I felt quite guilty regarding my own case of "whining" over not getting a position in Yellowstone for the summer of 1989. Yes, I wanted to go back to Yellowstone, but how could I complain about working another glorious season in the Great Smokies?

About two weeks prior to the beginning of the summer season, Joe Halladay called from Yellowstone. "Butch," he began, "you're in luck. One of our seasonals has made a last-minute decision to take an opening in the Tetons, so she can be closer to her parents who have a summer cabin south of Jackson. That opens up a spot for you this summer." "Joe," I responded, "that sounds great. Let me check with my supervisors to see if there is any way I can make this happen." I already knew how Stan felt about it, but still, I wanted to run it past my immediate supervisor, Glen Cardwell. I told Glen what had come up, and also what Stan had told me. "Glen, if my leaving would mess up your summer staffing, then I'll be glad to turn down the last-minute Yellowstone offer," I told him. "Butch, I know how badly you want to return to your beloved Yellowstone," Glen said. "Go ahead and accept the position. I'll take care of replacing you and there will be no hard feelings on our end."

After the David Ring sermon, I had made peace with myself over working a third summer in the Smokies, but now Margaret, my two daughters and I excitedly began making plans for making yet another journey across the nation's midsection to head to the Yellowstone high country! Looking back, I can say that the two summers spent working in the Smokies produced many wonderful memories for me and my family. The work was extremely rewarding, but so was the opportunity to spend the summers living right on the banks of the gorgeous Little River. My kids and I enjoyed swimming in some of the more remote stretches of this wonderful clear mountain stream. Just across the way was the old Wonderland Hotel, where my family and I spent many a relaxing evening in rocking chairs on the front porch, listening to the sound of crickets, and watching raccoons come and go.

While I was indeed critical of the way the park was run in some areas, I had met many dedicated employees who dearly loved the Smokies, and strived to protect the resources and serve the visitor. The interpretive programs were exceptional and of special note was the fact that the park had an excellent junior ranger program in place. By 1989 Yellowstone still did not have a junior ranger program. Later that summer we actually initiated a junior ranger program for the Old Faithful area, and it was modeled after the Smokies junior ranger program. Margaret provided the artwork, and it was guided into place with the help of Dan Ng, who was a permanent interpretive supervisor at Old Faithful. Kids of all ages could earn a button with the title, "Old Faithful Explorer." I feel certain that this initiative helped motivate the park to bring on board Yellowstone's own junior ranger program shortly thereafter. Of course, I was careful to avoid saying, "In the Great Smokies we did things *this* way. I had learned my lesson!

A grizzly in early spring moves to the warm geyser basins along the Firehole

Where the Grizzly Walks

During my first two summers in 1968 and 1969 working in Yellowstone for the old Yellowstone Park Company, I saw plenty of bears including grizzlies; however, they were all "garbage bears." All of the black bears were spotted along the roads begging for food. I saw grizzlies feeding on garbage at the dock behind the Canyon Lodge where I worked, and I also observed grizzlies feeding on garbage at the dump in West Yellowstone, Montana. Despite a lot of hiking and backpacking during those two summers, I never observed a single bear in the wild.

My very first observation of both a black bear and a grizzly bear in the wild in Yellowstone actually occurred on the same trip in June of 1971. Our old Yellowstone friends, Rod and Kathy Busby, were visiting Margaret and me in Great Falls, Montana, where I was stationed at Malmstrom Air Force Base. The four of us had planned to do some hiking and backpacking around our old stomping grounds at Canyon. Rod and I had become good friends with Ranger Tom Griffith during our two summers working at Canyon, so we stopped by the ranger station there to say hello. After exchanging pleasantries Ranger Griffith made us an offer that we couldn't refuse: "How would you guys like to go into Mary Mountain patrol cabin? I received word that it was broken into, and I'm too busy here in the front country to get out there to check it out." Naturally, we jumped at the chance.

About halfway in on our eleven mile trek across Hayden Valley, we spotted a small black bear which passed near us during our lunch stop in a small stand of trees. However, it was the next day that was truly magical. We actually found the cabin to be in fine shape, so we would be able to give Ranger Griffith a good report that the cabin was secure. We had decided to take the shorter eight-mile trail out to the Norris-Canyon road. But this trail traversed through a dense lodgepole forest, and this early in the summer we were soon up to our knees post-holing in snow. We pulled out our topo map and compass, and set an easterly course that would take us back out into the open valley, which was free of snow. As we approached the tree line, there ahead of us was the scene that perhaps best personifies Yellowstone's wild backcountry: two grizzlies digging beneath a snow bank out in an open meadow.

We really had the perfect scenario for viewing grizzlies in the wild: the bears were a good distance away; they were not aware of our presence; and they were out in the open, while we were standing along the edge of a forest. Of course, this was back before bear spray was available, and the best advice for dealing with a charging bear was to climb a tree. Nowadays bear experts do not recommend climbing a tree since bears have been known to simply climb right up and pull the hiker out of the tree. It is better to stand your ground, and slowly back away, all the while keeping your canister of bear spray ready. The best thing going for us, that still applies today, is the fact that we had four in our party. Bear attacks rarely, if ever, involve a group of four hikers together.

We spent about thirty minutes mesmerized by this our first observation of a grizzly in the wild. Finally, we realized we needed to make progress on our journey back out across Hayden Valley, and there was no way we were going to attempt to detour around those bears out in the open meadow. We hated to disturb their feeding, but we shouted "Hey, bear," and immediately both bears stood on their haunches, looked our way, raised their noses in an attempt to catch our scent, and then suddenly broke into a run away from us, eventually veering to the north, and disappearing into the forest.

I did not realize it at the time, but that sighting coincided with a very dark period in the history of the grizzly in Yellowstone. For several years the legendary brother biologist team of Frank and John Craighead had been conducting groundbreaking research on Yellowstone's grizzlies. They were finding that bears covered a huge distance looking for food, often going well beyond the park's boundaries, and also that most of the grizzlies in the park were depending on human food at garbage dumps, and any other place such as a picnic area or campground, where human food might be found. Given the number of injuries to visitors from bear incidents along the road, and in the campgrounds, the National Park Service in Yellowstone was in the process of removing all unnatural foods. The dumps were being closed, garbage cans were made bear-proof, and regulations against feeding bears were being strictly enforced.

That's when the big debate between the Craighead brothers and the Park Service amped up. Park officials had decided that the best way to stop the unnatural situation was to go "cold turkey," and immediately remove all access to human foods. The Craighead brothers strongly disagreed, saying that most bears were addicted to human foods, and such a sudden removal of foods would result in bears coming into increased contact with humans. The Craigheads favored a gradual phasing out of human foods. To go "cold turkey" would cause a serious safety issue, which would result in the death of most of the park's grizzlies.

When I began working as a seasonal interpretive ranger for the National Park Service in Yellowstone in 1974, the debate was at a fever pitch. My training sessions obviously favored the approach the park was taking. "If we continue to have human foods available to bears, that will be just that many more cubs that get raised on garbage," was often the reasoning given. However, while that is certainly true, the "cold turkey" approach did seem to carry the ramifications that the Craigheads had predicted. Grizzlies began searching for food in all the wrong places, and many bears were euthanized or otherwise removed from the ecosystem. The population was falling into a dark hole, and some biologists did not expect the bear to recover. At its lowest point the population was estimated to be around 136 in the entire Greater Yellowstone Ecosystem (GYE.) It is no wonder that despite the fact I was frequently taking long hikes and backpack trips in Yellowstone, I hardly ever saw a grizzly, and only rarely their sign.

Gradually this changed. The grizzly was designated as a threatened species under the Endangered Species Act in 1975, and efforts by government agencies and biologists succeeded in bringing the bear population back. Recent population estimates have centered around 700 bears in the GYE. And not surprisingly, I began to observe grizzly bears with a much greater frequency on my hikes and backpack trips. When I first came to Yellowstone, I had a great respect and fear of grizzlies, but it did not keep me from entering the backcountry (see "Are you a Stander or a Runner?" in first volume.) Today, I certainly recognize that the grizzly is potentially a very dangerous animal that can easily kill a human. However, it is a risk that I am willing to take. Really, unless you never venture out from your home, life's daily activities just about anywhere are full of risks from a myriad of potential accidents/incidents.

Despite the potential danger of a grizzly attack, my attitude over the years has been shaped by my many observations of bears in the backcountry. I have probably had a fairly close encounter with a grizzly bear at least twenty times, and each time the bear has turned away (I did have one close call which is detailed in the story above.) It just seems that the grizzly is simply out there doing its thing trying to find food, and as long as you give it space, and allow it to pursue natural foods, it isn't going to bother you. I very strongly believe that the best defense against a grizzly attack is to travel the backcountry with at least four members in your party. Beyond that just use common sense. Be aware of your surroundings and be alert. Don't have odorous foods anywhere near your tent, make noise when necessary so as not to surprise a bear at close range, and have your bear spray out and ready to use, and I just think the odds of a bear attack are extremely small—much smaller than the odds of having an accident traveling the park's roads.

I have often been asked by my backpacking friend Clyde Austin, who takes big backpack trips all over North America, "Butch, what's the matter with you? Why don't you ever backpack in the Sierras? The Colorado Rockies? The Sawtooth Mountains?" My answer to Clyde is always the same: "Clyde, when I'm not backpacking in grizzly country, the wilderness just does not seem wild enough for me." It is difficult to describe the feeling you get when you come across fresh grizzly tracks, claw marks or droppings; or especially when you observe a sow peacefully feeding with her cubs out in a meadow. To use a term popularized by a credit card commercial, those moments are simply *priceless!* Today, the grizzly bear occupies a land area that amounts to only 2% of its original range in the lower 48 states. Imagine that! So I guess it is no accident that most, not all, of my backpacking adventures have taken place within the

Greater Yellowstone Ecosystem and the so-called Northern Continental Divide Ecosystem in northern Montana.

I suppose I should be ecstatic about the recovery of the grizzly bear in the GYE. But instead, I am worried about the future of the grizzly. I have watched two of its primary food sources, whitebark pine seeds and cutthroat trout, practically disappear over a relatively short period of time (see "When the Yellowstone High Country was Green," and "Memories of the Yellowstone Cutthroat"). As the grizzly attempts to substitute more meat in its diet such as by going after elk, I see more and more conflicts with hunters that often result in the bear's death. The Yellowstone grizzly is basically trapped on an island with no successful corridor to other populations. Given the development of more and more "ranchettes" throughout the GYE, the bear's habitat is decreasing. And yet, there is a strong push to delist the grizzly, and open it up to trophy hunting. Some say that given the fact that bears are being spotted well away from their range over the past several decades is proof that the population has increased. I tend to agree with those biologists who think the bear is expanding its reaches because they are simply having to look harder and farther for food. I am of the opinion that the grizzly should not be delisted and subjected to a trophy hunt in the GYE. Grizzly bears are truly majestic animals. If you haven't had the opportunity to see one in the wild, then I strongly encourage you to read through the outstanding book, "Grizzlies of Pilgrim Creek," with photos by Tom Mangelson and text by Todd Wilkinson. Tom's photos in that book will work your conscious over regarding what we should do regarding the future of Yellowstone's grizzlies. Despite the past progress we have made, now is not the time to delist the grizzly bear. Also I would strongly suggest that most citizens in the states surrounding Yellowstone and throughout the U.S. would much prefer to see and photograph a live grizzly bear in the wild rather than kill one for a rug!

Finally, keep in mind that the grizzly in Yellowstone resides on an "island" ecosystem. As large as the Greater Yellowstone Ecosystem is at approximately 18 million acres, the grizzly needs wildlife corridors to connect with other populations. The GYE island is surrounded by private lands, communities and ranches, and the grizzly faces a daunting gauntlet to connect with other populations to the north. Wildlife advocates are working hard with multiple landowners and government agencies to create a "Yellowstone to Yukon" corridor that connects wild lands, and allows the diverse gene pool that grizzlies will need for long term survival. Given all of the challenges involved, we need to err on the side of caution, and not give in to pressures to hunt the great bear, even if it is delisted.

Humor in Uniform

I first came to Yellowstone in 1968 as a college kid attending Auburn University in Alabama, and had never been west of the Mississippi River. I was a complete greenhorn when it came to knowing *anything* about the Rocky Mountain West. I learned many lessons the hard way, several of which were detailed in my first volume, *Tracking the Spirit of Yellowstone*. Therefore, I have always resisted the temptation to make fun of visitors to Yellowstone, who oftentimes do or say things, simply because they don't know any better. After all, I did the same thing when I first came to the park.

For years the staff at the Old Faithful Visitor Education Center has kept a folder to record humorous or strange comments made by visitors from all over the world. Some of the comments are downright hilarious, but others are simply what I refer to as head scratchers. Folks have different senses of humor, so I'll let you, the reader, decide which of these visitor comments/questions are "head scratchers," and which are just downright funny:

"Is the Old Faithful Geyser always in the same place, or does it move around?"

"How long did it take the Park Service to construct the mound that Old Faithful is on?"

"Is it okay to throw my husband into Old Faithful?"

"Did the fires in 1988 cause Old Faithful to stop erupting?"

"If I see an animal standing in the middle of the road, should I stop?"

"Where are the places where you keep animals tied up for visitors to see?"

"I saw some buffalo in the river. Do they eat the fish?"

"We had to stop for fifteen minutes because of bison crossing the road. Can't you people keep them in corrals?"

"Where do you keep the caged bears?"

"Is there a certain time that you schedule the bison to cross the river?"

"Is that water in the hot pools?"

"Do you know when the glacier blows up?"

"I want to take the zip line over Old Faithful. Where do I go to make reservations?"

"Where did I come from to get here?"

"So, all of these pine trees you see here…are they aspens?"

"Last time I was here, Old Faithful was erupting at an angle. Did you do something to fix it?"

"Those fires here sure caused a terrible infestation of trees, didn't it?"

"Is it okay for me to step off of the boardwalk to take a photo of the "Stay on Boardwalk" sign?"

"Can you tell me where I can find Pragmatic Spring?" (The visitor was obviously looking for Grand Prismatic Spring at Midway Geyser Basin.)

"Bears are mellower in California because they graze in marijuana fields. You should introduce marijuana in the meadows here in Yellowstone."

"Say Ranger, we were driving through Lamar Valley, and we saw a bunch of bison. Their front was very shaggy but their rears had almost no hair. Do you shave their butts each year?"

In the visitor center there is an exhibit that shows the types of animals one can expect to see in the geyser basins, such as coyotes and killdeers, a bird commonly seen in the Old Faithful area. Overheard at this exhibit: Youngster to his Dad: "Dad, what is a killdeer?" Dad to youngster: "Well son, that's when a buffalo steps on a deer and kills it."

A visitor is attempting to drive his vehicle onto a paved foot/bicycle trail that leads out into the geyser basin, and is told by a ranger that he must turn around. Visitor: "But if I don't do what my GPS tells me I'll be lost!"

Fifteen minutes after each eruption of Old Faithful, we show a wonderful film, titled "A Symphony of Fire and Water," that illustrates how geysers work, and what geologists believe is under the ground at Old Faithful. Visitor to ranger at the desk: "Do you pump smell into the theater during the geyser movie?" Ranger to visitor, "No Ma'am we don't." Visitor: "Oh, then it must've been the man sitting in front of me." (Many thermal features in the park emit a sulfurous odor).

A lady walked up to the desk and exclaimed, "Looking at the yellow and orange glow of the volcanic lava at the Midway Volcano is so exciting." The ranger responded, "Actually Ma'am, that yellow and orange are bacteria mats in the runoff channels of the hot springs at Midway Geyser Basin."

One evening our Ranger presentation was on the topic of forest fires in Yellowstone. The Ranger at the desk made the following announcement: "Folks, please head into the auditorium. It's on fire."

A visitor standing in the lobby of the visitor center waiting for Old Faithful: "I hear a siren going off. Is that the warning signal that Old Faithful is about to erupt?" Ranger to visitor: "No Ma'am, that's just the sound of the hand dryers in the restroom."

Visitor to Ranger: "I want to see Morning Glory Pool." Ranger to visitor: "Yes sir, the trail starts right in front of the visitor center, and is about a 25 minute walk." Visitor to Ranger: "You mean I have to walk to see it? Don't you provide golf carts?"

In order to obtain a backcountry use permit, a visitor must go to the backcountry office, view a film on topics such as bear safety, stream crossings, regulations, and camping etiquette. Then the visitor must pore over maps, and submit a trip plan complete with campsites selected to the ranger who will check availability. Once the permit is issued, the backpacker is ready to head out into the backcountry. However one day a couple walked up to the desk and had this question for the ranger on duty: "Here is our backcountry permit. So where are we going?"

Over the years I have always marveled at how our ranger staff strives to help visitors in a courteous manner. Of course, there comes a time for the visitor center to close for the evening. Cash registers must be closed out, and the ranger staff has to shut down the visitor center, its exhibits, and lock up the building. It can be difficult to convince everyone to leave the building, especially if Old Faithful has just erupted. Once this has finally been accomplished, we often encounter visitors walking up to the door and tapping on the window. You never know if there is a serious problem, so I typically prop the door open, let them know that the building is closed for the day, but I also want to know their question. One evening during the winter of 2013 a lady said that she had a question. "Ma'am," I asked, "Are you staying at the lodge this evening?" "Yes," she replied. "Then please come see us when we open in the morning at 9:00 a.m." I remarked. "But I only have one quick question," she countered. "Okay then, what is it?" I asked. The lady gave me her quick question: "We are going to be in the park for five days." I need you to plan our trip." I responded, "Ma'am, that is indeed a quick question, but I'm afraid the answer is rather time consuming. Please let me do that for you in the morning." Sure enough, the lady was there bright and early the next morning, and we spent at least thirty minutes helping her plan her time in the park.

Old Faithful is the busiest spot in Yellowstone. I would assume that anyone visiting Yellowstone is going to be certain to witness an eruption of the world's most famous geyser. Given the high elevation at Old Faithful (7,737') and the high number of visitors, it is not unusual to have quite a few medical emergencies during the busy summer season. For serious medical issues the park utilizes helicopter life flights to quickly transport patients to Idaho Falls, Idaho. Some busy days might see several such life flights. During July of 2013 I had stopped by the Old Faithful Backcountry Office, which is actually inside the Old Faithful Ranger Station, to check with Ranger Bob Kistart regarding some backcountry campsites, when a lady walked into the office and asked, "Is this where we sign up for the scenic helicopter rides? "Ma'am," I responded, "believe me, this is one helicopter ride you do not want to take!"

Working at Old Faithful allows the ranger to come in contact with people not only from all over the United States, but from all over the world. Yellowstone truly is a world treasure. It is always fun to try to guess where visitors are from based on their accents. As a native of Alabama myself, I have certainly enjoyed the many guesses as to where *I* am from. Most visitors guess Texas. Accents really do vary from region to region. I am actually pretty good at guessing U.S. regional accents. Visitors from north Florida, South Carolina, Georgia, Alabama, middle to west Tennessee, Mississippi, Arkansas, Texas and Oklahoma have accents that are very similar. Louisianans are in a class by themselves, and are very easy to identify. So are folks from east Tennessee. Having lived there for 31 years, the mountain dialect is fascinating and bears no resemblance to the typical "southern accent" heard in Alabama, Georgia, etc. North Dakotans certainly have a distinct accent, and now that I live in Montana, I'm always intrigued how a "creek" is pronounced "crick." Some of the folks from New Jersey and New York are easy to recognize.

Having finally visited Australia and New Zealand in November of 2012, I'm now getting much better at differentiating the accents from those two countries and that of Great Britain. However, my story of humor involves my favorite accent, and that is the one from around Boston. I learned a valuable lesson one day about communicating to visitors with different regional accents, when I was giving a three-hour walk in a backcountry area not far from Old Faithful. Much of the walk was in an open, treeless area, so at about the halfway point, I would gather up my group of about twenty visitors, and announce our plans for a "restroom" break. Since we were out in the open, I would walk our group up to a ridge, and instruct the guys to head in one direction, and the ladies in the other. The rise of the terrain at this spot separated the two groups. There was one large tree down below, and I told everyone to meet at the tree after about five minutes. However, my mistake was that I had always called the break a "potty break." I guess I was emulating long-time ranger Sam Holbrook, whom I had heard use that term many times.

One day after I gave my directional instructions for our "potty break," I noticed that when the ladies headed down one side of the ridge, one male visitor followed them. I quickly walked down and said, "Sir, you need to follow me. The guys are going down the other side of the ridge." The man looked disappointed and said, "I thought you said we were going to have a potty!" The man was from Boston. He thought I had announced a PARTY with the ladies! After that incident, I never used the word "potty" again. It was simply a "bathroom" or "restroom" break!

Springtime at Old Faithful often produces some interesting reality checks for visitors. After all, many folks have just left warm climes with green vegetation and flowering shrubs and plants to come to a world of snow and ice. April and early May above 7000' in Yellowstone is an exciting time of transition from the stark, frigid state of winter to the very gradual and slow warm-up to spring. Oftentimes, winter hangs on much longer than most visitors who have not done their homework would ever dream. For example, the snowpack along most of the park's roads and trails can remain several feet deep well into May. The big lakes, such as Yellowstone, Lewis and Shoshone, are often still frozen through most of the month of May.

Several years ago I was working at Old Faithful in the "spring" of the year. The roads into Old Faithful along with the visitor center typically open for the season in mid-April. I had been working for several weeks, and by mid-May most of the lodges were open, and many of the seasonal concession employees had arrived. After getting off work I decided to drive up to the DeLacy Creek trailhead near the continental divide, and enjoy skiing the three miles to Shoshone Lake. There were about four feet of snow in the area, and Shoshone Lake was still frozen. When I reached the trailhead I was surprised to see another vehicle parked there. Usually in the afternoon this time of year, I had the trail to myself. I noticed that the car's license plates were from Oklahoma, and there was an employee sticker on the window, which meant the owner was working for the season in the park. However, what *really* surprised me was that there were no ski tracks. Rather, some poor soul was "post-holing" their way in the deep snow. Upon closer investigation it appeared that the individual was sinking all the way to his crotch with each step! I've done a bit of post-holing myself in Yellowstone (see "The Trip from Hell," in *Tracking the Spirit of Yellowstone*), so I know firsthand what an absolutely miserable experience it can be.

"Why in the world would anyone subject themselves to such suffering?" I thought to myself. "Once this person realized that the snow was too soft to support their weight, why wouldn't they turn around?" After skiing about one mile along the trail through the trees, I would typically bear right to ski out through the open meadows, so I could obtain better views of the lake in the distance, as well as Mount Sheridan to the south. When skiing in such areas during the spring, I am always extremely alert for grizzly bears, pack along bear spray, and carefully watch for their fresh sign, such as tracks or droppings. When I reached the two mile mark, I heard a frightening sound coming from over in the woods that sounded like an animal in distress. The hair stood up on my neck as I looked in every direction, expecting to see a grizzly sow and cub emerging from the timber into the meadow. Instead I saw the shape of a man in the woods struggling through the snow. "The post-holer!" I thought to myself.

I left the meadow and skied over to this figure off in the woods to satisfy my curiosity. As I got closer I observed a poor fellow struggling mightily, and emitting a sad sounding groan with each sinking step in the snow. When I reached him I noticed that he was wearing blue jeans (now soaked), with a day pack, and a fishing rod on his shoulder. Suddenly, I had it all figured out. The young fellow from Oklahoma looked up at me with the saddest expression as I reached him, but said nothing. "Hello," I began. "I'm an off-duty ranger at Old Faithful. I'll bet you're on your way to fish in Shoshone Lake aren't you?" "Yeesssss," the poor fellow almost squeaked to me. "And," I continued, "I'll bet you didn't know that Shoshone Lake is still completely frozen over." "Noooo," he moaned in a pitiful high pitched voice. "And I'll bet you didn't know that you need a fishing permit to fish in Yellowstone, and that the fishing season doesn't open in the park for several more weeks?" I added. "Nooo," came the weak, sad reply.

At this point I offered to ski back along with him to be sure he made it back in one piece, which he eventually did. This fellow had obviously never been to Yellowstone, had left Oklahoma in very warm spring-like conditions, and probably was excited when he saw such a large lake as Shoshone on his park map. I didn't ask him what type of fish he expected to catch. He may have had some big plugs to go after large bass like they catch in lakes back in Oklahoma! I have gotten some really big laughs telling this story over the years, but being a native of Alabama, I could truly empathize with this poor fellow. It is indeed a shock to the system to leave the warm April/May climes of the South or Midwest, and enter what is essentially still a winter wonderland high on the Yellowstone Plateau!

Sometimes, international visitors fly into Salt Lake City, rent a car, and come to the park in April and May expecting summer-like conditions. Here are some of the questions we receive from such visitors: Question: "Can I go swimming in Yellowstone Lake?" Answer: "No sir, it is still frozen." Question: "Where are some good trails near here to hike?" Answer: "Did you bring along your skis or snowshoes?" Question: "We just got here. Where is the best spot to view wildflowers? Answer: "The peak of the flower season is about two months away."

Since my oldest daughter is a travel planner, I typically have a pat answer when visitors get upset to find that so many roads, trails, facilities and activities are weeks away from being available for use: "Sir, you need to hire a better travel agent!" After all, if a visitor is not going to do the homework himself regarding planning a trip to a national park in the Northern Rockies, then why not consult an expert in the travel industry who can provide accurate information?

Of course, humorous incidents with visitors and employees are not just limited to Yellowstone. I found that out during the two seasons I worked at Great Smoky Mountains National Park in 1987 and 1988. Perhaps the strangest thing involved the peak blooming season of rhododendron in the park, a spectacular flowering shrub found throughout the Smokies. There are basically two types of rhododendron in the park: the rosebay at mid to lower elevations, which tend to bloom in mid-July, and the Catawba rhododendron found in higher elevations, which bloom about the third week of June. One day in May I was working the desk at Sugarlands Visitor Center, when an enraged gentleman walked in, banged his fist on the desk, and exclaimed in a very loud voice, "Alright, WHERE ARE THEY?" I had absolutely no idea what this visitor was talking about, but I knew he was very upset, and I needed to proceed with caution. "Sir, what is it you are looking for?" I asked. "I came here just to see the blooming rhododendron! *Where are they*?" he shouted. It turns out that this visitor had called the park to find the precise dates for the peak bloom of the rhododendron. Unfortunately, his call had been directed to park headquarters rather than one of the park's visitor centers. So instead of speaking to a park ranger, he ended up speaking to a secretary. When he asked his question as to when the rhododendron bloomed, the secretary simply looked out the window and replied, "Well, it looks like they are in full bloom right now." Unfortunately, the secretary was looking at some ornamental hybrids from a nursery that are commonly planted for home landscaping. These do indeed bloom in May, but regrettably the secretary did not know the difference between the wild rhododendrons in the mountains, from the nursery-bred ornamental variety, and inadvertently provided the wrong information to this man who had driven all the way from Dallas, Texas to experience the lavish blooms of the high mountain rhododendron.

After hearing this man's sad tale, and seeing just how angry he was, I first explained to him how he had received the misinformation, but then I told him we would do our best to make it up to him for our mistake. I took the man to our break room, poured him a cup of coffee, and told him I would be right back. I then called our park's assistant chief naturalist, Don Defoe, and told him the story. Don, a first-rate naturalist, was also committed to customer service. "Bring the gentleman over to my office," he said. I escorted the visitor over to Don's office, where he found a sack full of books and brochures awaiting him. Don proceeded to give the man his personal phone number. "Next time you want to make a visit to the Smokies for any reason, call me personally," he said. I'll never forget that lesson in outstanding customer service that Don provided, but I also learned just how easy it is for us to "mess up." All NPS employees are on the same team. We are there to serve the visitor, but in a large park things can happen. Obviously, the man's initial phone call was routed to the wrong office, and the secretary should have directed his call to a visitor center for information on park vegetation.

On another day a visitor walked up to the front desk, and stated that he had just been stung by a bee, and wondered if we had any ointment like "sting-ease" to relieve the pain. I was working with an extremely knowledgeable ranger by the name of Rick Noseworthy, who had spent many seasons in the Smokies, and knew much more about this park than I did. Rick asked the man if he could see his hand. When the visitor held it up we noticed two holes about ¾ inch apart. "Uh-oh," I thought. "I'm going to let Rick handle this one!" I knew that this man had been bitten by a snake, not an insect. The park had two venomous snakes, the timber rattler and the copperhead. We rarely had serious injuries from snake bites, but the potential was certainly present. Rick then asked the man what he was doing when he got "stung." The man replied that he was reaching for something under one of the old historical structures nearby. That comment pretty much confirmed what we already knew. What happened next was a strong demonstration of the power of the mind. Up to this point this man appeared to be feeling just fine, but that was about to change. Rick told him, "Sir, I'm afraid this is not a bee sting. It appears that you have been bitten by a copperhead snake." The man instantly turned white as a sheet, his eyes rolled back in his head, and he began to topple over backwards. We ran over to catch him before he hit the floor, and then called for one of our park medics. As it turned out the man was administered some medicine and first aid and suffered no long-term injury.

Of course, sometimes the joke was not on the visitor, but rather on me. During my two summers in the Smokies I fouled up on several occasions. After all, I had worked fifteen summers in Yellowstone, and even though my home was only an hour's drive from my work location, it took me awhile to learn several things. For example, during my first week of work, my supervisor sent me out at night to post some flyers in the campground announcing our upcoming programs. I walked out without a flashlight, and quickly realized just how much darker it is in a Smokies campground than it is in a Yellowstone campground. I figured I could find my way to the restroom, where I was supposed to place the poster. With no moon and all of the deciduous trees, there is simply no darker place to be found than nighttime in the Great Smoky Mountains, unless perhaps your light goes out in a cave! On my way to the restroom I just about kissed the face of a black bear! Thankfully, it fled in one direction, as I was hopping three feet off the ground in another direction!

Toward the end of the season my supervisor asked me if I would be willing to work weekends during the busy month of October at Sugarlands, and continue to give evening programs at Elkmont campground. I jumped at the chance. By late August I was back teaching in the classroom at Walters State Community College, an hour's drive away, but I enjoyed my work as a park ranger so much I was thrilled to extend my season. However, I was somewhat unprepared for "leaf peepers" season in October, when the spectacular color change occurs in the mountains. Typically I allowed no more than 90 minutes to drive from my home in Morristown to Sugarlands Visitor Center in the park. However, I had never tried to enter the park during "leaf peeper" season, and in mid-October I found myself in total gridlock in the tourist trap town of Pigeon Forge. I was due at work at the visitor center at 1:00 p.m. There were no cell phones back then, so I got out of my vehicle and placed a call from a service station to Sugarlands. I told them of my plight. My supervisor Terry replied, "See you around 5:00 p.m." "What do you mean?" I asked. "Well," not only do we have peak color season, but Pigeon Forge is having a classic car show. You should have taken the back roads."

When I finally arrived I barely had time to head up to the campground for my evening program. All summer I had given my programs at night in just a short sleeve shirt, but this was October, and I had forgotten just how cold it can get at night in the mountains. I just about froze that night as I stammered and shivered through my presentation. Then, if that wasn't bad enough, the coup de gras for a pretty miserable day occurred when I opened up the little storage shed behind the screen to store the slide projector. There must have been 100 snakes all curled up in a bundle right at my feet when I entered the small shed. These were not poisonous snakes, and I guess they were simply massing together to keep warm, but the sight of this many snakes caused me to jump so high I hit my head on one of the cross beams. As choice words filled the air, several of the campers looked back up the trail to see what all the commotion was about. Needless to say, the next year when my supervisor asked me to work October weekends in the park, I figured there were not enough backroads in existence to find my way down there and back, so I politely declined!

One of the great benefits of being a park ranger is not just working in a gorgeous outdoor setting, but also interacting with visitors from all over the world as well as fellow employees who share the same passion as you for protecting and interpreting our national parks. Humor is a big part of the reward that comes with this fabulous job.

The Value of Public Lands

In my first volume I detailed the value of public lands from my perspective of growing up in Alabama, a state which has few public lands near my home town of Montgomery. Practically all of the natural outdoor areas that I cherished, and spent so much of my boyhood in are now gone. The open space areas near the neighborhood where I grew up that contained ponds, streams and forests, have all been developed into subdivisions or shopping centers. The wild areas along Jordan and Martin Lakes now all contain summer homes. I made the case that when I first came to Yellowstone and discovered natural areas on public lands that are protected and preserved for present and future generations, it was no wonder that I found it to be a life changing experience.

In 2009 Timothy Egan authored the *Big Burn,* a book that I had assumed from its title simply detailed the large forest fires that occurred in Idaho and Montana during the summer of 1910. In fact, Egan covered much more than that. His book documents the incredible accomplishments by President Theodore Roosevelt to protect and conserve magnificent lands throughout much of the West through the establishment of national monuments and national forests. His battles to make these lands public were anything but easy. He had to stand up to the most wealthy and powerful individuals, corporations, and members of Congress who wanted to exploit these lands for the profit for a few. Roosevelt was a proud Republican who took pride in protecting the interests of the common citizens from being run over by the greed for profits by a small but powerful and wealthy minority.

From a political standpoint I have always considered myself a conservative and an Independent. I certainly believe in the wise and prudent use of our tax dollars, and holding on to traditional values. Along those lines, what could be more *conservative* than *conserving* our nation's wonderful outdoor natural heritage for our children and grandchildren?

Just during my lifetime our nation's population has more than doubled. Our National Parks, Monuments and Wilderness Areas provide a critical refuge for so many of our citizens who live in congested cities. These areas provide a soothing, therapeutic tonic and relief to the body, spirit and soul. I have often expressed gratitude to our forefathers who worked so hard to set aside many of our fabulous public lands that we enjoy today. Not too many decades ago our nation's politicians seemed to agree on the importance of public lands for our citizens. After all our free enterprise system simply cannot do it all. It can deliver us a Disneyworld, but it cannot deliver us national parks, national forests and wilderness areas.

In addition to the loss of natural areas that I enjoyed in my youth in Alabama and along the panhandle of Florida, I witnessed the insidious degradation of wild country and open spaces in the mountains of East Tennessee during the 31 years that I lived near the Great Smoky Mountains. If anyone truly wants to see the contrast between private property and public property when it comes to protecting natural resources, simply drive through Pigeon Forge, Tennessee—perhaps the nation's foremost capital of billboards and tackiness, into the foothills parkway that leads into the national park. You are immediately transformed from gaudy, unending strip development to being completely surrounded by a green curtain of vegetation. Author Michael Frome documented this sad contradiction well in his classic book, *Strangers in High Places*.

During my two summers working at Sugarlands Visitor Center in Great Smoky Mountains National Park, I would often visit the basement where some interesting artifacts and documents were kept. I found a topographic map that depicted the original land area proposed for the national park, which was established in 1934. The park was supposed to include many of the foothills on the Tennessee side of the park, such as those in the adjoining Wears Valley. Tragically, this did not happen. The park's boundaries were pulled south back to the steep mountainous terrain. When we moved to East Tennessee in 1976, Wears Valley was mostly rural and undeveloped farmland with the beautiful backdrop of the Great Smoky Mountains, and for the most part had only a dirt road running through it. Over the decades I watched development spread throughout the valley, and up the mountain slopes like a cancer, transforming what had been a beautiful pastoral scene into garish concentrations of "mountain cabins" that are like pimples and warts on an otherwise beautiful face. Now when you hike the Cove Mountain trail that runs along the boundary of the national park, on the south side you have wonderful protected forest, mountains, and streams. To the north is an unending array of scars on the land with roads gouged into the sides of the mountains.

Despite the critical importance that the majority of America's citizens place on public lands, we are again witnessing the "Sagebrush Rebellion" era all over again. In my home state of Montana, several Republican state legislators have been involved with well-funded organizations which are no more than front groups for a few very wealthy individuals and corporations that want to see an end to federal ownership of land, such as in our national forests. The names of these organizations sound innocuous enough—"Americans for Prosperity," the "American Lands Council," the "American Legislative Exchange Council." These organizations say that they want to transfer the ownership of federal lands to the state. However, Montana state agencies do not want the politicians to force this on them for good reason. Experts warn that there is no way that states such as Montana could afford to manage these lands. Firefighting expenses alone would overwhelm a state's budget. Most knowledgeable observers agree that if federal lands were transferred to the states, it would only be a matter of time before the states would be forced to sell them to wealthy individuals and corporations. That's when the "No Trespassing" signs would begin to go up. Many citizens are convinced this is the ultimate goal of the above-mentioned organizations.

During the winter of 2015 conservationists in the state had heard enough of such talk, and organized a "Public Lands Rally" on President's Day, February 16, in the rotunda of the state capitol in Helena. Over 500 citizens came from all ends of the state to protest the movement to transfer federal lands to the state. Margaret and I decided to take the 90 mile drive, and attend the rally. Conservation organizations present to protest the transfer of lands ranged from the Rocky Mountain Elk Foundation to the Montana Wilderness Association to many sportsmen groups. Folks carrying all sorts of signs and placards were packed into the rotunda as Governor Steve Bullock prepared to speak. Along with the dozens of hand-painted signs that contained such messages as "Keep Your Hands Off Our Public Lands," I noticed a single fancy sign that had been produced by the American Lands Council and contained a map of the U.S. depicting federal lands in red. The slogan at the top of the sign read "Transferring Public Lands = Better Access and Better Productivity." The man carrying the sign walked down next to me and stood behind the podium, hoping to get his sign photographed by the hordes of media covering the event, even though he appeared to be the only one out of 500 who supported the transfer of public land. The governor was not ready to speak yet, so I turned to the man and asked, "Where in Montana are you from?" No answer. I tried again, "Better Access and Productivity for whom?" Again, no answer. I looked at his elaborate sign which showed almost no federal lands in Texas, then asked him, "If you think this is such a great idea, why don't you move to Texas?" No answer. Finally I asked him, "Are you being paid to be here today?" To which he replied, "I am from Utah and I have just as much right as you do to be here!"

The gentleman was absolutely correct, though I did point out to him that he should attempt to organize his own rally and see how much support he could garner, to which he did not reply. It appeared obvious to me that this man was most likely being paid by the American Lands Council, which is based in Utah, to attend this rally and hold up the expensive signs that had been produced. Fortunately, Governor Bullock, a Democrat, blasted the political movement to transfer public lands and exclaimed to the crowd, "Our public lands are not part of the problem – they are part of the solution. I'm pleased to stand before you and say that as governor, I'll do everything to ensure that wholesale transfers of public land will not occur. Not on my watch." As I looked around at the huge crowd and recalled that polls in the state found that 75% of Montanans were opposed to the land transfer, I wondered to myself, "How did this ever become a partisan issue? As an Independent myself, why aren't Republican legislators opposed to this movement?" For that I had no answer.

The same efforts are taking place by some members of Congress. For example, the Land and Water Conservation Fund, which utilizes royalties from off-shore drilling to acquire critical wildlife habitat and unique natural areas, has proved to be an admirable program with bi-partisan support for over 50 years. However, even this popular program has been in the crosshairs of Republican members of Congress who are opposed to any increase in public ownership of land.

So just as we witnessed in the early 1900s during the presidency of Theodore Roosevelt, and again during the Sagebrush Rebellion era of the late 1970s and early 1980s, there are wealthy and powerful interests being represented by politicians on the state and federal level that are calling not only for not adding anymore public lands, but actually reducing them. This in the face of a continually growing population that is creating more and more pressure on our existing national parks, monuments and forests. Members of Congress, again all Republicans, are working overtime to take away the authority of the President of the United States to establish national monuments on existing federally-owned land. Some of our nation's most beloved national parks began as national monuments, including Grand Teton, Grand Canyon, Acadia, Zion, Olympic, and many others. Congress often lacks the political courage and foresight to set aside a national park, therefore it is critical that the President retain the authority to create a national monument. Otherwise, instead of an Arches National Park (which was established in 1929 as a national monument) we might instead have a field of open pit mines and drill rigs.

The year 2016 marks the Centennial Year for the National Park Service. As the NPS begins its second century of stewardship of our national parklands—often referred to as "American's Best Idea," the agency has initiated the "Find Your Park" program. Some long-time park visitors mused that the program should have been called "Find Another Park" to steer folks away from the so-called crown jewel parks, and seek out less popular parks. One thing is for certain, as more and more of American's national parks are becoming overcrowded, the last thing we need Congress to do is remove the long-standing authority of our President to designate new national monuments!

To see such short-sighted politicians working hard to dismantle our public lands can be very discouraging. However, some things never change. Our nation had the same battles at the turn of the century. Theodore Roosevelt looked at our nation's natural heritage and vowed to protect it for our children and grandchildren. He fought the good fight against those who looked at those same resources for the extraction of profits, nothing more. One has to wonder, where are the Roosevelt Republicans today?

During August 2015 I was in Grand Teton National Park on a camping trip, when U.S. Senator Ted Cruz (R) of Texas visited Jackson, Wyoming for a fund-raising event for his presidential campaign. Jackson is the summer home to some very wealthy people, including several who fly in on their private jets. So it is a logical place for some politicians to raise money. About three weeks prior to Cruz's visit, presidential candidate Ben Carson (R) also held a fundraising event in Jackson. The following day after Cruz's visit, I read in Jackson newspapers that he had ridiculed the public ownership of land in Jackson Hole, and that it should be privately developed. He went on to say that this worked well in his state of Texas. I don't know how folks in Texas feel about having such a small amount of public lands, but I am certain that up in the Northern Rocky Mountain States his idea would not be well-received.

There is no question that public lands are a treasured resource that we need to protect for future generations, as well as continue to protect more natural areas as parks, monuments or wilderness designation. We live in a democracy. The one way to lose our cherished public lands and natural areas is for good men and women to not engage, and casually remain on the sidelines, doing nothing to prevent it. When I hear a politician on the state or federal level refer to citizens who are working to protect our natural outdoor heritage as "radical environmentalists," I'm reminded of a comment made by Carol Ruckdeschel in the excellent book *Untamed* by Will Harlan. Carol has devoted most of her life working to protect the wilderness of Cumberland Island, now a national park along the coast of Georgia. Carol has been called a radical by those who would like to develop Cumberland Island for profit. She made the excellent point that only 2% of the land area in the contiguous United States is protected as wilderness. "So just who is the radical?" Carol asked. "The one trying to protect the tiny amount of wilderness we have left? Or the one who wants to develop and destroy it for profit?" I have to agree with Carol, and frankly I don't apologize for having a passion for preserving wild country. If you share that same passion, then by all means, do not sit idly by while some politicians are attacking the concept of protecting wild country and public lands. Enjoy our public lands, but get involved and engaged to protect and preserve them for our future generations.

EPILOGUE

In my 43 years of working as a seasonal ranger, I have continually been impressed by the passion and love that visitors from all over the world have for Yellowstone. Whether I am on rove in the Upper Geyser Basin, working at the desk at the Old Faithful Visitor Education Center, or hiking a trail in the backcountry, I see that sense of wonder in their eyes and facial expressions, I hear it in their excited conversations. It is obvious to me that Yellowstone's natural wonders have an uplifting and therapeutic effect on folks, many of whom reside in congested cities.

As an interpretive ranger, I try to impart what I feel is a critical message to our visitors and it is this: First, Yellowstone cannot take care of itself. It requires attention and care from its owners, the American people. For example, Yellowstone is not owned by only Wyoming, Idaho, and Montana. If someone out on the west boundary in Idaho, 15 miles away from Old Faithful Geyser, advocates drilling for energy to make a profit, it is important for Yellowstone's constituents all over the nation (and indeed world, for Yellowstone is truly a world treasure) to take action to prevent the possible destruction of Yellowstone's geysers. I always urge visitors to keep up with the issues that might negatively impact Yellowstone by continually checking the park's website, and also staying involved with organizations that strive to support and protect Yellowstone, listed in the Appendix.

Second, I urge visitors to cultivate their passion for Yellowstone by taking that passion back to their home turf. As our population continues to grow and more youngsters are tempted to substitute their smart phones for the wonders of nature, we need to take care of natural areas near our homes, wherever that may be. In addition to protecting and preserving units managed by the National Park Service, we need to also get involved with our local and state parks, nature preserves, wildlife refuges, national forests, and all wild lands. This is one reason that I included in this book several adventures from wild country beyond Yellowstone.

In this day and age of technology and congestion, we need wild country more than ever, and wild country needs us. It will take an engaged constituency to stand up to the demands from those interests that would harm wilderness. Take a close look at the appendix. If you love wild country that the Greater Yellowstone Ecosystem represents, please get involved and stay involved. Future generations will thank us.

Orville E. Bach, Jr

Old Faithful, Yellowstone National Park

April 25, 2016

Appendix

The following organizations work to protect, preserve, and/or support Yellowstone National Park and the Greater Yellowstone Ecosystem:

The Yellowstone Association
www.yellowstoneassociation.org

The Yellowstone Park Foundation
www.ypf.org

The Greater Yellowstone Coalition
www.greateryellowstone.org

The National Parks Conservation Association
www.npca.org

The Sierra Club
www.sierra.org

The Wilderness Society
www.wilderness.org

The National Audubon Society
www.audubon.org

The National Wildlife Federation
www.nwf.org

Earthjustice
www.earthjustice.org

The Natural Resources Defense Council
www.nrdc.org

The Nature Conservancy
www.nature.org

The Geyser Observation and Study Association (GOSA)
www.geyserstudy.org